PAOLO LIVERANI, GIANDOMENICO SPINOLA
WITH A CONTRIBUTION BY PIETRO ZANDER

THE VATICAN NECROPOLES
Rome's City of the Dead

INTRODUCTION BY
FRANCESCO BURANELLI

MUSEI VATICANI

LIBRERIA EDITRICE VATICANA

BREPOLS

International copyright © 2010
by Editoriale Jaca Book SpA, Milano
Libreria Editrice Vaticana, Città del Vaticano
Musei Vaticani, Città del Vaticano

First published in Italy in 2010 by
Editoriale Jaca Book SpA, Milano
Libreria Editrice Vaticana, Città del Vaticano
Musei Vaticani, Città del Vaticano
First published in English by
Brepols Publishers

Original title
LE NECROPOLI VATICANE
LA CITTÀ DEI MORTI DI ROMA
Translated from the Italian by
Saskia Stevens and Victoria Noel-Johnson

For the images of the Necropoles on the Via Triumphalis
© Musei Vaticani
Foto Archivio Fotografico Musei Vaticani, A. Brachetti / G. Lattanzi

For the images of the Necropoles under St. Peter's Basilica
© Fabbrica di San Pietro in Vaticano

ISBN 978-2-503-53578-4
D/2010/0095/176

Contents

INTRODUCTION

"The Eternal City": this is the epithet that, probably more than any other, sums up the very essence of Rome: in antiquity, already called *Urbs*, "the City" *par excellence*. Rome, with its multimillenial history, succeeds in offering an image of historic and architectural continuity that only knows few equals in the world, despite living in alternating vicissitudes.

The gradual stratification and enlargement of the city has created a unique urban texture which, with an uninterrupted continuity and life, is capable of documenting the "eternity" of Rome, from the first agglomerates of the proto-historic huts of the legendary Rome founded by Romulus, traditionally dated to 21 April 753 BC, to the metropolis of today. In this astonishing reality, we support the gradual expansion of the city, articulated by the perimeters of the defensive walls that in particular historical periods, demarcated the territory like concentric circles. New buildings are constructed on top of old ones, streets are repaved, raising their levels and whole quarters are designed and built, often maintaining very old orientations. Rome has seen a continuous development that, in the course of centuries, has created this unique city of more than four million inhabitants in which we live today. Part of the "collateral effects" of urban expansion has been, already since antiquity, the systematic destruction of the *necropoleis*, those endless cities of the dead that were initially located outside the built-up area, first, on high grounds and in surrounding valleys, then, along the consular roads to become gradually occupied by the city of the living. This is the reason why tombs from the Early Regal Period were discovered in the area of the Forum Romanum, while tombs from the Orientalising, Archaic and Republican Period were already on the Esquiline, far away from the primitive settlements, and which were in their turn obliterated by buildings from later periods. Not to mention the Imperial burial grounds that, along the consular roads, extended across Rome's countryside until some miles outside the Aurelianic wall, which brought about the first contraction inside the new defensive perimeter.

Some demographic information should be added to these synthetic topographic considerations, in order to realise, with informal data, the millions of tombs that have disappeared.

At the time of the Etruscan kings (around the sixth century AD) Rome's population was calculated at approximately 30,000 inhabitants. It grew rapidly, as three centuries later, there were almost 190,000 residents, reaching the number of circa 1,500,000 in the second century AD. Rome, the capital of the Empire, became the most crowded city of the ancient world and remained such until the first invasions of the Visigoths and Vandals at the beginning of the fifth century AD.

This brief introduction is simply meant to underline the importance of the conservation and protection of the archaeological remains, whether it concerns isolated tombs or larger sections of *necropoleis* which, unfortunately, according to a misleading modern compromise of safeguard, are very often regularly excavated, documented and then removed to make way for the city's expansion. The result of such a *modus operandi* has been the permanent and systematic cancellation of endless "cities of the dead" with the consequent loss of a large quantity of historic and cultural data, handed down by the *pietas* of family members who, with a surprising resemblance to what happens at our cemeteries today, documented with a moving sentimental sincerity not only the general characteristics of their loved ones, but also the human accomplishments of the deceased, in particular their *cursus honorum*, an inexhaustible source of knowledge for the reconstruction of ancient history and the organisation of Roman society.

It seems incredible, especially if we compare it to the important nearby cities of ancient Etruria, *Latium Vetus* or *Magna Graecia*, that Rome, capital of the Empire, existing as a city for three thousand years, had millions of inhabitants - amongst which kings, consuls, emperors, senators, generals, writers, but also popes and saints that all created history, as well as freedmen and slaves - has not been able to preserve, if not in the smallest part, its own *necropoleis*. Only few and sporadic testimonies have been preserved of those that through the centuries must have been the most extensive cities of the dead; to get a faint idea of the archaeological patrimony that has been lost, it would be opportune to visit the *necropoleis* of nearby Ostia or of the archaeological sites of Pompeii, for instance, a little further away, and then apply those local realities to the grandeur of Rome.

For this reason, the *necropoleis* that have come to light on various occasions in the Vatican area during the twentieth century, and have been integrally turned into an on-site museum thanks to the vision of the Vatican authorities, who were advised by archaeological experts, have become of great importance for the historic knowledge of the city.

An "in-house protection system" of a remarkable precision that even today constitutes an example of a vigilant and cautious safeguard, is rewarded by the continuous attention of visitors that go to the excavations of the so-called "Vatican *necropoleis*" under St. Peter's Basilica and to the sections of the *necropoleis* along the *Via Triumphalis*, commonly named the *necropoleis* of the Autoparco and Santa Rosa.

The excavations were carried out in the years 1940-1947 and subsequently between 1953 and 1957 during the papacy of Pope Pius XII (Eugenio Pacelli, 1939-1958), to bring to light the "Vatican necropolis", a monumental stretch of the necropolis along the Via Cornelia that had luckily been preserved under the central nave of St. Peter's basilica. The excavations started with the death of Pope Pius XI (Achille Ratti, 1922-1939) who had asked in his testament to be buried in the Vatican Grottoes; during the construction work that entailed the lowering of the floor by approximately 80 centimetres, the elegant cornice of a funerary building was discovered. The architectural element was still *in situ* and was part of the decoration of what would later be known as mausoleum F, or of the *Tullii* and the *Caetennii Maiores*. From this moment, the excavations continued during the pontificate of Pius XII, bringing to light twenty-two rich funerary monuments, splendidly preserved on both sides of a narrow street. However, the most remarkable discovery that has since then developed an historical and archaeological interest, and a religious veneration that is unequalled, is the identification of the "tomb of Peter": a complex sequence of funerary structures, of which the epigraphic and archaeological testimonies make it possible to recognise the veneration – uninterrupted for two thousand years – of the Apostle's tomb. In the middle of Michelangelo's dome, under Bernini's baldachin of the Confession's altar, almost perfectly "in plumb", lie in an ancient necropolis the remains of the "red wall" on which the inscription "Πέτρ[ος] / ἔνι", "Peter is here" was found. The Vatican necropolis has been the first and visionary example of turning an ancient necropolis into an on-site museum, and today it is open to the public thanks to the application of very advanced and sophisticated climate control technologies that allow the perfect preservation of the ancient structures and artefacts.

Even if many pages have already been written about the charm and magic of subterranean Rome, and even if at a specialist level the vast necropolis on the north-western slope of the Vatican hill skirted by the ancient *Via Triumphalis* had been known to scholars for centuries, the excitement one experiences upon entering the area of the Autoparco and the Santa Rosa Parking in the heart of the Vatican is very great, and one clearly perceives crossing two thousand years of history at one fell swoop. In two large underground spaces, on both sides of a modern street, are enclosed more than four hundred tombs, one on top of another along the slope of the hill, taking up the smallest remaining spaces and datable to between the first and fourth century AD.

Rich *aediculae* decorated with mosaics and stuccoes together with poor burials directly placed in the ground, occupy the area in such density that almost seemed impossible to the archaeologists who for the first time, were able to carry out scientific excavations and define the limits of the burials, often even placed one on top of the other.

It concerns a section of the pagan necropolis that was located along a stretch of road that since the earliest days ran from Rome to Veii. As a perpetual reminder of the conquest of the Etruscan city and the defeat of a fierce enemy, the Romans decided to call the stretch closest to Rome *Via Triumphalis*, along the urban tract of which – between the *Pons Neronianus* and the Capitoline Hill – for centuries, triumphant generals led their magnificent processions. On the hillside of the Vatican hill that dominated the extra-urban route, an endless cemetery developed over the centuries, the remains of which were often discovered during occasional excavations or archaeological campaigns carried out scientifically.

Until the first excavation in 1956, the Vatican authorities decided, on the example of what had been done for the necropolis under St. Peter's basilica, the complete on-site preservation of single tombs and grave goods as they were brought to light.

The necropolis along the *Via Triumphalis*, together with the Vatican necropolis, therefore became one of the most important testimonies of Rome's ancient *necropoleis*, not only for its extent but also for the state of preservation of the tombs. It is a rich archaeological complex with an impressive amount of data concerning the social structure and funerary rituals of ancient Rome.

For these reasons, the direction of the Vatican Museums, also in charge of the archaeological preservation of the Vatican, immediately pointed out that when, in November 2001 during a meeting of the *Consiglio dei Direttori del Governatorato dello Stato della Città del Vaticano*, the plan was presented for a large underground parking in the area of the Piazzale di Santa Rosa, the discovery of a Roman necropolis was to be expected in the area: a continuation of the burial grounds that had already been discovered during the construction of the nearby Autoparco. Following the announcement, it was established that scientific coordinators of the Vatican Museums coordinators would intervene on the construction site whenever archaeological discoveries were made. As a result, the archaeologists of the Direction of the Vatican Museums could intervene when they were alerted by the news of discoveries, by excavating a large area and protecting a conspicuous number of tombs that would reveal a new and very important section of the necropolis along the ancient *Via Triumphalis*, which, from an archaeological perspective, was a perfect continuation of the tombs already excavated in the areas of the Galea Fountain and the Annona, and of the funerary grounds under the Autoparco, discovered in the years 1956-58.

At the end of the construction works in 2006, the excavation and its systemisation were presented by the author of this introduction during a well-attended ceremony as part of the celebrations of the five hundredth anniversary of the Vatican Museums. Ever since, thousands of visitors have put in requests to visit this extraordinary place in which stones and inscriptions tell us about an ancient world, long ago, yet close to our sentiments and our painful perception of parting.

The meticulous mentioning of the years, months and days of loved ones, the documentation on stone of their names, *gentes*, families, trades and professions, are all indications that it was very important, like today, to save their presence from oblivion, as if they wanted to remind the visitors and people passing by – in that moment and for the centuries to come – that right there, on that particular spot, was buried *"Tiberius Natronius Venustus 4 years old…"* whose face with the finest features was sculpted in marble, talks to us about the senselessness of a child's death, that one should praise the *"sanctitas"* of Cocceia Marciana, *honesta foemina*; that *Tiberius Claudius Optatus*, an important man and *tabularius a patrimoniis* of the emperor Nero, wept for the loss of his daughter *Flora*; and that a young slave with a hooded mantle on his shoulders would have waited forever for his young master who would never return home, sitting with a burning lamp and sleeping on the marble.

For this reason, I am proud to be able to announce today, while I am writing these few lines, that plans have been made to finally proceed to the solution I was in due course hoping for: the reunification of the two sectors of the *necropoleis* thanks to excavations under the street that separates the two areas on the surface.

Francesco Buranelli
Secretary of the Pontifical Commission
for the Cultural Heritage of the Church

Chapter One
Topographic Setting

Previous pages:
1. Plan of the Vatican, indicating the necropoleis.

One cannot discuss the Vatican *Necropoleis* without looking at their topographical context. They were located in the periphery of Imperial Rome, an area that became renowned, however, in Late Antiquity thanks to one of its more humble tombs: the one of a fisherman from the provinces, who was probably executed by the emperor Nero in the days after the great fire that destroyed large parts of the city in AD 64. On top of this tomb the world's largest Christian basilica would rise. The word "Vatican" would gradually come to represent one of the most important centres of Christianity until it became the seat of the bishop of Rome and of a State, the dimensions of which do not compare to its fame.

As a start, it is essential to explore Rome's earliest history when it started to develop as a city. This involved not only an increase in population, but also saw the development of an organised topography and space, and a com-

plex and stratified society. It is also the period in which the territories of the various communities – urban or less urban – were defined, that were drawn to the lower course of the river Tiber. It is an era that mythology ascribes to the first kings of Rome who were responsible for the organisation of the city. At this point, the *Ager Vaticanus* also comes into the picture, that already in the days of Pliny the Elder in the first century AD, however, had become a feature that was probably only known to antiquarians. Pliny[1], in fact, describes the *ager* – that is, the area – as a stretch of land along the right hand bank of the river Tiber (the *ripa Veientana*, on the Etruscan side of the river). It started somewhere between *Crustumerium* and Fidene on the left hand bank of the river, and continued further south for a dozen kilometres where it included the Gianicolo Hill, called "Vatican Hill" by the poet Horace.[2] (fig. 2)

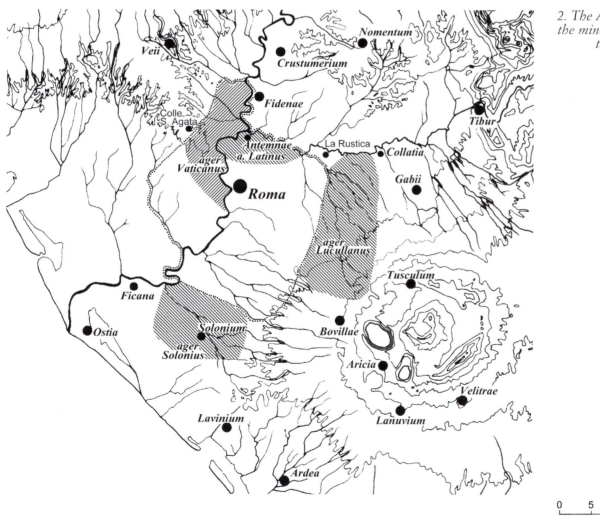

2. The Ager Romanus Antiquus and the minor neighbouring territories at the end of the Iron Age (from Liverani 1999).

The *Vaticanum* possibly also included the area even further south, the current quarter of Trastevere, or at least the part that was included by the Aurelianic wall in the Imperial Period. The same Pliny the Elder[3], in fact, located Cincinnatus' patch of land "*in Vaticano*", on the left hand bank facing the ancient military port of Rome across the river.[4] Until a few years ago the *Navalia*, which was the name of the harbour area, were thought to have been located further north, towards the *Campus Martius*.[5] The recent identification of the *Navalia* in the large Republican structure preserved at the foot of the Aventine Hill, previously identified as the *Porticus Aemilia*, has put the traditional ideas regarding its location under discussion once again.[6]

Leaving aside its exact extent, the *Ager Vaticanus* must have been the territory of a community that became part of Rome relatively early, from the Regal Period onwards, giving us a glimpse of the geopolitical situation in early Latium that appears to be much more fragmented than in the historic age in the absolute sense. In this period, other territories similar in size and status (*ager* Latinus, Lucullanus and Solonius) are known to have existed immediately inside or outside Rome's primitive boundaries that would soon, however, integrate with the main historical cities and, eventually, with Rome itself.[7]

This situation, which already in the age of Pliny was the legacy of a past no longer considered important, changed in the second century AD. From this moment onwards, one no longer talks about the *Ager Vaticanus*, but only the toponym *Vaticanum* is used, very much reduced in size. Based on a number of ancient sources we can narrow down the *Vaticanum* area to the Vatican Hill and the actual St Peter's Square, basically the area now known as Vatican City.[8] The earliest reference is found on a famous inscription from the necropolis underneath St. Peter's Basilica[9]: on the facade of tomb A, the easternmost tomb in the excavated area, we find an inscription containing a summary of the owner's last wishes, a certain Gaius Popilius Heracla (*cfr.* table 2, p. 43), who requested to be buried "*in Vatic[ano] ad Circum*". It may be obvious that such an indication would only make sense if it refers to a rather limited territory and not to an *ager* that stretches out for kilometres; in addition, the position is defined in relation to the Vatican Circus to which we will return shortly. First it is necessary to conclude the discussion on the actual extent of the new toponym: one should consider the possibility that the area also included the current Via della Conciliazione. A late commentator on

Horace, pseudo-Acron who wrote in the first half of the fifth century AD, located a pyramidal funerary monument, randomly called the *sepulcrum Scipionis* that was still visible on the corner of the Via della Conciliazione and the Via della Traspontina at the beginning of the Renaissance, "*in Vaticano*".[10] It is possible, however, that this source only gave a rough indication of the area, using, for simplicity's sake, the most common toponym for the neighbourhood as a general reference point. One should therefore be cautious in including the Via della Conciliazione in the *Vaticanum*.

The *Ager Vaticanus* was an area that was not particularly popular because of its vicinity to the river Tiber and probably the frequent flooding of the river banks. It even had the reputation of being unhealthy[11] and of producing bad wine.[12] The *Vaticanum*, on the other hand, was crossed by rather important roads and constituted a zone for the *horti* and suburban villas of Rome's nobility

thanks to its vicinity to the city. In the Imperial Period, a number of bridges connected the *Vaticanum* with Rome: the oldest bridge possibly dates back to the reign of Caligula, who probably had it constructed to have quick access to the *horti* he inherited from his mother Agrippina. In the Middle Ages, the bridge was called *Pons Neronianus*[13] according to the then common tendency to attribute everything that was part of the *Vaticanum* area to the infamous emperor who was guilty for burning down Rome and martyring Peter. The bridge was only granted a short life, as it no longer appears in the third century AD in the list of bridges of the Regionary Catalogues. The bridge was probably destroyed for defensive reasons when the Aurelianic wall was constructed. Its pillars were still clearly visible in the eighteenth century[14] and also today: when there is low water, one can see them under the water's surface immediately downstream of the current Vittorio Emanuele bridge (fig. 5). The pillars remain visible to such an extent that a few years ago, an inexperienced journalist tried to get a scoop in an attempt to make them pass for an unpublished discovery. The *Pons Aelius*, or Aelian Bridge[15], remained a secure connection between the two river banks. It was constructed by the emperor Hadrian to make his funerary monument easily accessible and is still in use today after many reconstructions and restorations, albeit under a different name: the Ponte Sant'Angelo (fig. 6). It was in fact the presence of the emperor's tomb, in front of the bridgehead on the right hand side of the river bank that protected it in periods of political and military instability. From the beginning of the Gothic Wars in the sixth century AD, the tomb was transformed into a fortalice that finally became into the impregnable Castel Sant'Angelo that we all know.

Across these bridges one could not only access the Vatican, but also get onto two important thoroughfares that started from an uncertain location on the current St Peter's Square and along which the *necropoleis*, that are discussed in this volume, developed. The *Via Triumphalis* headed north towards Monte Mario and the Etruscan town Veii (nowadays Isola Farnese), while the Via Cornelia and a branch of the Via Aurelia, that for the first stretch coincided, ran westwards towards another important Etruscan neighbouring town: *Caere* (today Cerveteri). The location of the *Vaticanum* made the area much desired, not only for suburban property of Rome's nobility – which allowed the owners to enjoy the leisure of country life at a short distance from the *Urbs* – but also

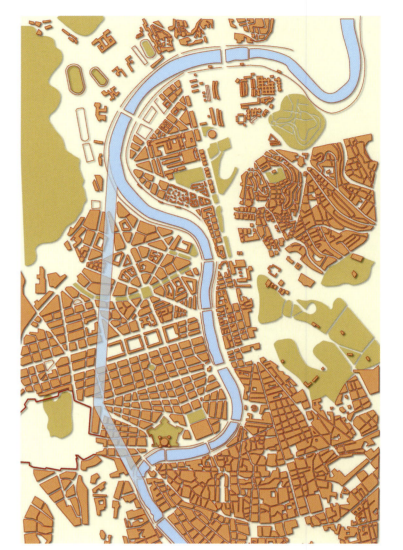

for urban development projects. Caesar had conceived a magnificent development plan and in the summer of 45 BC, less than a year before his assassination, he presented the *Lex de Urbe Augenda*, a law concerning the city's expansion. According to Cicero it foresaw that "the course of the Tiber was to be diverted from the Milvian Bridge along the Vatican hills; the *Campus Martius* was to be built over, and the Vatican was to be a sort of *Campus Martius*."[16] To change the course of the Tiber in a western direction, Caesar had already hired a Greek engineer. One look at the map allows us to imagine the general outline of the plan (fig. 4): taking into account the presence of Monte Mario directly overlooking the river Tiber, the new riverbed would have had to begin just south-west of the Milvian Bridge. One can imagine that the chosen course would have followed a line close to the current Viale Angelico, bending in a south-eastern direction opposite the Piazza del Risorgimento, skimming the

5. *Pillars of the* Pons Neronianus *that emerge from the river Tiber in the summer, downstream of the Vittorio Emanuele Bridge.*

6. *The Sant'Angelo Bridge and the tomb of Hadrian – today Castel Sant'Angelo.*

Vatican Hill and joining the old course immediately after the current Vittorio Emanuele II Bridge. This way it would have cut off a wide bend, allowing the current of the river to increase, while the area of the Vatican plain, combined with that of the *Campus Martius* and with the land enclosed by the bend of the Tiber at the foot of the hills of Parioli further north, would have tripled in size, opening the road for large scale urban developments. It concerned one of the most imaginative plans of Caesar that none of the other emperors after him, however, felt like resuming.

As a result, the hydrogeology of the Vatican was spared and the area remained subdivided into various properties: already at the time of Caesar the *Horti* of Scapula, that appealed very much to Cicero, were laid out at the spot where the river would have have been diverted. The proprietor of the *Horti* was probably Titus Quintius Scapula, a follower of Pompey the Great who committed suicide immediately after having been defeated by Caesar at the battle of Munda, a Spanish town not far from modern Cordoba. It is likely that his possessions came on the market at a relatively good price considering the political disgrace of its proprietor. Cicero dreamed of constructing a tomb there for his beloved daughter who died at a young age. He had to compete, however, with another rich potential buyer, the Plebeian Tribune Lucius Roscius Otho.[17] Who got the property in the end, we do not know for certain.

The main properties, however, were those that ended up in the hands of the Imperial family: the *Horti* of Agrippina Maior, inherited by her son Caligula, and, further to the east, the *Horti* of Domitia. The former must have occupied the Vatican valley that spread out between St Peter's basilica and the Via Cornelia-Aurelia, extending towards the river Tiber until the area near the already cited *Pons Neronianus*.[18] Right in the centre of these *Horti*, in the valley, Caligula laid out his circus, probably partly built in stone and partly in wood. In the middle of the circus he placed a colossal obelisk that he had brought from Alexandria by a boat especially built for this purpose. The obelisk remained at its original spot even many years after the circus had fallen into disuse, until Pope Sixtus V ordered the architect Fontana to transfer it to the centre of St Peter's square in front of the new Renaissance basilica.[19]

The second property just mentioned was located further towards the east, beyond the limits of the *Vaticanum* in the stricter sense. The *Horti* of Domitia would later become famous because Hadrian would build his tomb there. For the purpose of the argument, it is necessary to be more specific about this tomb: first of all, even though this type of monument is called a "mausoleum", as it is in specialist literature, from a philological point of view the name is completely arbitrary. In the ancient sources the word is never used, because in the first three centuries AD the only mausoleum in Rome was that of Augustus. It was not until the fourth century AD that the word acquires the significance of "imperial tomb" and only then the mention of the mausoleum of Saint Helen, of Constantia, of Honorius and Maria and of various members of the ruling family in general begins to appear.[20] By then, however, the tomb of Hadrian had been full for a while: after the burials of Julia Domna, the wife of Septimius Severus, and her son Geta, no more burials were added.

The second specification concerns the Domitia after whom the property was named. In the handbooks basically two hypotheses are suggested: she could be the first wife of Passienus Crispus and paternal aunt of Nero, who had her killed in AD 59 and took hold of her possessions;[21] on the other hand, she could have been Domitia Longina, wife of Domitian.[22]

In reality there is a third simpler and more satisfying possibility that emerges from recent studies on Hadrian's family.[23] The family ties of this emperor have only been recently clarified,[24] identifying Domitia Paulina Lucilla the Older as his mother, while his half-sister was Domitia Calvisia Lucilla the Younger, who, in turn, was also the mother of Marcus Aurelius. At this point, the idea that Hadrian constructed his tomb inside the *horti* he inherited from his mother would seem only natural, without having to hypothesise any intermediate and rather complex passing of property.[25]

To conclude the discussion on the *Horti* of Domitia and its famous burials, it is necessary to add one more aspect that, although it will be studied in detail elsewhere, needs to be touched upon here briefly. Jean-Claude Grenier's[26] recent new reading of the hieroglyphs on the obelisk that once embellished the Circus Varianus (but has stood on the Pincian hill since 1822) (fig. 7) has opened the way for some important insights. The obelisk, as already known, was commissioned by Hadrian. He had it inscribed in honour of his beloved ous who drowned in the river Nile in AD 130 in a tragic accident. The Egyptian text mentions the tomb of Antinous, but the passage in question (on the southern side, column A) had a small lacuna that has now been most satisfyingly completed.[27] The translation of the relevant passage as proposed by the latest editor is as follows: "The Very Fortunate, who is in the afterlife and who rests in this consecrated place that is located inside the *Horti* owned by the *princeps* in Rome." Without going into a detailed philological discussion, it suffices to raise a few points: first of all, the fact that – whatever Antinous would have thought of it – the inscription describes him as "Very Fortunate", meaning "he who is summoned by the gods", according to a concept that could be paraphrased by the famous verse of Menander: "he who is beloved in heaven dies young." Moreover, it confirms that the obelisk marked the tomb of the young man which was located in one of the emperor's properties in Rome. The Egyption term *sḫt*, that translates to "gardens", can be considered the equivalent of the Latin "*horti*". The editor therefore proposes that the *horti* may refer to the

Horti of Domitia where Hadrian was preparing his own tomb, or, alternatively, to the *Horti* Sallustiani.[28] (fig. 8) The latter was probably the emperors' preferred property. It was located in an area between the Porta Pinciana and the Porta Salaria, while on the north side it coincided more or less with the line of the later Aurelianic wall. The southern limit of the property corresponded approximately to the current Via XX Settembre. Many Egyptian and Egyptianising sculptures were in fact found in this area: first of all, the colossal granite statues of Queen Tuya, mother of Ramses II, of the pharaoh Amasis, of Ptolomy II Philadelphus, of Arsinoe II and of an anonymous princess. Today these statues are located in the Museo Gregoriano Egizio in the Vatican[29] and in the Albani Collection.[30] The statue of the hippopotamus, today in the Ny Carlsberg Glyptotek, was also found here.[31] Even more important is the obelisk, dominating the staircase of the Trinità ai Monti[32] since the nineteenth century. The pedestal of the obelisk, however, was dis-

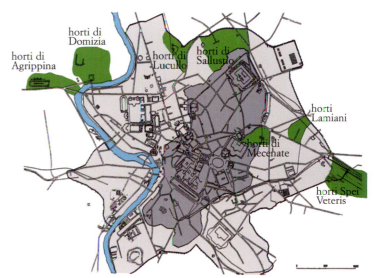

7. *The Antinous' obelisk on the Pincian Hill.*
8. *The Imperial Horti of ancient Rome.*

covered in 1911 on the corner of Via Sardegna and Via Toscana.[33]

The new reading of the hieroglyphs puts an end to old interpretations that established the famous Villa Adriana near Tivoli as the imperial property mentioned in the text. A more recent suggestion for the property, the so-called *Adonaea* gardens that would have been located on the Palatine hill[34], has also been rejected, based on recent archaeological research and a reassessment of the documentation.[35]

Having to choose between the *Horti* of Domitia and those of Sallust, one without doubt would pick the first. Besides the presence of Hadrian's tomb, which at the time of the obelisk's manufacture must have been already under construction, it has become clear that only the *Horti* of Domitia are located outside the *pomerium*[36], the sacro-legal boundary that demarcated the limit between city and territory, between civil and military power and, crucial to this argument, between the world of the living and the world of the dead. In the Imperial Period there has only been one certain exception[37] to this ancient law, already present in the Twelve Tables from the beginning of the Republic, stating that nobody should be buried inside the city: the burial of Trajan, whose ashes were deposited in the small chamber in the base of his column between the Basilica Ulpia and the so-called libraries of his forum complex.

In brief, the "consecrated space", that is the tomb of Antinous, was probably located on the right hand side of the river Tiber, not far from Hadrian's monumental tomb to somehow continue the bond that existed between them in life, also in death. It may be obvious, moreover, that there is no connection between the Circus Varianus, where the obelisk was found in the southeast of the city, and Antinous' tomb. Instead, we should consider a reuse of the monument by the Severan family, the emperors that laid out the *Horti Spei Veteri* (the *horti* near the ancient temple of Hope) in the vicinity of the current basilica of Sante Croce in Gerusalemme. On that occasion, they would have transferred the prestigious ornament to the *spina* of the circus, imitating what had already been done at the Circus Maximus and at the circus of Caligula and Nero. This happened at a time when the veneration of Antinous had ceased to exist, possibly during the reign of Heliogabalus.[38] On the other hand, only an emperor could give permission to move such a monument, and only under two sets of circumstances: first of all, the transfer of the monument must have taken

place between two imperial properties; secondly, the spoliation of a tomb was prohibited by sacred law as a rule, but exceptions could be made by the only person who had authority in this field, the *pontifex maximus*, the highest power in Roman religion. The given prerogatives that came with this office, from the end of the Republican Period until the late fourth century AD, were reserved for the emperor himself. In the end, when the Aurelianic wall was constructed, the Circus Varianus and Antinous' obelisk were excluded from the city and were damaged during the siege of Totila's Goths in AD 547 as they were unprotected.

Let us return to the Vatican area. If the area that is now crossed by the Via della Conciliazione also belonged to the *Vaticanum*, it is important to mention at least a few other important late-Republican or early-Imperial funerary monuments. The first, in the shape of a pyramid, has already been mentioned: besides its rather arbitrary name, *Sepulcrum Scipionis*, the monument was known in the Mediaeval Period as *Memoria Romuli* or *Meta Romuli*. It has been compared to the sepulchral pyramid that until today has been standing next to Porta San Paolo, and despite the fact that it carries the name of its proprietor Gaius Cestius, it was analogously given the name *Meta Remi*, as a reference to the two mythical founders of the *Urbs*. Despite some recent hypotheses[39], we do not know the real owner of the Vatican pyramid.

Next to the Vatican pyramid, a tomb of two storeys with a circular floor plan was constructed, which features in late-Mediaeval drawings. It probably concerns the monument that from the twelfth century onwards is referred to as the Tiburtinus or Terebinthus of Nero[40], even though by then it must have been already in a bad state of preservation. The first name, Tiburtinus, is likely to derive from the monument's original panelling in travertine. The second, besides the common tendency to attribute anything Roman in the Vatican to Nero, originates in the scholarly identification of a Terebinth shrub that would have arisen on the spot of the apostle's tomb according to the Greek account of Pseudo-Marcellus[41], the last and most comprehensive edition of the apocryphal acts of Peter from the sixth century. In other sources, however, from the twelfth century, the monument is called the "Obelisk of Nero." [42]

At the foot of the Vatican hill a monumental structure arose that, more than anything else, characterised the *Horti* of Agripina: the aforementioned Circus of Caligula and Nero. To summarize a complex series of events, the circus was restored by Nero, who spent much of his time there showing off as a charioteer. Nearby, he also constructed a wooden theatre which was used for the final rehearsals of his vocal performances. According to one of the three stories that circulated about the event, Nero would also have used this particular theatre to sing about the mythical fire of Troy, while he watched the real thing taking place in Rome, falling to the flames in AD 64.[43] Immediately after the fire, the emperor opened his gardens in the Vatican to the homeless that escaped the devastation. He used the circus and the *horti* for the cruelly spectacular executions of Christians: they were blamed for the disaster, used as scapegoats in the notorious persecutions in which also the apostle Peter was killed.

It is not easy to reconstruct the appearance and position of the circus: for certain, it must have occupied the valley between the Vatican hill and the Via Aurelia-Cornelia, with an east-west orientation. Also in this case, however, one should critically review the current reconstructions of the building that have even made their way into popular literature. In an important study, Filippo Magi[44] reconstructed a rather large circus: approximately 580 meters long and almost 100 meters wide. In his reconstruction, the circus would have stretched out between the southern *propylaea* of St Peter's Square and the church of Santo Stefano degli Abissini, behind St Peter's basilica. The difficulty in identifying the structure is undoubtedly connected to the fact that the building was completely buried: nine meters separate the current paving from the race track of the first century AD.[45]

To summarise the few certainties we do have: besides the orientation and level of the circus, we know that the original position of the obelisk was in the centre of the *spina*, the low central barrier that divided the track lengthways, allowing the chariots to race around it. The dimensions suggested by Magi, however, seem excessive and do not correspond to the little data we have from excavations: the walls that are located under the southern *propylaea* almost certainly belonged to the substructures of the area's terracing, and not to the circus itself or the *carceres* – the starting boxes of the chariots – as Magi believed. Moreover, underneath Santo Stefano we find Roman tombs seven meters above the level of the circus' racetrack[46] and regarding the supposed position of the building on the north side under the current St Peter's Square, a tomb was found nine meters deep,[47] but no trace of the circus' stands.

Elements that would potentially help us improve our knowledge on the plan of the circus, which was not granted a long life anyway, are evidently lacking. The excavations carried out by Castagnoli to find the obelisk's foundation in the Piazza dei Protomartiri Romani[48] (cfr. table 5 p. 46), in fact, confirmed that the racetrack fell into disuse and was already occupied by chamber tombs in the second half of the second century AD; within the first years of the third century AD, moreover, the circus was buried under almost three meters of soil. It must have been a planned operation with the purpose of changing the area's function. At the same time, it would indicate the imperial family's loss of interest in the area. In the second century AD, the *Horti* of Agrippina are no longer mentioned in the sources and its functions were transferred to other *horti*: the fact that the *Horti* of Domitia and those of Sallust were close to the city centre and more luxurious must have persuaded the emperors to make this move.

The area was then left for the construction of tombs, and one in particular of remarkable dimensions – approximately 30 meters in diameter – was built in the centre of the space once taken up by the Circus. Even in this case, we cannot name the owner of the tomb, because in Late Antiquity it was elevated and connected to St Peter's basilica. It was dedicated to Saint Andrew, brother of Peter and used as a side entrance to the basilica. Later, it served as a sacristy until its demolition in 1777.[49] The person who built the circular funerary monument in the beginning of the third century AD, a date indicated by brick stamps discovered in the structure, must certainly have been very important, as no comparable monument, besides those of the imperial family, can be found.

The funerary purpose would become the main function of the *Vaticanum* area, but it was not the only one. The presence of a sanctuary dedicated to the mystery cult of *Magna Mater*, the Great Mother Cybele from the East, between the second and fourth century AD, was of great importance. It was called the *Phrygianum*, as the goddess was of Phrygian origin, but was known amongst the worshippers as the *Vaticanum*, obviously referring to a particular meaning that has nothing to do with the word as discussed earlier. In fact, *Vaticanum* became the name *par excellence* for Cybele's sanctuary. Also outside of Rome: two inscriptions from Lyon (ancient *Lugdunum*) and Kastel near Mainz (*Castrum Mattiacorum*), refer to the local sanctuaries of *Magna Mater* as *Vaticanum*[50] and *Mons Vaticanus*[51] respectively. It thus copies – albeit on a smaller scale – the phenomenon we can also observe for the temple of Jupiter, Juno and Minerva in various colonies of Rome: it was named the *Capitolium*, after the grand temple on the Capitoline Hill in Rome.[52]

Apart from a few references in the ancient sources, the *Phrygianum* is mainly known from various epigraphic dedications (fig. 9) all unfortunately discovered outside of their original context. They commemorate the sacrifice of a bull (*taurobolium*), which was considered to be a purification and redemption ritual by the followers. A rather *grand-guignolesque* description of the ritual is given by Prudentius[53], the controversial Christian poet in the fourth century AD, according to whom the ritual consisted of some sort of baptism of blood: the bull's throat was cut above a trench covered by a wooden grille, below which the follower stood and was drenched by the victim's blood. Recently, however, a comprehensive study of the documents has called this suspiciously controversial version into serious question.[54] In any case, this cult – despite having its ups and downs – coexisted with the Christian basilica dedicated to the main apostle, at least until AD 391 when the emperor Theodosius decreed the closure of pagan cult places. Judging from some of the descriptions, it is likely that the *Phrygianum* consisted of an open area containing shrines dedicated to Cybele, Attis and possibly other divinities of her circle – like the types we know from the *Campus* of the goddess at Ostia – and that it was positioned at a higher level than the basilica.

Also uphill from the basilica, where the landscape was scenic and more salubrious, we should locate the property of Quintus Aurelius Symmachus, one of the most influential pagan senators a the end of the fourth century AD, and of his son-in-law Nicomachus Flavianus, who are both mentioned in Symmachus' letters.[55]

In the end, the construction of St Peter's basilica completely changed the equilibrium of the area as well as the focal point of the city. It kept, however, at least for a while, a funerary function. It is true that the *necropoleis* surrounding the basilica were gradually abandoned and there are hardly any funerary remains that can be traced back to the beginning of the fifth century.[56] However, this is a common phenomenon that repeats itself, with small variations, in the whole territory surrounding the city.

At the same time, however, it was precisely the presence of the apostle and his cult that was the incentive for the Christians to be buried as closely as possible to the saint's tomb. In the fourth century, a primarily Christian necropolis is attested to located in the area immediately to the west, uphill from the basilica. Unfortunately, the necropolis was excavated accidentally and without scientific inspection. The excavations took place in the first half of the nineteenth century during the exploitation of the Vannutelli quarry, where clay was extracted for the kiln nearby. Various inscriptions[57] were discovered, as well as a couple of Paleo-Christian sarcophagi[58], which are all housed in the Vatican Museum today. Among the inscriptions the small stele of *Licinia Amias*[59] is particularly noteworthy. The stele's date is disputed: it is generally dated to about AD 200 and considered the earliest evidence for a Christian burial in the area outside the basilica. In recent years, however, this idea has probably been challenged too radically and without solid arguments.[60]

In any case, at the beginning of the fifth century at the latest, the *necropoleis*, under discussion in the present book, went out of use. The burials that took place afterwards would be closely connected to the basilica, from the sepulchre of Junius Bassus[61], to the burial chamber of the Probi-Anici[62], to the tomb of Honorius, Maria and of the imperial family in the rotunda of Saint Petronilla at the end of the southern transept of the basilica[63], until eventually the primarily ecclesiastic burials in the basilica itself.

9. Altar of the Phrygianum *(Vatican Museums).*

CHAPTER TWO
THE RITUALS: ANTHROPOLOGICAL
AND RELIGIOUS ASPECTS

On page 22:
1. The Autoparco Necropolis, general overview.

The following chapters will present examples of rich archaeological data regarding funerary customs. Unfortunately, the abundance of material evidence does not correspond to the amount of information we find in literary and epigraphic sources on the topic. The latter two are, however, precisely the sources on which we would rely to find explanations for issues arising from the excavations. Although it might seem anomalous, we have no source that clarifies, for example, the reason for the transition from the rite of cremation to that of inhumation.[1] The archaeological data in the *necropoleis* allows us to observe a clear prevalence of cremations in the Late Republican and Early Imperial Period, until the beginning of the second century AD. Subsequently, inhumation gradually took over as the main funerary rite and the *necropoleis* filled up with burials in graves and, for the more wealthy subjects, in marble sarcophagi.

If we use the burials from the Galea area as a case study, we can observe a rather clear development: tomb 1b, dated to about AD 125, was constructed as a *columbarium* to be used exclusively for cremations. The two inhumations found in the mosaic floor belong to a secondary phase in the third century AD when the *columbarium* was reused. Tomb 1a, from about AD 130-140, is unfortunately only partly preserved, but present a large number of funerary urns, about 40, against only one *forma* and a terracotta sarcophagus, reaching a total of five inhumations.[2] A slightly different ratio is also found for tomb 11, dated to AD 140-150, in which three quarters were cremations versus a quarter of inhumations.[3] The four chamber tombs on the lower terrace present a chronology of half a century later that is reflected in a further loss of balance between the two rites. Tomb 8, the oldest one datable to AD 160-180, seems to show a ratio of one to two between cremation and inhumation.[4] The fact that the back wall and part of the south side of the tomb are missing, however, make a reliable evaluation difficult. The ratio is more or less constant in tombs 6 and 7 from about AD 180-190.[5] Finally, tomb 2, built between AD 180-190 but rebuilt around the mid-third century AD, does not contain cremations in the original phase or in the secondary phase, but only inhumations.[6] The transition from one rite to the other has therefore been very gradual and cremations have still been attested for the third century AD, for example in the area of the Autoparco. The complete disappearance of the older rite is certainly related to the success of Christianity, which on one hand accepted the Jewish tradition, but on the other hand nurtured

respect towards the human body as the temple of the Holy Spirit. Such a contribution nevertheless sanctioned the end of a process already clearly started. The last known cremation in the Roman archaeological record with a securable date is right in the Vatican: the cremation of Trebellena Flacilla whose marble cinerary urn in burial T contained a Constantinian coin from AD 317-318[7], so shortly after the edict of AD 313 in which Constantine allowed the Christians to practise their own religion.

The literary sources are rather informative regarding the associated rituals: the display of the corpse, the funeral and the whole public dimension of the funerary ritual. The latter aspect in particular made it possible to exhibit, strengthen or reaffirm the status of the household by publicly bestowing honours upon the deceased.[8] The information about the private side of the ritual, however, is meagre, fragmentary and often incoherent. It concerns customs that were known to all members of society and it was therefore not regarded as necessary or interesting enough to record them or pass them on. Moreover, Roman religion did not constitutionally have a comprehensive theological system, but rather tended to codify the outlines of the common rituals that assisted in regulating life at critical moments of death and the passing of generations, which mediated in defining the relationship between the gods and the people, the hierarchy within these two respective groups and, finally, the relations between the living and the dead. Roman religion is about pragmatics rather than theoretical philosophy, which did not provide any normative indications for the beliefs in the Afterlife or more specific methods of survival after death: in short, all those existential questions which would be impossible not to wonder about today. Those things were certainly present in the ancient culture, but depended on personal convictions or family traditions, and could exist side by side or completely superimpose very different solutions, about which the archaeological data provide indications to be used only with considerable caution.

This picture seems to be confirmed by the various nuances that one senses, for example, inside the same necropolis under the Vatican basilica. Here we find very different expressions within the scope of a few meters: the burial of Flavius Agricola in tomb R, for example, shows an outlook on death similar to a somewhat popular version of Epicureanism. In the "Tomb of the Egyptians", on the other hand, the cultural references of the family seem, without overrating the iconographic evidence of the frescoes, susceptible to oriental customs. Finally, in the "Tomb of the Valerii", the household was particularly keen on displaying its knowledge of classical culture – literature and rhetoric – that is, as far as one can judge from the choices of the decorative programme.

Firstly, we must attempt to see what the rituals were, of which, until now, only a framework could be sketched through archaeology, that is, based on the funerary structures excavated in the various *necropoleis* studied. By separating the funerary rituals from those that periodically commemorated the deceased[9], we shall begin by affirming that the discovered traces of ritual activity by no means refers to a rigid custom, but rather to a model that could be adjusted to the economic situation and the social position of the deceased's family.

To examine therefore, the funeral rituals: according to Cicero, a sow was sacrificed in the vicinity of the tomb[10] a ritual of great significance as it established the tomb as such; it is likely that in the case of a cremation, offerings such as meat, were deposited on top of the funeral pyre.[11] Ceres was not a deity related to the underworld, but in her capacity as goddess of the earth she welcomed the body of the deceased, in a similar way that she welcomed the seeds of the crops, for example. In other words, this goddess presided over the space in which the assimilation of the deceased by the *Manes* took place. It does therefore not concern a funerary sacrifice in the strict sense of the word. However, the deceased had not passed into the world of the dead yet, because otherwise it would have been necessary to make a burnt-offering, that is, a kind of sacrifice that was usually made to the gods of the underworld. While during a normal sacrifice the participants of the ritual could, and had to, eat the meat of the sacrificial animal, at the sacrifice to the gods of the underworld everything had to be completely burnt – as the Greek word "*holocaustos*" indicates – because the living could not share anything with the gods of the realm of the dead. The meat of the sacrificial animals was then divided between Ceres, who received the entrails (*exta*), the deceased and the family, in a banquet which during the last two centuries of the Republic was called the *silicernium*. Once the common meal had been consumed, the funeral pyre was lit and the body to be cremated was placed on top. After the fire had gone out and the ashes cooled, the remains of the bones were gathered, washed and placed inside an urn.[12] In the case of inhumations, however, one can imagine that the deceased's share of the

sacrificial animal would have been burnt on a brazier next to the tomb.

Subsequently, there was a nine day mourning period[13], or rather an eight day period according to the modern calculation, as the ancients counted both the starting day and the end day. At the end they made two sacrifices: a burnt-offering to the *Manes* of the deceased, the gods of the underworld, and the sacrifice of a ram to the *Lares*, the protective gods of the family. Finally, the *cena novemdialis* took place, this time near the house: it was the banquet of exactly the "the ninth day." This put an end to the mourning period and reunited the family with the rest of the community, so that they could invite friends and neighbours or, in the case of very important people, a great crowd of people that could include as many as the whole city. The logic behind these rituals is obvious: they accompanied the deceased in his passage to the Afterlife. First, they separated the deceased from his family and united him with the dead – the sacrifice to the *Manes* was particularly important in this context. Subsequently, the family returned to the community of the living. The various stages were also emphasized by the choice of clothes: at the beginning of the mourning period the male family members wore the *toga pulla*, a toga in a dark blackish or brown colour. In the period between the death of the family member and the burial, the women, on the other hand, used to wear the *ricinum*, later called the *mafurtium*, a veil that covered the head and shoulders.[14] During the funeral they would have to wear a cloak that was also *pullus*: a dark colour like the male togas. At the same time, the deceased was dressed in his best clothes, almost like an inversion of the roles: the deceased still appeared to belong to the world of the living, while the vicinity to the world of the dead was visually branded on the family members. Only at the end of the mourning period did the family members return to wearing their normal clothes, when they had regained their role in the society of the living and could return to their businesses or magistracies.

The *Parentalia* (the feast of the dead celebrated every year between 13 and 21 February and described rather comprehensively by Virgil[15] and Ovid[16]) varied only slightly as an institution. After the initial celebrations of the cycle (the proper *Parentalia* in the strictest sense of the word) there was an eight day mourning period that preceded the sacrifice combined with a banquet at the tomb in honour of the deceased (*Feralia*). The following day, a second banquet was held that marked the end of the mourning and reunit-

ed the families. The format of the first part was therefore similar to the one already seen at the funeral rituals. In the richest and most ostentatious cases, the first banquet near the tomb could also entail the celebration of funerary games. The inscription of Quintus Cominius Abascantus from Misenum in Campania[17] records in detail the funds left by the deceased for such celebrations, providing the prices for the contestants and the costs for the organisation of the games, the oil, the flowers to decorate the tomb (violets and roses)[18], as well as the banquet that was to be offered in the *triclinium*, that by explicit request would be held on the terrace of the tomb[19] and, naturally, the sacrifice in his honour. The second banquet, on the other hand, that was held near the house in order to reunite the family and conclude the celebrations, took place on 22 February. The celebration was known as *Charistia* or *Cara cognatio* and consisted of a sacrifice to the *Lares*, but according to Ovid also concerned the living. In Rome in the Christian Period, the pagan feast was replaced by the celebration of Saint Peter's Chair.[20]

The final type of celebration that was dedicated to the dead was not fixed. It was a festival that only lasted one day and could be connected to an anniversary: the *Parentatio*. It consisted of a commemorative sacrifice, or rather a burnt-offering, to the *Manes* of the deceased, but without the banquet.

Returning to the archaeological data, it is easy enough to identify the material confirming the rituals described above. The evidence concerns most of all the funerary banquets that were held near the tomb during the *Parentalia*, as those held during the funeral had to take place rather close to the funerary pyre. More often than not there are indications that the terrace on top of some of the tombs under the Vatican basilica (tombs E, F, H, L, O) could have accommodated the funerary banquets. For the more modest tombs, one should imagine provisional and makeshift arrangements. In the necropolis from Portus near Ostia, there is evidence for the presence of masonry *triclinium* beds in front of the tombs (figs 3 and 4).[21] In the necropolis under Saint Peter's basilica in the area in front of tomb H, a well has been preserved, which clearly must have served these funerary rituals. Evidence, moreover, for the custom of decorating the tombs with flowers is found in painted and sculpted decorations: roses can be identified at various tombs.[22] These could be related to the *Rosalia* that were celebrated in May or June: a festival during which roses were brought to the tombs of the loved ones.[23]

Furthermore, on funerary altars that were needed to burn the part of the sacrifice dedicated to the dead, we often find carved festoons and garlands of flowers and fruit. It was not a delicate kind of decoration on its own: the concept of decoration in antiquity was completely different to ours today. In other words, the subject of a painted of sculpted decoration had to thematically and functionally fit with the function of the space in which it was situated or with the object it adorned. The flower festoons on the altars were therefore no other than the stone version, so to speak, of the garlands that actually accompanied the rituals of the dead. On the altars of Lucius Passienus Optatus and Passiena Prima, for example, in the Santa Rosa Necropolis, evidence can be easily found, even though it is not always clearly visible.[24] Above the cornice one still finds small holes with traces of hooks that coincide with the ends of the carved garlands: during festivities they were used to hang real flower garlands from, which replaced those in marble. The latter would have seemed more realistic, by the way, because of the use of colour which was once commonly and abundantly applied on white marble, but has mostly disappeared by now. There are only a few examples on which traces of this chromatic treatment have been preserved, for example on the lid of the sarcophagus of *[F]l(avia) Vera e Aur(elia) Agrippina* of the Tomb of the Sarcophagi in the Santa Rosa Necropolis.

The evidence for the periodical visits of the deceased's family has been preserved particularly well in the same Santa Rosa Necropolis, due to the fact that at least part of the burial ground was prematurely buried by a landslide sometime in the Hadrianic Period. In a corner of the small *columbarium* XVI, for example, three small jugs, in Latin "*urceoli*", were found, similar to those depicted on the left side of each altar. They were needed to pour libations of wine, oil or milk for the dead. A considerable number of oil lamps, moreover, was found close to the small urns, immediately above the terracotta lids that sealed the *ollae*, the containers in the shape of a pot that, walled into the niches of a *columbarium*, provided the most common receptacle for the ashes of the dead (figs 5-10). The custom to light an oil lamp over the remains of a dead family member is also attested for other burial sites. At Ostia[25] the custom may not be frequently attested, but for other Italian *necropoleis*, such as Angera[26] near Varese and Voghenza[27] near Ferrara, there is ample evidence.

Several testimonies, mainly epigraphic, have been preserved that contain instructions for the heirs concerning the lighting arrangement: this range from those who were most concerned for the upkeep of their final resting place and asked for a daily lighting[28] or even continuous lighting[29], to others who ordered an oil lamp to be lit three times a month[30] at the Calends, the Nones and the Ides[31],

as well as to more moderate examples of only one lighting every other month.[32]

A final, omnipresent piece of evidence purporting to the sacrifices made in honour of the dead springs from the need to physically maintain a communication channel with them. This happened mainly via a terracotta tube that from the ground's surface, reached down to the cinerary urn or even the grave, in order that the libations could arrive at the ashes or the corpse. This ritual must have been of considerable importance since people made sure that, when the ownership of the land changed, access to their own dead was guaranteed anyway, as for example the inscription of *columbarium* 7 of the Autoparco Necropolis demonstrates.[33] To maintain this direct access, the evident hygienic inconveniences that must have arisen from placing a tube in an inhumation were at the same time overlooked.

Preserving the essence of one's own identity was a constant concern in Roman culture, and also in the context of a tomb. Such concern manifested itself first of all by the use of inscriptions carved in marble. They could also be simply painted, as is evident, for example, in *columbarium* 1 in the Autoparco Necropolis.[34] All the names that were probably painted on the small slabs under the niches have disappeared. The owner's name has been preserved, however, on the only slab that was also inscribed. In addition, the identity of a Roman also had a fundamental social component, as the role he played during his life was often mentioned besides his name: in the socially most eminent cases, one would list one's *curriculum* (to coin a modern saying), or at least the work he carried out, even if he had been a simple slave. Also the physical features of the deceased would be preserved, when means allowed it; some tombs show a strong concern from the owners in this matter. In the "Tomb of the Valerii" under the Vatican basilica, in particular, we find replicas of the deceased in a stucco statue, in a high-relief marble portrait, in a funerary mask made directly from the face of the corpse and in a portrait that may have been inspired by this image.[35] In the other *necropoleis* that were used by families or social groups of lesser economic means, portraits are less common: it is worth mentioning the small Tiberius Natronius Venustus in the Santa Rosa Necropolis[36] or the stele of Ma with his son Crescens in the Autoparco Necropolis[37], or even the portraits recognisable on sarcophagi.

Just like the inscriptions in the most elaborate examples

5, 6. Grave goods from the Santa Rosa Necropolis: at the bottom, three urceoli for libations from tomb XVI.

7, 10. Oil lamps from tombs of the Santa Rosa Necropolis.

could give rise to poetic and rhetorical exercises that sometimes contained texts of a certain literary value, the images of the deceased allowed a rather similar metaphorical game, even if it was realised in a language that had possibilities and restraints different from those of the written word. The figurative message may at the same time have been vaguer, but it was also more intuitive and suggestive, at least for those who, unlike today's modern observer, were part of the same culture and the same collective imagery.

Being depicted on horseback in a lively hunting scene, like Valerinus Vasatulus on his sarcophagus, does not necessarily mean the young man buried in the necropolis under the Vatican basilica was a skilful hunter.[38] In the Roman figurative language, hunting represented virtue, and this was simply the message that the observers of the relief immediately and intuitively understood. In some cases one finds the deceased dressed like divine character: though, this did not mean to display a pretension for deification or the devotion to a particular deity. If a husband dedicated a portrait to his wife in which she was dressed like Venus, it only meant that the deceased had the grace and beauty of the goddess: a metaphor similar to the words that would affectionately have described her as his Venus.[39] In other examples, placing the portrait of the deceased on the body of a classic mythical and well known figure, helped to insert human matters in a more elevated setting, which could also be tragic, but which had been transfigure by myth and literature to allow the projection of private and personal matters in a framework and order that made them expressible and, in a way, significant, besides obviously making the pain of those who remained tolerable. Secondly, an expression thus codified according to a rhetoric of a strongly formalised image attests to the eyes of the spectator the high cultural and social level of the deceased and his family circle.

Instead, something that has always puzzled the scholars studying these images is that, in certain cases, the portrait of the deceased has been only drafted and unfinished, in an otherwise completely finished relief. This is, for example, the case for the already mentioned sarcophagus of Valerinus Vasatulus[40], but also for the sarcophagus with a portrait on a *clipeus* supported by two winged victory figures found in the Tomb of the Sarcophagi (VIII) in the Santa Rosa Necropolis.[41] Many have strived over this phenomenon and there is a vast and sound bibliography on the topic[42]: considering the length of time it would take to manufacture a sarcophagus, the easiest explana-

tion has been the hypothesis that there would have been a mass production of sarcophagi already finished at the workshop of the sculptor. At the time of the funeral, the family of the deceased could choose the most appropriate sarcophagus type. Due to contingent reasons of various kinds, one did not always have the chance or possibility to finish the work and have the portrait of the deceased himself carved on the rough-hewn head. A similar explanation, in itself completely valid, clashes however with the observation that examples exist, like the "Dogmatic" sarcophagus[43], today in the Pio Cristiano Museum in the Vatican (fig. 11): their extraordinary dimensions and unique choice of iconographic repertoire make it unlikely that they were made without a specific commission. Others have suggested that the sarcophagus might have been prepared during life, as was common, moreover, for the whole tomb. Out of some sort of superstition, however, the client did not want to be portrayed on his sarcophagus as deceased. Finally, there are more imaginative theories that audaciously project postmodern concerns on ancient mentality. They would perceive the unfinished portraits as a weakening of the identifying character of the portrait, as if that were no longer necessary, in a sort of identity crisis.

In reality, leaving out the accidental motives that could prevent a portrait from being finished, the whole issue becomes more understandable if one considers it from the opposite point of view, that is, the identifying role of the portrait which, within the figurative language, is in every respect equal to the function of the name itself. Indeed, one cannot ignore the fact that a large number of sarcophagi, despite having a slab that would contain the name of the deceased, were left without an inscription and therefore present a similar phenomenon from the epigraphic side. In the second case, one could naturally argue that the inscription could have been painted and subsequently disappeared. As a matter of fact, we know of a series of sarcophagi that have a sculpted portrait but no inscription. The opposite is rather rare. In fact, I can only think of one case to my knowledge: the sarcophagus of Maconiana Severiana.[44]

The assumption that the identity of the name and portrait would have corresponded from a functional and semiotic point of view is rather based on intuition. It is possible, however, to support this assertion with further arguments. Among the various possible ones, it will suffice to mention just a few: the first is the comparison with the feature that is well known in Roman archaeology, the

11. *The so-called Dogmatic Sarcophagus from St. Paul's Basilica, Pio Cristiano Museum in the Vatican (Photographic Archive of the Vatican Museums).*

damnatio memoriae. It was a measure that was taken against private persons and emperors, for example Nero or Domitian, who committed particular crimes or were disgraced. When someone was struck by such as measure, the portraits and inscriptions bearing his name would be erased from public monuments in order to remove the public memory. In addition, one could also mention a famous line in the Gospel of Matthew in which Christ, referring to the money payable to Caesar, asks the Pharisees and the Herodians: "Of whom is this portrait and inscription?" [45] From this context it is clear that these two elements, the name of the emperor and his portrait on the *denarius*, were considered equivalent.

Starting from the assumption of the corresponding name and image and returning to the issue of the unfinished portrait on sarcophagi, one can mention that in the inscriptions from the late Republic and early Empire – particularly those stating the ownership of the burial and listing the names of those who were entitled to use the tomb – the Romans were attentive to specify those who were living and those who had already passed away. Next to the names of the living they carved a V, an abbreviation of *vivus*, and next to the dead the Greek letter Θ, an abbreviation that defined *theta nigrum* and stood for θ(ανῶν) or θ(άναθος), indicating that a person had died. In later periods we find different situations, but they correspond to the same logic and similar concerns: in early Christian and early Mediaeval mosaics, for example, there is a clear iconographic distinction between the saints that wore an aureole, and the devotee, for example a priest who was still alive at the time of the dedication, whose head was inserted in a square nimbus. This highlighted his presence, and at the same time distinguished him from those who were already in the beatific condition in the sight of God. These examples could be developed further, but it will suffice here to simply add a story from a letter of Paulinus of Nola, the holy bishop from the fifth century.[46] His friend Sulpicius Severus asked him for a portrait to put in the baptistery of his two basilicas at *Primuliacum* in Gaul, in front of the one of Saint Martin of Tours. At first, Paulinus refused determinedly[47], but later on he complied to the his friend's request, on the condition that there would be two inscriptions next to the portraits to avoid misunderstandings. According to the texts proposed by the same Paulinus, Saint Martin would have been represented by the heavenly man (according to the famous expression of Saint Paul). For Paulinus, on the other hand, the penitent sinner, the old earthly man, we

can refer to the second of his poems sent to Severus: "The venerable portrait of the man shows Martin / the second image reproduces the humble Paulinus".[48] In this context the word humble is used etymologically from *humus*, that is, still connected to the earth.[49]

In other words, Paulinus feared that the placement of his portrait next to that of a most revered saint, like Saint Martin, would lead to an equivalence between the two, and would cause the real prayers to be directed to the living bishop instead of to the saint.

Beyond the moral and proper Christian concerns, we cannot refrain from recognising the same kind of mechanism that is found in pagan sarcophagi. Having the name or portrait carved on a sarcophagus did not only designate its owner but also confirmed the presence inside the tomb if no other specific indications were available. During the *Parentalia* or other private celebrations (*parentationes*) it could have caused misunderstandings, running the risk that the members of the *familia* could have made sacrifices not only for the deceased but also for the living. The risk was not completely theoretical if one considers that fact that the *familia* could contain, besides the direct family, like in the modern meaning of the word family, also slaves and freedmen with their respective families, and could end up consisting of a rather large group. Such a ritual error should not be seen according to the Christian moral categories, but as something that changed the *status* of the participants involved. It mixed up the roles and created disorder in a tie that was fundamental in ancient culture, that is, properly in the strict distinction between the living and the dead that, as we have seen, was precisely articulated in the funerary and sacrificial rituals described above.

We can therefore conclude that the provident Roman concerned himself with preparing his own tomb and that of his family in advance, choosing also the necessary sarcophagi, but leaving the inscription blank and the portrait unfinished. The ups and downs of life could alter the choices that were carefully made. One could think of ordinary events, such as a premature death of the youngest members of the family, which could change the destination of the sarcophagi. Quite frequently, in fact, we discover portraits that were drafted for a woman, but reworked as a male portrait or vice-versa. A death while travelling, for example, could make it difficult or even impossible to return the corpse. Yet another reason for the change of a sarcophagus' destination could be matrimony, when a daughter passed into another family and was therefore buried in another tomb, or a second marriage of a widow who would follow her second husband to the grave.[50] This specific case can possibly be proved since we have some examples in which a sarcophagus for two carries a double portrait on the front. Only the facial features of one of the two spouses are finished while the other one remains in rough outline. To give more concrete examples, one could think of the sarcophagus of Flavius Faustinus, who died his AD 354 (fig. 12). His sarcophagus is preserved in the Pio Cristiano museum in the Vatican and has a *clipeus* with a portrait of Faustinus completely finished, whereas the portrait of his wife next to it is only roughly carved.[51] In the Museo Nazionale Romano we find a similar example[52]: on the coffin of the sarcophagus, miracles of Christ have been depicted, but there is no inscription on the name slab, while the side panels contain *clipei*: the one of the left has a portrait of a praying woman completely finished, while the one of the right shows a male portrait only roughly carved. Finally, there is the sarcophagus of Pullius Peregrinus[53], in the Torlonia collection. It shows a finished portrait of Peregrinus while the one of the muse in front of him, which was obviously reserved for his wife, is only roughly carved.

Among the numerous themes for deliberation that emerge from the study of the excavations of this necropolis, one more piece of evidence deserves attention. On itself it is unpretentious and hardly conspicuous, but that is exactly the reason why it is difficult to find comparisons in similar *necropoleis*. Moreover, it also creates a space for methodological considerations regarding the limits of archaeological documentation. An area in the Santa Rosa Necropolis contained a series of small ditches filled with ashes without any trace of cinerary urns or grave goods, except in a few cases where nails were found together with the ashes.[54] It was demonstrated, moreover, that those ashes did not come from a funeral pyre, like those ditches of a certain width found in central European *necropoleis*, but of smaller quantities, comparable to those found in more common urns. Moreover, even though nails with apotropaeic functions have been attested in some burials[55], their isolated presence together with the complete lack of any other item that came with the burial would suggest a different interpretation. One should remember that among the marble cinerary urns there are many examples of urns that imitate a type in perishable material. There are a rather large number of small urns on four feet that obviously imitate wooden boxes.[56] Therefore, the presence of nails could be easily explained thinking precisely of those cinerary urns made in wood. The version in stone could be a more durable and expensive imitation that maintained the shape considered traditional, such as the wooden coffins for inhumations that were found in the *necropoleis* of Portus, near Ostia.[57] In other examples, it seems that wicker baskets

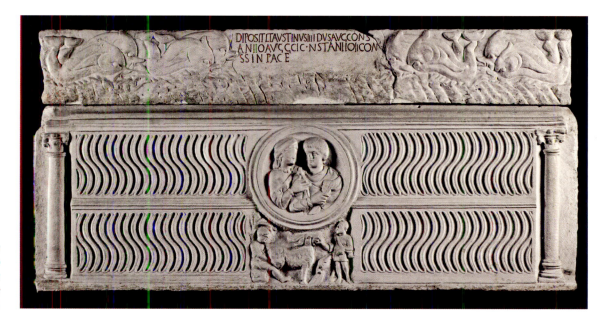

12. Sarcophagus of Flavius Faustinus, Pio Cristiano Museum in the Vatican (Photographic Archive of the Vatican Museums).

were used: this type is also represented by marble urns, imitating the shape of the baskets, both in Rome[58], but even more frequently in the region of Aquileia.[59] (fig. 13) Comparable examples were discovered in other parts of the Empire, for example in Trier or in Britannia[60], but it would seem they were not previously found in central Italy. If this hypothesis were true, one would obviously have to imagine that the ashes were initially wrapped in a piece of cloth[61] to make sure the remains of the deceased would not be filtered through the fissures of the basket. The fact that evidence for this type of urn passed unnoticed until now, could be due to the preservation of the context, the nature of the soil and the very frailty of the remains. Even though their consistency is scarce, they serve to prove the existence of an even greater differentiation among burials than could only have been suspected until now. More or less elaborate tomb buildings could be used for burials, enriched with decorations in fresco, in stucco or in stone, in which the human remains would be collected in urns or marble sarcophagi; and finally, at the other end of the social scale, extremely poor funerary deposits were made, like the ones described above. If the proposed interpretation is correct, we would be obliged to hypothesize the existence of other preparations in perishable materials. For example, *stelae* or small enclosures realised in wood or with hedges could not have survived until now, which therefore changes our perception of the funerary phenomenon to some degree, preventing us

from recognising the burials of the socially weakest class. At the same time, it is necessary to underline, however, that the internal subdivision of the *necropoleis* was not subject to strict planning, that is, at least for those areas under examination. It is clear that the area under the Vatican basilica was a preferred area for burials of a certain economic and social level. Simultaneously, however, a certain heterogeneity can be established in the other nuclei, which may be partially explained by chronological differences that are not always easy to understand. In any case, in close proximity, burials of a certain standing are found that strained to use the space in a rational way, as well as burials that irregularly took up the space available, or at least considered as such, alongside very poor burial areas containing cremations in wooden urns (if the interpretation proposed above would be correct) and later inhumations without grave goods which were barely covered by a few reused brick tiles.

In conclusion, considering these observations, though they are synthetic rather than systematic, through a closer examination of the clear evidence given by some fundamental choices made in ancient culture in regard to death, it is possible to catch a glimpse of the wide variety of choices, attitudes and beliefs, as well as an extremely varied and complex social and cultural stratification. This is the reason why the study of *necropoleis* and Roman funerary customs is so important for the understanding of the city of the living.

13. Cinerary urn imitating a wicker basket, Aquileia, National Archaeological Museum.

14. Santa Rosa Necropolis, view of the north-western section.

15. Santa Rosa Necropolis, view of the south-eastern inhumation area

On the following pages:
16. Santa Rosa Necropolis, tomb III, niche with stucco decoration depicting Medea and the Pleiades.

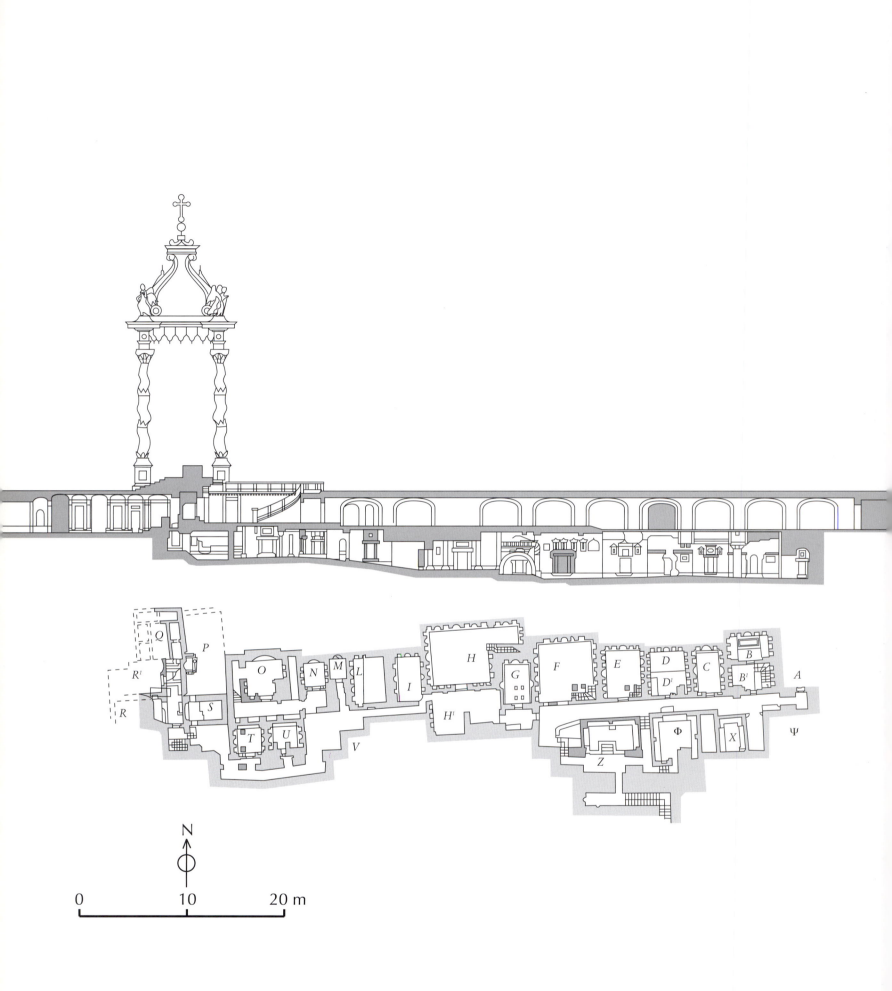

CHAPTER THREE
THE NECROPOLIS UNDER ST. PETER'S BASILICA

The necropolis excavated under St. Peter's Basilica is, without a doubt, the most famous one in the area; one could even say it is the Vatican necropolis *par excellence.* This is certainly not only due to the historic importance of the excavation, but also to its topographical and archaeological value. No other necropolis in Rome can match up to its quality and high state of preservation. The necropolis is, however, even more famous for the presence of an extraordinary tomb: the one of the apostle Peter, the main generator for the construction of the basilica above and, subsequently, the entire monumental Vatican complex.

As a result, the chapter dealing with this area needs to focus on a series of problems that are essential for a broader understanding of the complex significance of the excavations, even if they at times go beyond the topic related to burials and the usual archaeological problems. The excavations have drawn the attention of many specialists from various disciplines and a vast bibliography has built up over the years. Just consider the fact that in 1964 a volume of 260 pages was needed to collect the 870 publications written until this time about the problems that had arisen from these discoveries.[1] Today, forty-five years later, a volume of similar size would not suffice to review the studies that have come out since.

It is evident, on the other hand, that these topics can only be covered in a synthetic and highly selective manner. By studying them together, however, some connections can be made that would be missed otherwise by too detailed a study. Moreover, one can get a better general understanding of the discussion on the topic so far. On the other hand, the discussion will only be occasionally referred to the basilica when it is necessary to understand the general problems, as there is another volume planned in this series, dedicated completely to it.

At the time of Nero, the southern slope of the Vatican hill continued all the way down to the outer limit of the Circus. In this period, however, this part of the hill was not yet occupied by monumental tombs. They would appear, if ever, in the area further east, closer to the *Pons Neronianus*, or further south, in the area located between the Circus and the Via Cornelia-Aurelia. In fact, both the pyramid that was built at the beginning of the Via della Conciliazione – the so-called *Meta Romuli* – and the adjacent circular tomb that, again in the Mediaeval Period was called *Tiburtinus* or *Terebintus* of Nero, are dated to the Late Republican or Augustan Period.[2] South of the Circus, a burial chamber was discovered by Magi during the construction of the Audience Hall Paolo VI[3]: the tomb is a *columbarium*, a sepulchre used, at least initially, only for cremations. The threshold of the door on the south side, opening towards the nearby Via Cornelia-Aurelia, is located on the same level as the arena of the Vatican circus and the monument has been dated to the period between Nero and Domitian – thus the second half of the first century AD. One could hypothesize that traces of another similar tomb were preserved, not far off, marked by the funerary inscription of Tiberius Claudius Abascantus, Tiberius Iulus Tyrus and Nonius Stratonice[4], datable to the same period. The inscription, that has disappeared today, was discovered further to the east in the first decades of the sixteenth century, when the Palazzo of Cardinal Lorenzo Pucci, that would later be the seat of the Holy Office, today the Congregation for the Doctrine of Faith, was enlarged.

Only in the second century AD, when space was no longer available in the vicinity of the bridge and along the Via Cornelia, the tombs of the necropolis started to occupy the slopes of the hill, lining up north of the Circus. They represent the oldest excavated monumental tombs in the area (tombs A-G, O, S, cfr. Fig. 1) built between the age of Hadrian and the first years of the reign of Antoninus Pius, along a narrow path that the excavators called *iter* and that today still constitutes the east-west axis of the burial ground.

If we look at the relative chronology of the funerary chambers and the way they are built against each other, it becomes evident that the occupation of the area started from the east and that tomb A, the tomb of Popilius Heracla (fig. 2) the inscription of which tells us it has been built "*in Vatica(no) ad Circum*"[5], is not only the easternmost tomb, but also the oldest one. At the time of its construction, moreover, tomb Ψ did not exist yet. It presently sits in front of tomb A, blocking its view towards the valley. The indication *ad Circum* could therefore refer to a more specific meaning: "on the edge of the Circus area". We could even say, without pushing things too far, that Heracla's relatives, gathered on the terrace on top of the tomb for the funerary ceremonies, could enjoy the chariot races that took place on the track below, a few metres towards the south. Only in the second half of the second century AD, as already mentioned, the Circus was abandoned and occupied by tombs, one of which was found directly behind the foundation of the obelisk (fig. 5).[6] The tombs encroached upon or even extended beyond the limit of the *iter*, towards the valley

2. Inscription of the tomb of Popilius Heraclca in the Vatican Necropolis.

*On the following pages:
3. View of the* iter *that runs across the Vatican Necropolis in east-western direction; the first floor of tomb F.*

(tombs H, U, T, R).[7] Let us return, however, to the beginning, when the Circus was still fully functioning. In the Neronian Period, this building and the surrounding gardens were the setting for the persecutions with which the emperor intended to punish the Christians for the fire that destroyed large parts of the city in AD 64. Some Christians were crucified, others burned like human torches, some were torn to pieces by animals while re-enacting a mythological pantomime.[8]

According to a large number of scholars, the apostle Peter was also crucified during these persecutions.[9] Saint Jerome[10], however, offers a different chronology, referring in his turn to the *Chronographia* of Eusebius of Caesarea (now lost): according to these writers the martyrdom of Peter took place three years later, in AD 67. The difference is obviously not substantial, but there are many more problems surrounding this event that have been passionately debated. However, a more objective point of view may now be possible, taking into account some of the recent discoveries.

4. The iter *of the Vatican Necropolis during the excavations before the reconstruction of the Grottoes' paving (1941-42).*
5. Axonometric drawing of the excavations at the base of the Vatican Obelisk with the adjacent tombs (from Castagnoli 1959-60).

6. Axonometric drawing of the area around Courtyard P (from Esplorazioni *1951).*

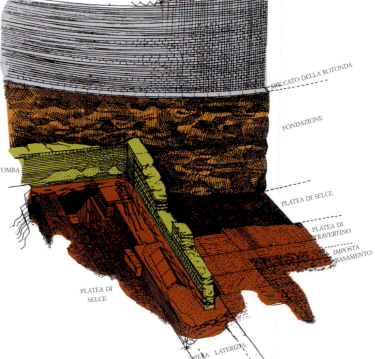

THE TOMB OF SAINT PETER

Until now, only the overall development of the necropolis has been discussed, focussing on monumental tombs from the Hadrianic Period onwards. The possibility of finding humble tombs from an earlier period, however, has not been considered: this is actually the case for the tomb inside which the remains of the apostle Peter were supposedly buried. Because of its complexity, Peter's tomb deserves a more detailed discussion.

The first reference to the burial of the apostle is by the already abovementioned Eusebius of Caesarea, the first Church historian.[11] He quotes Gaius, a priest who wrote, in about AD 200, the Disputes or Dialogues against Proclus, a Montanist heretic, who boasted about the tomb of the apostle (or the deacon) Philip at Hierapolis in Phrygia. Gaius, however, sets it against the *tropaea*, the "trophies" of the apostles Peter and Paul, visible in the

Vatican and along the Via Ostiense respectively. Based on the context, the word *tropaea* is a reference to the tombs of the two apostles, whose martyrdom equalled the triumph of faith over death and sin.

Two large-scale and complex excavations under the paving of the Vatican Grottoes took place during the pontificate of Pius XII (1940-49, 1953-57) (figs 5,6) and brought to light a series of very important archaeological data, often difficult to interpret. Today, the western half of the basilica consists of three levels (fig. 2). The first level corresponds to the floor level of the current church, but immediately below we find the area of the Grottoes where artefacts related to the basilica's history are preserved, as well as several papal tombs. The floor level of this area is essentially that of the Constantinian basilica which the Renaissance church intended to preserve, at least in its first designs. However, when Antonio da Sangallo the Younger became the architect of the direction of the

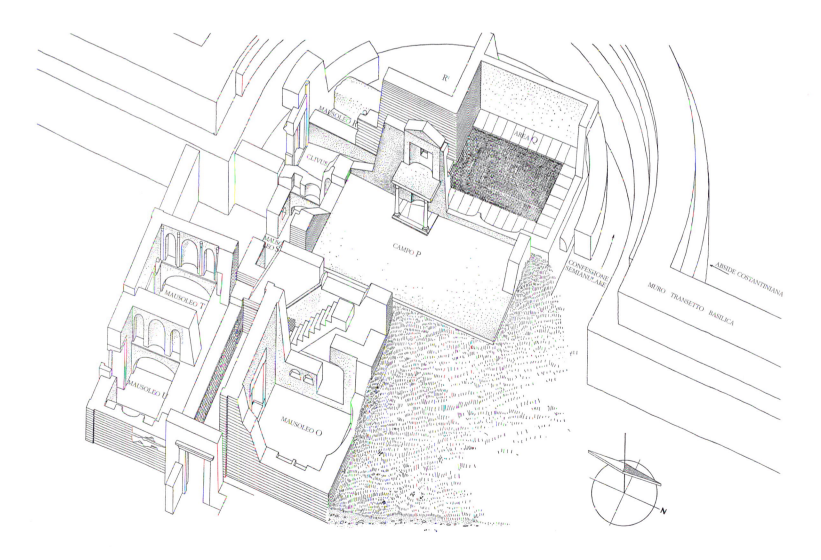

Fabric of Saint Peter (1520) he brought about some important changes to the original design of Bramante. Besides strengthening the pilasters of the cupola, and so abolishing the large niches, he also decided to give the naves a more classical layout. To that end, the floor was elevated by circa three meters, supported by a series of vaults that created accessible spaces: the famous Vatican Grottoes. In the previous century, Pope Pius XII decided to lower the floor level in order to enlarge the available space: that is when the Roman tombs, which had already been briefly sighted in the previous centuries, started to appear (fig. 4). Despite the difficulties caused by the Second World War, the pope decided to start excavating, and the tombs that are now visible on the third and deepest level, were brought to light. The architectural history of the basilica explains, moreover, why the excavations ended on the eastern side at tomb A, that of Popilius Heracla: beyond it, we find Maderno's extension of the basilica. To increase the capacity of the church, Maderno changed the Greek cross layout and turned it into a Latin cross floor plan. The entire eastern side of the building respects the floor level as set by Sangallo, but its paving is resting on an earthwork instead of arches. This means that in the event of continuing the excavations in the direction of the basilica's entrance, the digging would not be as easy as the previous ones that took place under the Grottoes' arches, as it would involve dismantling the paving of the basilica and would therefore interfere with the church's celebration of the liturgy.

The excavations that were carried out in the area immediately surrounding the papal altar and partly even directly underneath it, revealed an extremely complicated situation, but, to be very short, it brought to light an open courtyard among the other funerary buildings: the so-called "Campo P".[12] (fig. 6) Although the state of preservation was partly compromised by the foundations of structures in later centuries, among which the columns of the bronze baldachin of Bernini, it is possible to identify a boundary wall on the western side of the open area, simply called the "red wall", because of the colour of its plaster. Behind it ran a small street uphill (named *clivus* by the excavators), which allowed access to the adjacent funerary enclosure Q. East of the red wall, that opened to Courtyard P, stood a simple aedicule with two columns that framed two superimposed niches, cut out in the same red wall (figs. 9-10). On the same vertical axis, a third subterranean niche was added, about which I will expand shortly.

For now, it suffices to say that the aedicule, the red wall and the small street running at the back were all built in one phase, the chronology of which could be deduced based on a series of brick stamps, produced at the latest in AD 161.[13] The aedicule, moreover, was immediately identified as the "trophy" mentioned by Gaius. The two columns, one of which is no longer in place today, had to support a marble slab to give prominence to the larger niche. Above this sort of console, the imprints of which also remain in the red wall, there was a smaller second niche containing a small window. The top of the aedicule is not preserved and the reconstruction of a triangular tympanum (fig. 7) is purely indicative and hypothetical. The larger niche coincides today with the Niche of the *Pallia* (fig. 8) in the Confession below the altar. This niche, that is, that appears to be covered with a mediaeval mosaic (very integrated) showing Christ, in which the *pallia* were stored – that is, the short stoles of the archbishops – before they were delivered as a *symbol* of a particularly tight bond which connected them to the apostolic seat of Peter.

In correspondence to the aedicule and under the ancient street level, one finds a ditch which is also partly inserted in the foundation of the red wall, forming the third, already mentioned, subterranean niche, which was of a rather irregular shape. The ditch, in which one would expect to find the relics of the apostle, was in fact disturbed and did not contain human remains. Around the aedicule, a number of deposits were discovered from various time periods (fig. 14). The two oldest ones antedate the monumentalization of Courtyard P: the first is tomb θ, a ditch covered by tiles *a cappuccina*, one of which contains a brick stamp from the Vespasianic Period. This chronological indication does not, however, seem to be secure as the level at which the tomb is found is relatively high and would suggest a period somewhat later. In this case, the tile containing the brick stamp could have been reused.[14] The dating of tomb γ is more reliable. It concerns a very deep terracotta coffin, covered by tiles and a walled structure that can be dated to the years AD 115-123, once more thanks to a brick stamp.[15]

In a phase subsequent to the construction of the "trophy of Gaius" a wall was inserted, moving the right column. It concerned wall *g*, also called the wall of the graffiti, because it contained a large number of devotional graffiti (figs. 11-13). This wall abutted the red wall, but not at a perfectly right angle, and contained a *loculus* cut out after its construction. The excavators found this *loculus*,

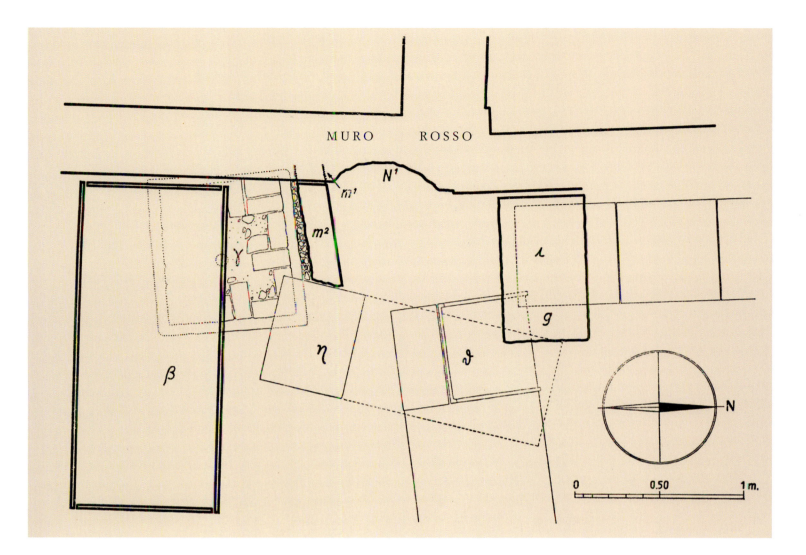

MURO   ROSSO

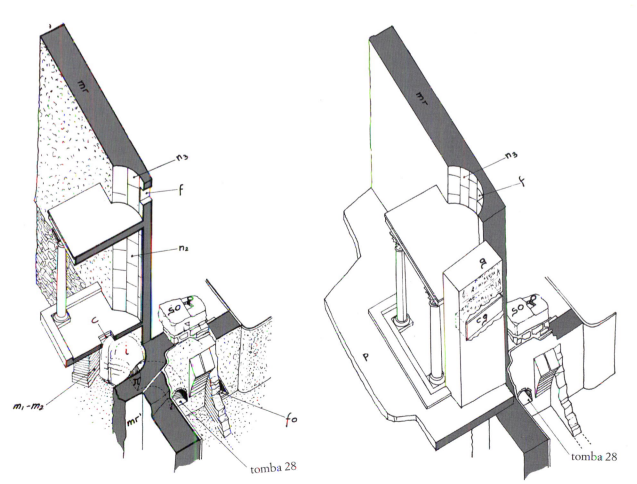

8. *Mosaic with a depiction of Christ in the Niche of the* Pallia.

9. *Plan of the "Trophy of Gaius" (from* Esplorazioni *1951).*

10. *Axonometric section drawing of the trophy with the three niches above (from Prandi).*

11. *Axonometric section drawing of the trophy with the addition of wall* g *(from Prandi).*

tomba 28

covered on the inside with marble slabs, to be essentially empty. Some years later, however, the well-known epigraphist Margherita Guarducci began to study the graffiti left on wall *g* by the ancient pilgrims. Based on the testimonies of Giovanni Segoni head of the workmen that worked at the excavations, Guarducci believed that a box in the storeroom could be identified as containing bones, which would have been removed from the *loculus* without the knowledge of the archaeologists. According to her reconstruction, these bones would been Peter's – in a period that is difficult to fix but in any case before the intervention of Constantine who had the trophy enclosed by a sort of security wall: the so-called *memoria*. The bones would have been exhumed from the ditch and placed in the *loculus*, after they had been wrapped in a purple cloth with gold threads, of which still some traces exist.[16]

To support this interpretation, Guarducci used a graffito as evidence (figs. 15, 16), which originated in the plaster cover of the red wall, where it was abutted by wall *g*. Unfortunately, it was not found *in situ*. On it, there are two highly suggestive Greek words, which Guarducci completed as: Πέτδ[ος] ἔνι, "Peter is here." The two words, which are the only attestation of Peter's name among the hundreds of graffiti present, are located on the edge of a lacuna, which makes it impossible to completely exclude different readings.[17]

Some final elements can be brought forth regarding Guarducci's hypothesis: first of all, an observation that deserves a close inspection. The Constantinian basilica was built with the "Trophy of Gaius" as the focal point in the apse. The orientation of the church, however, does not correspond to that of the necropolis or the circus, but diverges a few degrees from it. This diversion should be verifiable in wall *g*, which was also included in the Constantinian *memoria*. It was exactly on this small wall, however, that the architects of the emperor and Pope Sylvester would have based the orientation of the construction and, which in their eyes, was of extraordinary importance.[18] However, also this argument is not decisive as – if verified – it would only prove that at the beginning of the fourth century AD the *loculus* was highly regarded and would, for that, reason be interpreted as the apostle's burial.

Recent research on the tomb of Saint Paul in the basilica on the Via Ostiense is more interesting.[19] In fact, here, under the papal altar in the middle of the transept, a marble chest was found and, according to all evidence, it concerns a sarcophagus. It is not located on the original Constantinian level, but on the elevated floor level of the late fourth century, that is, of the second basilica built by Theodosius. If this reading, that presents itself immediately, is correct, it would concern the corpse of the apostle that would have been exhumed from its original bur-

14. *Plan of Courtyard P and the surrounding area with inhumations (from Prandi).*
15. *Plaster fragment with the graffito* pétros éni.
16. *Drawing of the graffito* pétros éni.

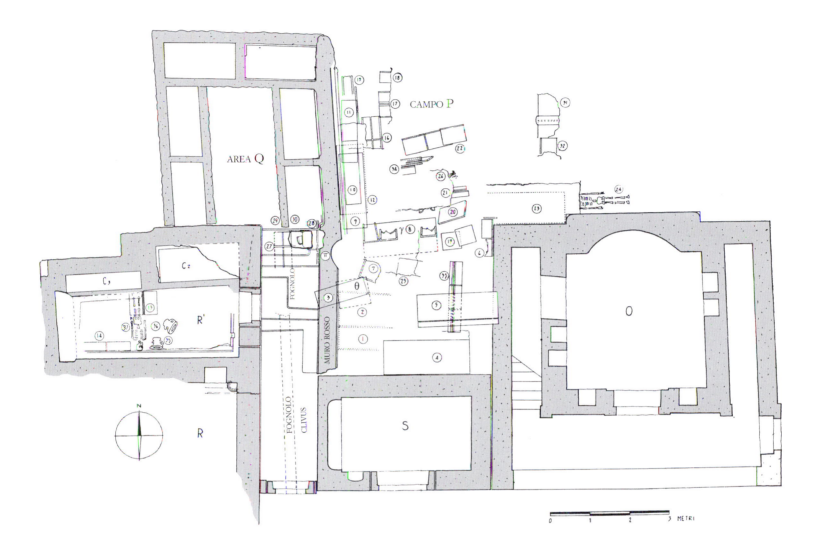

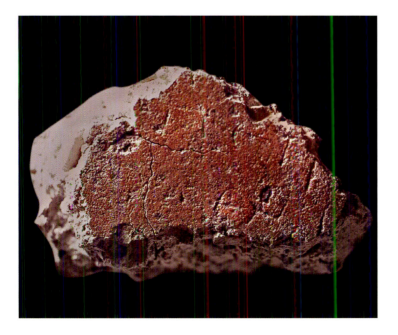

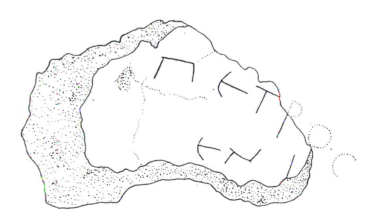

ial place and raised to a level that was compatible with the new architectural layout of the church: in other words, an elevation that did not change its position within the church. Moreover, exactly while these lines are being written, it has been announced that via an endoscopy, a few remains of bones and two clothes have been found inside the sarcophagus: a purple linen cloth interwoven with golden threads and a second blue cloth.[20] Observing the situation as a whole, one can only recall the one reconstructed by Guarducci for the bones of Saint Peter, also maintaining the chronological difference between the two exhumations.

These are the main data that scholars, dealing with the issue, have interpreted in many different ways.[21] As is understandable, not all scholars accepted Guarducci's reconstruction. The criticism ranges from the negation of the bones' identification, considering that the complex circumstances described above between the excavation and the eventful discovery do not provide a completely unproblematic situation, to more radical attitudes that also deny the initial presence of a deposit in the trench underneath the trophy.[22] One of the main problems is the fact that between the death of the apostle (AD 64 or 67) and the first subsequent secure date (the construction of the "Trophy of Gaius", say before AD 161) there is a gap of about a century for which there are no literary of archaeological data that would help us to understand how the memory of the burial could have been preserved without a recurring liturgy or some sort of registration. We know in fact, that around the mid third century AD, the celebration of the apostle's festival on June 29 did not take place in the Vatican but near the catacombs that are now known as those of Saint Sebastian on the Via Appia.[23] The festival of Saint Paul, on the other hand, was at the same time celebrated on the Via Ostiense, therefore near his tomb. At the catacombs of Saint Sebastian, a complex was found with a portico and rooms for banquets (fig. 17), on the walls of which graffiti were discovered invoking the apostles Peter and Paul.[24]

One can respond to this important observation in various ways: first of all, it is logical that the cult of the martyrs would only have started to flourish at a moment during the Church's existence when the first serious theological disagreements and heresies had started to be examined, as only then the importance of the apostolic tradition was recognised. In other words, there was a need to appeal to the founders of the community as guarantors of the transmission of faith's patrimony. The "Trophy of Gaius" in the Vatican represents, in fact, the first archaeological evidence of such a cult, like, on a textual level, the passion of Saint Policarp, bishop in Asia Minor, which is dated to

the same period. Secondly, it is not impossible that a memory is orally passed on for a century: in human terms, a century corresponds to three generations and can be covered by a single passage of information from grandparent to grandchild.[25] Finally, Stefan Heid's new interpretation for Ignatius of Antioch's letter to the Romans should be considered.[26] Around AD 110 the bishop was transferred to Rome, condemned to the wild animals in the Circus. He wrote an important letter to the Romans begging them to do nothing that would impede his martyrdom: then he would be a disciple of Jesus Christ, when the world would not see his body.[27] With this type of martyrdom it is inherent that the world would not see his body as, devoured by the wild animals, he would not have a tomb and could therefore not be venerated. Ignatius continued, comparing his insignificance as a prisoner to the dignity of the apostles Peter and Paul: apostles were deemed free as they had already faced their martyrdom. If all the consequences of this comparison are drawn, there is a further implication: the saint from Antioch wanted to suggestively show that he did not in itself want a tomb surrounded by veneration, like those of the apos-

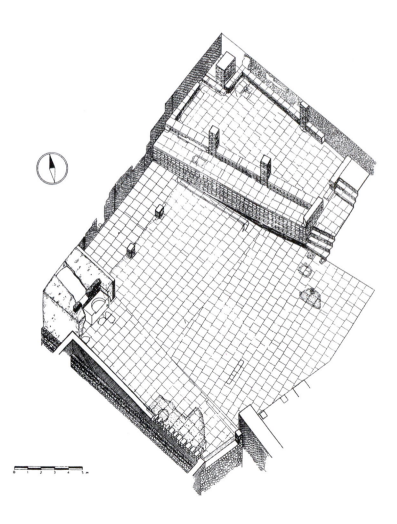

tles Peter and Paul. This subtle deduction therefore offers the testimony that we are looking for, right in the middle of that century for which references to the apostolic tomb are lacking.

This discussion has been particularly heated in the past years, but that is at least partly due to not having the various levels of the problem sufficiently distinguished.[28] It is necessary to recognise at least three levels: the historic level of Peter's death in Rome, the archaeological one of the tomb's identification and, finally, the last one considering the devotion to the relics.

If the matter is set in these terms, it is immediately evident that the first level is by far the most important: this is the hard core of the tradition that, even though it is often allusive and hardly explicit, is nevertheless coherent in reporting Peter's death in Rome during the reign of Nero. This fact is by now no longer seriously doubted and, with one exception, scholars of various inclinations, both catholic and protestant, agree on this after all.[29]

For the second level, that of the identification of the tomb, we have the reasonable certainty that it was identified as the "Trophy of Gaius" already around the mid second century. For the period before, we have seen the various interpretations that have been proposed and the complex issues. At the same time, however, it has been acknowledged that, all things considered, there are no motives to deny *a priori* the possibility, and that the scholars' various viewpoints are significantly dependant on the likelihood they attribute to the later tradition.

Finally, regarding the identification of the relics, we have no certainties, but without wanting to underrate the importance of the devotional aspect, the level of this discourse must be considered subordinate to the previous ones. In other words, the problem of identification of the bones does not compromise the historic reconstruction, the significance and ecclesial role of the bishop of Rome, or, finally, the importance of the Vatican basilica.

THE NECROPOLIS

Now the initial issues have been explained, the moment has arrived to examine the necropolis. At this point, it is useful to make a first terminological observation. Current literature traditionally talks about "mausolea", referring to the burial chambers of which they are composed. This term, however, is not correct and will be avoided here. The Latin term, if anything, is *monumentum*, in the sense that it is a memory to the deceased. The term is found in the already mentioned inscription of Popilius Heracla, in which it refers in fact to the tomb. In Rome, on the other

hand, there was only one mausoleum in the first three centuries AD, the one of Augustus.[30] Not even the famous tomb of Hadrian, which is very often called a mausoleum in scientific and popular literature, is named such in the ancient sources.[31] The term mausoleum is only effectively used in the Roman territories of Northern Africa to designate funerary chambers that are similar to those in Vatican necropolis. It is evident, however, that it concerns a regional and provincial use of the word.[32] In Rome, on the other hand, the term would only evolve at the beginning of the fourth century AD when it is exclusively used to specify imperial tombs, and therefore has a very limited meaning.

In the previous pages, the vast landfill that covered the necropolis has been mentioned. It is necessary, however, to discuss its origins more explicitly. At the beginning the necropolis was mainly pagan, apart from the "Trophy of Gaius", and only at the very end it began to show traces of Christian burials. When Constantine conquered Rome, having eliminated his rival Maxentius at the battle of the Milvian Bridge (AD 312), he proclaimed religious tolerance in the Edict of Milan (AD 313), granting the Church the freedom of faith. One of his first concerns was to give support and visibility to this new religious community that finally emerged from the shadows already rather firmly structured. However, it was essentially without a cult place in which the congregation of believers could come together for the liturgy and to recognise itself as a community.

This is when the construction of various basilicas started, among which in Rome the first must have been the cathedral dedicated to the Saviour, subsequently called Saint John in Lateran. Almost immediately, however, he turned his attention to the place where tradition located the tomb of the apostle Peter. The prestige and significance of this martyr were the main reasons for the extraordinary dimensions of the building that had to overcome major technical and legal obstacles, in that he did not want to touch the burial location in any way. It was located on the hillside that bore a double slope: steep in north-south direction and less steep in east-west direction. Moreover, the presence of the necropolis all around the tombs, of which were protected by law and custom, was not a small problem. Regarding one of the typical contradictions in this time of transformation, to construct the largest Christian basilica, Constantine had to act as Pontifex Maximus: the highest priestly authority in pagan religion and expert in sacred law. In this capacity he could therefore authorise the colossal building works that entailed the excavation of the hill, uphill from the tomb and the burial of the others downhill until a level of at least seven meters was reached to create the substructures and the large platform on which Saint Peter would rise (fig. 19).

It is thanks to this burial that the necropolis, compared to the majority of other similar examples, was extraordinarily well preserved. The tombs of the necropolis were occasionally sighted during the construction of the Renaissance basilica, during the works in the Confession (fig. 18) and, finally, when works took place around the pontifical altar to build the bronze baldachin of Bernini in 1626.[33] Among these discoveries – some of the most important ones will be discussed later – the sarcophagus of Junius Bassus is mentioned, which was found during the papacy of Clemens VIII (1597) during the enlargement of the Confession.[34] The deceased was a person at the peak of his political career in his day: at the time of the emperor Constantius II, in AD 359, he was made Urban Prefect of Rome at the age of 42, but he died the same year.[35]

The sarcophagus is a cornerstone for Early Christian art (fig. 20), both for its secure date, for the high quality of its reliefs and, finally, for the complexity of the figurative programme. On the front there is a series of scenes from the Old and New Testament, arranged in two superimposed registers, both enclosed by an architectural cornice in the tradition of the sarcophagi with columns. The scene is not in chronological or narrative order, but the Saviour is represented in the centre. In the upper register we find the key scene: Christ, young and without a beard, is depicted in a variation to the so-called *Traditio legis*, or Christ the Lawgiver, scheme. With his left hand, Christ hands over the new law to Peter, who presided over the apostolic community, while on his left is Paul, the other Pillar of the Church of Rome. It is on this depiction of the two saint martyrs that the Church founded its apostolic origins and its authority among the other local churches. Christ (fig. 21) is turned directly towards the spectator,

expressed by the frontality of his pose that was insistently used in Late Antique and Early Christian art. At the same time, he summons the spectator and stands out thanks to the authority of his pose. Despite his juvenile features, he is seated raised on a step on a type of throne with carved lion legs. At his feet there, is a bearded figure that emerges from the ground. Half his body is shown and his head is covered by a billowing cloak that draws an arch, held at the end by his two hands. It is a representation of Heaven, or in Greek, of the *Kosmos*, which derives from Roman art, but was reused as a symbol to confer the Saviour sovereignty over the universe and the new law, a value that transcends time and space.

The representations on the front of the sarcophagus can be read as references to St. Peter's Basilica and its decoration: unlike the *aediculae* that enclose the scenes on the side, the two in the centre of both registers that contain an image of Christ are the only ones that are flanked by columns decorated by vine branches in low relief, in between which are depicted *putti* that are harvesting grapes. It is easy to recognise in them the columns decorated with vine that surround the tomb of the apostle Peter in the apse of the basilica and which, according to the *Liber Pontificalis* (34.16), the same Constantine had imported from the East. Until today, they can be admired, inserted in the upper niches of the four pillars that support the cupola[36]: they constitute a clear allusion to the tomb of Peter to the extent that the same Bernini was inspired by it when he built his bronze baldachin. The iconography of Christ, on the other hand, seated on the *Kosmos* while handing over the law, seems to be a synthetic allusion to two mosaics that ornate the basilica: the one on the triumphal arch that divided the nave from the transept with Christ seated on the globe of the world, and the other in the apse where the *Traditio legis* scheme would be used.[37]

To continue the examination of the upper register, flanking the central scene and in a significant example of parallelism, the left hand scene depicts the arrest of Peter and symmetrically, on the right, the arrest of Christ himself. On the far left side we find the sacrifice of Isaac, a character of Christ's redeeming sacrifice, and on the right side the judgement of Pontius Pilate. In the lower register Christ appears once again in the central scene, this time depicted at his entrance into Jerusalem. The used iconographic scheme subtly plays with the imagery familiar to the ancient spectator, to whom the entrance of Christ had to recall the *adventus* of the emperors (but also of high officials), that is their formal and ceremonial arrival to the city in the presence of the population, the senate or Decurions. Such a reference was made, however, through a sort of counterpoint: the imperial chariot pulled by horses has been replaced by a simpler draught animal, a donkey. The whole scene alludes to an *adventus*,

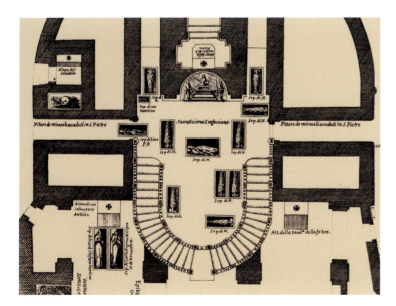

even royal one, but at the same time he is a bearer of peace and salvation that shuns the manifestation of a military triumph and earthly power.[38]

To the left of the lower register's central scene, we find a representation of Adam and Eve flanking the tree of good and evil. They are represented in a demure pose for having just committed the original sin that Christ had redeemed with his incarnation. On the far left there is Job seated in disgrace after having lost his fortune, his loved ones and his health: a symbol of man's state of pain, but also of his indestructible faith in God. On the right there is Daniel (with restored head) in the lions' den, another image of someone who completely trusts in God, while on the far right we find Paul who is being brought to martyrdom, a scene necessary to complement Peter's arrest already seen on the upper register.

On the whole, it concerns one of the most important sarcophagi of the time, a mirror of the high level of commissions. The workshop of sculptors responsible for it was capable of modifying traditional motives with a certain originality; the characters have been represented in a classical style that manifests itself in the choice of a still remarkable organic naturalism, if one considers the average contemporary sarcophagi production. The relief is unusually deep and the figures stand out against the background emphasised by the powerful *chiaroscuro*; the architectural cornice separates the scenes, distinguishes a relative hierarchy of importance among the scenes and scans the figurative rhythm, even if the distribution of the scenes takes the composite criteria into account and caused many discussions among the specialists.

The sarcophagus of Junius Bassus was discovered in the far west of the basilica, right at the apex of the apse in line with the Peter's tomb, and thus in a highly privileged location that can only be explained by the very high status of the deceased.

A, the tomb of Popilius Heracla

A coherent topographic examination of the necropolis needs to start at the very edge, with tomb A, the one of Popilius Heracla, already mentioned several times.[39] It suffices to dedicate only a few lines to this tomb: its important inscription has already been discussed on several occasions (cfr. table 2 p. 43). One could add that the inscription incorporates part of Heracla's testament containing exact instructions as to the construction of his tomb (*monumentum*). They included the financial resources that were to be used for the construction and also the place in which the tomb was to be built: in the Vatican in the vicinity of the circus "near the tomb of Ulpius Narcissus" which, as we can deduce, was buried a few meters to the east under the basilica's extension by Maderno. The price of the tomb, 6,000 sesterces, is also interesting: we do not know how rich the internal decoration was and also the complete dimensions can only be reconstructed based on comparisons to other tombs that have been fully excavated; only the entrance of the tomb has been excavated, squeezed in between the buttresses that contain the soil and support the structures above. It can be hypothesised, however, that it occupied an area of approximately 25 square meters and therefore did not belong to the largest and most impressive tombs.

However, as a comparison, the amount corresponds to five years' salary of a legionnaire[40], which on the one hand gives us an idea of the investment's scale that was needed for acquiring land and constructing a tomb building. On the other, it gives us an insight into the economic capacity that a certain number of freedmen could acquire.

In front of tomb A, at least two meters, there is another ancient wall: the one at the back of the tomb indicated with the Greek letter Ψ, which is part of the funerary

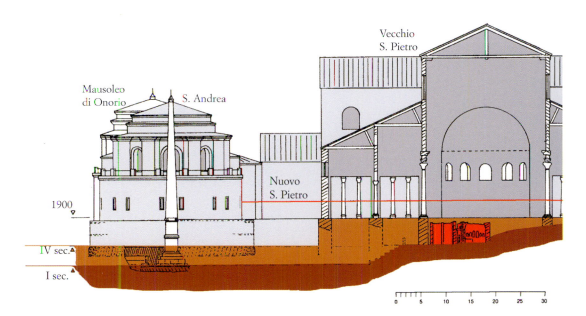

18. *Benedetto Drei,* Plan of the Vatican Grottoes *(1635) with the works around the Confession of Saint Peter.*
19. *Section of the Vatican Hill with the superimposition of the Constantinian basilica and the necropolis together with the various elevations of the terrain until the modern period (from Biering – von Hesberg 1987, modification by Liverani).*

20. *Sarcophagus of Junius Bassus, Saint Peter's basilica, Treasury Museum.*

21. *Sarcophagus of Junius Bassus, detail of Christ handing over the new law to Saint Peter in front of Saint Paul.*

chambers that were constructed at the end of the second century AD when the border with the circus area became less respected and the necropolis could occupy the space. Not even this tomb could be excavated, however, and only the north-west corner can be seen.[41]

B, the tomb of Fannia Redempta

From a chronological point of view, the next tomb was built against the western wall of tomb A at short intervals.[42] The name by which it is known does not actually correspond to its female founder, but basically to a woman who was buried there in a relatively later period and who was the wife of Aurelius Hermes, imperial freedman of possibly Septimius Severus and Caracalla.[43] We do not know the name of the original owners as the inscription next to the doorway was removed. When it was originally constructed at the time of the emperor Hadrian, the tomb consisted of two spaces: a courtyard surrounded by a wall of almost three meters high from which one would access the real chamber through a wide arch. The chamber, covered by a cross vault, showed the common division of the walls with alternating niches in the upper part, while the lower part was concealed by *arcosolia* that were added later (fig. 22). Only in a second phase, the funerary chamber was really clearly separated from the courtyard: around the mid-third century AD it was paved with a black and white mosaic in a rather schematic and rigid way, depicting two doves symmetrically arranged on each side of a crater, while the rest of the paving was decorated with slender spiral-woven vegetation. Simultaneously, underneath the arch, a wide travertine threshold was put in to mark the passage with the courtyard. In the course of the second half of the same century, the arch was blocked in with a wall in *opus listatum*, a type of masonry that could be constructed rather quickly and which has a typical outer facing of alternating layers of brick and tuff blocks. The passage was now secured by a door, while light entered through a number of windows cut in the top section of the arch. It is possible that in this moment the inscription, which was originally located to the right of the door of the courtyard, was moved to this wall which has a cavity above the architrave. At the same time, the *arcosolia* were built in the main chamber to house the inhumations that are visible in the lower part of the walls: in fact, in this period the cremation rite had almost disappeared and there was a need for new graves for burials.

In a final stage, close to the construction works of the Constantinian basilica, the door of the courtyard was closed and the wall raised to the level of the basilica. At the eastern part of the courtyard a small masonry staircase was constructed which, even if it was built in an awkward way, had to provide access to the tomb from above until the very end, that is, until the tomb was buried completely.

The pictorial decoration shows various phases which we must relate to the different reconstructions of the structure. The more refined pictures belong, without a doubt, to the first phase: in the central niche of the front wall on a white background we find a peacock, a characteristic attribute of Juno, in front of a crater, probably made of glass, filled with flowers and fruit. On the left wall, on the other hand, the central niche was decorated with symbols of Venus: we can recognise part of a golden make-up box, from which a dove takes a necklace, while a second dove is symmetrically sitting on the right hand side. On the box there is a sceptre with a crown of flowers, alluding to the goddess' powers. The corresponding niche on the right wall reveals a slight glimpse of a lance, possibly a reference to Mars.

Originally, the niches were framed by columns, like in tomb G, which must have been decorated by the same workshop, but these additions in stucco were removed during the redecoration in the second half of the third century. In the top section there are outstanding lunettes decorated with paintings of two birds flanked by cups on slender stands. The most interesting scheme, however, must be the one in the vault, which is still substantially preserved. The frescoes are organised in five cross shaped medallions of which the central and largest one still shows, even though it has partly disappeared: the *quadriga* of *Helios*, a divinity that was popular in the third century AD and that was depicted for three quarters with his right arm lifted holding a whip. He is dressed in a long-sleeved *chiton* and a purple mantle flapping behind his shoulders, while his head is framed by a circular nimbus. The other four medallions depict the four seasons: on the west there is probably spring and on the opposite side, autumn, while on the south side we find winter. The medallion depicting summer is lost.

In a second phase, as already mentioned, a subtle layer of lime was added to serve as a base for a new decoration. A good part of it is only documented by old photographs because the layer was removed during the first restorations that were aimed at recovering the first decoration

phase. It concerns a rather coarse style in which linear features divided the wall's surface on which images of birds and racemes were painted. As a contrast, the lower part of the wall including the *arcosolia* that were constructed on the same occasion had a faux marble decoration.

X, the tomb of "the Tulli and the Caetennii"

In front of tomb B, the small tomb *X* was constructed at the beginning of the third century AD. Its entrance has unfortunately been blocked by a sixteenth century foundation wall and access to it is therefore rather difficult, and can only happen via the vault which was broken through by the workers of Constantine.[44] This is unfortunate as it is one of the finest tombs of its period thanks to the richness and variety of the decorations, exceeded only by nearby tomb Φ. The tone is already set by the *opus sectile* paving in geometric patterns consisting of tiles of a dozen different marbles in various colours: Breccia marble from Skyros, Caristian marble, marble from Chios, Bigio marble from Capo Tenaro, Bardiglio from Luni, Ardesia, Breccia Corallina from the quarries in Bythinia, Pavonazetto from Phrygia, and the so-called African marble, which in reality comes from Teos in Asia Minor, and which the ancients called Lucullean marble. The walls contained two superimposed levels of *arcosolia* for inhumations, as by this time the incineration rite had fallen into disuse.

The upper *loculus* on the west wall was decorated with a racemes relief in stucco of a high quality. The walls are white to put more emphasis on the painted mythological scenes that decorate the *arcosolia*. In three of the *arcosolia*, in the lower register marine deities are depicted, above which red stripes are pending. These are stylizations that allude to garlands or ribbons. In particular, the northern *arcosolium* is dedicated to Venus' triumph. The goddess stands out in her nudity against a dark background of a drapery supported on the side by a marine centaur and a triton (fig. 23). On the left a small cupid is riding a dolphin through the waves while its counterpart on the right is now lost. The eastern *arcosolium* is in a worse state: one can only guess as to the identity of a cupid accompanied by two dolphins on the left, following a second cupid who is riding a hippocampus. In the middle there seems to be a Nereid wearing a red cloak riding a marine centaur, while the group on the far right is no longer understandable. The best preserved painting is the one in the western *arcosolium*: on the left, a cupid with blue wings opens the scene. It is sitting on a marine creature no longer identifiable with a body wound in coils, and follows a hippocampus, drawn in a sketchy manner that is puller by a marine centaur that is turned towards the centre of the composition (fig. 24). It is holding a pastoral staff and, on its left, a blue mantle is billowing up. Its body is stretched in two twisted coils, on top of which a Nereid is resting in a semi-reclined position. She is wearing a red cloak, which leaves her body uncovered from the waist up. The flesh in bright colour stands out from the colour of the clothes, of the greenish tone of the hippocampus and the blue of the waves. On the right, traces remain of another hippocampus mounted by a cupid.

We find more elaborate decorations in the *arcosolia* of the upper register that are framed by garlands of flowers and fruit, and on top of which birds are sitting. The variety in fruit alludes to the various seasons of the year: from spring to autumn. At the end of the garlands we find Sileni, and in the centre a mask of Pan, part of the well tested Dionysian repertoire. The paintings are unfortunately poorly preserved. This repertoire, however, corresponds to the theme of the main scenes inside the *arcosolia*. The best preserved painting is the one on the northern wall which depicts a rather complex scene: the discovery of Ariadne by Dionysos at Naxos (fig. 25). On the left, the Cretan heroine lies on one side holding up her left arm which is folded behind her head: according to the ancient iconographic traditions a pose suggesting sleep. Her naked torso sticks out above her red mantle while the dress, from the belt up, is of a dark yellow colour. The hem of the mantle is lifted by a satyr of the god's retinue, who, astonished, uncovers her both in the strict and metaphoric meaning of the word. The character turns towards Dionysus to get his attention and the god comes forward, supported by a young satyr. He is wearing a large mantle and holds a thyrsus in his left hand while the right one is stretched towards the sleeping young girl in a silent dialogue. Above the figure of Ariadne, in the background, a satyr appears half-hidden from behind a rock; on the far right of the composition, behind Dionysus, there are two more figures: a bearded Silenus and a Maenad.

Beneath the fresco, in the middle of the *loculus* there was once an *emblema*, a panel in the finest mosaic, which is unfortunately almost completely lost. Only visible is a background consisting of a curtain hanging on a colonnade, which must be a reference to the interior of a palace in which the scene was set, possibly borrowed from the tragic repertoire.

In the eastern *arcosolium*, we find a painting of the meeting between Mars and Rea Silvia. The colours have very much vanished but the outline of the figures can still be discerned. The vestal, who became pregnant with the twin founders of Rome by the god, is sleeping in a reversed scheme, but similar to that of Ariadne. Next to her, on the right hand edge of the image we find a male figure that must represent Sleep. In front of Rea, in the middle of the composition, the warrior god is observing the

23. *Tomb* **X**, *lower* arcosolium *along the north wall, the triumph of Venus.*

24. *Tomb* **X**, *lower* arcosolium *along the west wall, Nereids and marine centaurs.*

25. *Tomb* **X**, *upper* arcosolium *along the north wall, Dionysus and Ariadne.*

woman: he is wearing a helmet and is armed with a sword, lance and shield. The lower part of his body is wrapped in a scarlet mantle, the *paludamentum*, which symbolises military authority. A small cupid in front of him draws his attention to Rea. Halfway to the right we can distinguish a veiled female figure who is sitting down with her hand at her chin, a typical gesture for someone who is concerned: she can probably be interpreted as the goddess Vesta. Two small shepherd figures, though hardly visible, separate her from the god Mars.

The last scene, in the eastern *arcosolium*, is the most compromised one. It represents a Dionysian scene that may be related to the infancy of the god. Starting on the left we find a female figure that lifts her right forearm, possibly as a sign of astonishment, followed by a satyr who is carrying a child on his left arm. Further to the right there is a second female figure in a position similar to the first, who is looking at a swan at her feet. Beside her, there is a couple consisting of a draped female figure and a satyr. The scene is closed by a woman who bends down offering a basket of flowers.

There is clearly a differentiated decorative programme: in the lower part the *arcosolia* are decorated with marine themes – very common for sarcophagi of this period. The upper *arcosolia* contain decorations of complicated love stories in which a deity unites with a human being. It is a sort of figurative reflection that, using the mythological categories inherited by tradition, tries to place human life and comprehend its inevitable end in a bigger picture connecting the human and the divine, and attempts to make the pain for those who stay behind bearable, simultaneously giving hope to the deceased.

A precise dating of the tomb is difficult, as no brick stamps were found or other secure indications that could help establish a date. We would depend on an evaluation of the painting style, which for this period lacks clearly dated reference points. The figures are long and narrow and treated with some pretension of monumentality. The tall shading that accompanies the bodies does not give them a sense of true depth or volume. These features bring to mind, besides the paintings of nearby tomb Φ, the abduction of Proserpina in the *columbarium* of the *Caecilii* in Ostia[45], or even better, the scene of the Elysian Field in the *hypogaeum* of the *Ottavii*, slightly later[46], let alone some of the less known frescoes of the *Domus Transitoria* at the Palatine.[47] One could therefore imagine a Severan date at the beginning of the third century AD.[48]

C, the tomb of Lucius Tullius Zethus

From tomb C, constructed in *opus listatum* immediately after tomb B but still in the Hadrianic Period[49], we know the owner who features in the inscription above the entrance[50]: Lucius Tullius Zetus built it for his wife Tullia Athenais, for his children Tullia Secunda and Tullius Atheaeus as well as for his freedmen and freedwomen. The inscription is furthermore concerned with indicating the dimensions of the building's plot: 12 by 18 Roman feet, dimensions that can actually still be observed today (3.58 x 5.40 m.). It was a precaution that was often taken to avoid illegal encroachment and occupation of the plot. The inscription was crowned by a frieze that elegantly played with the difference in colour between the fired bricks while two small windows framed it.

The interior was rather simple: (fig.27) the tomb was covered by a barrel vault, its walls were plastered white and a mosaic with a Greek border and spiral vegetation in the background covered the floor. The mosaic mainly consists of black and white *tesserae*, but to enliven the details some coloured mosaic *tesserae* were used; in the centre of the floor there must have been an *emblema*, a more precious panel, which is unfortunately lost. Underneath the mosaic some incinerations must be located as the holes for the tubes suggest through which libations could be made during festivals for the dead. This way, they could participate in the celebrations as well.

The lower part of the lateral walls housed *arcosolia*, while the upper part contained niches for cremations. The back wall, on the other hand, was only used for cremations. The central niches were always the most important ones, double in height with an upper shell-shaped vault which must have been originally flanked by stucco columns like in tomb G. Above runs a crowning with alternating tympana and semicircular lunettes.

Against the back wall, the most honourable one, two cinerary altars were placed soon after the construction of the tomb. The one on the right contained the ashes of Tullius Athenaeus[51], while the one on the left shows a rather unusual inscription. Initially a text was inscribed which stated that Tullia Secunda's ashes were placed in the urn, the daughter of the tomb's owner.[52] In a subsequent moment, however, three lines were added that claimed that the mother transferred the cinerary urn to Passulena Secundina, probably a family member who was not part of the family in the strict sense, in that she has a different *gens* name. Tullia Secunda, in fact, married Marcus Caetennius Antigonus and was buried together with him in tomb F[53], which, as we will see later, also belonged to a branch of the family. The first text was therefore premature to say the least. As the last lines specify, the mother assigned the cinerary urn to Secundina, by this time destined to remain empty as the daughter Secunda had clearly followed her husband to another tomb. Although the mother's name is not mentioned, it is clear that it concerns Athenais and that it therefore must have happened after her husband Zethus had already passed away. In the meantime, the latter must have found a place in the urn in the centre of the wall, in the most important location, the inscription of which is unfortunately gone. It is possible that the lines related to Tullia Secunda would have been stuccoed over in the meantime to conceal them, as they did not correspond to reality. The fact that a tomb reserved for a family member gets another destination is not surprising, as some examples are also known from tomb H of the "*Valerii*". More difficult to explain is the fact that the name of the person would have been already inscribed on the urn, implicitly affirming the death to come, when those who were preparing their tomb made sure to point out that they took care of it while they were alive, as to prevent that the funerary rites would be addressed to persons who, not being dead, were not entitled to it.[54]

The original decoration is not well preserved and is partly covered by a repainting in a second phase. At the lower part, there must have been a plinth in faux marble. Above, on the east wall, there are faded traces of a hunting scene, while on the back wall, above the left cinerary urn, there is an image of a charioteer of the Blue team, the *factio Veneta*, one of the two main ones that competed for victories in the chariot races (fig. 26). The racer is holding up a crown in his right hand while his left must have held a palm branch, both symbols of victory. In front of him, one can guess the four horses pulling his chariot. It would seem likely that the circus scene extended over the whole wall: on the rest there are faded traces of a symmetrical chariot, which can possibly be attributed to a charioteer of the Green team, of the *factio Prasina*, main rival of the Blues in the circus races. In the centre we find a palm, symbol of victory from which two festoons are pending. Underneath one can recognise the original decoration of the wall's plinth, covered by cinerary urns that were placed there in a secondary phase, and which was replaced by a bush of squirting greenery painted in a rushed way. In the centre of the wall above the plinth there is a clear imprint of a gadrooned vase, probably in marble, which must have served as a cinerary urn.

The circus scene is one of the first examples, if not *the* first, of this theme used in a funerary context and raises a number of questions. On the one hand, we could read the hunting scene on the eastern wall as a *venatio* – a wild animal hunt, also offered as spectacles in the circus – and therefore hypothesize that Zethus, probably a freedman, was involved in organising these kind of spectacles. In this case, a link to the nearby circus of Caligula and Nero should not necessarily be assumed because, besides Zethus' private situation, the circus seems to have been in decline in the Hadrianic Period, possibly also because the attention the emperor paid to the *Horti* of Domitia was greater. A second possible reading of the paintings remains: that is, that animal hunts and circus games were interpreted from a private point of view, rather than as a professional reference. The hunt must therefore be seen as a symbol of virtue and the chariot races as symbols of victory and as a metaphor for life, a significance that finds numerous parallels in sarcophagi, with some evidence from as early as the Hadrianic Period.

Returning to the north wall, the paintings of the upper niches are nearly completely lost, except for those of the lower right niche where a peacock, Juno's symbol, can still be discerned. It is shown frontally together with a sceptre leaning against a column on its left. The other niches mainly contain decorations representing rural scenes or vegetation. Of the northernmost lower niches, however, the lateral walls towards the back, those that were immediately visible to the visitor facing the tomb, show traces of still lives with divine attributes: on the right, a golden helmet, a lance and a shield allude to Minerva, or even Mars, and on the left, a mountain goat with a sceptre at its side wrapped with fluttering bands, are attributes of Dionysus.

The ceiling, which is only partially preserved, must have been most lively coloured. It was, in fact, decorated with coffers framed by stucco cornices with a reddish purple or black-dark bluish background against which vases and plant motifs stood out.

Tomb D

We do not know the name of the family who owned tomb

26. *Tomb C, north wall, charioteer of the Blue team.*

27. *Tomb C, the tomb of Lucius Tullius Zethus.*

D, constructed shortly after tomb C.[55] The inscription that must have been located next to the entrance way has not been preserved, because it was walled in by Constantinian workers who carried out consolidation works similar to those we have seen already in tomb B. Also, tomb D presented a similar articulation, albeit more simple, with an open entrance court surrounded by a wall almost three meters high, while only the funerary chamber further inside was covered by a vault. Therefore, for St. Peter's Basilica's construction site, the doorway was deprived from its travertine doorjambs and walled in, elevating all the walls until the new ground level. In addition, a series of amphora bodies – one set in the other forming a pipe – was inserted in the thickness of the blocked doorway to drain rain water from the higher level. The pipe became clearly visible through the gap that was reopened during the archaeological excavations. The interior was not richly decorated and part of the plaster has even fallen from the walls, revealing the internal wall's facing in *opus reticulatum mixtum* in tuff, with string courses and quoins in brick: a building technique very characteristic for the Trajanic and Hadrianic Period. The tomb was planned as a *columbarium*, that is, to exclusively house cremations. In a subsequent phase, during the reign of Septimius Severus, a burial was added in the south-western corner of the small entrance court, covered by three tiles containing brick stamps.[56] The walls contain a single row of niches: the two niches in the middle of the lateral walls of the small court and the one in the centre of the back wall, the only one having a semicircular shape, stand out in size. There was no paving, or better said, it was probably made of wooden planks.

Φ, tomb of the "Marcii"

Opposite tombs C and D runs the back wall of tomb Φ. It was built, like the others of the downhill row, at an advanced moment in the history of the necropolis, after the Circus had fallen into disuse. Its entrance is facing south towards the main road, like all the other tombs, but it opens at a lower level of a few steps compared to the path that separates it from C and D. It appears to have been constructed with a brick facing on the outside, enriched by square Corinthian pillars on the corners, and a facing of *opus listatum* on the inside, but completely decorated with frescoes and stuccoes. The building was covered by a cross vault, which was completely destroyed when the tomb was buried. The tomb mainly housed

inhumations, as the only niches for cremations are found in the walls near the entrance, on both sides of the doorway. Only the two superimposed niches on the western side of the door are still visible: the other two symmetrically placed on the east side have been destroyed together with the corner of the tomb, part of the facade and the doorway by the Renaissance foundations of the right colonnade of the central nave of St. Peter's Basilica. [57] On the facade, on both sides of the doorway, there must have been two coloured mosaic *emblemata*, sort of small pictures in fine mosaic made directly on *bipedales*: the typical Roman square brick named after its size of two feet by two feet. Only the mosaic on the left remains (fig. 28) as, also in this case, its pendant to the right of the doorway has disappeared because of the Renaissance foundations. The one that survived is only partly preserved, but it is a product of a remarkable delicacy for the period of its manufacture: it depicts the death of Pentheus[58], subject of the well-known tragedy by Euripides "The Bacchantes". The king of Thebes who did not allow the cult of Dionysus in the city, was killed and torn to pieces during a rite on Mount Cithaeron by Bacchantes: women who were possessed by the sacred rage of the god. The image only shows Pentheus having taken refuge in a pine tree besieged by Maenads who are armed with lances, swords and a tiger.

On the inside, the pavement consists of a beautiful geometric *opus sectile* floor of precious marble floor tiles, of the same type as the one already described in tomb X. Two rows of superimposed *arcosolia* fill the walls, in all, four on the lateral walls and two in the back.

The burials of the upper row are inserted into a sort of masonry box, the external walls of which are decorated in stucco imitating the front of a strigil sarcophagus, with the typical S-shaped parallel grooves on both sides of a central rectangular panel, on which the names of the deceased could be written. The east side of the tomb is best preserved, to the left for those who enter.

The walls and the part that remains of the vault are covered with a vivid red stucco that served as a background for the painted decoration. It clearly stands out chromatically from the bright marble floor and the background of the lower row *arcosolia*. On the spaces in between them there are traces of baskets with fruit and in the corners, faded human figures with their arms lifted and an aureole: a sort of *telamones*. On the western side above the *arcosolium*, there are traces of the left peacock that was part of a symmetrical couple, symbols of immortality. In front of it one can make out a yellow column with a staff

on top which must have supported a basket with fruit. On the inside of the lower *arcosolia*, the background is light blue and all the scenes have marine themes, like those we have already seen, moreover, in tomb X. In the northern *arcosolium*, hidden by the impressive sarcophagus in the middle, a marine retinue is painted, divided over two superimposed registers in an attempt to perspectively suggest a certain depth. In the lateral *arcosolia* (all decorated with scenes set on the banks of the river Nile, the heavenly river *par excellence*) the paintings of the two towards the back are still visible. Fish and various water birds can be discerned among the marshy reeds: particularly ducks, but also flamingos, swans and possibly a cormorant.

The *arcosolia* of the upper register, on the other hand, are framed by rich flower and fruit garlands supported by cupids hanging in the air (fig. 29). Birds are resting symmetrically in the lunettes, while in the space between one *arcosolium* and the other, two bearded Sileni with a nimbus (fig. 31), a sort of aureole particularly used in Late Antiquity for divine figures and, at times, imperial ones[59], emerge from cups of acanthus. Each of them is holding a vessel for wine, a *kantharos*, a kettledrum and a thyrsus in their right hands. Mythological scenes were painted in the lunettes, the ones with a red background unlike the lower ones, of which only those to the left of the entrance are still visible. It concerns the most important scenes of the whole decoration, which can be reconstructed thanks to excavation photographs when the legibility had not yet been compromised by the stratification of salts caused by rising damp. On the main side, the one on the north, we find a depiction of Dionysus discovering a sleeping Ariadne (fig. 32), a topic already seen in tomb X: on the right there is the Cretan princess in semi-reclined position, while on the opposite side in the middle, the god is standing out in an almost frontal pose; in the lunette of the left *arcosolium* on the east wall, the Roman parallel of the theme appears: the meeting between Rea Silvia and the god Mars, following the same model as we have already seen in tomb X. On the right lunette of the same wall, a theme typical of the afterlife is depicted: Hercules, on the left, presents king Admetus to his wife Alcestis, wrapped in a *chiton* and cloak (fig. 30). Following an oracle that ordained the death of the king, she offered herself in place of her husband. Hercules, however, had gone down to the gods of the Underworld and had snatched her away from the kingdom of the dead, bringing her back again to earth.

29. *Tomb Φ, the tomb of the Marcii, upper* arcosolium *along the west wall, reconstruction in watercolour by A. Levi (1945).*

30-32. Tomb Φ, tomb of the Marcii, upper
arcosolium *along the west wall, historic*
photograph of the pictorial decoration.

On the western side, the best preserved one, we find two unusual myths: in the left lunette, Hermes can be recognised by the *petasos*, the winged hat, and the *kerykeion*, his staff with two entwined snakes. In front of him we can distinguish three female figures, possibly the three daughters of Aglaurus and Cecrops, king of Athens: Herse, Aglaurus and Pandrosus. Behind him sits a cloaked figure. In the centre, between two of the daughters, there is a cylindrical shaped object, which can not be further identified. In the right lunette, one cannot but recognise Leda, depicted with her back for three quarters visible, while she turns round almost completely naked. Behind her there is a female servant and at the edges of the scene there are probably two personifications of places: a nymph lying down on the left and a young semi-naked man on the right.

Ultimately, the centre of the tomb is dominated by the large sarcophagus (fig. 33) that Quintus Marcius Hermes had built for him and his wife Marcia Thrasonis while he was still alive.[60] It is this impressive burial that has given the name to the complete tomb. The owner is depicted on the front of the cover on the left, with curly hair, wearing a toga and holding a scroll in his hand: an allusion to his administrative competence. Two winged cupids are supporting a veil behind him which, in the language of the period, was intended to exalt the figure. In the opposite half two winged Victories provide the same service to the wife, who is holding an apple or pomegranate in her left hand, a symbol of life and rebirth, while the gesture of the right hand could possibly be interpreted as the *tres digiti porrecti*, the three lifted fingers[61], a sign of address. The main coffin is a superb example of the late Severan age: a central niche, flanked by two spiral columns supporting an arch, frames the figure of a young drunken Dionysus leaning with his left hand on a thyrsus and holding with his right a two handled wine cup, a *kantharos*, while a young satyr on his side is holding him up. To the side there are two strigil-style panels, the gadrooned S-shaped decoration that we have already seen in the stucco of the upper *arcosolia*, while at the end a maenad and a satyr are playing and dancing completely enchanted by the god's ecstasy. The perfect and shiny polishing of the marble surfaces is striking, which gives it a slightly affected perfection.

The dating of the tomb cannot benefit from secure datable elements, and the stylistic arrangement of paintings from this period is still lacking tenets. The best parallels both thematically and stylistically have already been made with tomb X. Consequently, we should consider it more or less contemporary, dating it to the last years of the second and the beginning of the third century AD.

E, tomb of the "Aelii"

Despite the damage caused by the Constantinian construction site, the facade of tomb E still appears to be in a particularly good state (fig. 35).[62] The door jambs and the architrave of the door have been removed and as a result, the inscription that was inserted above and the right window are unfortunately gone as well. The facing in brick is nevertheless a very good example of the fineness that could be achieved in these cases. The *aediculae* that frame the lost inscription and the two small windows to the side are executed with taste, sculpting the brick itself to shape Corinthian capitals and cornices, playing at the same time with the differences in colour due to the firing of the bricks and creating, in the pilasters and side of the inscription, a twisted cord design with a simple yet effective result.

On the inside (fig. 34), the tomb was paved with a black and white mosaic of a simple design consisting of triangles, squares and lance-shaped elements. Some swastikas and solar symbols can also be identified. The walls, as usual, were divided in three *arcosolia* covering the graves for the inhumations in the lower zone, and niches for the cinerary urns in the upper part. The main niches were framed by small fluted columns in stucco, only partly preserved. Even higher, the final decorated zone under the vault consisted of a crowning of alternating triangular tympana and small arches. The walls are not completely symmetrical, however, because of the staircase with two flights that takes up part of the right wall and led to the terrace on top of the tomb where, in all likelihood, the funerary banquets were held.

In the *arcosolium* of the back wall, we find an inscription of Titus Aelius Tyrannus[63], imperial freedman, who was a secretary – *a commentariis* – in the administration of the Provincia Belgica. His burial must have been the most important one in the tomb and it was dedicated to him by his wife, Aelia Andria and his father-in-law Aelius Valerianus, who was also probably a member of the *familia Caesaris* himself: that is, of the group of imperial slaves. The wall decoration is predominantly of a white background: in the lower section, the *arcosolia* are decorated with faux marble. In the upper register, however, the main niches have a nice red background, while the small-

33. Tomb Φ, of the Marcii, sarcophagus of
Quintus Marcius Hermes.

34. Tomb E, interior.

35. Tomb E, detail of the facade.

74

36. Coffered ceiling of tomb E.

37. Tomb E, onyx oinochoe.

er rectangular ones are framed by red and violet lines, and show a variety of symmetrically arranged images in the background: cups on high cylindrical bases, fruit garlands, pinecones – a symbol of immortality and rebirth – torches, crowns of flowers, nets filled with petals hanging together with a pair of flutes, animals (deer and parrots).[64] In addition, the area above the niches on the west wall, touching the vault, is decorated with a flower basket, with a pair of peacocks symmetrically arranged on either side: in this case, meant as an allusion to the four seasons. On the back wall, however, on both sides of the shell-shaped vault of the niche we find yellow golden craters, symposium cups, next to which a grape is painted to underline the particular significance. Of the ceiling that was originally decorated with coffers of a dark background, only the sections in the corners are preserved (fig. 36), as it was removed by the construction workers of the Constantinian basilica to be able to bury the tomb during the foundation works.

Finally worth mentioning are a number of alabaster vases of a very high quality that were found in the niches: in particular an onyx jug (oinochoe) (fig. 37) decorated with a Medusa head at the base of the handle, and a crater in the same material. Both were still sealed as they were

used as cinerary urns. It concerns a rather common practise also referred to in the sources: for example, Papinius Statius, who wrote "the shiny onyx that encloses your bones in its lap."[65] While these vases must date back to the Hadrianic Period, a third, more simple urn in white marble was still embedded in one of the rectangular niches of the western wall and contained a coin of Julia Mamea (mother of the emperor Alexander Severus, AD 222-235).

The dating of the tomb is based on the style and sequence of the burials: the tomb of the "Aelii" was in fact constructed after tomb D, but before F. It should therefore be attributed to the last years of the Hadrianic Period (AD 117-138) or the very first of Antoninus Pius' reign (AD 138-161).

F, the tomb of the "Tullii and the Caetennii Maiores"

Tomb F, immediately constructed after tomb E and adjacent to it, was the first one to appear in January 1941 when construction works started to lower the pavement of the Vatican Grottoes.[66] Its dimensions are substantial, second only to those of the tomb of the "Valerii". The façade, however, shows a curious lack of symmetry. The doorway has been shifted towards the right in respect to the central axis, while the cornice of the inscription above, which is unfortunately lost, and the adjacent little windows are perfectly centred. This is caused by the internal stairs that started immediately to the right of the entrance and wound via two flights, also along the east wall, to the upper terrace which was probably used for the funerary banquets, like in tombs E and H.

Above the doorway, of which the jambs and the large travertine architrave are preserved, the cornice containing the main inscription and the adjacent windows are superiorly decorated with a crowning of plant volutes and palmettes in brick of a lighter shade than the wall's facing (fig. 39). To the side, there are two final decorative panels: on the left, a brick panel sculpted in very low relief which represents a partridge in a rural setting (fig. 38); the panel on the right, unfortunately rather damaged, depicts a building playing again with the brighter and darker shades of the bricks. It concerns an architectural complex which cannot be easily fit in the common typology: in the lower half, a podium with a large staircase can be recognised. The stairs ascended between two flanks depicted in perspective, on top of which ran colonnades. On the upper floor, but still at the first level, there must have been two columns that supported the ceiling, possibly a coffered vault that was designed around a central point. In the centre, an opening was probably made to provide light on the landing of the internal staircase.

The removal of the inscription, the marble decorations of

the window and the damage to the architectural panels were probably caused by the Constantinian construction works, during which the necropolis was buried to create the foundation terrace of the Vatican basilica.

On the inside, the original pavement is only partly preserved and consisted of a black and white mosaic with plant motives. Along the main sides, a series of marble slabs with holes were inserted: they were opening for tubes which led to the cremations underneath the paving, and served to distribute liquid offerings during the annual rituals for the dead.

The walls were divided in the usual *arcosolia* (fig. 40), in the lower part for housing inhumations and niches in the upper level for cremations. This part in particular, however, was clearly articulated and richly decorated with very lively colours, thus abandoning the light background used in other tombs. The long sides each housed two semicircular niches of double height with a vault decorated with a shell. The vault of the niche was flanked by small stucco columns, no longer preserved, and crowned by a trabeation topped by a tympanum. In between, there were smaller rectangular niches, placed one above the other. The back wall only contained one large niche, clearly the most important one of the building. It was superiorly crowned by a tympanum and inserted into an apsidal arch with a painted vault, which amplified the architectural emphasis, repeating the effect on a larger scale and immediately attracting the attention of the visitor.

The scene painted in the apsidal vault has been recently restored. It recovered the legibility of the image that was very dark beforehand. The upper left side is unfortunately missing, but the surviving fragments are sufficient to understand the topic (fig. 41). It represents the birth of the goddess Venus, who rises from the waves, seated on a violet cloak (the upper body is lost). She is flanked by two tritons that emerge with their upper bodies from the sea (the one on the left is nearly completely lost). The effect must have been magnificent, which was increased by its conspicuous position. The scene is probably the oldest one that used this type of iconography, which later on often found its way into sarcophagi reliefs.[67]

On the west side, on the other hand, above the niches we find a bucolic scene in the centre of which a ram and bull stand out between low trees and shrubs (fig. 42). The scene is likely to have continued on the entrance wall, the least richly decorated, where one can still discern a partridge, and trees with other birds.

The vault was destroyed by the Constantinian workers,

but enough is preserved to reconstruct its overall design: a cross vault decorated by coffers.

The *arcosolia* have a white background decorated with flowers and birds, while the external walls that frame them are deep purple, on which candelabras and delicate white swans stand out, holding slender symmetrically arranged garlands. This decoration, however, was concealed on the west side and at the back when new masonry counters were constructed along the walls in front of the *arcosolia* to create space for new burials. The most recent burial among those is the one on the east side, which has produced brick stamps from the beginning of the fourth century AD[68], shortly before the moment in which the necropolis became buried under the Constantinian basilica.

In the middle of the chamber, however, we find a document dating back to the first generation of users, that of the founders: here, a funerary altar dedicated to Marcus Caetennius Antigonus and his wife Tullia Secunda dominates the space.[69] The latter was the daughter of Lucius Tullius Zethus whom we have already met in the discus-

*41. The birth of Venus, fresco of the apsidal
vault of the north wall of tomb F.*

40. Interior of tomb F.

42. Bucolic scene, west wall of tomb F.

43. Christian funerary inscription of Aemilia Gorgonia, tomb F.

sion of tomb C, where, as mentioned above, a cinerary altar has been preserved that was originally made for her, but was subsequently given to another family member.[70] Tomb F therefore originally belonged to the *Caetennii* and there are, in fact, various inscriptions preserved that are related to members of this family: in the left niche of the back wall we find the small urn of Marcus Caetennius Tertius, a freedman of the family[71]; in a niche in the east wall there is the small urn of Marcus Caetennius Ganymedis[72], another freedman, and in the right niche on the north wall the small urn of a third freedman, Marcus Caetennius Chryseros, was located.[73]

Through the marriage of Tullia Secunda, the *Tulli*, although already being the owners of tomb C, evidently obtained the right to also be buried in tomb F. In the middle of the counter, built against the back wall, we find an inscription that may have closed the *loculus* behind it and which records the burial of the nineteen year old Lucius Tullius Hermadion[74], buried by his homonymous father. He had reserved for himself a small urn[75] with a *tabula ansata* held by two cupids that was located in the same tomb in the central niche of the back wall. It is interesting to note the passing of generations and rituals: we are likely to be in the third century AD: the father chose the old rite of cremation for himself, while the son preferred inhumation, which by then was established as the prevalent rite.

Some further names appeared from outside the two families, with which it is possible to reconstruct the relationship with the other deceased. To the burial of the young Hermadion, a second burial was added of which the inscription, in a rather incorrect Latin, was carved in the space that had remained vacant to the right of the original slab: it concerns the burial of the twenty-five year old Siricius, buried by his wife[76] and who probably passed away between the late third and early fourth century AD. In the same counter, on the western edge, there is a slab that closed a terracotta sarcophagus and which records a child of six years, Marcus Aurelius Hieron, son of a homonymous re-enlisted veteran of Marcus Aurelius.[77] On the right wall, on the other hand, in the northernmost *arcosolium*, we find a long inscription with which Aurelia Eutychiane dedicated the burial of her husband Aurelius Nemesius, proudly proclaiming his musical gifts and his function of *magister chori orchistopalae et pantimorum*: that is, head of a choir that accompanied acrobatic dances and pantomime.[78]

Ultimately, there is even a Christian burial, probably from the beginning of the fourth century AD: a grave dug in the paving was covered by a slab containing the inscription of Aemilia Gorgonia[79], buried at the age of twenty-eight by her husband (fig. 43). Besides the typical terminology (*anima dulcis, dormit in pace*), the figurative decoration also identifies the young woman as a Christian: on the left we can distinguish a woman drawing water from a well, a symbol of eternal life. However, it does not concern the evangelic episode of the Samaritan at the well, which must have influenced the scene iconographically, but the deceased herself as is specified by the caption above: *Anima dulcis / Gorgonia*. Underneath the main text, two doves frontally displayed frame an invocation in smaller font with a final salute of the husband: "I built it for the sweetest wife."

From a chronological perspective, the tomb is well-dated thanks to various brick stamps that date back to AD 140-150. Also, the change in iconography and choice of colour that dominate the frescoes can be considered representative for the stylistic evolution that took place in the period between the reigns of Hadrian and Antoninus Pius.

Z, the tomb of the "Egyptians" [80]

Opposite tombs E and F, in the row further downhill, we find a funerary chamber which is particularly interesting because of its figurative programme, unique in the Roman panorama. It arose on the original slope of the Vatican hill, at a lower level in respect to the path, the *iter* that crossed the entire necropolis, from which it was averted opening up towards the valley. The wall of the entrance no longer exists as it was cut off when the foundation for the southern colonnade of the basilica's central nave was constructed. In fact, an ancient opening of the construction site in those foundations provides access today to the tomb and the entire necropolis.

The structure of the tomb is rather simple because, having been constructed at the end of the second century AD when inhumation was the prevalent rite, there was no need to anticipate the crowded articulation of the walls with small niches that were necessary for housing cremations. Along each of the three walls[81] (fig. 44) there are two *arcosolia* that are repeated on an upper level to contain sarcophagi, as already seen in a simplified version in tombs X and Φ. The chamber is covered by a rib vault and has windows at the top of each wall. The paving consisted of marble slabs of which only small fragments are preserved on the north side, which resemble the decorative scheme of tomb Φ. The only boss on the walls is a pilaster between the two *arcosolia* of the back wall, the function of which is not clear.

The walls are covered with a stucco of a uniform red-orange background. This is again clearly different from the bright walls of the Hadrianic tradition, or the strong contrasts typical for the Antonine Period (tomb F).

The interpretation of these frescoes has improved enormously after the recent restorations and maybe only the excavators were able to observe the frescoes equally well. In any case, due to the phenomenon of rising damp and its successive evaporation that deposits salt on the surfaces, forming an ever-thickening whitish film, the images remained for decennia forms that were difficult to decipher.

Today a division of the wall can be distinguished, horizontally subdivided by a red band that runs slightly above the top of the upper *arcosolia*. A clear, more subtle band runs higher up, at the bottom of the small windows, while other vertical lines frame the main figures. In the middle, we find a divine Egyptian figure that moves in profile towards the left (fig. 46). In his right hand he is holding the long sceptre *Uas* while his left clasps a lobed cross, the *Ankh*, the symbol of life. The torso is fitted with a sort of blue waistcoat decorated with *rishi* scales, while a short and tight skirt in the same colour is covered with triangles and rosettes. The head can be easily identified as Horus with its characteristic falcon beak and eye. The head is crowned by a solar disk. The figure seems to be standing on a low pedestal like a statue. Underneath the red band we find a delineated rectangle: it looks like a kind of pier or pedestal. The figure is framed in a large rectangle, defined by a clear line, the upper corners of which are crossed by a pending semicircle. To the side, two narrower panels contain two other figures: to the left, even though it has been reduced to a silhouette, the ox Apis with the solar disk between its horns can be recognised, turned towards Horus. On the right, however, we can possibly discern the image of a bird (maybe an Ibis?) placed on a socle. On the edge of the walls, there are two Gorgon's heads (fig. 45): completely normal for a Roman Imperial context.

A similar subdivision in fields has been applied to what remains of the lateral walls: based on excavation photographs, a sphinx has possibly been identified on the left, which, in order to be consistent with the other representations, could also be interpreted as Anubis (?), however,

having the appearance of a squatting jackal (fig. 47); the figure on the right is clearly recognisable as the god Thoth in the shape of a baboon. The god, also squatting and crowned by a solar disk between his horns, is turned towards the now-lost entrance to the tomb. Despite the scarcity of parallels, we should date the construction and decoration of the tomb to the early Severan Period, at the beginning of the third century AD, because of its relative chronology – the tomb slightly predates tomb Φ – and typology.

The first commentators were struck by the fact that the iconography of the main figures is derived from Egyptian figures, albeit with some naivety and clumsiness, that does not seem to have filtered through a Hellenistic-Roman reinterpretation. It was believed that the family who owned the tomb enjoyed a strong connection with Egypt and its culture, and had therefore supplied the workshop that made the frescoes with models.

The more recent studies, on the other hand, tend to nuance this statement, as there are some possible parallels with Pompeian paintings[82] or with the Late Antique marble intarsias of the basilica of Junius Bassus[83], that make the iconography in question less rare. One could therefore talk about the owners' interest in the Egyptian world and potentially in religious forms of Egyptian origin which would go with the lack of cremations, but it would not be wise to go beyond that.

This also means that one should not overemphasize the stylistic differences between the frescoes and the marble sarcophagi that have been found there – perfectly fitting with Roman production – as if the use of the latter ones would signify a change in the religious ideas of the family who owned the tomb.

More simply put, in Rome, Egyptianising sarcophagi did not exist, and furthermore, a personal participation in Egyptian cults did not exclude other more traditional religions – especially in the figurative choices that were also determined by other factors. A certain eclecticism in religious choices has in fact been attested in Rome, and besides, a sarcophagus of high quality was necessary to indicate the high social status of the deceased and, indirectly, of the family. The choice of mythological representations concerns a stable repertoire, which on the one hand showed a refined culture, but on the other made it possible to surround the grief with traditional stories that enabled parallels to be established between the human and temporary experience of the family, and the divine and timeless ones of the gods and heroes. In other words,

44. *Tomb Z, the tomb of the Egyptians, back wall.*

45. Tomb Z, head of Gorgon.

46. The god Horus, tomb Z, back wall.

this was a way of giving meaning to the critical passages of life – in this case, specifically the death of a family member – repositioning them in the light of categories which, even before being religious in the modern sense of the word, had the reassuring capacity and familiarity of an ancient tradition.

In the *arcosolia* of the tomb a number of sarcophagi are displayed. They are mainly strigil-type sarcophagi, that is, with the typical S-shaped symmetrically arranged grooves: a type that was very common in the third century AD. The S-shaped decoration was often alternated with illustrated panels placed at the ends and in the middle of the frontal field of the coffin. The front of the covers, however, repeats steady repertoires with retinues of mythological marine creatures. The most representative sarcophagus is certainly the one which has the myth of Ariadne depicted on the coffin (fig. 48). The daughter of the king of Crete, Minos, helped the hero Theseus to leave the Labyrinth after having killed the Minotaur. Full of love, she followed him, but was abandoned by him on the beach of the island of Naxos. After she had fallen into a deep sleep, she is found by the god Dionysus, who makes her his wife. The scene is of the highest quality and in a perfect state of preservation, which even makes it possible to appreciate traces of the original polychromy which is particularly obvious in the residues of red paint present on the cloak of Ariadne (fig. 49). The scene is skilfully constructed, with Dionysus approaching in his cart drawn by a centaur on the left end of illustration. Everything about the atmosphere exudes the divine drunkenness that filled everyone in the retinue, and which manifests itself in a submission to music and dance. Also in this general excitement, there is a moment of suspension of the rhythm in the centre of the scene. This is due to the presence of Ariadne, half naked in the classical sleeping pose with the right arm lifted above her head and her cloak that billows up to emphasize her gesture, and to create a setting for the beauty of her body. The maenads, satyrs and cupids of the retinue stop, enraptured, and turn towards the god who is about to arrive, to show him the discovery. The retinue also decorated the front of the cover, albeit in a lower relief. The Dionysian repertoire was without a doubt the most common one in this period and transmitted hope of rebirth and participation in the divine life as had happened to Ariadne. Whether it had only a metaphorical and poetic meaning or a strictly religious one, we do not know. The sarcophagus must be dated to the mid-Severan Period:

the most recent suggestions, in fact, tend to bring the date forwards compared to the initial later dating.[84]

In this tomb, a real change of religious orientation can only be found in a female burial of the second half of the third century AD, which is located under the *arcosolium* of the left wall in a terracotta sarcophagus. At the back of the *arcosolium*, an inscription was painted in red which, being already fragmentary and difficult to decipher at the time of its discovery, is now completely lost. The name was not recognisable but next to the inscription there were the characteristic symbols of Christian burials: the palm and the dove.[85]

G, the tomb of "the Teacher"

When tomb G was originally constructed, it was still a freestanding structure. Only in a second phase, tomb F was built against it on the right side and, even later, tomb H against the left and back.[86] It was one of the few tombs covered by a thatched roof instead of by a terrace. Some of the terracotta roof tiles were found during the excavations and various brick stamps[87] from the Hadrianic Period were identified, which makes it possible to securely date the whole building. At the moment, the façade and the interior of the tomb are only partly visible because of the later foundations: a reinforcement arch of the Constantinian construction site conceals a good part of the façade that was crowned by a row of large rosettes around a *patera*, and that played with bricks in various colours. The interior, however, is partly occupied by a foundation from the sixteenth century and some reinforced concrete pilasters that were added in 1948 during excavations for static requirements. Despite this, a good part of the tomb's frescoed vault is still preserved, except for the southern section that was punctured by Constantinian workers when they had to fill it up with soil.

On the inside, the walls have been divided in superimposed zones as usual: in the lower area *arcosolia* received inhumations and the upper area contained semicircular and rectangular niches in an alternating sequence to house cremations. In the middle of each wall, there is a niche of twice the height flanked by small columns and topped by a vault decorated by a shell. On both sides there are smaller niches on two levels, some of which have been walled in and repainted in a subsequent phase, probably very late towards the closure of the tomb. On the closed niches vases with flowers and birds were paint-

48. Sarcophagus with Dionysus and Ariadne, tomb Z.

49. Detail of the sarcophagus with Dionysus and Ariadne, traces of red paint.

ed in an impressionistic and rather hurried style. The repainting concerned the walls and possibly the vault extensively: a peacock in a frontal position, for example, was painted in the central niche of the northern wall. During the restorations that followed the excavation, a good part of the repainted layer was removed from the surface to recover the tomb's original aspect, and it was only documented by black and white photographs beforehand.

The first phase was painted with a very refined hand: the vault is decorated with festoons and panels enlivened by small animals, vases and plant elements, but attention is drawn first of all to an image painted above the central tympanum of the front wall, well visible as soon as one enters. It depicts a bearded figure depicted in a three-quarter pose, seated on a stool, while spreading out a scroll on a low table in front of him (fig. 50). He is wearing a wide garment in a pretentious violet-purple colour. In front of him, a smaller standing figure is waiting: a figurative method of underlining his lower hierarchic position. The brown colour of his clothes suggests, moreover, that he is wearing an everyday work outfit, a *tunica pulla*. At the time of the excavation the scene was interpreted as a teacher giving lessons to his student, and hence the name of the tomb of "the Teacher" was established. It is more likely, however, that it concerns an administrator who is busy controlling the accounts in front of a slave.

H, tomb of the "Valerii"

Tomb H, or the tomb of the "Valerii" is, without a doubt, the biggest and wealthiest tomb of the whole necropolis.[88] The building consists of an entrance court, the walls of which are covered with niches for cremations, evidently reserved for slaves and freedmen of the family. From the forecourt, one would access the main chamber, and the architrave above its doorway bears an inscription of the owner[89]: Gaius Valerius Herma, who built the tomb for himself, his wife Flavia Olympias and their children Valeria Maxima and Gaius Valerius Olympianus, as well as for his freedmen, freedwomen and their descendants – as was common.

Herma must have been a freedman, as we can deduce from the fact that he does not mention his patronymic in contrast to his wife. He must have acquired a reputable position having the means to construct a respected family tomb. In addition, he must also have achieved a certain cultural status, an aspect that is clearly brought forward

in the choice of the internal decoration that could possibly refer to an administrative career.

The interior of the tomb consists of a rather large chamber (fig. 52) with stairs on the right that provided access to the upper terrace, used for rituals and funerary banquets.[90] The tomb building was inserted between the two neighbouring tombs – tomb I of the "Quadriga" on the left, and tomb G of the "Teacher" on the right. This explains the L-shaped layout of the tomb, with a small room that extends behind tomb G.

The construction date can be established rather securely thanks to a brick stamp that was found *in situ*, datable between AD 155 and 161[91], while the style of the magnificent stuccoes and the portrait type of the tomb can be linked to the same period. The rich and complex decorative scheme of the chamber, in fact, knows no equal in Rome or Italy. While niches for cremations are still built in the wall of the entrance, similar to those in the entrance's forecourt, the other sides have a rather dynamic architectural articulation. The paving was covered with marble slabs but the lower zones of the walls contain paintings of faux polychrome marbles, in which the *arcosolia* for the first sarcophagi are opening up. Above this zone, the walls are covered with white stucco articulated in a lively play of alternating semicircular and square niches, which must have been the work of a high quality workshop that followed a refined and accurately planned decorative scheme.

The subdivision between the lower zone with the burials and the upper one with the stuccoes is clear, and does not simply involve a change in decoration, but also an implementation of different hierarchic and organisational criteria, as we will explore further later on.

The burials in the *arcosolia* of the back wall's (the northern wall) lower zone were assigned to the family of the owners. The owner, Gaius Valerius Herma, and his wife Flavia Olympias[92] must have been buried in the central *arcosolium*. The son Gaius Valerius Olympianus, who died as a child at the tender age of four, was buried in the left one, while the *arcosolium* on the right was reserved for the daughter, Valeria Maxima, who was hardly more fortunate than her brother, in that she lived to be twelve years. Premature deaths were rather frequent in Roman society where the infantile mortality was high. However, one could imagine that it was the death of those family members that pressed Herma to construct the tomb in the first place. That the children were already dead at the time of the tomb's construction, one can deduce from the

50. Tomb G, *detail of the fresco of the "Teacher"*.

51. Tomb H, the tomb of the Valerii, back wall.

52. *Tomb H,* the tomb of the Valerii, left wall.

reduced dimensions of their *arcosolia*: if this had not been the case, the place they were entitled to by law, would have been built to fit an adult. It is likely that also the wife was no longer living at the time, as only Herma is mentioned in the dedicatory inscription above the doorway. This situation has brought forward the hypothesis that the family fell victim to the deadly plague that reduced the population of the empire in AD 166.[93] However, shifting the date would start a chain reaction, complicating the building sequence of the nearby tombs that partly depend on this date. It should therefore be considered with caution and it is preferable to maintain the traditional date.

The decoration of the walls' upper part is without a doubt the one that draws the immediate attention of the tomb's visitor. The main niches contain stucco statues, each of them placed on a low base, which substitute and imitate more expensive marble statues. The most important figure must have been the one in the central niche of the front wall, indicated by its position and the large dimensions of the niche (fig. 51). Unfortunately, we only know that statue's 'shadow', or better said, its imprint on the background: the statue was destroyed by the Constantinian construction workers who – raising the level of the necropolis until the tombs' roofline – built the terrace on which the Constantinian St. Peter's Basilica rose in the 20s of the fourth century AD.[94] In order to do this, the workers took off the tombs' roofs and built transverse walls before proceeding with the landfill. This way a formwork structure was constructed that enclosed the soil, avoiding slides and subsiding, which could have undermined the stability of the building above. One of these walls – removed during the archaeological excavation – crossed through the middle of the funerary chamber. It passed through the doorway of which the door-jambs were removed, and have now been replaced by a modern restoration in masonry, continued on and ultimately abutted the wall right in the centre of the niche. We can reconstruct a male figure posing in heroic nudity, draped by a short mantle thrown behind his shoulders, passing over his forearms and falling down again to the side. The left hand must have held a staff, as a line of holes for the metal support that anchored it to the wall indicate. On his feet, he was wearing ankle-boots. As will become clear in a moment, it must be a divinity, the identification of which Apollo or Mercury have been proposed as they are both characters that are generally depicted with juvenile and slender features and a naked body. Other possibilities, however, should not be completely rejected.

In the rectangular niche immediately to the left, we find the remains of a statue of Minerva similar to the so-called Velletri-type. She can still be identified thanks to the helmet on her head, while the figure on the right is more dif-

ficult to interpret. The current figure has the head of Selene, as is easy to comprehend thanks to the crescent moon on her forehead. It concerns, however, an arbitrary integration from the time of the excavation. Recent restorations have further clarified any reasonable doubt that it does not concern the original head, slightly smaller, while the original one must have been covered with a veil of which one can still discern the traces in the background. Also in this case, we remain in doubt as to the identity of the figure due to insufficient characteristic elements. In any case, the presence of Minerva and the greater height of the central niche assures us that it concerns a divine triad. The hypothesis of identifying the central figure as Mercury – or the Greek Hermes – would fit with the funerary attributions of this god, who could also be represented as tutelary deity of the owner Herma, for the obvious reference in his *cognomen*. In the niches beside the triad rather different figures can be distinguished: two mature men in Greek clothes, wearing a mantle that leaves part of the chest uncovered. Their gazes converge at a central point in the room: the figure on the left seems slightly younger, has a beard and short, well-groomed hair. The right hand figure, on the other hand, appears to be older, with hair and a beard that are longer, more flowing and wavy. We should identify them as two philosophers, or maybe a philosopher on the right and a rhetorician on the left.[95] In a while, we will return to the association between philosophers and divinity. It has been pointed out that the vaults of these two niches contain decorations in bas-relief that are symmetrical: above the philosopher on the left we find a semi-reclined female figure whose lower body is wrapped in a mantle, while her upper body is naked from the belt up. Her hair is entwined with spikes and fruit and in her left hand she is holding a cornucopia. In the background, in very low relief, a rock and tree are outlined. In the niche of the right hand philosopher, however, we find a male figure in a symmetrical pose. He wears a long and wavy beard and hair sticks out like a crown of pincers framing his face. In his right hand he is holding an oar and in his left elbow rests an anchor. It is easy to identify the couple as personifications of Earth and the Ocean, which close, so to speak, the series of figures on the north wall as if placed between two brackets, giving them a sense of completeness that raises the significance to a cosmic reality, not entirely restricted to the family circle of the chamber in which they were enclosed.

The niches were separated by stucco herms which are unfortunately rather fragile and therefore for the major part lost. The best preserved examples are the ones that could have been reconstructed on the west wall. The edges of the northern wall are taken up by two superimposed smaller rectangular niches. They are not purely decorative, but the lower ones served to house two cinerary urns each. The background is stuccoed in bas-relief and in the upper register we find a running satyr – in a very bad state – and a maenad in the ecstasy of the Dionysian dance, holding a kettledrum (a sort of tambourine) in her left hand and a thyrsus in her right. In the lower niches, however, the symmetry is reversed. On the left, there is a running maenad carrying the thyrsus on her back and on the right there is a small dancing Pan clasping a syrinx (pan pipes) in his right hand and a wine amphora in his left, held at the tip as if it were a club.

To conclude the description, it is necessary to briefly sketch the continuation of the back wall on the right, in the small space behind tomb G. In the lower *arcosolium* Valeria Asia is buried, probably together with her patron Valerius Princeps, who must have been the brother of Valerius Herma. Above, the niche contains an only partly preserved image of *Hypnos* – an allusion to the sleep of death and maybe a promise of reawakening – while the upper vault is decorated with two cupids who, instead of the usual feathered wings, have bat wings adapted to nocturnal flights. They are holding a cornucopia which is made with an impasto technique – very unusual in Roman stuccoes – which has a golden shade like the poppies below, yet another allusion to the ultimate sleep. Next to the main niche, we also find two couples of smaller superimposed rectangular niches, with two satyrs and maenads alternating in a chiastic design. The east and west walls have a very different character in respect to the general design. On the east wall, immediately to the right of the entrance, there is space for a single full-height niche, to the sides of which we find the usual pairs of superimposed niches used for cremations. The figure that takes up the major niche is a man in toga, of mature age with signs of an advanced baldness, an inspired gaze and a half-closed mouth (fig. 53). Above, in the vault of the niche, the instruments of his profession are depicted in low-relief: a diptych of wax tablets for scholastic notes and exercises, a *stylus*, a small bowl – possibly for keeping the ink[96] – and a rod, maybe of a teacher. The figure's expression is in tune with these objects and the half-closed mouth suggests the act of reciting verses, dictating or giving lectures. In his left hand, he is holding a sort of a slab on which three letters are painted: [—-]MAE – today less well preserved – that have been interpreted as the genitive clause of the name: [HER]MAE. The figure could possibly be identified as the patron of Gaius Valerius Herma.[97]

A detail should be added that reinforces this suggestion: the toga is of a particular type, for which it is difficult to cite precise parallels.[98] It is rather shorter than the model used in the period of Marcus Aurelius. Moreover, while the *sinus* – the wide pleat falling back under the right knee – is compatible with the second century examples, the *balteus* – the hem that runs transversally on the chest

and that generally falls back with a soft pleat above the waistline – is as straight as the examples from the first century AD. One gets the impression that they wanted to depict an image out of fashion, if not completely old-fashioned, to indicate that the figure was part of a past generation and to possibly add a certain authority to his aspect. The patron of Herma, obviously, did not have to be buried in this tomb and is, in fact, not even mentioned in the inscription above the entrance. In the *arcosolium* below, Dynate is buried: the wife of Gaius Valerius Eutychas by authorization of Herma in the role of his patron.

Let us pass to the final side – the west side, to the left of the entrance. On this side there are three major niches: in the centre we find, as always, the most important figure. It concerns a togated male figure with his head covered, because he is depicted in the act of sacrifice: in his right hand he is, in fact, holding a *patera* for libations. The face is only partly preserved but one can recognise a bearded man. In the vault that closes the niches at the top, we find depictions in bas-relief of a small box next to a papyrus scroll partly unrolled on the left, and a case of *styli* with an incorporated inkpot: allusions to the figure's literary education. It must concern the owner of the tomb, Gaius Valerius Herma, solemnly depicted in the toga of a Roman citizen. One could add that – in contrast to his patron depicted on the front wall – his toga is perfectly in tone with the period. It speaks for itself that the former identification of the person in question with the emperor Marcus Aurelius[99] – sprung from a certain "Antonineness" – is no longer accepted in the light of both the context and a more strict methodology in the study of the portraits. In these examples, one speaks of an assimilation of the private portrait to the imperial one or, of a "period face" (*Zeitgesicht*) to characterise certain physiognomic models particularly popular in specific periods. The lateral niches on the left contained a young female figure. The objects depicted in the vault of the niche also support the identification: a *cista*, a small box that probably contained toiletries and an unguentary with perfume and a mirror, all objects of the womanly world that fit very well with a young unmarried girl waiting for her wedding. It must concern the daughter Valeria Maxima. The other niche contains the portrait of an older woman, above whom we find depictions of objects that suit a matron: a basket for wool, a spool and spindle and a circular non-identified object. Also in this case it is easy to recognise the figure: the wife of Herma, Flavia Olympias. The main niches are separated, as usual, by pairs of smaller superimposed rectangular niches that contained cremations and are decorated in the common Dionysian repertoire of alternating Satyrs and maenads. Noteworthy regarding this wall are the better preserved herms, placed to articulate the spaces. They are all of extremely skilful manufacture and are recovered partly thanks to the careful restoration of the last years.

Let us make an attempt for a synthesis: the areas of the upper parts of the wall show a clear subdivision between the back wall and the side walls. The former constitutes a sort of *lararium*, in which – next to the protecting divinities – there also two figures that in the eyes of Valerius Herma must have had a special function: they may have been two teachers, or two intellectual models, the work of whom constituted a privileged reference for his cultural education.[100] Such a mixture of divine and human is not that striking if one considers piety of this period that starts to mix proper religious aspects with philosophical education that, even if they remained abstract and academic, had an influence on the life style. This tendency fully developed in the Late Antique Period, bringing forth the characteristic hybrid form of civil piety, or of an allegorizing philosophy tending to mysticism, in which the literary and philosophical culture became more and more important not only for their spiritual qualities, but also as a sign of *status*, as a license of intellectual nobility that allowed a certain social rise, even if they did not belong to the nobility by birth. Characters such as Herma – and maybe already his patron – underline the control of a cultural tradition and of expressive forms of an elaborate and demanding literary and rhetorical technique: the only one that allowed them not only to get attention from the elite, but also to enter into the state administration that was progressively being controlled by bureaucrats educated at the schools of the empire, and less and less by magistrates who enjoyed a private education in the framework of familiar traditions of service to the *res publica*.

The persistence of cultural signs is, therefore, not read – with an inappropriate modernisation – as intellectual snobbery, but, more generally, in the framework of society's values of the day, impersonated at this historic moment by the same emperor Marcus Aurelius who was devoted to a strict philosophical discipline: one that was intended as a necessary foundation for his political action.

The lateral walls, as already seen, have been decidedly dedicated to the human side and to the owner of the funerary building: the founding family is lined up along the west wall. The wife and oldest daughter are standing next to the *pater familias*, while the youngest son is not depicted because of the very premature age at which he died. On the front wall there was an image that should probably be interpreted as the patron, whose footsteps –

judging from his professional attributes at least – were followed by the same Herma and were, in all likelihood, the origins of his own fortune.

If we return to what was outlined at the beginning of the tomb's description, it is more evident now what was meant by a differentiation in the hierarchy of the spaces. In brief, this was based on the fact that the figures depicted in the stucco sculptures of the upper part of the walls have no necessary or direct connection with the deceased buried in the lower *arcosolia*: Valerius Herma and his family are, in fact, represented on west wall, but buried in the north wall. This derives from the adoption of principles common in all Roman architecture, according to which the front wall of any complex – the most visible one – is therefore the most important and honourable one. To this first criterion, a strong need for symmetry as a principle for the organisation of space should be added. Because of this, the burial of the tomb's tutelary couple needed to be located in the central *arcosolium* of the back wall. However, if one looks at the upper zone, the one that is decorated, the priorities have shifted and the *pater familias* had to give up the most honourable position to characters that represent the tutelary deities and the moral and cultural references of the family.

It should be noted, moreover, that the image of the first generation of *Valerii* – so to speak – is insistently present: in the stucco statues of the east wall, in the inscription above the doorway and in the details on the *arcosolia*. Two marble portraits were, in fact, found in the chamber[101]: the first is a bearded male portrait whose hair is sculpted in thick and jutting tufts, strongly accentuated by the shadow play of the deep grooves, following the colouristic taste of the Antonine age (fig. 55). The second one is a female portrait, wearing a veil on her head retained by her left hand in an affected manner, her hair is divided in bands at the middle of her forehead, and on top of her head she had a more complex coiffure: a plait is wrapped in a turban, imitating the hairstyle that was in fashion at the court in the late Hadrianic and early Antonine Period (fig. 54). The expression is the authoritative yet reserved one of a matron, and from it springs the natural attribution of the two portraits to Valerius Herma and his wife Flavia Olympias, also considering their likeness to the surviving features of the stucco statues: the two heads must have been part of a relief placed at the entrance of the tomb. If a fragment of a foot, also found in the tomb, could be attributed to the same statue, we would have a relief of a complete figure rather

than of a simple couple of busts. It should also be noted that Olympias' hairstyle seems to be slightly retro, which would fit with the hypothesis expressed above that the tomb would have been built after her death. A second female portrait, this time a bust in stucco (fig. 57) was also found in the tomb and shows a strong likeness with the marble portrait: it can also, therefore, be identified as Olympias, even though she is depicted a little older: it has been suggested that this portrait would have been displayed near her grave, that is, near the central *arcosolium* of the north wall.[102]

A smaller bust in stucco of natural and fine manufacture represents, on the other hand, a young woman, which could give us the features of the daughter Valeria Maxima, but there is another small bust of a young boy (fig. 56), and it is very tempting to identify this with the young Gaius Valerius Olympianus.[103]

Even though the right side of the face is missing, the quality of the portrait is very high and it distinguishes itself by two further particulars. The first one is that – despite the short hairstyle of the boy – at the back of the head, on the right side, there is clearly a lock that stretches from the occipital bone to behind the ear. This is a common element of other boys' portraits and is traditionally interpreted as an assimilation of the boy with an image of the young Horus, a symbol of an initiation to the mystery cult of Isis, mother of the god. More recent systemized studies have demonstrated, however, that such a hairstyle – generally limited to boys under the age of ten – is also found in portraits of little girls, even in a smaller number, for which as assimilation with Horus is unrealistic. Moreover, boys having this characteristic lock are also found in connection with cults of other divinities such as Dionysus, Demeter and with the Eleusian Mysteries, and seem therefore interpretable in a more generic way. It should not be read as a real and proper symbol of initiation, but rather as a sign of confidence in one of the divinities just mentioned.[104] In children's funerary portraits this symbol expresses the hope that the divinity – whoever it is – takes care of the young deceased in the Afterlife, an interpretation that is strengthened in this case by abundant traces of gilding that covers the portrait: an element that gives an ennobling and heroizing air, and suggests a sense of belonging to a superior world. Stucco portraits are not very common, but probably also because of the fragility of the material only few examples have been preserved.[105] The set preserved in this tomb is therefore rather exceptional. Some fragments of a differ-

ent, yet related, type of depictions should be added: gypsum funerary masks made by casting a mould directly on the face of the deceased.[106] A first example represents the face of a boy of a few years old, which could have served as a model for the realisation of the gilded bust of Gaius Valerius Olympianus (fig. 59). Besides this mask, which is a positive obtained from a cast, there are two fragmentary moulds that are related to two other faces: the first one is taken from a bearded man and only the left half of the face is preserved. The second one consists of two components that fit together, and is taken from the face of a child not even one year old (fig. 58), of whom we have no other portraits and cannot hypothesize his name.

Similar masks were found in Rome and in various regions of the Empire (Lyon in France, Alexandria and Hermopolis in Egypt, El Djem and Sousse in Tunisia, Alacer do Sal in Portugal, and probably also in Athens and Lepcis Magna)[107], but another Vatican example should be added to those already mentioned, which is unfortunately lost. Pirro Ligorio, the famous architect and antiquarian of Pius IV, recorded that in 1543, during excavations for the foundations of a section of the Vatican walls, that of the Belvedere bastion, some Roman funerary buildings were discovered. In one of them, there was "a dead man who did not have his head on his neck but between his legs; and instead of the head, there was a shape or mould of gypsum in which his image was made, the kind that is used in the wardrobe of the Pope."[108]

As has been said already, in the tomb of the "Valerii" we can observe a remarkable persistence in conserving the physical image and physiognomic features of the deceased. One should also remember that during the excavations, some inhumations turned out to have been submitted to a treatment that meant to preserve or extend the integrity of the body, probably a kind of simplified mummification in respect to the Egyptian practice.[109] This is all the more interesting as there is still abundant evidence for cremations in the same tomb, a rite that seemed to have been reserved for the less favoured members of the *familia*: slaves, and possibly less important freedmen.

This observation pushed for another investigation of the spiritual concepts of this group of deceased, also bearing in mind the long period of use of the tomb. The tomb building was, in fact, not only built for the family members of Herma in a strict sense, but was constructed with a broader expectation: it could house 170 burials, but until its burial underneath the Constantinian basilica, it

56. *Stucco male portrait with traces of gilding, Gaius Valerius Olympianus (?).*
57 *Stucco female portrait, Valeria Maxima (?).*

58. *Infant's funerary mask.*
59. *Infant's funerary mask, Gaius Valerius Olympianus (?).*

reached *de facto*, a total number of 250. Regarding the spirituality and the cultural orientation of the founder's family, some remarks have already been made. Some have taken the interpretations further in recognising an Egyptianising component[110] based on the presence of mummified bodies, funerary masks – a common practice in Egypt – the boy with the lock of hair, the old identification of the statue in the back wall as Selene, a possible assimilation between Minerva and Isis and, finally, a relation between the Dionysian motives of Satyrs and maenads and the cult of Isis. All these arguments however, seem fragile: some – as has been outlined – have been refuted based on further observations, while others are not sufficiently decoded.[111]

It therefore remains difficult to identify the religious or philosophical motivations of the family's funerary customs with precision. It is more interesting to observe some indications that put forward the idea that some of his members became Christian in the last phase of the tomb's use. In this case, the tomb would have had a particular value as it was located very close to the tomb of the apostle Peter. It concerns three different testimonies that call for a critical discussion in order to be correctly interpreted.

Sarcophagi were placed in the centre of the funerary chamber once the spaces that were originally provided for in the *arcosolia* were exhausted. Among these, there is a sarcophagus of a remarkably high quality, currently displayed in the entrance court of the tomb (fig. 160).[112] Based on its typological and stylistic features, the sarcophagus can be dated to around AD 270. On the coffin, we find a scene that was very popular in the funerary production in those years: a animated lion hunt, with a young horseman wearing a short beard as the protagonist at the centre of the scene. This must be the deceased, who was not necessarily keen on safari: in the Roman figurative language, the hunt was a symbol of virtue in the sense of physical valour and courage. The cover, however, had, as always, a much lower and less accurate relief and there are some that have doubted, maybe wrongfully, its original pertinence to the coffin: a *tabula ansata* supported by two winged cupids contains the dedicatory inscription in the centre. On the left, there is a cart pulled by two oxen loaded with animals that were killed during hunting, while on the left two *genii* with a burning torch – symbol of life – are supporting a veil that serves as a background of a bust of which the face is not finished. On the far right, a peacock is depicted, a symbol of immortality.

Unfinished portraits were very common in sarcophagi of this period, in that they were only finished off with the portrait of the deceased when it was effectively used, that is, when it received the corpse.[113] In this example, the portrait on the cover was not finished and, in any case, it would have needed to be radically reworked as it was prepared as a female portrait, therefore inadequate for the actual user of the sarcophagus and the decidedly male topic of the decoration. It was considered sufficient to finish off the head of the horseman in the main decoration in the centre of the coffin, and to carve the dedicatory inscription on the over. It reads: "To the Gods of the Underworld. Valerius Vasatulus lived 31 years, 3 months, 10 days and 3 hours. His wife Valeria Florentia built it for her husband, who had a well-deserving heart. His burial took place on September 7."[114] There are no clear signs in the complex of the deceased's belief. As it concerns a sarcophagus from the late third century – a period in which Christian art is taking its first steps and is hardly recognisable as such – the inscription and representation respect all the usual conventions in the Roman world, like the exact registration of the duration of life, which probably had implications for the horoscope of the deceased, and the mentioning of the *Manes*, the gods of the Underworld. This element would seem typically pagan, if it was not for the fact that its use must have been a conventional element by then, possibly autonomously added by the sculptors of the sarcophagi because its presence would qualify the tomb as *res sacra*, and placed it under the protection of law and customs.

There are in fact more than a hundred examples of Christian tombs among the oldest ones that use this formula.[115] What is nevertheless important, for the Christian examples, is the fact that the name of the deceased following the formula *DM* was in the nominative or dative clause, and therefore detached from whatever preceded it. If, on the other hand, it had been in the genitive clause, the dedication would have addressed the *Manes* of the deceased himself, which was obviously incompatible with Christian belief. In the present case, the formula *DM* on its own is not really discriminatory in the Christian sense or in the pagan and we must therefore return to examine the ensemble together.

As we have seen, at a first glance the sarcophagus seems to respect all the conventions of pagan monuments or, as one should state more correctly, of profane monuments. Some small details have raised the suspicion that Valerius could have been a Christian[116]: the presence of two

60. Sarcophagus depicting a lion hunt from the tomb of the Valerii.

Following pages:
61. Area in front of tomb H; in the centre, at the bottom, there is the opening of the well to draw water necessary for the funerary rites.

carved palmettes in the upper corners of the *tabula ansata*, as well as the qualification *benemerenti* in the inscription and above all, the mentioning of the *depositio*, that is, the day of the burial which for Christians meant the beginning of the new life.

The first two criteria are really very fragile and would not survive a serious examination, while traditionally more importance is given to the presence of the *depositio*'s date. Also in this case, however, a more systematic study has shown that among the pre-Constantinian inscriptions this indication is found in both Christian and profane inscriptions, in which it is even statistically prevalent: only in a later period it becomes an effectively characteristic symbol of Christian epigraphy, especially in the Roman sphere.[117] We are therefore forced, in doubt, to revoke the supposed Christianity of this person.

A second inscription from the tomb of the "*Valerii*" is clearer, but also has its limits: the one of Flavius Istatilius Olympius[118], who died at 35 and is praised for his cheerful spirit averse to quarrels. In the first line, next to the name of the deceased, appears the Christogram, that is, the abbreviation consisting of the two Greek letters *Chi* and *Rho*, the first two of Christ's name. The margin of doubt that remains does not concern the Christian faith of Olympius, but, if anything, the pertinence of the inscription of a deposit in the tomb. The exact context of the discovery is, in fact, unknown, excluding the fact that is was discovered in a secondary phase, after the excavations had finished during the restorations that took place in the years 1953-54.[119] Moreover, the Christogram is an element that in the pre-Constantinian Period only appeared in very few dubious cases, or as an abbreviation and not as a symbol.[120] The example in question should therefore be dated to the very short period between the battle at the Milvian Bridge in AD 312 and the construction of the basilica, which, as has already been indicated, is dated to the 20s of the fourth century AD.[121] Therefore, a margin of doubt remains regarding its real relevance to the epigraphic component of the tomb, or if one should not rather consider that it came from burials that were dug in the paving of the basilica in a subsequent period.

A final document, certainly the most remarkable one, also has its interpretative difficulties: it consists of drawings and inscriptions in the central niches of the back wall, to the left of the leg of the stucco divine figure (now lost), as discussed above. Two heads sketched in a rather schematic way can be distinguished one above the other, accompanied by some charcoal inscriptions. Guarducci[122], the well-known epigrapher already mentioned in relation to St. Peter's tomb, interpreted the lower head as an image of Peter and the upper one as Christ. Next to the latter, a group of symbols that are hard to interpret should be read as an abbreviation of *Chr(istus)*, while on

both sides of the head the scholar recognised further inscriptions consisting of tiny symbols, partly superimposed, which she interpreted as references to Christ containing complex theological allusions. Next to Peter's face, she identified another simpler inscription, grammatically incorrect, which, in the unravelling of the abbreviations and the additions proposed by the editor, would recite: "Peter, pray Jesus Christ for the holy Christians buried near your body!"[123] The two heads are still visible today because they were drawn before the inscriptions with a pigment to which an organic binding agent was added as very recent research carried out with multispectral photographs has demonstrated.[124] The charcoal inscriptions, without a binding agent, however, disappeared rather soon and only old photographs remain. These can obviously not replace a direct examination, particularly if one considers the difficulties of reading and interpreting these documents. For this reason, nobody has ventured to verify the proposed reading since, which remains therefore in a sort of epigraphic limbo.

The further interpretation offered by Guarducci, and which therefore would concern testimonies (at least for the oldest inscriptions) of the late third century of people that visited the tomb[125], has also been put under discussion: it actually seems simpler to consider that they were made by one of the workers of the Constantinian construction site, drawn in the years or maybe months in which the tomb was about to be buried. Otherwise it would be strange that similar inscriptions were drawn at the foot of the statue of Mercury or of a similar pagan deity.[126] The most important indications for Christianisation in the necropolis should therefore be sought elsewhere.

I, the tomb of the "Quadriga"

The tomb of the "*Quadriga*"[127] was placed in the oldest row of tombs, the one uphill, and is only accessible through an opening that was made in 1946 in the southeast corner[128] that allowed it to be emptied, and provided access. The façade was, in fact, incorporated in a Constantinian foundation wall that also reused the doorjambs of the original doorway. The dimensions of the chamber are modest compared to the adjacent tombs, but its state of preservation is rather good, especially after the recent restorations. In particular, the mosaic painting is almost completely preserved, which has given its name

to the tomb and of which only the northern edge is damaged due to a trench that was opened in a late phase.

It concerns a black and white mosaic in which a characteristic funerary theme can be easily recognised: Pluto, the god of the underworld, abducts Persephone, carrying her off in his *quadriga*, followed by Hermes the god who, among numerous other functions, also accompanied the spirits to the Afterlife (fig. 62). According to the myth, Persephone's mother – Demeter the goddess of the earth, fertility and the harvest – withdrew to Mount Olympus after the abduction, and the earth turned arid and unproductive. The gods came together to decide to give her back her daughter, but in the meantime she had eaten a seed of the pomegranate offered by Pluto. It was too short to keep her forever in the Underworld, but at the same time, the young girl still had accepted something from the Underworld. The impartial decision was that she would spend six months with her mother and six with her husband: this is supposed to be the origin of the turning of the seasons.

The scene occupies the central rectangle of the paving. The band that served as a cornice is decorated on the entrance side by two tigers heraldically placed on both sides of a crater. On the long sides, we find hunting scenes of lions chasing gazelles spaced out by flower baskets that illusionistically correspond to the similar ones painted in the middle of the lateral walls. The rapture of Persephone is a theme widely used in funerary art until very late[129]: in this case, the style is sketchy, with white lines to indicate the internal details of the figures that are outlined with a certain confidence, but without excessive attention to the volumes; moreover, the figure of Hermes seems to be juxtaposed in a way not completely integrated with the rest of the illustration, in respect to both the dimensions and the frontal and rather theatrical pose, which is in contrast with the dynamism of the *quadriga*. Such characteristics, together with considerations of better comparisons – in particular on the mosaic with a similar subject from the Via Portuense[130] – point towards a date in the Late-Antonine Period, contemporary with the second decorative phase of the frescoes.

The walls are organised following the usual system, but the dimensions of the tomb only allowed for the construction of two *arcosolia*, one in each of the lateral walls. In the centre of the back wall, a semicircular niche with a shell-shaped vault – marked by a perimetric blue band – stands out (fig. 64): its position is further exalted by the arrangement between stucco spiral columns that support

62. *Mosaic with the abduction of Persephone.*

Following pages:
63. Tomb I, the "Tomb of the Quadriga",
left wall, detail with female figure.
64. Tomb I, the "Tomb of the Quadriga",
back wall.

65. Tomb I, fresco with a peacock.

a triangular pediment. The background of the niche stands out because of its lively red colour, and to its side there are two smaller rectangular niches, above which we find frescoed panels, also on a red background. These panels contain mythological scenes in tone with the surroundings: their legibility has been strongly compromised by the technique in which they were made: a tempera painting added in a secondary phase on a red background. Recent restorations have only partly recuperated the lost details. On the right we find the duo Hercules and Alcestis, the protagonists of a myth about death and resurrection: Admetus, having forgotten a sacrifice to Artemis, was supposed to have died, but Apollo allowed him to be replaced by a family member. His wife Alcestis offered herself in his place, but Hercules, guest of Admetus, having fought *Thanatos* (Death) managed to snatch her away and return her to her husband. On the panel left of the niche we find a second couple, consisting of a seated and abandoned figure on its right, dressed only in a mantle and behind him a figure in a frontal pose. The interpretation has been very much disputed. The first publisher of the painting recognised its coherence with the general theme of the decoration, the death of the same Alcestis.[131] The last restoration has clarified, however, that the reclined figure is male, and an alternative, more advanced interpretation would therefore be preferable: that is, the death of Adonis next to Aphrodite.[132]

The lateral walls show a similar articulation, but the state of preservation and the lack of unambiguous characteristics make an identification of the silhouettes in the panels immediately to the right and left of the entrance – the only ones that are decorated – even more difficult. To the left, in fact, we find a female figure with a fluttering dress and a ribbon or garland in her hands (fig. 63) which has been interpreted as a Season[133] – this is questionable, as the figure is without her usual companions – or, according to other, as Laodamia.[134] After the restoration, a standing male figure became visible in the panel immediately to the left, reduced to little more than a shade. On the front wall, however, in a symmetrical position, another male figure is depicted on his feet and naked – with only a cloak over his left shoulder – while he is leaning on his lance: the image is clearly of a hero, but also here the opinions are divided: it could be Admetus[135], husband of Alcestis for reasons of coherence with the rest of the decoration, or Protesilaos, the husband of Laodamia, who died at the walls of Troy, for which his wife[136] was granted another day with him by the gods.

Above the lateral niches, on a white background of blooming meadows with birds we find depictions of a peacock (fig. 65) and a duck, while on the back wall a red panel is decorated with a candelabra between two swans, while the light background of the wall is filled with various types of birds. One could think of allegorical images that allude to deities: the swans could then be connected to Apollo, the peacock to Juno and the duck to Venus. Fragments of a coffered vault have survived, decorated with stuccoes in relief on a background of lively colours: one could guess the presence of the personifications of the seasons.

As has been indicated, the frescoes of the tomb show two subsequent decorative phases, in all likelihood chronologically not far apart. Of the first phase, only few fragments have survived, which date back to the moment of the tomb's construction in about AD 160 – in any case, in a moment immediately after the construction of tomb H, of the "*Valerii*", against which it was built; the decoration that is currently visible – including the mosaic floor – is essentially of the second phase, about ten years later.

L, the tomb of the "Caetennii Minores"

Tomb L was constructed in brick after tomb I of the "*Quadriga*" but before tomb M of the "*Iulii*" that used its western wall.[137] It could be dated to before the third quarter of the second century AD. The tomb's name derives from the fact that its owners were related to the *Caetennii* of tomb F, but the funerary chamber is smaller. At the time of the excavation the façade was completely covered by a wall from the Constantinian construction site of the basilica: a wall that cut the *iter* in half, which connected the entire necropolis in an east-west direction. Only in 1946, three years later, could the passage that is currently passable be opened, revealing the front of the building. Above the doorway, we find the main inscription, between two small slit windows and framed by a terracotta egg and dart cornice: the dedication is made to the *Manes* of Caetennia Hygia, who died at the age of twenty-one by the father Marcus Caetennius Hymnus and the brother Marcus Caetennius Proculus. A small relief is mounted above the inscription, which depicts an axe flanked by two small amphorae; on the right of the façade, a panel can be recognised that was walled in by the Constantinian workers: it must have belonged to a small window that brought in light to the landing of the staircase the led to the upper terrace – in a similar way to tomb F. It could also have been part of a marble relief that was removed during the work at the construction site during the Constantinian Period and added to the masonry. Today, this detail is hidden by a modern arch that was built for static reasons. The doorjambs in travertine still report the dimensions of the tomb: 13 feet wide on the front and 19 feet deep (*in agro*).

The interior is only partly excavated; over half of it was filled by the wide wall that constituted the chain of foundations on which the so-called triumphal arch of the Constantinian basilica was built. It is the arch which allowed the passage between the main nave and the pseudo-transept in which the Constantinian *memoria* of Peter's tomb was located. To the north, built against the back of the same tomb, the foundation can be seen together with a short tract of a raised wall that belonged to a late exedra, of which the significance is not clear.[138] It was possible anyway to excavate along the inside of the east wall, which provided at least an idea of the internal architecture. The pavement was destroyed but the walls were articulated according to the traditional scheme: *arcosolia* in the lower parts, and niches for cremations in the upper registers. In the upper zone, we find an alternating pattern of full-height niches with shell-shaped vaults flanked by stucco columns and square niches superimposed on two levels. It was all covered by a trabeation crowned by alternating triangular and semicircular tympana. A brickstamp from AD 142 was found in the northern tympanum which offers a *terminus post quem*.[139] The discovery was not as useful as it would seem, because – as already discussed – the tomb was built after the one of the "*Quadriga*", and therefore at least twenty years later than the brickstamp's date.

In 1942, an inscription was found outside its original context. It was dedicated to the *Manes* of Caetennia Procla, who died at the age of twenty-one, by her husband Marcus Aurelius Filetus. Based on the name one could hypothesize a relationship with the Caetennius Proculus who, together with his father, dedicated the tomb in question.[140] Given the state of the tomb, however, it is not possible to find a final confirmation.

M, the tomb of the "Iulii" or of Christ the Sun

Tomb M is the smallest tomb in the necropolis[141], but at the same time one of the most famous in the history of Christian art: it appears regularly in all the textbooks because of its mosaic vault. In contrast to the majority of the tombs, tomb M was already sighted in the Renaissance when construction work took place in the basilica: in 1574, a sort of small portico was going to be built in front of the altar of Pope Sixtus I that stood immediately to the right of the presbyterial area.[142] During the excavation for the foundation of two columns, "a beautiful tomb was found (…) all in ancient mosaic with figures that looked like horses, one would think it belonged to noblemen (…) Near the window of the said tomb or chamber there was a marble slab with holes to provide light, and in the middle of the said slab, there were these letters."[143] The document continues with the transcription of the main inscription of the tomb that was dedicated to the young Iulius Tarpeianus who died when he was not even two years old, by his parents Iulia Palatina and Maximus.[144] Since the boy has his mother's name and his father is no nobleman, Palatina

must have been a freedwoman who married a slave. The tomb was built in a passage that remained between the tomb L and N, taking advantage of their external walls connected with two load-bearing brick walls and covered by a low cross vault. Its pagan origins are demonstrated by the only niche at the back which contained two cremations, and was walled in during the second decoration phase. Apart from that, only inhumations were found under the pavement that was missing: on the central axis a sort of subterranean *arcosolium* was found, hardly larger than half a meter with a burial; and on both sides, there were two more graves, each with two superimposed burials, separated from the central one by erected bricks. Above ground level, close to the east wall, there was another inhumation: coffin *t*.

The first phase of the tomb is difficult to date because the original decoration is completely concealed by the successive decoration; a *terminus post quem* is provided by the construction of the adjacent tombs, but a margin of uncertainty remains and the presence of cremations could lean towards a date before the second half of the second century AD. For the profound renovation of the decoration, however, we do have major indications that also correspond to a shift in the religious orientation of the proprietor's family.

The socle of the walls presents rather severe and sober decorations that imitate a facing of marble slabs. The background is light dark or red lists, while the panels or circles in the centre of the various fields are yellow – an allusion to Numidian marble. The most interesting decoration, however, is located in the upper zone of the walls and in the vault. The latter is best preserved, in spite of a central hole – the one the Renaissance discoverers saw – and the loss of a third of the *tesserae* in the north-west corners. Also, the *tesserae* of the wall decoration have nearly all fallen off the wall, but fortunately the image is still perfectly legible thanks to the *sinopia*, the detailed preparatory drawing of the mosaic. In the vault, there is a youthful figure with a nimbus and radiant crown wearing a long garment girded at the chest, and a fluttering cloak. The figure, turning slightly to its left, is holding the globe in its left hand, while it proceeds on a *quadriga* pulled by white horses, started off at full gallop from east to west. The background consists of yellow *tesserae* and is vivified by lush vines that spread its branches across the whole surface, leaving only an octagonal shaped field in the middle for the *quadriga*. Some of the *tesserae* of the divine charioteer's aureole and the garment are gilded. If we would only have this scene, we would have immediately identified it as a traditional image of *Helios*, the sun that crosses the sky represented in his course.[145] Nevertheless, the scenes that are still legible on the walls, which are now visible thanks to the restoration that removed the abundant salifications from the surfaces,

67. *Tomb M, the tomb of the Iulii, north wall with a socle in faux marble and a sinopia of a mosaic depicting a fisherman.*

68. *Tomb M, the tomb of the Iulii, right wall with a socle in faux marble and a sinopia of a mosaic depicting Jonah swallowed by the whale.*

69. Tomb N, cinerary urn of Gaius Clodius Romanus, detail of the left side.

70. Tomb N, cinerary urn of Gaius Clodius Romanus, detail of the right side.

steer the interpretation in a different direction. The silhouettes of three scenes can still be recognised, all surrounded by the omnipresent vine branches: on the left, one can discern a good shepherd (fig. 67) whose lower part is unfortunately missing, carrying a sheep on his shoulders, with a second one at his feet, hardly visible; the design of the back wall is much better preserved: it shows a fisherman who has just caught a large fish on his hook, while a second one swims next to the first, getting away. On the right wall, finally, we find the most complex but also most telling scene: on a ship with the prow turned towards the right, two sailors raise their arms, while a third figure falls in the water into the jaws of a sea monster. It is the scene of Jonas who was swallowed by a whale (fig. 68) in which – according to the bible – he remained for three days: it symbolises the death and resurrection of Christ. Nothing in the other two scenes – studied in isolation – seems to refer in an unambiguous way to Christianity. In fact, in the course of the third century AD, images of shepherds with sheep on their shoulders, and fishermen, are part of a bucolic repertoire that is common in the imagery of sarcophagi, which gradually replaces mythological depictions that were used before. Only Jonas is sufficiently typical not to be attributed to any other repertoire than a Christian one, even though it is depicted in a traditional classical scheme. This cornerstone brings about a change in the reading of the entire complex: the shepherd and the fisherman – who in a pagan setting could have been interpreted as a duo alluding to the earth and sea – acquire clear characteristics of the New Testament. We can then identify them as the Good Shepherd from the evangelic parable, while the image of the fisherman of souls is used frequently in the New Testament, without even counting the significance of the fish as a Christological and Eucharistic symbol. At this point, the chariot of *Helios* must also be semantically revisited from a Christian viewpoint and should be understood as Christ the Sun, of whom ample evidence exists in the Patrology, albeit with various accentuations.[146]

The dating of this extraordinary cycle sways in the second half of the third century[147]: it is a moment in which Christian art is seen shaping its repertoire. It clearly starts from the pre-existing vocabulary of the classical tradition, searching for the most fitting figurative themes, but also for those that can be used neutrally from a religious point of view, or that can be utilised in a new visual language, loaded with new meanings. It is a process that can be completely compared to the one that took place in literature, when the Church Fathers used a well-considered selection of the arms of classical rhetoric to express a new symbolical and ideal world and a new sensibility, putting these instruments to use in the homiletics, apologetics and the catechesis.[148]

The tomb is of an extraordinary value, in that it is the first Christian mosaic, and represents an essential link for understanding the initial development of this art. Later on, in the course of the fourth century AD, the character that rises in the sky on a wagon would be used not only on sarcophagi, in particular for the image of the prophet Elijah ascending into heaven[149], but also – in one example – for a monumental mosaic: the one of the Sant'Aquilino chapel in basilica of San Lorenzo in Milan. Its reading is controversial, but according to some it would represent Christ *Sol Invictus*.[150]

In the end, the choice of this particular iconography attests the presence of a family which converted to Christianity, probably in its entirety: as seen in the other burials further to the east, Christian burials are rather rare, hardly conspicuous and often slightly later.[151] It is difficult to choose between two different hypotheses to comprehend the choices of this family: one could imagine that the owners of a family tomb converted and decided to transform the decoration in a way that agreed more with their faith, or that a new family took over the ownership of the tomb, which could have even been chosen for its spiritual attraction: the vicinity of Peter's tomb.

N, the tomb of the "Aebutii *and the* Volusii"

The excavations of the 40s of the previous century could not reveal much more of this funerary chamber than its façade (fig. 72). The interior was occupied by pilaster that served as a support for the large status of Pope Pius VI, sculpted by Canova and placed in the middle of the Confession, in front of the papal altar in the basilica above. Only in 1979, when the statue was moved to the eastern edge of the Grottoes, was the pilaster destroyed – liberating the space.[152]

The inscription on the façade is particularly interesting as it contains two texts on two superimposed levels, but from the same period. The first inscription is dedicated to Marcus Aebutius Charito, who built the tomb for himself when he was still alive – reserving it also for his freedmen, as was common, but without naming other members of the family, which could indicate that he remained single.

When the funerary building was still in construction, another family must have joined in: the second dedication is, in fact, to the *Manes* of Gaius Clodius Romanus, nineteen years old, by his parents Lucius Volusius Successus and Volusia Megiste who declared to have acquired half of the tomb (*in parte dimidia*).[153]

When the inside of the tomb was excavated, the urn of Romanus[154] was found in the central niche of the right wall. It was a square urn with an inscription on the front that repeated the dedication of the main inscription (fig. 71). On the sides, however, there are representations of two ointment flasks closed with a cap on the left (fig. 69) and a *thymiaterion* (an incense burner in an elaborate chalice shape) on the right, together with an oil lamp (fig. 70). It concerns a rather uncommon iconography, but for the ointments flasks – besides the one depicted in stucco

in the niche of Valeria Maxima in tomb H – one could refer to an urn from Lucca dated to the second half of the first century AD[155], while the *thymiaterion* could be linked to two supports visible on a Roman urn from the late first or early second century AD.[156] Of particular interest is the coin from the Trajanic-Hadrianic Period[157] that was found inside the urn, that could raise the dating of the tomb initially established by the first excavators based on a rather weak argument: the relation between the amount of wall footings in the tomb in question, and the adjacent tombs. A relatively late date, however, one finds in harmony with the parallels mentioned above for the urn, as well as with the frescoes on the inside which, even though they are destroyed, show a vegetation repertoire on a white background with garlands, flowers and, above the door, a beautiful plant candelabra: all elements that one could date to the Hadrianic Period. In addition, the presence of only one *arcosolium* per inhumations in the back wall, would suggest a moment in which the cremation rite is still clearly prevalent.

For the remainder, the lateral walls are articulated with niches of alternating semicircular and square shapes on two levels. The back wall above the *arcosolium*, however, contains a large niche with shell-shaped cover above which two peacocks were painted: symbols of immortality, seen already in other frescoes from the necropolis.[158] The barrel vault is only very fragmentarily preserved, as is the paving in black and white mosaic, decorated with plant spirals.

Finally, it should be mentioned that during the excavations a beautiful Early Christian sarcophagus (fig. 73) was discovered from the first quarter of the fourth century AD[159] in front of the tomb at the height of the inscription of the façade, which was obviously lowered in a burial in the paving of the basilica. It contains a continuous frieze depicting the characteristic trilogy of Peter (the baptism of his gaolers, the prediction of the denial and the arrest), scenes from the New Testament (the healing of the blind man and the *Hemorroissa*, the resurrection of Lazarus) as well as from the Old Testament (Moses receives the Ten Commandments, Daniel poisons the dragon of the Babylonians, the sacrifice of Isaac). In the centre of the coffin stands a praying female figure, which must be interpreted as the tutelary of the burial. The cover, however, shows the scenes of Jonas thrown in the sea and the three young girls in the furnace on both sides of the inscription which, unfortunately, does not contain a name.

72. Tomb N, part of the entrance.
73. Early-Christian sarcophagus from the period of Constantine with scenes from the Old and New Testament.

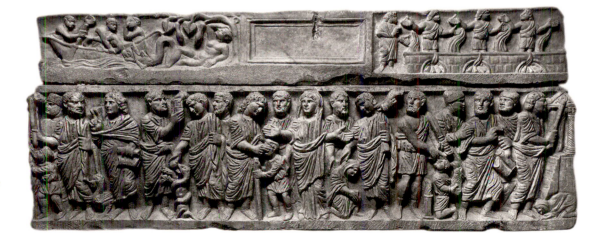

Previous pages:
74. Small piazza in front of tombs N, M and L with
the Constantinian foundation wall.

Tomb V and the area in front of tomb N

In front of tombs L and M one can discern the north-west corner of tomb V[160], which can not be examined, as the transverse foundation wall of the triumphal arch already discussed in the context of tomb L, runs through it. Its entrance opens towards the south, like all the tombs in the row further downhill, and it must also have a dating in common: not before the second half of the second century AD.

Corresponding to these tombs, the *iter*, which, coming from the east, served the necropolis separating the two rows of tombs, was blocked by tombs for sarcophagi, built in masonry and transversely placed against a side of tomb L of the "*Caetennii* minores", but which are no longer preserved today. Traces of these tombs are still visible on the other side of the path and also on the northern wall of tomb V, which, in its turn, was built against these tombs. As tomb V was built after tomb L, we also get this way to a date towards the late second century AD. If one was taking the *iter* at this moment, one would have needed to take a deviation, going around south of tomb V to reach the small piazza that was paved with bricks. On the north side tombs M, N and O opened to the piazza, while tomb U defined it on the west side. Against the latter one, other tombs with superimposed coffins were built of which traces remain on the curtain wall, still narrowing the open space.

In the end, the small piazza would be blocked by walls of the Constantinian construction site (fig. 74) that served to harness the landfill for the raising of the terrace upon which the basilica would be built: part of the wall that connected the south-western corner of tomb L with the south-eastern corner of the enclosure O is still visible.

O, tomb of the "Matucci"

Tomb O was already sighted in 1822 during the works for the foundation that needed to support the statue of Pope Pius VI in the middle of the Confession, in front of the papal altar.[161] The foundation did only permit a very partial exploration during the excavations of the 40s of the previous century, as was the case for the adjacent tomb N.[162] Only in 1979, the moving of the statue made it possible to enter it completely.

From an architectural point of view, the tomb is rather original compared to the other tombs in the same necropolis: on the front and to the sides, the funerary chamber is surrounded by an enclosure that forms a sort of perimetric corridor with an off-centre access at the south-eastern corner and with a masonry staircase that led to the upper terrace on the west side. While the chamber is constructed in brick, the enclosure is built in *opus reticulatum mixtum* – the typical Roman masonry with tuff stones arranged in a net-like pattern at an angle of 45° – with toothing and quoining in brick, a technique typical for the Trajanic-Hadrianic Period. The fact that during the construction only niches for cremations were planned is another indication for dating the tomb; moreover, just a glance at the general plan clearly reveals how the southern wall of the enclosure is precisely aligned with the same line as the front of the older tombs that were built further to the east (A-G). It indicates that, when the tomb was built in the Hadrianic Period, the circus further to the south was still in use, conditioning the position of the tombs.[163] This date has also been confirmed by a brick-stamp on a *bipedalis* found in the window to the left of the dedicatory inscription, above the entrance to the chamber.[164]

The inscription is dedicated to the patron Titus Matuccius Pallas by his two freedmen, Titus Matuccius Entimus and Titus Matuccius Zmaragdus, who were weavers or merchants in linen cloths.[165] The interior of the tomb is rather austere: the paving, which is only partly preserved, was in brick; the vault, also only fragmentarily preserved, was a cross vault. The walls are articulated by yellow and green squares, separated by large purple bands, embellished by a simple white plant decoration. The lateral walls contain niches for cremations on two levels, but in two of those on the east side, children's burials were added at a later moment. The wall to the right of the doorway had another doorway that gave access to the space under the staircase, the walls of which were decorated in the usual pattern of large alternating green and yellow panels, except for the wall that contained the doorway which was frescoed with roses on a white background. In a secondary phase, this passage was occupied by a large terracotta sarcophagus and the access was walled in. In the end, the staircase was destroyed by burials lowered from above, that is, from the paving of the basilica. Also the back wall of the main chamber was concealed by burials lowered from above that have been removed to restore the original situation: a wide but shallow niche (fig. 75) with a vault decorated with frescoes on a blue background, which are unfortunately completely lost. One could imagine a marine scene similar to the one

75. *Niche in the back wall of tomb O.*

in the niche at the back of tomb F. On the lower part of the walls, on the other hand, we find two yellow panels alternating with garlands with a central green panel; there was also a low counter in the lower part, probably destined to contain the urn of the patron Titus Matuccius Pallas, which would have been located in the most honourable position. Under the staircase some fragments of inscriptions were found, one of which must originate in the tomb itself as it preserves the dedication to Titus Matuccius Demetrius who died at the age of twenty-four, made by his freedman Titus Matuccius Hermaiscus.[166]

T, the tomb of "Trebellena Flaccilla"

Tomb T was constructed together with the adjacent tomb U with which it shared dimensions, type and decoration.[167] Both tombs are built against the south wall of the enclosure of tomb O, but also come out later than tomb S, as a drain that runs along the latter was cut by their construction.

The exterior has a facing in brick, while the interior is built in *opus listatum* with alternating courses in brick and tuff; the paving was covered with marble slabs. The name derives form the discovery of an urn in a niche immediately to the left of the entrance, which now stands in a very obvious position, on display (fig. 76).

As a matter of fact, the deceased would not have any motive for her own fame and the urn is made of a reused piece of marble. Its form is very simple: a *tabula ansata*

occupies the whole front, which contains the dedication to the *Manes* of Trebellena Flaccilla, made by her mother Valeria Tecina. The name of the latter has brought forward the idea that there was a possible connection with the *Valerii* of tomb H. That *gens* name, however, is rather common and the dating of the burial very late, as will become evident.

The urn is interesting because inside, a Constantinian coin was found among the ashes from the mint from Lyons, datable to AD 317-318: it not only concerns therefore one of the latest burials before the construction of the basilica[168], of which it constitutes one of the most precise *termini post quem*, but it is also one of the latest cremations known from Rome. To explain this fact, we should think of a particular traditionalism of the pagan stamp, or rather one should imagine that the person died outside Rome, and to return the remains of the deceased to the family tomb, cremation could have been chosen for practical reasons.

We do not know the first founder of the tomb, because the main inscription on the facade is lost. The only other inscription that probably originates from the tomb is the dedication – pertaining to an *arcosolium* – made by Samiaria Hermocratia for her husband Decimus Laelius Alexander and her twenty years old son Decimus Laelius Lucilianus.[169]

On the inside the tomb contains *arcosolia* along the sides and the back, while higher up, the lateral walls have a central niche with a shell-shaped vault framed by stucco

Following pages:
79. Tomb U.
80. Left wall: in the arcosolium *the depiction of an eagle grasping a snake; in the upper niche a depiction of* Lucifer.

81. Right wall: in the arcosolium *the depiction of a peacock; in the upper niche a depiction of* Vesper.

columns and flanked by two smaller superimposed square niches. The colours of the walls are lively: red and yellow are the prevailing colours. On the background of the central niche on the right, there is a painting of a head of Dionysus from which plant spirals spring that spread to the sides, and on each of which a bird is sitting. In the smaller square niches we find a chalice of greenery with a bird and rose branches. In the western *arcosolium* a panther is depicted chasing a stag with wide antlers (fig. 77), unfortunately reduced to a silhouette by now: in the excavation photographs the trees that formed the landscape in the background are still visible. The symmetrical eastern *arcosolium* is closed and in front of it a counter was placed, the front of which is illegible. In the centre of the upper part of the back wall there must have been the depiction of a group of which only part of a cupid is recognisable, while on the right a dolphin has been preserved that twined around Neptune's trident.

As for the dating of the tomb, we can rely on the structural relations with the other nearby tombs, the taste for background in strong colours and an impressionistic technique that suggests a late Antonine or maybe late second century AD date.[170]

Tomb U

Regarding structure, dimensions and building technique, tomb U is completely similar to its twin, tomb T.[171] The

distribution of the niches and the choice of colours are also repeated (fig. 79), but in the case of tomb U, the paintings are better preserved and legible, especially after recent restorations. All *arcosolia* are painted with depictions of animals on a bright background: in the *arcosolium* in front of the entrance, two flying turtledoves facing one another (fig. 78): the *arcosolium* on the right is decorated with a peacock that moves towards the left between two saplings (fig. 81) and the one on the left, partly missing, shows an eagle that plunges on a snake (fig. 80). As for the upper register of the wall, the one at the back was heavily damaged by the Renaissance foundation that only permits the identification of the legs of a horse moving towards the left. More interesting is the decoration in the central niches of the lateral walls: in the one on the west, we find an image of a young man – sketched with a skilful and quick hand – dressed only in a fluttering mantle, seated on a white horse going upwards towards the left. In his hand he is holding a torch and his head, accentuated by an aureole, is crowned by a star: the character can be easily recognised as *Lucifer*, the morning star (fig. 82). In front of him, in the opposite niche, there is less well preserved shape, but still easy to reconstruct. It depicts his symmetrical companion, *Vesper*, who rides downwards towards the right: the evening star. The only anomaly is that one would expect them to be in a reversed position: *Lucifer* is, in fact, depicted on the side of the sunset and *Vesper* vice versa. But perhaps we are asking too much of the painter whose intention was only to decorate

76. Small urn of Trebellena Flaccilla.
77. Fresco of the western arcosolium *of tomb T.*
78. Tomb U, arcosolium *of the back wall with a dove in flight.*

82. *Detail of the left wall niche with the star* Lucifer.
83. *Plan of the superimposition of the necropolis and the structures of the Confession (from Prandi 1963).*

THE NECROPOLIS UNDER ST. PETER'S BASILICA

the tomb using allusions to the similarity between sunrise and sunset – like in the *arcosolia* the eagle that seizes the snake alludes to Jupiter, while the peacock is a reference to his divine wife Juno. In the smaller square niches to the side, we find a decoration already seen in tomb T with rose branches on a white background and a chalice of greenery. The dating is the same as its twin tomb.

S, the tomb of Flavius Agricola

Moving around tomb T and U from the south, one runs into tomb S, which, as already mentioned[172], was built before prior to those. We are getting closer to the most important area of the necropolis, in the centre of which the "Trophy of Gaius" is located, as already discussed. As a result, however, the funerary chamber of tomb S and of the other tombs that will subsequently be explored are also the most damaged ones, either because of later burials – it was in fact a much desired privilege in the Late Antique and Mediaeval Period to be buried close to the apostle – or due to the construction of the Confession

with its semicircular corridor and the connected chapels (fig. 83), let alone the baldachin that was built in 1626 by Pope Urban VIII Barberini after the design of Gianlorenzo Bernini, which still constitutes one of the most characteristic parts of the basilica.

The latter invention particularly deserves a brief excurse: not only to explain its interference with the Roman structures, which has been brought up many times, but also for the peculiar interest in the vicissitude and some discoveries that were made on this occasion that integrate both the archaeological and historic panorama of the necropolis.[173]

Already previously, in the sixteenth and early seventeenth centuries, inscriptions and tombs had been found in this critical area.[174] However, when the foundations were made for the four colossal bronze columns that were to support the baroque baldachin, there was a lively discussion about the awe that was aroused by the prospect of getting close to the tomb of the apostle. The Archive of the Vatican Library has preserved some traces of these disputes: letters that opposed the idea[175], statements that were in favour of the undertaking[176] and historic

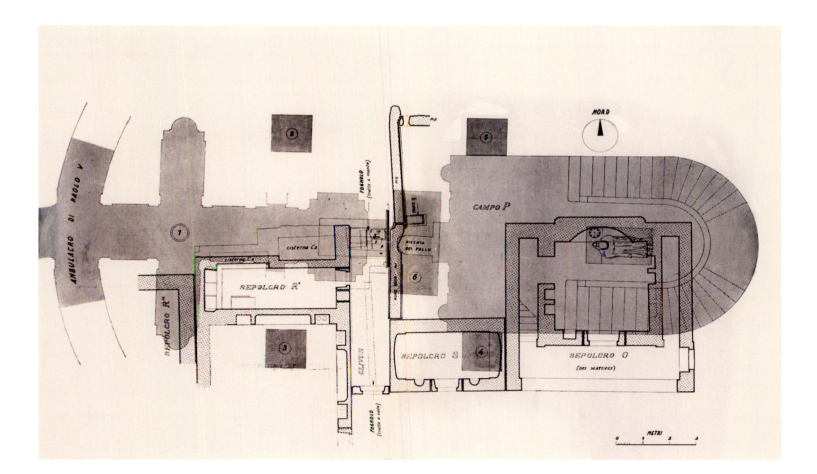

reports.[177] The most interesting documents, however, are the reports that were compiled at the excavation itself, with an eye for detail and true accuracy that was remarkable for that time. It was a sign of extraordinary interest (and in some cases of fear) that all levels of the Holy See were feeding on this undertaking. There is a document in Latin of the Capitoline notary Giovanni Battista Nardone[178] and one in Italian of Ugo Ubaldi[179], to which we can add the more concise notes of Torrigio's diary.[180] The works were followed by some canons of St. Peter appointed for the purpose, who were the only ones authorized to put their hands on the remains, the bones and the finds. Even canon Antonio Maria Aldobrandini was forced to submit written requests to be able to visit the excavations.[181]

The precautions and discussions forced some adjustments to the Berninian project which explains, for example, the irregular rectangular plan of the baldachin.[182] Most interesting from an archaeological point of view, however, are the discoveries that are referred to in the documentation and, in particular, the ones that were made inside tomb S. Here, the statue was found of a person, lying down on a *kline*, a dining couch, according to a funerary portrait type common in the Middle Imperial Period. The man is wrapped in a mantle that leaves the upper part of his body uncovered, holding a cup for libations in his left hand and in his right, brought to his head, a crown of flowers. His bearded face has features and the characteristic style of the Antonine Period, and could be dated to about AD 160.[183]

What struck the contemporaries was the inscription on his tomb, which not only gives us the name of the deceased, but also calls upon him to speak; it is Flavius Agricola himself who apostrophizes the reader and spectator directly by a short composition in elegiac couplets:

"Tivoli is my home town, Flavius Agricola my name:
yes, I'm the one you see reclining here;
just as I did all the years of life Fate granted me,
taking good care of my little soul and never running short on wine.
Primitiva, my darling wife, died before me,
she too a Flavian, chaste worshipper of Isis,
attentive to my needs and of graceful appearance.
We spent thirty blissful years together;
as a comfort she left me her son, Aurelius Primitivus,
to tend to our house with dutiful affection,
and so, herself released from care, she has kept a welcome for me forever.

Friends who read this, do my bidding.
Mix the wine, drink deep, wreathed in flowers
and do not refuse to make love to pretty girls.
When death comes, earth and fire devour all."[184]

The composition combines a direct and explicit language with some refinements and puns: the first line, for example, plays with the *gens* name. It could also be very well translated as: "Tivoli is my home town, I am a farmer and my name is Flavius", and further on, advantage is taken of the wife's *cognomen*, insisting on her earlier death with rather pedantic alliteration (*"Praecessitque prior Primitiva"*). Finally, in the final recommendations to the friends that stay behind, the urging to drink a lot and to crown the head with flowers is reinforced by the personal example, given that his image is doing exactly the same. These were not the aspects, however, that struck the Papal court most. It was rather, so to speak, the popular Epicureanism represented by the composition that invited observers to enjoy life as much as possible and to welcome the joys offered by beautiful girls. It clearly embarrassed someone who cultivated a simple philosophy, so incongruous with the sanctity of the place and the vicinity of the relics of the apostle that were buried so nearby. The statue ended up in the collection of the Barberini family until, at the beginning of the last century, through a commercial antiquarian, it was exported outside of Italy to find a less austere destination. The inscription was destroyed after the discovery, but fortunately not without having been copied first. Of the statue, however, old drawings have survived that made a secure identification possible.

We also find traces of the seventeenth century's excavations in a *poliandrion*, a receptacle that piteously contained the human remains found during the foundation works and which was recognised during the archaeological excavations of the 40s.[185] Even though the latter intervention was carried out with considerable limitations caused by the Berninian foundations, it was possible to ascertain that the tomb had been built to house both inhumations and cremations: *arcosolia* were seen along the west and north wall, while marble slabs with holes were inserted in the marble floor that made it possible to pour libations to the deceased buried in the urns under the floor. In the upper registers of the walls, moreover, traces have been preserved that suggest the common articulation in niches of alternating rectangular and semi-circular shapes. The ones on the west wall were later destroyed, however, to create space for an inhumation.

84-85. *Infant's sarcophagus of the* lenos-*type from tomb S.*

The relative chronology with the nearby tombs and the portrait style of Agricola date the tomb to about the mid second century AD.

Tomb R

To the west of tomb S runs a private uphill path – called *clivus* by the excavators – that separated S from tomb R. Not much remains of the funerary chamber of the latter: already cut by the foundations for the semicircular crypt of the mediaeval basilica, it was glimpsed at during the construction works around the Confession in 1615, while the foundation of the south-western column of the Bernini baldachin filled it up for the most part.[186]

In any case, it was possible to discern the common subdivision of the walls: on the lower levels there were *arcosolia* and in the upper parts of the walls, niches in between stucco columns, decorated with plant motifs. Only in a second phase, a cavity was created below the original paving, 2.30 meters deep: a sort of crypt that was progressively filled up with burials from above. The excavators of the previous century realised with a certain astonishment and fear that the column of the baldachin is basically standing on a void.

Once the ancient owners of the tomb had exhausted the space of the crypt, three more sarcophagi were placed on the paving of the chamber. The first one is particularly significant: not only in itself, but also for the chronology of the tomb's occupation (fig. 84). It concerns a coffin with strigil-style decoration on the front panel. In the centre, two figures on a base – imitating a sculptural ensemble – are framed by an arch. They represent Meleager and Atalanta: two of the most famous hunters of the mythical Calidonian boar hunt, showing a rather unusual iconography for this version. The front of the cover, however, contains a more common decorative repertoire: next to the panel for the inscription – that was unfortunately never added, or only painted and therefore now lost – a row of marine creatures unfolded: to the left, *ketoi* (a kind of marine snake) and to the right, tritons. On the inside, an adult was buried with a child. Together with their remains, coins were found from various periods: the oldest one dates back to Domitian, while the two oldest ones are from the reign of Septimius Severus[187], datable to AD 193 and 194 respectively. However, because of the treatment of the eyes of the two heroes, the hair of Meleager as well as Atalanta's dress, the coffin must be dated slightly earlier[188] – to the decade AD 180-

190. We are therefore dealing with a reuse of the tomb, or with two subsequent burials. In the latter case, the coins must have been added together with the second burial.

Together with the sarcophagus, a second children's burial was found. It was an egg-shaped coffin with strigil-type decorations, and on the front it had two panels to the side with depictions of the deceased attended to by a maid (figs. 84-85): on the left, the deceased is sitting in a chair with a lyre, and on the right she is sitting on a stool next to a sundial. A third sarcophagus was almost completely without decoration, with a panel without inscription on the coffin and vine branches on the cover. As for the building history of the tombs directly to the north, the path and the two northern enclosures – Q and Courtyard P – tomb R must be dated immediately after the mid-second century AD. Further to the west, one can catch a glimpse of scarce remains that have been interpreted as an additional funerary chamber – completely destroyed – that was called R'.

Tomb R'

Aligned with the facade of tomb R, immediately north but on a higher level due to the natural incline of the terrain, lies tomb R', almost completely destroyed by the foundations of the central corridor of the Confession and by burials lowered down in the paving from the Constantinian basilica.[189]

Little more than the façade of the tomb building has been preserved. From the few remains that have survived, it seems to have been a rather irregular funerary chamber, with the entrance side on the *clivus* narrower than the one at the back where an *arcosolium* was used for various superimposed burials, separated from one another by brick tiles. The first and deepest one, therefore the one that dates the tomb, was covered by tiles, one of which had a brick stamp, datable between the years AD 146 and 161[190], and identical to five examples that were found in the small drain below the *clivus*. The cover of the successive burial that was placed on top contained a brick stamp from the period between the reign of Marcus Aurelius and the Severan Period and a second one from the age of Marcus Aurelius (AD 161-180).[191] Next to tomb R' was a cistern and the tomb itself is built on top of earlier structures. Their function is not completely clear but they contained burials, one of which had a brick stamp that can be dated to the years AD 138-141.[192]

Among the late burials that were lowered down from

89. Clivus: *detail of the entrance to enclosure Q and the rear of the red wall.*

above, one is still visible *in situ*: an early Christian sarcophagus inserted in the wall that divided R from R', of which the coffin also encroaches upon the *clivus* in front of it (fig. 86). The front of the sarcophagus turned towards the south, that is, visible from tomb R, has strigil-style decorations with, in the centre, the portraits of a couple inserted in a *clypeus* (a disk in the shape of a shield, an ancient honorary shape, fig. 87) set above an idyllic scene of a shepherd milking a sheep. On the edges there are images of the apostles Peter and Paul (fig. 88).[193] The coffin that still contains two corpses can stylistically be dated to the second quarter of the fourth century, but must have been reused in a later period as the cover does not fit comfortably and does not seem to be the original one.

Enclosure Q

Even further north than R' lies an open air enclosure that could only be excavated with difficulty, and which turned out to be largely destroyed by the foundations of the central corridor of the Confession, the Clementine chapel and the north-western column of Bernini's baldachin.[194] The enclosure was constructed in brick, paved with a mosaic consisting of large flint *tesserae* and designed to only hold inhumations that were placed in *arcosolia* along the walls. There was no cover and the access was through a door at the northern limit of the *clivus* (fig. 89). To the east, the perimeter wall coincided with the northern continuation of the red wall of Courtyard P, which was discussed at the beginning of this chapter. The structure seems to date back to around the mid-third century AD. Enclosure Q is constructed on top of earlier structures, like tomb R': probably a cistern, contemporary to the construction of the *clivus*, the red wall and tomb R'.

Courtyard P

We have finally returned to the location from which this chapter started, to the open air area that was limited to the west by the *clivus* and enclosure Q, and to the south by tomb S. The discussion on St. Peter's tomb will not be repeated and a more detailed description of the various

phases of the discovered structures would be possible, but would not bring more clarity in a necessarily synthetic discourse such as this. It suffices to say in conclusion, that this area of the necropolis – leaving out the isolated burials of Courtyard P – must have been occupied in the course of a few years starting from the south and the west. As we have seen, in the Hadrianic Period there were, in fact, cisterns that were partly reused for burials in the area that was taken up by tomb R'. Therefore, tomb S was built, then tomb R and eventually, towards AD 160, the complex of the *clivus*, to the east defined by the red wall with access to the west of the new tomb R' and to the north of a cistern later replaced by enclosure Q.

In these building activities the Christian community also took part, monumentalising the place that was venerated as the tomb of the apostle. That is, it must have happened on the hand due to the greater and accrued awareness of the apostle's importance as a guarantor of the faith of the Roman community itself and as a direct intermediary with the teaching of Christ. On the other – and this aspect should not be underestimated – it protected the venerated location against expansion of the necropolis and gave it a status that was also recognisable by the pagan visitors of the area, in a way to avoid possible desecrations and damages.

There was no access to Courtyard P from the *iter* – the main axis of this section of the necropolis as far as we know it – nor from the *clivus* that finished at enclosure Q, but necessarily via a route that passed uphill from the northern row of tombs. There are no indications that imply that the necropolis in this area further north was as densely built up, but in any case, the available space in Courtyard P does not suggest that large numbers of believers participated in the commemorations that took place here. This aspect of space-availability is an argument to keep in mind when the celebration of the festivities of the Saints Peter and Paul on June 29 is discussed, which, as already mentioned[195], for Saint Paul would have been held at the location of his burial on the Via Ostiense at least from AD 258 onwards, while for Saint Peter, people would still go to the catacombs, now called the ones of Saint Sebastian, on the Via Appia.

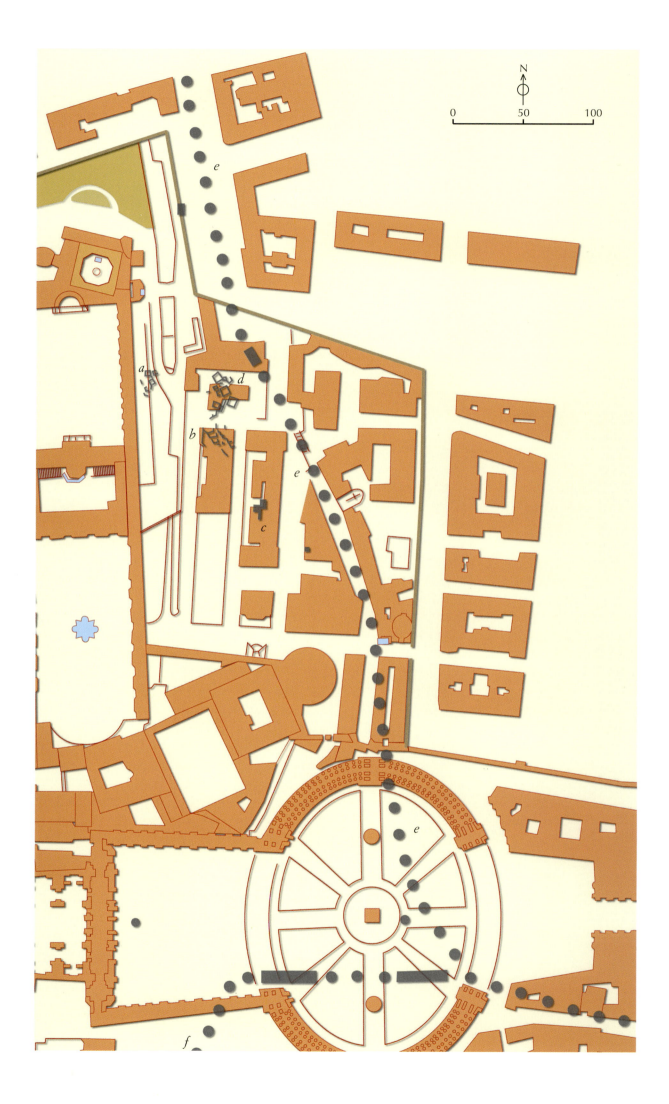

Chapter Four
The Vatican Necropolis on the *Via Triumphalis*

Topographical Introduction

In the out-of-town area, the ancient *Via Triumphalis* originated from the northern bank of the River Tiber, starting from the first *Pons Neronianus* (bridge) and then the *Pons Aelius*, at the height of Hadrian's tomb.[1] The road came off the *Via Cornelia* at an unknown point but probably where St. Peter's square is located today, in order to head northwards, passing through the valley below the Vatican hill in the direction towards Monte Mario; at the height of Giustiniana (VI mile), the *Via Triumphalis* met with the *Via Cassia-Clodia* which passed immediately to the west of Veii. Therefore, the original course corresponded, more or less, to the ancient *Via Veientana* but presumably did so after the destruction of this Etruscan city thanks to Furio Camillo (396 BC), when it changed its name to *Triumphalis*. By means of a bridge or a ford, it seems that it linked up inner Rome with a porticoed road that ended with the ancient Republican *Porta Triumphalis* itself[2] at the slope of the Capitoline Hill. During the Imperial Period, the *Via Triumphalis* bore an importance that was essentially linked to that of local traffic, reducing its significance in favour of the suburban stretch of the *Via Cassia-Clodia* which crossed the River Tiber at the Milvian Bridge. It nevertheless still appears on the *Tabula Peutingeriana*, a medieval copy of a topographical map which dates back to AD 325-362[3], when the road is shown as linking Rome to St. Peter's Basilica.

In order to understand the area's anthropisation better, one should recall here how the Vatican hill – like Rome's other hills – is of volcanic origin. Its nucleus foresaw the geological superimposition of sterile clays and tuff banks whilst the more superficial layers were composed of sand and gravel which had been deposited by prehistoric floods caused by the River Tiber. Thus, great instability followed with a strong predisposition for landslides and subsidence. Due to its geological nature, the sharply sloping area was not well suited to a concentrated suburban building settlement but was rather better suited for the cultivation of vegetables and vines as well as burials, as would be expected.[4] The use of this area for such things did not prevent, however, the rise of private and imperial suburban dwellings, which were presumably [accompanied by] relative hill stations.[5]

For the entire Republican Period, this first stretch of the *Via Triumphalis* was thus inserted into a rather inhospitable landscape; the Vatican Hill must have been quite uncivilised, forest-like and uncultivated whilst the zones located at the bottom of the valley and the neighbouring areas were flat country yet also marshy and were subject to frequent overflowing from the River Tiber. It is not by chance that the citizen road network – which passed by the heart of Rome on the left bank – was connected to the Trasteverian quarter on the other bank further south of Rome, at the slopes of the Janiculum Hill. This was done by means of a series of bridges which favoured building development and the urban expansion of that area. Following on, this Vatican trans-Tiber area where the quarter of Prati is now located, was gradually occupied by a series of tombs, some of which were of great importance, first amongst which was the so-called medieval pyramid *Meta Romuli* that was erected roughly where the entrance of the modern *Via della Conciliazione* is located today. It was destroyed during the papacy of Pope Alexander VI (1492-1503).[6] What is particularly noteworthy, however, is the burial ground of the Emperor Hadrian that was later transformed into Castel Sant'Angelo.[7] This type of phenomenon continued to happen during the course of the centuries that followed and burial grounds were overlaid with other burial grounds. In particular, up until the 16th century, numerous finds of a great necropolis were discovered in Vatican City.[8] They were found at irregular intervals, ranging from the height of the hill along the north-east slopes to the valley, corresponding to the first stretch of the *Via Triumphalis*. A minor road network came off from this street: it was made up of short and tortuous digressions as well as a series of small and steep slip roads, which joined up with one another and allowed access to the burial grounds. The earliest phase that we are able to identify starts as early as the Augustan Period, when the first tombs were documented with certainty: tombs that were placed along the Vatican Hill without a precise building program. The most ancient burials were individual ones, burials and cremations that took place there where the ground allowed it: a levelling of the slope, a razing, a clearing amongst the vegetation without prearranged orientation or an organic urban project. The early burial period, therefore, did not foresee clear changes to the land and tombs seemed to adapt to the orography of the hills, their positions almost being dictated by the natural curves and bends of the hill. In some cases, one can note the gravitation or a link towards the second road network which originated from the *Via Triumphalis*. The most ancient tombs must have been located on both sides of the *Via Triumphalis*, occupying the neighbouring areas with several rows deep. Then, it was preferred to move to a "panoramic zone", as attested by some burials of the Augustan Period, which are positioned just below the hill's summit in close proximity to the 17th century "Galea" mountain. In this area of the Vatican – the so-called Belvedere of the 15th century small palazzo of Pope Innocent VIII Cybo (1484-1492) – some sporadic discoveries made between the start of the 16th century and the early 20th century are documented. Unfortunately, however, it is not always possible to accurately place them topographically.[9] At the same time, one recalls the rediscovery of a small part of the necropolis in 1840 in an area that was generally known at the time as the "Belvedere Meadow".[10] Other minor parts of the same necropolis came to light during the building work that took place underneath the Vatican Post Office[11], the Swiss St. Pellegrino[12], the St. Damascus courtyard[13], the electric warehouse[14] and *Via Leone IV*, which is located immediately beyond the borders of the Vatican City.[15]

Some works have brought about the discovery of bigger entities which – where possible – have provided the opportunity of more detailed studies and the possibility of turning the excavation areas into an on-site museum. If we follow the topographical location (going from the summit down towards the valley), we can include the Galea area discovered during the 1930s by Enrico Josi and expanded further during the excavations which were carried out in 1994.[16] This area is situated in the Autoparco's basement and was found by Filippo Magi between 1956-1958 and is located directly below the current structure of the Vatican Annona which was excavated by Enrico Josi in 1930 – it is now only occasionally accessible by means of a narrow trap door. In addition, we can add the necropolis area that was discovered during the recent construction works for the Santa Rosa Car Park during the 2003 excavations.[17] These areas of the Vatican Necropolis along the *Via Triumphalis* will be described individually in the following paragraphs with the aim of establishing their coming about, development and the end of sepulchral structures and funerary practices (plate 1).

In general, even if the exact origin of this necropolis has not been determined, it is, however, possible to document its existence from the end of the first century BC and follow its development until the early years of the fourth century AD when, around AD 320, the Constantinian Basilica was built over St. Peter's tomb, just a few hundred metres further south. Perhaps the construction of this imposing cultural structure – the cradle of Roman Christianity – sped up the end of the funerary function of this part of the Vatican, whilst it was only in the area of the new Basilica that they continued with burials. For centuries, the *Via Triumphalis* continued to act as a pathway for pilgrims who reached the First among the Apostles' Tomb from the north-east. It was thus always frequently used. It is not by chance that traces of life dating back to the Late Middle Ages attest the transformation of chamber tombs (located closest to the road) into stables and narrow shelters.[18]

Furthermore, the combination of progressive swamping of the valley area and the superimposition of frequent sediments from the hill also resulted in the burial of the reused tombs and thus caused their complete abandonment. During the Late Medieval period, little interfered with the buried bodies: as aforementioned, the hill's north-east summit was subjected to important works only

from the late 15th century onwards when Popo Innocent VIII's Palazzetto del Belvedere was built. Other great building projects would follow in the subsequent centuries. Indications for the new occupation of the area can be found in various tunnels that were built to pillage buried ancient structures, destined to procure construction material, and in various cuts and levelling measures owed to the construction of the gardens' terracing. The importance of these burial contexts is not based on the preciousness and the quality of the tombs and their relative treasures but their exceptional state of conservation. What is more, a great number of inscriptions, altars, urns, sarcophagi and various furnishings were discovered; these contexts were often still intact and *in situ*.

The same tombs – at least the most ancient ones – not uncommonly came to light as a result of landslides or land fills. As such, the structure's decorative display, comprised of mosaics, frescoes and stucco remained in a good state of preservation. We are not dealing with works of art that are of a very high quality but rather signs of life and taste which can be followed diacronically in their development spanning over a period of more than 300 years. On the other hand, the deceased who were buried on this side of the *Via Triumphalis*, do not appear to have been particularly rich: they mainly belonged to a social class that we could define as lower middle class. Above all, slaves and freedmen chose this sloped location as their abode for the afterlife even if many of them belonged to the Emperor's vast and influential *familia* (family). It occurs in just one case – the rich tomb VIII (of sarcophagi) found in the Santa Rosa area – where the discovery of a family tomb is documented as including a family member who belonged to the Equestrian Order. The inscriptions, decorations and treasures suggest they belonged to people of different backgrounds and of common or unusual trades. Furthermore, one can make a calculated guess as to their connections with religion, philosophy and different traditions: the history of the life and hopes of men emerges from their tombs. Therefore, all the conditions required for a reconstruction of a particularly interesting and articulated historical-social structure, are present. In addition, it has provided the opportunity of studying some aspects of funerary ritual in greater depth which hither to had been little documented about.

The Galea Area

The area of the *Via Triumphalis* necropolis referred to as the area "of the Galea" was named after the homonymous fountain located behind the Palazzetto del Belvedere of Pope Innocent VIII Cybo (1484-1492). The fountain was built using a great basin during the papacy of Pope Clement IX (1667-1669) at whose centre was

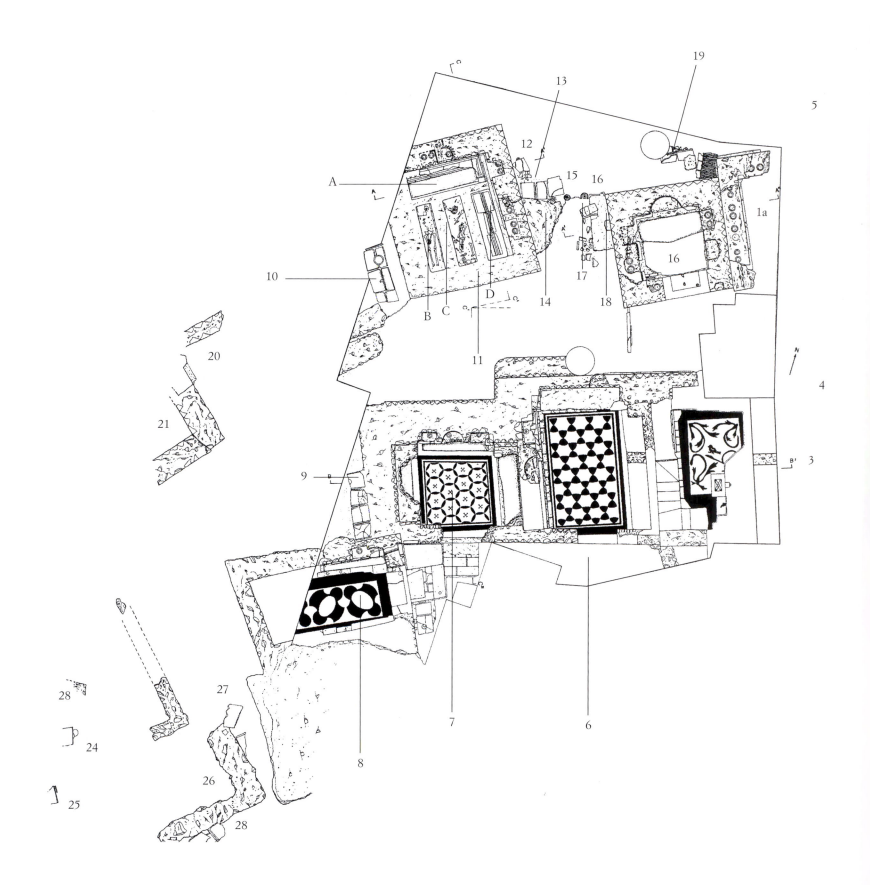

placed a model of a galleon that was made during the papacy of Pope Paul V (1605-1621). This galleon was made of lead with bronze finishing touches based on a design by Carlo Maderno. Jets of water spring from the canons, masts, banners and buglers on the ship's stern that, once activated, create a series of water games destined to enliven a small park of little trees and small hedges. Indeed, during the 17th century, the valley area of Bramante's very long Corridor was intended as a garden, organised on different terrace levels and partly used as a vegetable garden. Various views of it have been recorded, amongst which we can note a 1615 engraving by Maggi and Mascardi. Post-antiquity interventions in this area are considered rather limited and only allow us to document some 16th century shafts which were intended for recovering building material that was then reused for new pontifical buildings as well as the realisation of escarpments and buttresses for the terracing. As a consequence, until the excavation works in the 1930s, the area had almost been entirely left intact from an archaeological point of view, sealed by the garden's soil.

It was following the Lateran Treaty of 1929 that the area was subjected to a series of building works which were necessary for the internal reorganisation of the new small Vatican City State. First of all, a primary requirement appeared to be the realisation of a more articulated road network. As a result, a few essential excavations were carried out for the new percourses and connections, which simultaneously provided the opportunity of making some important finds. In particular, between May and September 1930, a road was built that would join the north-east of the State with the Belvedere's summit area. Whilst levelling and making the pathway, the first chamber tombs (which were immediately described and included in the first edition by Josi) were discovered just a few metres downhill from the Galea Fountain.[19] The tombs were found without their lids and were partly cut off due to the creation of the garden terraces. They were positioned over several rows along the incline, which sloped down from the area that would later become Bramante's Staircase. The ancient terracing seems to have been distributed over a minor road network with the odd slip road connected by means of sharply sloped side ramps.[20] Unfortunately, three funerary chambers and part of a fourth were destroyed for the construction of the modern road network; one tomb, and the side of two others, however, were conserved within wide arches under the modern terrace.

Between 1994 and 1995, new excavations were undertaken in the same site. These were necessary for the creation of the Vatican Museum's Sale of Publications and Reproductions Office. As such, the archaeological area discovered during the 1930s was opened up. The discovery of new tombs has allowed one to check their fairly regular arrangement over three ancient terraces of lay-bys and spaces which were once occupied by individual tombs (cremation and burial interment).[21] The realisation of the warehouse resulted in some sacrifices, such as the partial demolition of the few remaining remains found on the upper terrace or their obliteration under the modern structures. But it also allowed the archaeological area to be isolated within a new building. Armed with more advanced and suitable means, one was thus able to proceed with new excavations as well as a series of restoration interventions which carried on until 2005.[22]

In the other neighbouring areas of the Vatican Hill summit, other discoveries have recently been made that belong to the same necropolis. In 1995, a superficial excavation carried out whilst rearranging the flower bed in front of the Galea Fountain brought to light a cinerary urn lid decorated with little birds and small acroterial palmettes.[23] During the 1998-2000 works carried out for the Jubilee Year, other discoveries were made in connection with the tombs found at the summit of the Vatican; these occurred during excavations for the construction of the new entrance to the Vatican Museums[24] and the realisation of the new refreshment bar.[25]

The three terraces of the Galea area are occupied by tombs which are chronologically close to one another; it should naturally be presumed that at least one other terrace located further up and numerous terraces further downhill once existed (plate 2). Indeed, the building up of this area appears to have started from the summit and gradually proceeded with spaces that are located further downwards, with some adjustments due to the irregular shape of the slope. Amongst those identified so far, the most elevated terrace occupies a narrow space behind the foundations of the gallery what is today the Museo Chiaramonti. The tombs discovered here belong to the Augustan Period and the first decades of the first century AD. As already mentioned, they are therefore the most ancient tombs of the area. Some chamber tombs have been conserved at foundation level with cinerary urns and graves dug into the pavement that were intended for burials on overlying levels (*formae*). At the side, a few poor burial interments can be found: in one case, the grave was covered over by a series of *bipedales*, two of which bear a stamp dating back to the first century AD.[26] The underlying terrace marks a jump in height of almost 1.5 metres and a chronological leap of a century. The dating of all of the tombs is actually contained to the first half of the second century AD, and in particular to AD 120-150. Six chamber tombs have been identified, as well as two containers of bones, four tombs *a semicappuccina* (a sort of small roof constructed of a single row of tiles placed against the adjacent wall), and three cremations in terracotta cinerary urns (characteristic ovoid vases which constitute the most diffused type of container for holding ashes during the Roman Period).

Tomb 5, which is located behind Pope Gregory XVI's fountain[27], is located next to Tomb 1a of which the east side has been conserved – the rest was destroyed during the construction of the road.[28] The rectangular room[29] made of brick contained eight cinerary urns and a niche holding another two funerary urns on the northern side which are set into the counter located behind the wall. Photographs taken during excavations headed by Josi[30] show something else: along the northern side was another niche with two cinerary urns and, below it, a terracotta sarcophagus, whilst on the east wall a *forma* held four or five interments. The tomb rests upon *columbarium* 1b (dated around AD 125). Due to the prevalence of cremations over burials, they can be dated to around AD 130-140.

Columbarium 1b seems older than the intermediate terrace: it is of an almost square format and measures approximately 3 metres each side. It was built to hold three rows of two niches on each lateral wall (plate 3).[31] At the centre of the bottom side is a niche that is bigger than the others, presumably intended for the tombs' titular couple, whilst the entrance wall contained smaller niches. One can thus count a total number of 28 cremations. The room's internal decoration comprised of a small brick cornice and an elegant series of decorative motifs made of stucco that still bear traces of colour. The precarious state of conservation only allows one to guess which figures were placed within faux architecture inside of the niches. The floor was made up of a black and white mosaic but today only a few mosaic *tesserae* remain in the corners close to the travertine threshold. Two burial graves during the second half of the third century AD destroyed the rest.[32] The tomb's door was protected from possible landslides or the rain by a slab that was inserted at an angle in the ground in front of the threshold.

In the north-west angle of the *columbarium*, a brick was found bearing the stamp *Paetinus* and *Apronianus* (dated AD 123).[33] Therefore, the tomb was built after this date but prior to the 'box' tombs 17 and 18 – perhaps two bone containers – that were leaning against it. These tiny sepulchral monuments are made of bricks lined with mortar, plastered and painted red. A pierced marble slab,

placed within a small painted niche, allowed libations to be poured inside of tomb 17. Inside of the 'box', a brick bears a second stamp similar to the previous one mentioned.[34] In the adjacent and contemporary tomb, Tomb 18, a low-relief stele contains the portrait of a young boy with a short fringe that was particularly fashionable during the Trajanic Period (AD 98-117).[35] Below, we read the text which reveals the identity of this deceased youth: a 13 year old boy by the name of *Publius Cornelius Protoctetus* (plate 4). It is possible that the stele might relate to an earlier burial of the young boy, who was perhaps originally interred in a grave and whose remains were then moved and placed in the bone container a few years later. The father *Eutychus'* dedication to his son *Protoctetus* and the woman *Protocenina* leads one to believe that the 'box' Tomb 17 relates to the latter.

A short path, which passes in front of *columbarium* 1b and Tomb 11's two bone containers and is linked by a ramp behind Tomb 11, connects the intermediate terrace with the upper terrace. During the second quarter of second century AD (that is just before the construction of Tomb 11), the path did not exist and the area appears to have been empty. A series of cremations were carried out in this area. Of these, three clay cinerary urns lay underground with the libation tube inserted through the pierced lid (funerary urns 14, 15 and 16).[36]

Around AD 140-150, Tomb 11 was built (of quadrangular form and measuring c. 3.5 x 4 m) used for mixed rites (plate 5).[37] Made up of mixed brick and small blocks of tuff, two or three rows of niches stand on the walls whilst underneath the pavement floor stand four *formae* which contain four or five interred remains each. Three *formae* are placed longitudinally after the entrance whilst the fourth is placed horizontally to the wall behind. A terracotta sarcophagus placed on a travertine shelf lies above it. All of the internal spaces were covered in white plaster-work and traces of fresco decoration, containing a series of red squares along the skirting board and red and green floral plant shoots have been found in the niches and above them.

Some grave goods (small *amphorae*, terracotta incense holders, chalices and glass balsam holders) were placed in the niches, above the lids of funerary urns, whilst a bronze *applique* with a valve made of shell and other ceramic objects have been rediscovered in the *formae*. The *formae* were closed off by a layer of bricks, which simultaneously acted as the floor; in the east *forma*, a hooded cover was found which presumably closed off the wooden coffin. Everything was sealed by a small mosaic floor consisting of white mosaic tiles crossed by a black strip. It probably counts as one of the last depositions in the tomb, dating back to the second half of the second century AD when available spaces were starting to get used up.[38] Originally, 52 cremations and 16 interments

3. Galea area, columbarium 1b.

4. *Galea area, stele of the young boy Publius Cornelius Protoctetus.*

5. *Galea area, Tomb 11.*

were calculated. Almost two generations must have used this burial ground which was in use until the end of the second century AD. Although the lack of inscriptions prevents one from being absolutely certain, it appears that the property belonged to a funerary college[39] rather than to a family. These funerary colleges were a type of cooperative in which members, belonging to the lower middle class, paid a contribution for a tomb to be built, acquiring, as such, one or more *loculi*. In addition, financial contributions regularly paid by the deceased relatives guaranteed the tomb's maintenance as well as the carrying out of ceremonies in remembrance of the dead.

Tomb 11 became an object of attraction due to various burials it housed. Apart from Tomb 19 *a semicappuccina* (which was constructed behind Tombs 1a and 1b), the Tombs 12 and 13 *a semicappuccina* lie to the east of Tomb 11, whilst Tomb 10 is located along its west side.[40] The latter is a grave covered by *sesquipedales*[41] placed flat, whilst a Dressel 2-4 type amphora one lies on top of it in direct correspondence to the face of the deceased below. Indeed, only the tip is missing which, when inserted vertically, allowed libations to be poured. This type of wine amphora provides us with just a rough chronological indication as it was produced over a wide period of time that spanned from the beginning of the first century AD through to the middle of the second century AD. A stamp (dating to around AD 120) that appears on the brick lid provides little new information as it is a reused element.[42] As a result, by comparing it to Tomb 11, a later date for this tomb has been determined, dating it to the middle of the second century AD, like nearby burial tombs. There is little else to add about the subject of tombs located on the intermediate terrace, other than the presence of other individual burials and chamber tombs in a nearby area: these have been partly identified close to the west border of the excavation site. In particular, chamber tombs of 20 and 21 are recognisable: they were used for mixed rites and are dated to around the middle of the second century AD, as well as Tombs 22, 23 and 26 which belong to the early Imperial Period, together with individual burial tombs 24, 24 and 27 which alternatively are generally dated to first century AD. All of the most inner tombs found in this area are now covered by the modern warehouse.

The lower terrace is made up of a rather more defined and stable structure. A wide foundation wall (with a screen constructed of little blocks of Cappellaccio tuff[43]) protected the area from possible landslides deriving from the earth of the intermediate terrace and, at the same time, acts as the back wall for a row of at least five chamber tombs. The tomb located furthest downhill from the other series, was discovered during the excavations carried out in the 1930s: Tomb 4.[44] The partly reconstructed walls (built in *opus reticulatum mixtum* in Cappellaccio tuff and strips of bricks) bear a small cornice made of brick in the upper part and *arcosolia* with *formae* in the lower part.[45] Both the technique and plan of the room must have been similar to that of the adjacent Tomb 3, which is also only known of through sparse photographs and information compiled in the 1930s. The only element which differentiates this tomb from the previous one is the fact that several fragments of a fresco (a series of floral motifs on a pale background) exist on the back wall of an *arcosolium*.[46]

The position and structure of these two tombs is similar to that of adjacent tombs 2, 6 and 7 which are conserved and accessible today. They make up what was an organic project, dated around AD 180-190, when at least five tombs were built in sequence and completely restructured a sixth sepulchre, Tomb 8. These tombs, which were originally covered by a geometric black and white mosaic floor, share the long and wide back wall, as well as lateral walls they sometimes shared. Furthermore, all of them face (directly or by means of a short open-air front court) onto the same road network and are decorated by an elegant brick cornice at the front consisting of a sequence of various mouldings: a continuous *cyma* moulding, an astragal, a frieze with dentils, and an Ionic *cyma*, as well as a series of neck and listel mouldings.[47] The tombs could be accessed by way of a short flight of steps consisting of three large steps (due to the road network being located about a metre below). This change in level was deemed necessary in order to safeguard the tombs from infiltrations of rain and landslides. The project foresaw both cremations (ashes placed in terracotta containers affixed at the corners or placed on the floor of a niche) and buried interments (placed inside *formae* found underneath the *arcosolia*). The latter ritual was the most prevalent. Such characteristics seem more suitable to a repartition of burial chambers shared by members of a funerary college. But, as is also the case here, the absence of important inscriptions prevents one from establishing possible relationships once shared between the deceased.

Tomb 2 seems to have been built earlier than Tomb 3 and, judging from Josi's notes and photos taken, it was abutted at a later moment. It presents two clear and dis-

tinct building phases: the first, which is assignable to around AD 180-190, is related to the layout of the entire formation of funerary structures, whilst the second dates to the middle of the third century AD.[48] Based on a rectangular plan[49], it originally housed a bench and two *arcosolia* along the lateral walls and one *arcosolium* on the back wall, under which *formae* were placed for five superimposed burials. Remains of funerary urns, however, have not been found, unlike in other tombs where they are affixed at the corners. Based on a comparison with tombs in the sequence, the floor must have consisted of a mosaic "rug" made up of geometric motifs made from black and white mosaic tiles during the first phase.

The second phase, which is attributable to the mid-third century AD, radically changed the tomb's structure.[50] The mosaic floor was completely removed. An underground chamber was created about 2.60 metres below the original floor and exposed the foundation's entire perimetre. The flight of steps that provided access to the structure immediately starts to the left of the entrance, turn at 90° degrees and descend with another four steps. Thus, with another right-hand bend consisting of two steps, one reaches the *hypogaeum*. In order to create these steps, the first *forma* on the left wall with its relative *arcosolium* and bench had to be sacrificed. Inside this small underground environment, an *arcosolium* on the back wall was uncovered, under which was found a *forma* containing interments. However, on the opposite wall, there is an unexcavated tomb *a cappuccino* of which the gable-wise set bricks remain embedded in the walls, whilst a large chest tomb is positioned in front of the steps. This was a particular type of burial that consisted in placing interments inside of a sort of brick trunk.[51] The floor is made of mosaic but the digging of a grave for a subsequent burial has resulted in leaving just a few remnants of it behind.

The pictorial fresco decoration is much better conserved and its location corresponds to the last bend of the stairs. Here, there is a high soccle coloured red upon which is a square containing a pink shoot. Internally, the pictorial decoration is divided over three different registers. In the lower part, there is the high soccle, constructed of squares with red stripes and various geometric motifs in faux marble *crustae* in the background (amongst which large red circular shields at the centre and green *peltae* inserted diagonally at the corners (plate 6). The walls and the vault are articulated by stylised faux architecture, realised with thin red and green strips. As such, compartments were created within which little figures are suspended: in particular, when one enters at the right a rampant antelope, a female figure in mid-flight (she is probably an Aura) on the arch wall that divides the two sections with a small plant below, whilst on the left there is a face painted in a *clipeus* (perhaps a *gorgoneion*) between two birds in flight (plate 7).

The decoration inside the *arcosolium* is different. On the back wall, framed by two subtle red garlands that slope down and are "curtain-like" open, appears a religious subject: an altar is placed on an uneven terrain upon which a flame burns. Immediately to the right we find a small green column upon which lies a red mantle, a brown and yellow shield and a lance whilst to the left there is brown and yellow element that is not entirely decipherable (plate 8). Shortly before the underarch, one sees linear squares in red, yellow and green with an almond-shaped frame at the top inside which an aquatic bird is caught about to fly off. At the sides of the underarch are, instead, two green marine horses.

The subjects described find various comparisons in the pictorial production of the second century AD, but stylistically they match stylised and "moderately impressionistic" expressions only known from the late Severan Period onwards, persisting until the end of the third century AD.[52] Particularly similar, for example, are the figurative themes and architectural partitions belonging to the tomb of the *Ottavii* in an area that is far off from the *Via Triumphalis* (now the National Roman Museum)[53], as well as in two parts of Villa Piccola, located underneath St. Sebastian on the *Via Appia*[54], dated to the first half of the third century AD. Between the second half of the third century and the start of the fourth century AD, the decorations can be linked to paintings found in some of the rooms of the *domus* underneath the church of "San Giovanni e San Paolo" on the Caelian Hill[55], and to some at Ostia (in room VII Room of the House of the Yellow Walls and at the *thermopolium* in the *Via della Casa di Diana*).[56]

In the first section of the small *hypogaeum*, the figure of Aura in flight is missing her head due to a gap caused by an unauthorised tomb opening. In fact, a little above it is a small rectangular niche which presumably once bore an inscription or decorative or religious element. This element was removed when a 16th-17th century long shaft was dug out which, after having affected the tombs nearby and the upper plane of Tomb 2, also destroyed the *hypogaeum*'s vault. This shaft was built to retrieve precious material which then could be reused. Consequently, one can also attribute this event to the damage done to an infant's sarcophagus found in the *hypogaeum* during the 1930s excavations.[57] A subject conventionally called the "Island of the Blessed" is sculpted in low-relief on the coffin – a subject that is composed of small boats with cupids captured in sea-life activity, in a port context (presumably Alexandria in Egypt).[58] A semi-reclined figure of a young deceased person (of an unrefined face) can be seen at the centre. The sarcophagus, which is dated around AD 300, represents one of the latest examples of a funerary use in the entire Galea area (plate 9).

The construction of the *hypogaeum* naturally also

7. Galea area, Tomb 2, hypogeum with frescoes and an arcosolium at the back.

8. *Galea area, Tomb 2, hypogeum, detail of the* arcosolium's *frescoes.*
9. *Galea area, infant's sarcophagus depicting the "Island of the Blessed", discovered in Tomb 2.*

THE VATICAN NECROPOLIS ON THE *VIA TRIUMPHALIS*

involved the re-laying of the upper room's floor.[59] Re-using the original mosaic tiles, a mosaic "rug" floor was realised that was framed by a series of thin marble slabs. Following a wide black banner, the refigured subject was placed on a white background with an invitation to go beyond the threshold on the inside. The mosaic decoration is comprised of four tufts of acanthus which diagonally come off from the corners of the room in order to converge towards the centre, where a small bird (perhaps a blackbird) perches on a branch (plate 10). As with the frescoes, this subject matter was also rather diffused in the course of the second century AD.[60] However, one finds better stylistic comparisons in the production of the following century as shown by the Ostian mosaics of the Insula dell'Aquila,[61] the *Schola* of Trajan[62], and those of Tomb 55 and the little portico of Tomb 34 in the Isola Sacra necropolis.[63]

New tombs added during the course of the third century AD do not seem to have been added to this upper room. As a consequence, one can hypothesise the room's transformation into an ante-chamber used for funerary practices, such as *refrigeria*, periodic banquets held in commemoration of the deceased. The period between the two phases can be calculated as the equivalent of about three generations but it is not possible to establish whether the building transformations refer to the re-use of an abandoned tomb or a prolonged use by the same family or funerary college who were the owners during the first phase.[64]

Tomb 6 opens up next to it, a tomb that is similar in form and size[65] to Tomb 2 with which it shares a lateral wall and the continuation of the back wall.[66] In front of the tomb there are two small walls parallel to one another and placed perpendicularly to the tomb's outer corners. They seem to form a very small open-air courtyard overlooking the path that joins the terrace.[67] The previously discussed 16th-17th century shaft built for plundering from Tomb 2 also allowed for the removal of the threshold and entrance jambs, thus damaging the first stretch of mosaic floor. The lateral walls were also knocked down during the undertaking of this underground work. In any case, on the basis of that which has survived, one can reconstruct the existence of two *arcosolia* with three niches above on each of the lateral walls. These niches comprise of a large semicircular one positioned at the centre with two funerary urns and two smaller rectangular niches containing one funerary urn. Under each *arcosolium* is a *forma* which was used for the deposition of five burials.

The back wall contains a large *arcosolium* with a usual *forma* underneath and a bench below which was meant to bear the sarcophagus. This wall conserves ephemeral traces of a decoration in blue bands.

The mosaic floor is of a certain interest: it is a "rug" whose border is made up of brick and whose interior is filled with black and white mosaic tiles in the form of an illusionary geometric motif (plate 11). Wide hexagonal white flowers with six black petals come off at the intersection of stripes. This motif finds numerous comparisons: in particular, one recalls the Ostian floors such as that of the *Domus* of the Fish[68] and that of Trajan's *Schola*[69], which are generally dated to the third century AD. In the current context, we can arrive at an earlier dating thanks to the discovery of two brick-stamps. Placed so as to create a division between two sepulchres found inside one of the *formae*, these bricks cover the lower burial, which is the oldest one, of the second *forma* on the left side of the room. The stamp makes mention of the *figlinae Publinianae* in the *praedium* of *Aemilia Severa*, a *clarissima femina* (that is a woman belonging to a senatorial family) who is known to have lived in Rome between AD 190-210.[70] As this is repeated on two different bricks, it provides a credible chronological indication as to when the sepulchre was first occupied.[71] No material dating to after the mid-third century AD has been found in the tomb. As such, one can hypothesise that the tomb was used for little more than half a century (between AD 180-190 and 250).

Tomb 7 concludes the series of tombs placed along the same wall of the terrace.[72] This wall has a recess which corresponds to that of Tomb 11's entrance – it is an older one but was clearly still used at the time. As a result, the dimensions of Tomb 7 were reduced so that it had an almost square form.[73] In the lower part of the lateral walls and the back wall there are three *arcosolia*, and in the upper part we find two counters for sarcophagi in the lateral walls and three niches in the back wall. As is common, the central semicircular niche is wider and contains two funerary urns whilst the lateral niches have a rectangular form and contain one funerary urn each. The walls are covered in white plaster-work; a thin red strip marks the border of the *arcosolia* whilst grey-green colour plant motifs (which are unfortunately badly conserved) decorate the upper spaces.

A mosaic was discovered at the centre of the room although it had been smashed due to the collapse of the vault; the reason for this collapse can be linked to the cre-

10. Galea area, Tomb 2.

11. Galea area, Tomb 6.

12. Galea area, Tomb 7.

13. Galea area, Tomb 8.

ation of a 16th-17th century shaft which originally contained two tunnels for removing materials as previously described: the first tunnel turns towards the east and crosses Tombs 6 and 2 whilst the second one, which was dug in a south-westernly direction, penetrates Tomb 8 and surpasses it. As is the case here once again, the tomb's door jambs and threshold were removed by means of this tunnel, thus damaging part of the mosaic. The mosaic "rug" is framed by a band of small marble slabs which frame two strips of black mosaic tiles. Its centre contains a black and white geometric motif (plate 12). As seen previously, it creates a decorative illusionist game which can be seen at the intersection of several interlinked circles. "Olive leaves" are formed at the superimposition which mark out white hexagons coming off from the concave sides with flowers in the form of a cross in the background. This decorative taste – created by the superimposition of curvilinear geometric elements – characterises a large part of the mosaic production of the second century AD.[74] The same inspirational concept is, in fact, detectable in some mosaics that date between AD 130-150 as seen, for example, in the back triclinium of the *Hospitalia* at Hadrian's Villa[75] and in a *sacellum* along the Decumanus at Ostia.[76] However, one also finds floors that are created with marble insets, such as the one recently found in the Cisterna di Latina territory.[77]

Several inscriptions have been discovered inside the burial chamber which could be related to the deceased of the tomb.[78] The chronology of the materials found during the excavation of the room suggests, once again, that the tomb was abandoned early on around the middle of the third century AD (perhaps due to a landslide coming down from the hill's summit). Tomb 8 is the westernmost tomb discovered in the lower terrace. The tomb is not placed parallel to the terrace wall but transversally to it. Its entrance opens to the east and is turned at almost a 90° angle compared to the chamber tombs previously described.[79] As a consequence, one needs to hypothesise that the lower terrace track finished with this tomb or that here it turned at a right-angle in order to then descend with a ramp towards a terrace below. The room has an orientation that is much closer to that of the most ancient tombs belonging to the intermediate terrace (above all, Tombs 11, 22 and 26). What is more, its internal structure is irregular as if it had to adapt to predetermined spaces.

These topographical and structural anomalies could have been caused by a pre-existing factor: some walls corresponding to the corner that touches Tomb 7 indeed seem to have formed part of a previous tomb[80], a sepulchre that was almost completely levelled and rebuilt during AD 180-190. Another element that relates to this earlier tomb is perhaps the discovery of a structure that stands against the tomb's lower part (presumably belonging to the first phase). It is built in *sequipedales* and could have acted as a table for ritual banquets or, most likely, a sort of *cupa*, a burial placed inside the walls. Two bricks in this structure bearing a stamp dating to AD 80-100, could date the tomb's earlier phase.[81]

The front is covered in red plaster-work and contains three steps to access it. The internal room, as previously mentioned, has an elongated and slightly trapezoidal plan.[82] The back of the room is not currently visible as it remains under the floor of the modern warehouse (plate 13). The tomb's left wall was partially destroyed by the 16th–17th century spoliation shaft. It is possible, however, to reconstruct two *arcosolia* along the lateral walls with *formae* below, and three niches above. With regard to the back wall – of which only the top is visible – one can imagine a single *arcosolium* with a niche above that contained the remains of two incinerated bodies.

Again, the black and white mosaic floor is praiseworthy and belongs to a period contemporary to that of the nearby tombs (about AD 180-190) or shortly afterwards. The mosaic "rug" is framed by a border of marble slabs and a wide and irregular band of black mosaic tiles. As seen with the adjacent tombs, the central motif is created through the use of changes in colour at the intersection areas of undulating stripes. Here, they produce a series of white ovals, which are placed in a diagonal position with an alternate pattern; the ovals are marked out by *peltae* and rectangles with concave and convex sides. The decorative motif bears several variants that were particularly used in the first half of the second century AD. The mosaic of Room C of a Roman villa at Lanuvio is identical with the exception of some decorative elements (amongst which animals) that appear on the inside of the ovals.[83] With regard to the composition and illusionist imposition only, one recalls two similar mosaics in Rome: the first is a floor of a *domus* near S. Paolo alla Regola [84] and in some rooms of the *Paedagogium*[85], whilst the second is a mosaic found at Ostia in corridor D of the *Domus* of Apuleius .[86] A final comparison can be made with the mosaic found in the *frigidarium* of the great baths of Aquileia[87] (dated mid-third century AD) which attests to the motif's prolonged use. These comparative datings of the mosaic seem to contrast with the fact that Tomb 7 (AD 180-190) rests on Tomb 8, which therefore predates it. It follows that even during the second phase, the sepulchre was slightly earlier compared to the rank of tombs previously described and the mosaic constitutes a particularly early example of this motif executed around AD 170-180. The burial of the tomb happened over a period of time: thin layers of gravel and clay cover the steps and thus also enter inside it. The tomb's abandonment, which took place by the middle of the third century AD, seems prior to the completion of the available funerary spaces. This was perhaps due to its unconformity.

A stele of particular interest was discovered in the area opposite the stairs of Tombs 7 and 8. This stele bears two inscriptions which are opposite one another but on the same side: the first (which is probably dated to the mid-first century AD) was carved starting from the slab's original upper margin, whilst the second (which was added at least a century later when the slab was reused) was alternatively sculpted starting on the slab's original lower margin after it had been turned upside down. The oldest of the two inscriptions – which bears an elegantly written text full of rich allusions – commemorates *Antonia Titiana*: the epitaph is addressed to the deceased in the first person, commencing with "Here is the *rogus* of Antonia Titiana" – for "*rogus*" one does not mean *ustrinum* (the place of the pyre) but rather the burial place – and followed by a poetic description of the deceased's

Roman origins. Before mentioning the "*sanctissimus*" husband *Marcus Nonius Pythagora*, the inscription notes how the wife has left a small son and brother, who seems to be defined as a flute player even though other possible interpretations exist.[88] This aspect calls to mind *prothesis* ceremonies (the showing of the deceased), when hired professional female mourners and, in fact, flute players participated in the *lamentationes*. An example that illustrates this rite is portrayed in a sculpted relief of the *Haterii* tomb (late first– early second century AD) (I).

As has been described, the burials of the intermediate terrace and those of the lower terrace seem to have been effected by early hill subsidence. Indeed, the ceramic materials that have been found inside of them do not date later than the middle of the third century AD. On this basis, one can imagine that once the occupation of the *formae* had been completed and the funerary urns used for a period lasting two generations, many tombs were abandoned and progressively filled with earth from a series of landslides, which was never removed again. And finally, during the second half of the third century AD, only Tombs 1b and 2 survived. These were both aligned in the same way but positioned on different terraces. The former, *columbarium* 1b, was reused for burials, roughly damaging the mosaic pavement and various niches on the walls to make way for improvised *arcosolia* to be used for new depositions. The latter tomb was transformed and the internal space was transformed and redecorated more elegantly, with the addition of a frescoed *hypogaeum*. One can maintain that this area, positioned on at least two terraces of an unknown length, was less exposed to the hill's early powerful landslides around the middle of the third century AD; perhaps the tombs that were positioned further inside somehow protected the ones slightly further out. Additionally, their fitness for habitation could have favoured their reuse until the early fourth century AD.

The Autoparco Necropolis

About fifty metres to the south-east (therefore further downhill than the Galea area), there is the Autoparco area, which consists of terraces for tombs on a level about 15 metres lower. (see plate 1 on p. 140). This part of the Vatican Necropolis on the *Via Triumphalis* was discovered during the construction works of the Vatican Car Park during 1956-58.[89] The scale and importance of the discoveries resulted in an excavation directed by Filippo Magi who, at the end of the construction works, also

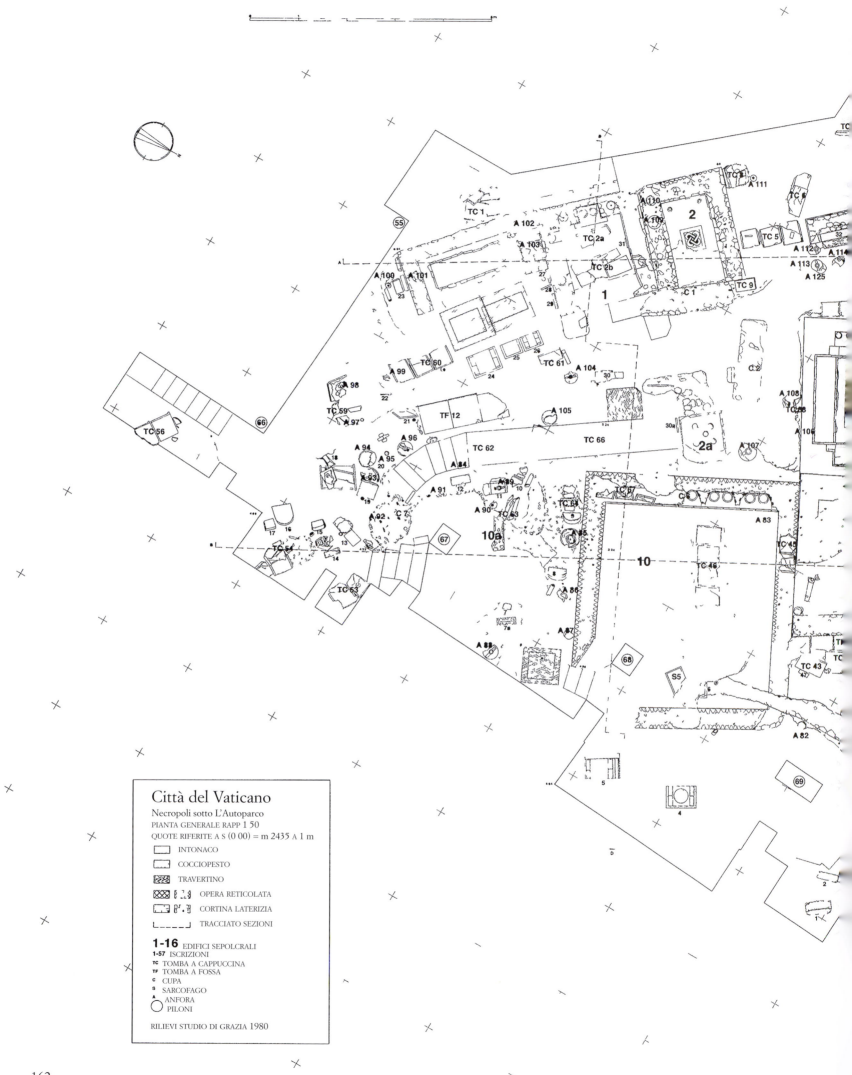

Città del Vaticano

Necropoli sotto L'Autoparco

PIANTA GENERALE RAPP 1 50

QUOTE RIFERITE A S (0 00) = m 2435 A 1 m

INTONACO	
COCCIOPESTO	
TRAVERTINO	
OPERA RETICOLATA	
CORTINA LATERIZIA	
TRACCIATO SEZIONI	

1-16 EDIFICI SEPOLCRALI

1-57 ISCRIZIONI

TC TOMBA A CAPPUCCINA

TF TOMBA A FOSSA

C CUPA

S SARCOFAGO

A ANFORA

○ PILONI

RILIEVI STUDIO DI GRAZIA 1980

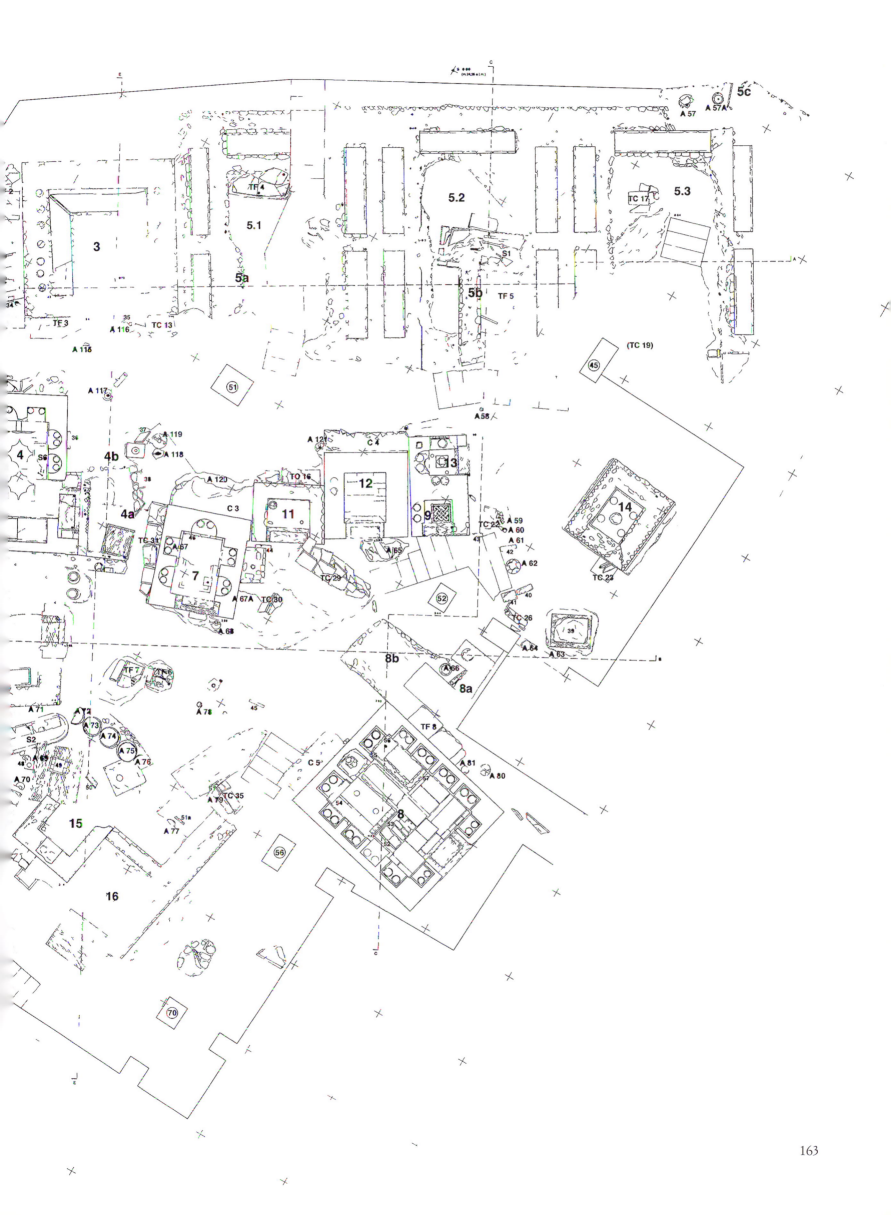

coordinated the first restorations, the preparation and the creation of an on-site museum of the archaeological area. As with areas nearby, the Autoparco area is characterised by a series of shallow terraces upon which numerous chamber tombs were built next to individual sepulchres (plate 14). In the area that was investigated four terraces have been identified. These terraces cannot always be clearly distinguished, however, as the differences in height between them vary: in some areas, they tend to be joined together and in other periods they seem to be partly placed on top of each other. The spaces appear to be very constrained and one should bear in mind that in just under 20 metres, there is a difference in height of over 5 metres with an average slope of around 30%. Along the steep slope between one terrace and another, a great number of individual tombs (both for cremation and interment) appeared which, over the course of time, were built on top of each other, cut across or were covered by one another. About 20 funerary monuments, 68 tombs *a cappuccina* (perhaps covered by slabs placed gable-wise), 12 grave tombs with a flat cover, 6 sarcophagi, 7 *cupae* (individual "box" tombs) and a great number of cremations on funerary altars or in cinerary urns, which were buried in the ground and marked by *stelae* and *cippi* (memorial stones), have been found in this complex (plate 15).

It should be remembered that the irregularity of these artificial levels is due to its subordination to the hill's orography and was also conditioned by its progressive occupation. In fact, the terraces started in the area closest to the *Via Triumphalis* at what was probably about 10 metres further downhill and, with time, proceeded to move upwards following and adapting to the terrain's inundations. Furthermore, one needs to consider that every time an upper space was occupied, the earth that was removed had to be dumped to one side or on a lower terrace, thus respecting earlier tombs that were still in use. The lack of any kind of general planning for these burial spaces, the instability of the land and the constrictions imposed by the hill's orography and pre-existing factors, are not only the cause of this irregular creation of terraces but also the tombs' different orientations and forms (plate 16). The Vatican Hill's instable "hat-like" geological conformation only partly allowed for a regularisation of the slope which was periodically subjected to a series of landslides. In particular, one notes the landslide that took place during the Flavian Period (AD 69-96) which covered a large part of the tombs that were in use

at that time. This landslide that was bigger than most, made subsequent building work necessary which was then also subjected to other hill subsidence.

The chronology of this necropolis appears to be more contained compared to that of adjacent areas. A period spanning almost two centuries, ranging from the middle of the first century AD to the middle, or the second half of the third century AD has been suggested. In particular, five main phases have been identified: the first phase spans the period of the mid-first century AD to the reign of Vespasian (AD 69-79); the second phase lasts for the remainder of the Flavian Period (AD 79-96); the third phase includes the reigns of Nerva (AD 96-98), Trajan (AD 98-117) and Hadrian (AD 117-138); the fourth phase spans the Antonine Period (AD 138-192); and the fifth phase starts with the Severan Period (end of the second century AD) and continues until the second half of the third century AD. Some monetary finds go beyond this chronological dating and fall into the second half of the third century AD although they do not relate to new sepulchral structures but only to some individual burials. Considering the hill's progressive and uninterrupted sepulchral occupation, without a real solution of continuity or extensive building projects, these phases should therefore be considered more or less conventional. In light of all the reasons outlined above, we will now chronologically examine this part of the necropolis, starting with the tombs closest to the *Via Triumphalis* (plate 17).

The first tombs to have been documented in this area date to the years immediately following the middle of the first century AD. In particular, two funerary altars dating to the middle of the first century AD or two decades later were found in the part of the lower terrace which is the flattest part of the entire area: Altar 5 bears a dedication to *Marcus Valerius Amandus*, who was perhaps a freedman of the noble family of the *Marci Valerii Messallae*[90] and externally shows two small iron nails for holding up a plant garland; Altar 4 is dedicated to *Marcus Oppius Receptus* and is hollow on the inside in order to hold ashes.[91] Several travertine *stelae* that are roughly contemporary have been placed at the sides.

A second terrace is slightly higher which during this period, the mid-first or second half of the first century AD, contained a few masonry tombs and a greater number of individual burials. During Nero's reign (AD 52-68), Tomb 10 was built somewhat uphill of Altars 4 and 5: it was a great open-air sepulchral area enclosed by a wall made of *opus reticulatum* with brick courses, which was

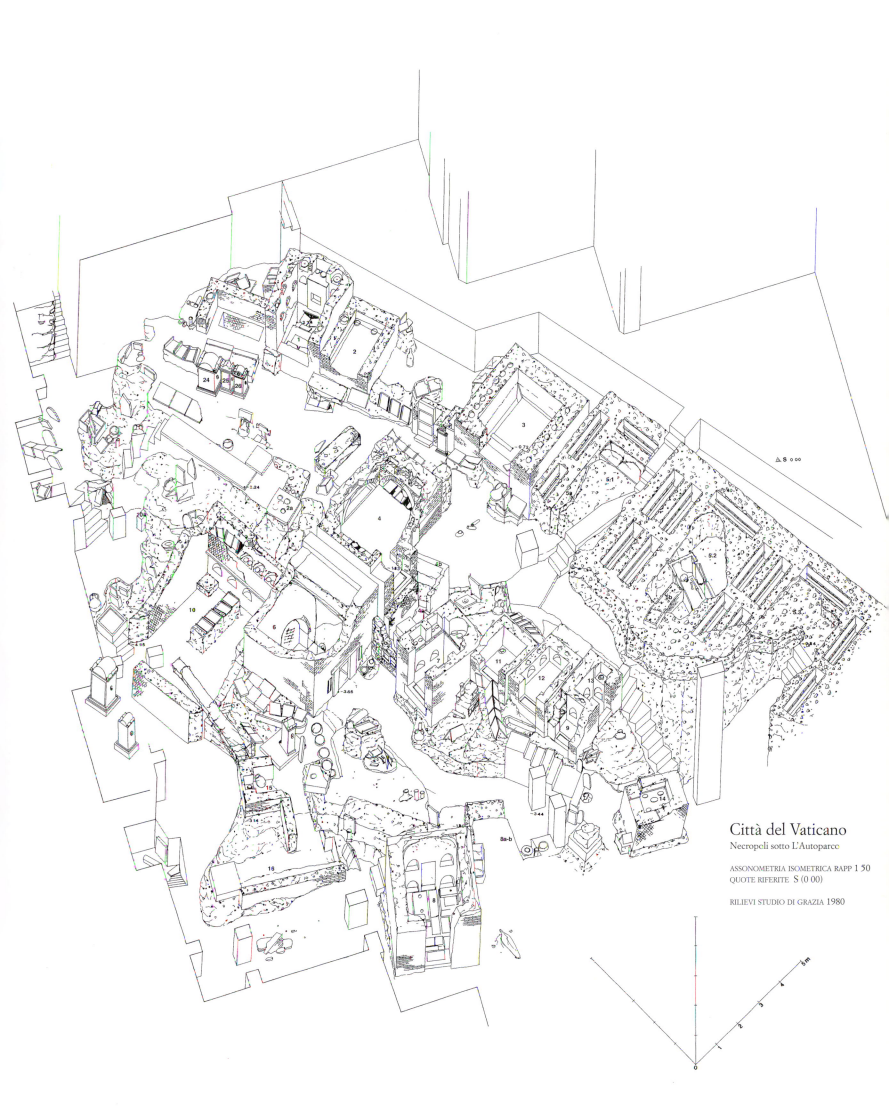

Città del Vaticano
Necropoli sotto L'Autoparco

ASSONOMETRIA ISOMETRICA RAPP 1 50
QUOTE RIFERITE S (0 00)

RILIEVI STUDIO DI GRAZIA 1980

16. *Autoparco area, panorama of the central area taken from above.*

17. Autoparco area, panorama of the central area taken from below.

18. Autoparco area, tomb with enclosure 10.

externally covered by red plaster (plate 18).[92] The enclosure is deprived of entrances and windows. Consequently, access was only possible by means of a wooden ladder that was possibly lowered from the alley uphill of the tomb. Two rows comprising of five niches were placed on this side, each containing two terracotta funerary urns for a total of 20 deceased. Already by the beginning of the second century AD, the enclosure was in a state of abandon. A few decades afterwards, it gradually started to fill up with earth, thus becoming a sort of almost level embankment which was then used for burial tombs (*cupa*-style or burials *a cappuccina*).

Still in the Neronian Period, another enclosure (4a) was built a little further west and at a slightly higher level but much smaller in size. It consisted of a low wall in tuff *opus reticulatum* covered in red plaster.[93] The back wall contained a row of three niches for funerary urns and, at the same time, served as a buttress in order to withstand the earth above. Inside, a travertine base once bore a *cippus* (memorial stone) or an altar upon which the tomb's dedication was written. Considering the enclosure's limited height, the dedication must have been visible and legible from the outside. Enclosure 4a survived the construction of the nearby *columbaria* 6 and 7 (dated to AD 60-80 and AD 110-120 respectively) but was buried and damaged during the building of *columbarium* 4 at the end of the second century AD.[94] One can thus deduce that it was frequented until at least the early decades of the second century AD.

Columbarium 6 is situated immediately after the two enclosures of the Neronian Period just described, since it used the right wall of Enclosure 10 as its back wall and adjusted its front to the corner of Enclosure 4a. These pre-existing conditions resulted in the burial chamber's curious trapezoidal shape with its back wall being wider than the entrance wall. The structure, in *opus reticlatum mixtum* that was originally covered in red plaster, opens onto the small piazza opposite with a low doorway made of travertine and two small windows. The panel for the inscription with the (missing) dedication is positioned above the doorway (plate 19).[95] Only a single row of niches appears inside: three side niches containing two cinerary urns each and two niches with just one cinerary urn on the wall of the entrance; on the back wall (which is reduced in size due to Enclosure 10) contains an *arcosolium*. The *opus signinum* floor contains incisions, which have been interpreted as drains for water which infiltrated the tomb. The *opus signinum* floor contains a terracotta sarcophagus along the left side (dated to the second century AD). As such, one can deduce that this tomb's floor belongs to a secondary phase.

The burial chamber was also furnished with an interesting fresco: both on the walls and on the barrel vault where a type of pavilion inside a *viridarium* (a small garden) was painted, consisting of a frame of red cross-beams and grid-work with ribbons hanging down tied onto them. At the bottom, bushes with long green leaves and red flowers rise up (plate 20). These are ornamental motifs that were particularly diffused in tombs dating to the second half of the second century and the third century AD, but they are rather rare in funerary contexts of the second half of the first century AD, such as the one just described.[96] Amongst the numerous ceramic finds made inside the tomb was also a series of oil lamps dating to the first half or middle of the second century AD. This leads one to believe that this tomb was used for a long period of time, perhaps 70-80 years. However, one can not exclude the possibility that the tomb could have been reused after its abandonment and the first phase of infill.[97] Both the steep slope on the left side of Enclosure 10 and the small level space downhill from chamber tomb 6, contain a series of cremation burials that were dug directly into the ground. These were often marked by a marble or travertine stele which bore a dedication to the deceased. These tombs are generally dated to the second half of first century AD and, after having been filled in, new individual tombs were built on top of them, being burials this time. Based on these uses of land, a convergence of these tombs of the middle or second half of first century AD can be identified towards two nearby areas where the slope was more level: the first is located close to Altars 4 and 5, whilst the second L-shaped one is positioned in front of and to the side of Tombs 4 and 6.

Still in the Neronian Period, *columbarium* 8 was built in front of *columbarium* 6 but at a slightly lower level: it counts as the best preserved and richest tomb discovered in the area.[98] The tomb, which has an external facing in brick and an internal one in *opus reticulatum mixtum*, faces north with the previously described tombs positioned behind it and presenting itself with a different orientation. One can thus deduce that it was accessed by a different route, perhaps via a ramp that was located between the Autoparco and Santa Rosa. In the burial chamber, two rows of niches comprising a total of 38 cinerary urns has been found. These cinerary urns were positioned rather irregularly due to the different requirements of the user and some subsequent changes to the design. In the right part, the central niche was enlarged so it could contain four cinerary urns. It was decorated with a polychrome wall mosaic framed by a row of shells (*cardium edule* shells or cockles). On the opposite wall on the left, a niche destined for the burial of a young boy was created in a secondary phase, vertically uniting the two superimposed niches.

The tomb's decoration is distinctly articulated by brick cornices that frame the stucco appliques and frescoes. A series of geometric motifs can be appreciated amongst the latter – painted in red, yellow and green – which are

placed side by side ivy tendrils, acanthus shoots and a basket of fruit. At the centre of the back wall there is a small *aedicula* framed by a brick cornice, whilst the vault is decorated by a stucco half-shell. Inside it there is a small headless statue, also made of stucco, which represents a seated person dressed in a heavy tunic and mantle. The figure's hands rest on his lap, holding a double wax tablet and a stylus: it would appear that he represents a scribe at work, perhaps even portraying the main user of the tomb or perhaps the administrator of the funerary college (plate 21). Indeed, the six inscriptions found *in situ* in this sepulchre prove that the tomb was occupied by people who were not related to one another but were presumably members of a college.[99] In this case, one can determine that the tomb and its relative *collegium* remained active for almost half a century until the early decades of the second century AD. Amongst the deceased, a certain *Eros* is mentioned. He was a *servus atriensis* (a sort of porter) of the *Horti Serviliani*; this estate was an Imperial property that is mentioned in several occasions on sepulchral inscriptions of this area during the Neronian Period, which should presumably be located not too far away from the *Via Triumphalis*.[100] Another two inscribed slabs relate, on the other hand, to two chests that held cremations which were made during a secondary phase. In particular, the left one still has its beautiful lid which is made from a slab of alabaster which bears two circular holes to allow for the insertion of ashes and plugs made of the same stone. There is also a small altar made of alabaster which can be found inside of the burial chambers, directly in front of the entrance. The realisation of other cremation tombs (located underneath the marble slabs of the floor) also belong to this secondary phase, which can be dated to before the beginning of the second century AD.

Some traces of occupation dating back to the Neronian Period have even been found on the slope of the car park area's higher level. A sort of shallow plateau characterises this upper part of the excavation site. Here, a series of tombs (which are positioned with the hill's slope behind them and appear on a slightly higher level) is placed next to a small piazza and linked by a pathway. They are dated to the second half of the first century AD. Stele 32 stands out amongst the others due its high level of quality: it is actually a small marble *aedicule* and is dedicated by *Nunnius*, a *servus saltuarius* of Emperor Nero (and as such in charge of the imperial estate, the *saltus*), to his wife *Ma* (a woman who takes her name from a Capadocian divinity) and his son *Crescens* (plate 23).[101]

The text is inscribed at the base of the stele whilst the upper part bears sculpted busts of the deceased and is crowned by an elegant pediment with birds that drink from a basin. The young boy sports a pageboy's head of hair with a full fringe that falls over his forehead, a hairstyle that was rather fashionable during Nero's reign. The woman sports a hair-do that followed a trend adopted by Nero's mother, Agrippina the Younger (plate 22). In front of the stele, two *amphorae* are fixed in the ground, which are presumably openings for making libations to the two deceased. Along the same path but more southeasterly, Stele 28 can be found dated to around AD 50-60. Its inscription contains a dedication to *Verecunda*, a servant (*ancilla*) in a temple for Venus in the *Horti Serviliani*, and her husband *Saturninus*, a slave at the Latin Library (perhaps related to the aforementioned *Horti Serviliani*).[102] This new reference to the *Horti Serviliani*, where the slave *Eros* also worked who was buried in *columbarium* 8, confirms the close relationship shared between the various deceased with some imperial properties (presumably located close to the *Via Triumphalis*) during this first phase of the necropolis. From these very *horti*, the Emperor Nero seems to have embarked upon his tragic escape from Rome in AD 68.[103]

Next to Stele 28, slightly moved back, there is a base upon which three altars are placed (24, 25 and 26). This base has been moved several times (in ancient times and once again during the 1958 excavations) due to a lack of space (plate 24).[104] In chronological order: the first altar (24) is located to the far left of the series, was built around AD 60-70 and is dedicated to *Iulia Tryphera* and *Tiberius Iulius Atimetus, patronus carissimus* (thus the patron and probably also the woman's husband); the second altar (26) is positioned to the far right and bears a dedication to *Iulia Threpte*, the daughter of the aforementioned couple, and to her husband *Caius Valerius Hymnus*; the third altar (25) is placed in the middle and features a dedication by the young widow *Iulia Threpte*, with perhaps less care and passion, to her second husband *Lucius Maecius Onesimus*. The three altars span a period of about two decades and the originally planned spaces around them were obligatorily reduced, partly due to the realisation of other individual tombs. If *Iulia Threpte* had initially manifested her desire to be buried next to her first husband, by the time of the second dedication, she had moved the altars and changed her mind: her second husband is no longer defined as "*dulcissimus*" (very sweet) nor contains the word "*sibi*" ("for herself"), which would have indicated

22. Autoparco area, stele of Nunnius, detail showing the busts of his son Crescens and his wife Ma.

23. *Autoparco area, alleyway*
containing the stele of Nunnius.

24. *Autoparco area, altars dedicated by Iulia Threpte to her parents and her two husbands.*

25. *Autoparco area, interior of columbarium 1.*

that she had prepared the tomb for herself in that place. A few years later, space was recuperated for the construction of two chamber tombs on this narrow small piazza by means of cutting into a small part of the hill's slope. The small *columbarium* 1 (a sepulchre built of brick and almost square in shape) was built immediately next to the *Vereconda* stele (dated to around AD 70-90).[105] The *columbarium* was initially only meant to be used for cremations. To this end, numerous rows of niches were built into the walls to hold the walled-in cinerary urns (plate 25). A risalit emerges from the centre of the back wall, consisting of an *aedicula* that is bigger than the others for the titular couple of the tomb, and of a second lower niche with a tube that led libations to a coffin under the floor. Two small boxes made of masonry appear at the sides that are only linked to the exterior of the tomb by means of an opening at the back. In correspondence with the niches, thin marble small slabs were affixed which must have carried the painted name of the proprietor but which has disappeared over time. Only one of these marble slabs, being inscribed, still bears the dedication to *Quintus Sentius Philetus*, who died at 45 years of age.[106] The decorative apparatus consists of small stucco cornices and frescoed floral motifs. However, almost nothing of the original mosaic floor has survived due to its removal during the first half of the third century AD in order to dig graves for two young boys. Recently, one of these two sepulchres has resurfaced behind the threshold. It belongs to a baby who possibly died of hydrocephaly. Inside the grave, the so-called obol for Charon was discovered, a coin placed in the mouth of the deceased to pay for his journey to the Underworld.[107] In this case, it is an "as" dated to AD 211-222 which attests to the tomb being reused well after its original construction.

At the same time, *columbarium* 3 was built a little to the left of the *Nunnius* stele (32). This *columbarium* also consists of an almost square burial chamber made of brick which must have been externally covered in red plaster. It was originally planned for cremations only, but not long after its construction it also began to house burials[108]: graves were dug for the tombs *a cappuccina* at the bottom of the walls that were articulated with niches that held cinerary urns; other graves were dug below the floor which was originally made of mosaic and marble slabs. Plant motifs placed under a series of red stripes stand out on the white plastered walls.

During the following years, numerous burials abutted the *columbarium*: simple cremations, such as stele 35, or cremations placed inside a small cubic structure such as the one marked by *stelae* 33 and 34 of the *Aufidii*.[109] The entire small piazza was therefore occupied by various individual tombs that were sometimes marked by *stelae* or *cippi* (memorial stones) and at other times by tubes or parts of *amphorae* used for libations. Amongst these, it is

worth mentioning a grave with a terracotta sarcophagus in the shape of a tub that bears a stamp which dates to before AD 79 and that, over a century later, was incorporated into the foundations of Tomb 5.[110]

A little further downhill we find an area that was occupied during the Flavian Period. This area consists of several cremations protected by parts of amphora, a tomb *a cappuccina* and some burials marked out *stelae* (40, 41, 42, 43 and 95).[111] Here, towards the end of the first century AD, *columbarium* 14 was built with Altar 39 in front of the entrance but placed with a different orientation.[112] The small tomb building was built on top of an older tomb *a cappuccina*[113] and is constructed in *opus reticulatum* in tuff with toothing in brick. The inside is plastered in white with a red band. The cinerary urns were placed at the corners under the floor level. A fifth cavity, located at the centre of the floor, is of greater dimension and one could subsequently hypothesise that this particular one might have been used for ritual libations. This type of internal distribution is also seen in tombs XXV, XXXV and XX (of *Alcimus*) found in the nearby Santa Rosa area that are only slightly older.

During the first decades of the second century AD, a new building phase characterised the small piazza north-west of the tombs 4a, 6 and 10. Various small cubic-shaped *columbaria* were built in this period, meant to cater for the rite of cremation. The space inside was intensely exploited: on the inside (measuring about a square metre of surfaces), a dense series of niches opens on the walls' surfaces, whilst other cinerary urns are embedded below the floor. These "cubic" *columbaria* (tombs 11, 12 and 9) were placed next to one another facing in an easterly direction whilst the most external one of the series, Tomb 13, opens towards the north where an open space leads one to believe that this was originally once occupied by a wide ramp (plate 26). The façades of these *columbaria* are placed further back than *columbarium* 7 (of *Antigonus*) which was built afterwards.

The most ancient tomb of the series is *columbarium* 12. It was built at the beginning of the second century AD in an isolated position and is located about three metres from Enclosure 4a. On its south side, *columbarium* 11 followed by *columbarium* 7 are built against it whilst the double *columbarium* 9/13 abuts it on the north side.[114] The façade of this series of tombs was constructed with a brick facing of excellent quality, of thin red bricks bound by a thin layer of mortar. This type of facing was made to remain visible, while its continuation along the lateral walls was rather less well constructed since it was covered by a thick layer of plaster painted red.

The access to the small *columbarium* 12 occurred by means of a small door of which the travertine threshold remains. In reality, given its reduced dimensions, one entered on all fours or otherwise one simply had to lean

26. *Autoparco area, Tombs 12 and 9-13 from above.*

Following pages:
27. *Autoparco area, interior of Tomb 12.*
28. *Autoparco area, Tomb 12, detail of the fresco.*

into the building in order to carry out the funerary ceremony in honour of the deceased. Two rows of two niches (each containing one or two cinerary urns) appear along the walls whilst the back wall foresaw two niches of larger dimensions which bore just one cinerary urn each (plate 27). On this same back wall much of the valuable fresco decoration has survived: a series of red and brown frames on white plaster delineate the painted area that itself was framed by a stucco listel and thin red stripes; inside the panel we find two subtle plant candelabra painted in red with little perching birds (plate 28). A rather similar type of decoration can be seen in *columbarium* 3 in the area of the Annona (see *infra*) and, given its proximity and contemporanity to the other two tombs, one could suspect that the same hand was employed for the decoration. It features an evolution of the "candelabra style" which originated half a century earlier, dated to between the late third and the fourth Pompeian style (middle of the first century AD). This style continued with varying degrees of quality until the end of the first half of the second century AD.[115] The marble floor, which features a small stretch of *opus sectile* at the entrance, is subsequent to the realisation of new cremations below the floor: this second phase occurred before the end of the middle of the second century AD.

The double *columbarium* 9/13 comprises of a single building block divided into two small rooms of very reduced dimensions. They are built from brick and are arranged in an L-shaped common wall which divided them into two (see plate 26 on page 181). *Columbarium* 9[116] repeats the structure of the bigger tombs but on a very reduced scale. Compared to the other *columbaria* discussed, the mosaic floor (made of black and white mosaic tiles) contains a geometric motif known as "Salomon's knot" – a sort of plait that creates the illusion that it has no start or finish. It is for this very reason that it is interpreted as an allegory of immortality or alternatively, it is possible to read an apotropaic value in its "labyrinthine" pattern.[117] A tube for libations that journey towards a cremation under the floor is framed in the corner of the central mosaic panel.

Columbarium 11 abuts the south of *columbarium* 12 and aligns with the front of the previous tomb's façade.[118] The space is particularly narrow here resulting in the exploitation of the south wall belonging to *columbarium* 12 in order to be able to create a niche (the only one present in the small tomb). This niche does not contain cinerary urns made of masonry but only a shelf to place urns and furnishings upon. As is the case here too, the tomb's pictorial decoration is only vaguely deducible from that which remains: a series of plant motifs painted red and green (most of which have faded) seems to be arranged over the white plaster of the walls. On the other hand, absolutely nothing remains of the floor which was com-

31. Autoparco area, columbaria *1 and 2 from above.*
32. Autoparco area, asbestos cloth.
33. Autoparco area, tomb a cappuccina.

pletely removed by the digging of small graves for new cremations. A stele (now exhibited in the lapidary above) assists us in our interpretation of the family dynamics found in the tomb: it bears a dedication to a young boy called *Quintus Muttienus Atimetus* who died at little over a year's old.[119] A second dedication to a younger brother appears at the bottom of the same stele who was given the same name and whom, unfortunately, suffered the same sort of fate with a premature death. One can retain that the parents also wanted to be buried next to these unlucky youths, with the positioning of their funerary urns below the demolished floor. An unfinished statuette of a cupid carrying a vase on his back – a subject frequently used in the decoration of fountains and gardens – was discovered in front of *columbarium* 9, just a few metres away from it (plate 29). It is thought that this iconography which does not usually appear on funerary sculpture, might have instead been reinterpreted and found to be well matched for the burial of the young boys. As such, it is believed that this sculpture came from this very tomb.[120]

Shortly afterwards, *columbarium* 7 was built. It is the last of this series and was constructed with an external facing in brick whilst *opus reticulatum mixtum* was used on the inside. The small tomb was built against the side of *columbarium* 11 but was placed in a more forward position towards the centre of the small piazza.[121] The tomb, which is marked by a stele bearing the dedication of *Titus Manius Antigonus* to himself and his sons, was erected on top of an earlier burial that is mentioned on the same stele. At the point of construction, the stele was incorporated into the back wall, and the text was modified accordingly.[122] In fact, the inscription posted by *Antigonus* whilst he was still alive, specifies a sort of right of way in order to reach the burials of *Apuleia Atticilla* and *Apuleius Valens*, together with the imperial slave *Eutychus* and *Claudia Epiteusis*. One is able to deduce, therefore, that an early inscription on the stele refers to these four cremations – accessible for libations via an amphora and a tube in the niche located in the bottom left-hand corner. When *Antigonus* bought the area in order to build his family tomb, he must have had to reuse the old stele in accordance with an agreement that established the right of transfer for the relatives of the two *Apuleii* (perhaps mother and son) and of the two other deceased (plate 31).[123]

The walls of the small burial chamber are covered in white plaster upon which are painted red and yellow bands which highlight the architectural partitions, and are framed by stucco elements. A series of stucco fragments with traces of painting and gilding, that were found during an excavation, allow one to also reconstruct a lacunar ceiling bearing relief-work motifs. The black and white mosaic floor seems to belong to a second phase due to the presence of various imprints relating to a previous pavement with marble slabs. In turn, the mosaic "rug" is broken off halfway down the tomb as it was probably cut by the construction of subsequent tombs. Two rows of niches appear on the walls, alternating between rectangular and semicircular ones. A particular scene appears on the upper niche on the back wall, which is bigger than the others and was presumably used for the couple who owned the tomb. The decoration is made of stucco and is difficult to understand due to its poor condition. The surviving fragments appear to rule out a mythological subject: it is more likely that it depicts *Antigonus*' profession.[124]

The small piazza located behind these small *columbaria* of the early second century AD, was gradually occupied by a series of individual underground tombs. The earliest were cremations placed inside cinerary urns that were placed directly into the ground or in terracotta containers or *amphorae*. During the following decades, various burials in simple graves, tombs *a cappuccina* or terracotta sarcophagi, were made alongside them.[125] For the entire second century AD until the middle of the following century, all available spaces were gradually occupied by these individual tombs. Graves were placed inside or close to masonry tombs and spaces already occupied by tombs that had subsequently been buried were then exploited, reusing all that was deemed useful in order to house and commemorate the newly deceased.[126]

Tomb 35, close to the south-east corner of *columbarium* 8, is indicative of the tomb type *a cappuccina*. Its entire development is detectable due to an exposed section of it in the ground (plate 33). A stele related to the burial stands out the original level of the terrain, and even though a large part of the inscription is missing, it still bears an indication of the measurements of the plot dedicated to the deceased. Three tubes appear at the bottom of the inscription (which are inserted vertically on top of one another) that led libations towards the deceased's face. The deceased was buried in a 1.4 metre deep grave and is covered by a series of bricks set gable-wise (*cappuccina* style or tile tent form).[127]

A sheet of asbestos was found in Well 69. It was found 5 metres down, folded into mortar (unfortunately lost) and is now exhibited in the archeological area between two glass panels on the wall (plate 32).[128] In the past, it was believed that this rare product – a fabric made of a fireproof mineral fibre – was needed during cremations in order to isolate the bodies from the wood that consumed it. But in at least one of three or four documented cases, it was placed with an interred body inside the sarcophagus. Magi therefore believed that it acted as a type of *funebres tunicae* as mentioned by Pliny (*Naturalis Historia*, 19, 19) that was very precious and difficult to weave. At this point, the material's incorruptibility was meant as an allegorical wish of immortality for the deceased person who would have worn it as a shroud. Some recent tests seem to point towards a type of asbestos with particularly long fibres which was therefore easier to weave (and not carcinogenic!) and which has not been attested in Italian soil, but would rather be of Spanish origin.

After the regularisation of this intermediate plateau, available spaces on the shallow terraces for the construction of new masonry tombs seem to have been exhausted in the Autoparco area. Indeed, the chamber tombs that are about to be described were always built on top of tombs that had previously been abandoned. *Columbarium* 2 was built around the middle of second century AD on the upper terrace next to *Columbarium* 1, which had been abandoned by then, and on top of other cremation tombs dating from the first century AD and the first half of second century AD (plate 31).[129] In turn, *columbarium* 2 was razed until it was almost the height of the floor level due to the cut of the slope in order to make way for the construction of subsequent tombs. As a result, its state of conservation only allows us to identify it as a rectangular room with rows of niches on the walls. Sporadic traces of fresco decoration, specifically vertical red stripes with plant motifs, can be found on the walls. Only a mosaic "rug" of black mosaic presumably constituted the original floor. However, during a second phase, the floor was redone following the insertion of new cremations, decorating it with the apotropaic motif of Salomon's knot already described.

A series of burials *a cappuccina* or *semi-cappuccina* (with just one side of sloping tiles) were soon set up against *columbarium* 2, whilst a good example of a painted red *cupa* can be seen in front of its entrance on the other side of the pathway.[130] *Cupae* (known as "*botti*" in Latin) are a particular type of tomb: the deceased was placed inside a brick *loculus* which was covered or incorporated in a small plastered trunk-like structure (figs. II-IV). These "*botti*" were used predominantly between the II and third century AD, above all in Mediterranean Africa, Spain, Dacia and Italy.[131] In the nearby *cupa* 7, which probably belonged to a scribed from the second century AD, precious grave goods were found that were meant to accompany the deceased person with the tools of his trade. An "as" dating to AD 85 (a coin that must have circulated, nonetheless, for many decades) was found in this tomb as well as a cylindrical bronze inkwell, a bronze oval small cup, another cup in the shape of a shell, a thin metallic

II, III, IV Portus, tomb "a cupa".

34. Autoparco area, grave goods from the scribe's tomb.

sheet, a small bone spatula, a hemispherical pumice stone, two small glass vases, some styli, as well as organic material that no longer remains (such as a possible *volumen*, wax tablet) (plate 34).[132] These grave goods are now conserved in a glass show case inside the archaeological area. Tomb 4, which was constructed a few years after *columbarium 2*, is found in close proximity to the latter and shows many good parallels with Tombs 6, 7 and 8 of the Galea area. As such, it has also been dated to around AD 170-190.[133] Tomb 4 has an irregularly square plan respecting the layout of earlier tombs, such as *columbarium 6* or stele 36.[134] Alternatively, Enclosure 4a did not fair so well and has now been completely levelled to such a point that above it is the former's entrance (positioned at the small piazza's southern corner) but at a level quite a lot higher compared to the cubic-type *columbaria* of the early second century AD. The outer walls are made of brick covered in red plaster whilst on the inside, they consist of bricks and small *tufelli*. The tomb was intended for mixed rite: three *arcosolia* can be found on the lateral walls under which *formae* contains four or five burials (placed on top of each other) that are divided by marble slabs or *bipedales* (characteristic square bricks measuring 2 feet each side, or 60 cm). Two cinerary urns can be seen in the niches located in the upper part of the walls whilst immediately after the entrance is an infant's sarcophagus made of terracotta that rests on the floor (plate 35). As seen in contemporary tombs of the Galea area, this tomb's floor also consists of a geometric mosaic bearing an illustionist motif of black and white mosaic tiles. The design emerges from the intersection of circles and squares which generate octagons from the concave sides that are inscribed within squares with alternating black and white gaps.[135] The decorative scheme continues on the walls, painted in fresco on white plaster: geometric partitions alternate with one another like a series of red and ochre stripes, an *oscillum* [136] with ribbons, a sort of pelta (small crescent-shaped shield) and plant and figurative elements, such as small red and green roses and a small ochre-coloured bird with a black head and wings. Tomb 4 was used for many decades, surviving the numerous landslides which occurred along the slope during the third century AD. In order to prevent the tomb being buried, a small wall was built at an angle immediately beyond the threshold, which reused various materials that even included two parts of marble cinerary urns.[137] The prolonged use of this tomb is confirmed by the discovery of a coin pertaining to the wife of Lucius Verus, Lucilla (AD 161-169), near the threshold, two coins in the terracotta sarcophagus of the infant including one of Commodus (an "as" of AD 192), another two coins inside of two *formae,* one of which dates to Septimius Severus (perhaps an as of AD 194) and the other to Gallienus (an Antoninianus of AD 268).

The complex of Tomb 5 concludes the building phases of the Autoparco area, dated to the late second– first half of the third century AD. Its walls have now been levelled to below floor level with the exclusion of the north-west corner, which is still partly conserved.[138] As is also the case here, its construction involved cutting or building on top of older tombs. This is well demonstrated by the already discussed tub-shaped sarcophagus made of terracotta (bearing a stamp that is prior to AD 79), which was incorporated into the tomb's foundations. The structure of Tomb 5, comprised of a facing of small tuff blocks, is located in the northern part of the highest terrace. It consists of three identical rooms placed next to one another facing the valley on the pathway which runs through the necropolis from north-west to south-east, but at a raised level. Each of the burial chambers is articulated by the presence of two *arcosolia* which are placed along the lateral walls as well as one *arcosolium* along the back wall, making a total of around 60 burials. This amount of space appears more suitable for a funerary college[139] rather than for family use: a final judgement is difficult to reach due to the fact that the graves were found empty, whilst an accumulation of exhumed bones was found collected inside the *forma* that corresponds to the best preserved corner. It is therefore also possible that this series of tomb buildings was not systematically used.[140] It is worth mentioning that the rather curious recycling of an old "*tegola mammata*" (a wall tile with spacers creating a cavity between the wall and the tile) for creating a division inside a *forma*, which bears the footprint of a human foot and that of a dog and bird next to it, which were impressed in it whilst the clay was still wet.

Tomb building 5 has many parallels in its internal layout (such as in the choice of construction materials) with some series of tombs of nearby areas that more or less belong to the same period. In particular, Tombs 2, 6, 7 and 8 of the Galea area, Tombs 6, 7 and 8 of the Annona area and two series of Tombs, VII and XV in the north and IX, XXIX and XII in the south of the Santa Rosa area. The second tomb series at the Santa Rosa area, which is located at least 5 metres further north, could even be connected to the present series of tombs, despite having a different orientation. One can thus deduce that the same manual labourers (or at least the same building companies) were used for an extensive building project which, during the Antonine or Severan Periods, attempted to organise the various terraces and different areas of the necropolis along the *Via Triumphalis* with greater coherence.

Various fragments of statues and sculptures in general (amongst which are two small busts of charioteers) are preserved In the showcases and the lapidary as well as lamps, incense holders, glass balsam holders, terracotta ware for libations, nails for wooden crates, buttons and other finds from the excavations: all are connected to the

36. Autoparco area, carved bones.

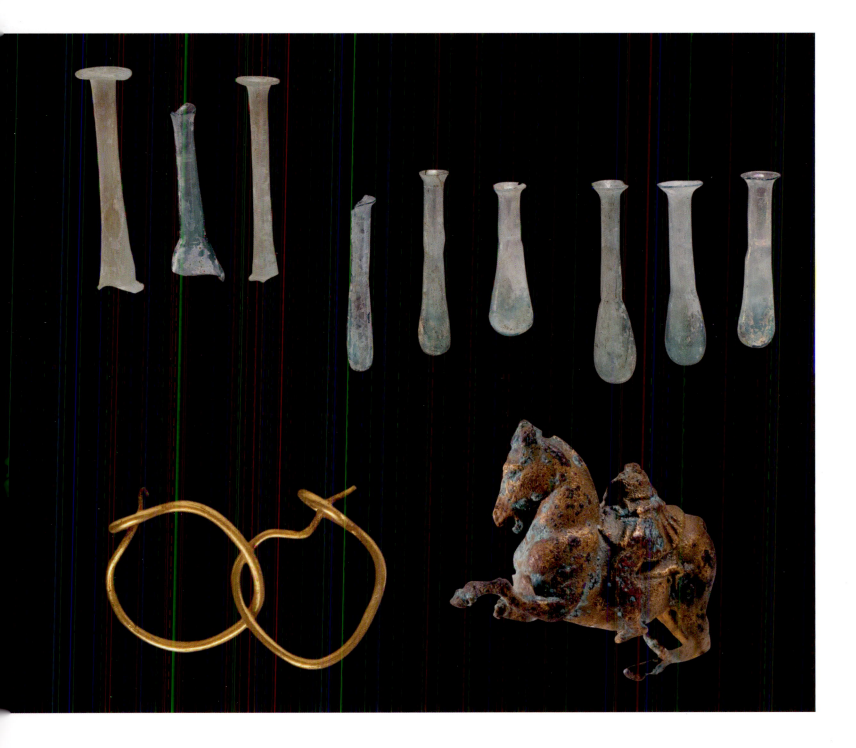

37. *Autoparco area, glass* unguentaria *(chrism jars).*
38. *Autoparco area, gold earrings.*
39. *Autoparco area, bronze statuette of an Amazon.*

40.-44. *Autoparco area, oil lamps.*

45. *Autoparco area, oil lamp with bust of Isis as a handle.*

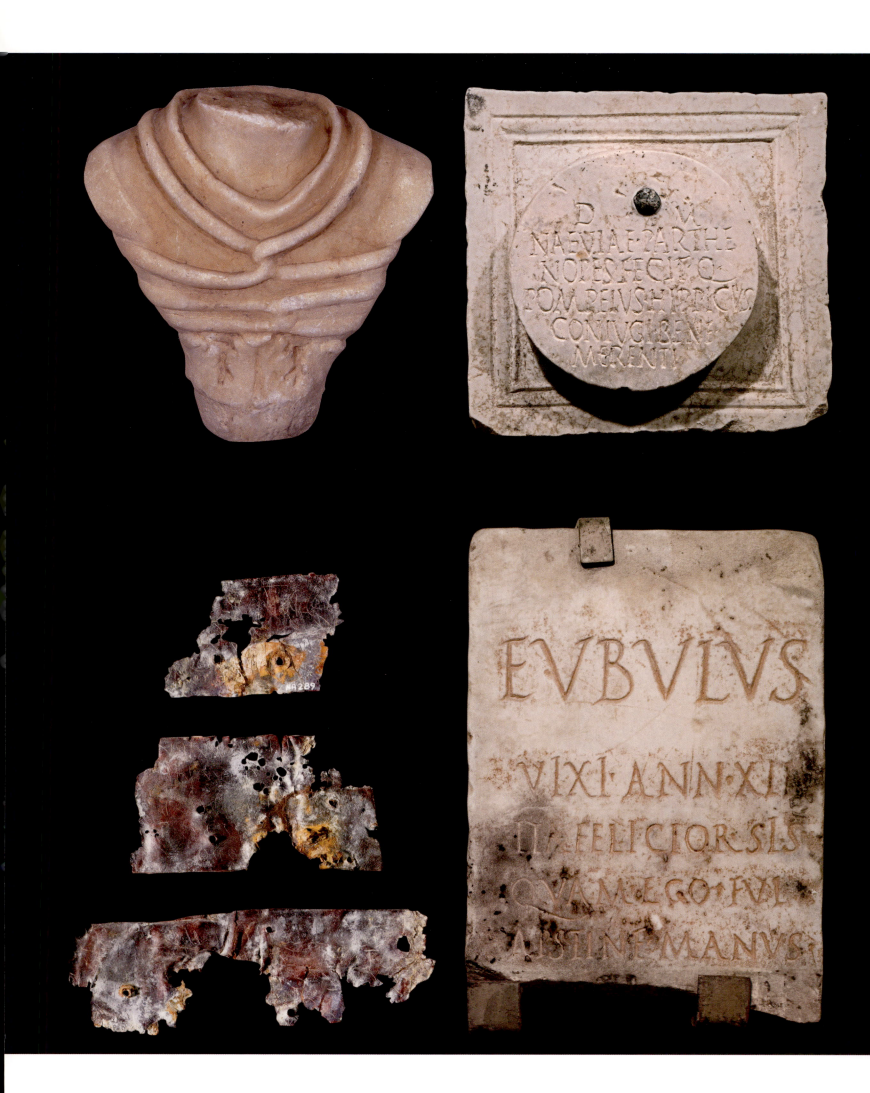

burials and the cult of death. Unfortunately, however, the exact find context is not known for all of them (plates 36-45). Amongst the exhibited materials, it is worth mentioning four *defixiones*[141]: thin sheets of lead which were often folded and bear inscriptions of curses that some people entrusted to the deceased, as an intermediary, as they carried such messages to the gods of the Underworld. They wished every sort of illness or disgrace for the person they hated, but almost never death (plate 48). Two *defixiones* lack the context in which they were rediscovered, whilst a third small sheet was found under a skull in Tomb 4 and a fourth near the cinerary urn close to stele 32 (belonging to *Nunnius*).

A series of bricks containing brick stamps have been mounted on the walls of the archaeological area as well as a number of *stelae*, inscribed slabs, cinerary urns, fragments of sarcophagi, and architectural decorations, all of which are unable to be contextualised or relocated *in situ*. Amongst these some objects are particularly curious and worth mentioning. For example, a lid of a cinerary

urn was found, which contains a hole for libations that is covered by a marble disk upon which the name of the deceased is inscribed and turns by means of a linchpin[142], or the inscription of *Eubulus*, a deceased young boy, who wishes the passerby a better fate than his and then asks them the courtesy of not tampering with his tomb (plate 46, 47, 49).[143] Beyond their historic-artistic interest, these testimonies give us an exceptional insight into the necropolis' social, or rather human, composition.

The Annona Area

One of the areas of the necropolis closest to the *Via Triumphalis* is the one of the Annona area. The area got its name from the Annona building that was constructed in the early 1930s to contain warehouses of alimentary products and spaces for their resale. During the summer of 1930, Enrico Josi oversaw all of the excavations that, after the Lateran Treaty[144], had to create spaces for the infrastructure of the new Vatican City State. As a result, parallel to the discoveries being made in the Galea area, the tombs of the Annona area and nearby areas, located between today's *Via della Tipografia* and *Via del Pellegrino*, were brought to light. This level area at the bottom of the valley, of which 630 square metres has been excavated, also spread out towards the buildings of the Vatican press, the *Tipografia Poliglotta*, and the doctor's surgery. Its topographical location indicates that it must have been close to the *Via Triumphalis*, of which only a short stretch has been retrieved, corresponding to today's *Via del Pellegrino*. The excavation resulted in the discovery of more than 30 tombs of which at least 23 are well recognisable even if rather little is conserved of them. This is due to the fact that, following the construction of the Annona building, a large part of this area of the necropolis was destroyed and the few surviving tombs are currently only visible through a narrow trapdoor located in the warehouses of the modern building. In particular, only Tombs 2 and 3 are almost completely preserved, whilst Tombs 1, 4, 5, 10 and 22 are partially incorporated into modern structures; the rest has been lost (plate 50).[145]

This excavation of the 1930s was also scarcely documented. Josi left few notes and various photographs, both panoramic and of particular details. Using this as a basis, an attempt has been made to reconstruct the overall topography, history and structure of this part of the necropolis (plates 51, 52).[146] Due to these limitations, the analysis of the burial structures is in part only indicative

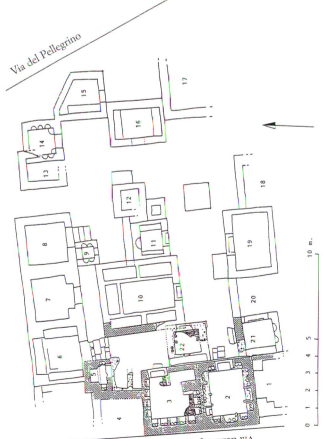

and only a few direct verifications could be made.[147] Some additional investigations and updates can be carried out, above all, with the examination of the close relationship that exists with tombs of nearby areas. In particular, the recent excavation of the Santa Rosa area allowed very close comparisons to be made as well as perceive common building phases.

As with the areas previously described, the gradual occupation of the adjacent areas to the *Via Triumphalis* resulted in a series of supports, cuts and superimpositions that were difficult to organise into clearly distinguishable phases. One can document with certainty the presence of tombs from the middle of the first century AD onwards, whilst the last tombs were built before the middle of the third century AD, even if one is able to detect a funerary frequentation of the site until the beginning of the fourth century AD. Subsequently, the construction of St. Peter's Basilica predominantly contributed to the transit of pilgrims in the area, given that the *Via Triumphalis* remained one of the main paths of access from the north. In any case, one can conventionally recognise several chronological phases of occupation: *columbarium* 14, the oldest found in the necropolis, is attributable to the middle of the first century AD; *columbaria* 1, 2, 3, 4 and 12 and Tombs 21, 22 and 23 can be assigned to the second half of the first century AD – beginning of the second century AD; Tombs 11, 15 and 19 can be generally dated to the mid or second half of the second century AD; whilst the tomb series 6, 7 and 8, the late *columbarium* 9 and Tombs 5, 13, 16, 17, 18, 20 and finally tomb 10 (which is probably not as old) belong to the last long phase that took place between the end of the second century AD and the first half of the third century AD. With regard to individual tombs, minor tombs and those that are only partially uncovered, their chronological dating is still somewhat uncertain due to the lack of concrete data relating to the context in which they were discovered during excavations. As aforementioned, the most ancient tomb found in this area of the necropolis is *columbarium* 14, which was built around the middle of the first century AD. It is found on the north-eastern top of the great levelled clearing in an area close to the *Via Triumphalis*.

The photos of the 1930s make it possible to at least roughly identify the layout and structure of the tomb.[148] It had a more or less square plan[149] and was built of brick whilst it was covered in light plaster on the inside. The entrance was located at the centre of the northern side, the only side not to contain niches. On the back wall and the lateral walls, one notes several rows of niches that contain built in cinerary urns: the larger central niches contained two urns, while the lateral niches only had one. Another cinerary urn was found inside a little masonry trunk positioned in the left corner of the back wall. With regard to the floor, only its concrete preparation in which

ducts were still visible remained. By digging further down, Josi discovered six Dressel 20 type *amphorae*, a container for transporting oil imported from *Baetica* (in Spain)[150], a commodity produced before the early Flavian Period which were then reused as cinerary urns (plate 58).[151] A part of tomb 13 was subsequently integrated into the western side of this tomb.

The *columbarium* must have certainly been flanked by other tombs, but the subsequent building phases prevent us from identifying them, with the exception of some individual structures underneath the late Tomb 10, at the centre of the excavation area, as well as a large marble base which belonged to a destroyed monumental funerary altar which was erected in front of Tomb 11 and *columbarium* 12.[152] It is only on the opposite south-west side of the piazza that one can identify tombs that were built slightly later than *columbarium* 14: these are *columbarium* 21 and 22, which date to the second half of the first century AD or the very beginning of the following century. The two tombs have a similar internal layout, were constructed to the same height, they are aligned in the same direction and both open up towards the east: the travertine thresholds of the doors still remain. They must have been built together on a slight slope which reared up behind them.

Columbarium 21 is a small structure of a square layout constructed of brick.[153] The lateral walls are covered with rows of niches bearing walled in cinerary urns, whilst the back wall contains an *arcosolium* with a *forma* underneath for housing burials. Two frescoed peacocks appear at the back of the *arcosolium* whilst at the sides one can see a basket full of fruit (plate 54). The floor is constructed of a mosaic "rug" with black and white geometric decoration. Along the walls, the mosaic frames the tube feeds that communicate with the cremations underneath the floor. The ornamental motif is based on an illusionist game of squares and lozenges that intersect, creating an octagon and other geometric elements next to one another. Both the subject of the *arcosolium*'s fresco and the mosaic's decorative motif find numerous analogies with works of the second century AD or, even, after that. Amongst possible comparisons with the fresco, one can mention (by virtue of its proximity) the fresco executed in Tomb VIII ("of the Sarcophagi") of the Santa Rosa area, which is dated, however, to the start of the third century AD and is different in style. More refined examples can be found at Ostia dating to the second half of the first century AD and the early decades of the second century AD.[154] In reality, it is really the *columbarium*'s structure that suggests a dating between the end of the first century AD and the start of the second century AD: the prevalence of the cremation rite, using just one *forma* on the back wall, is comparable with that of *columbarium* III ("of the Stuccoes") of the Santa Rosa area. It is also very similar to the decorative schema and is therefore dated to this period.[155] In a subsequent moment, the *columbarium* was levelled to the ground and a funerary structure made up of small blocks of tuff were built on top of it on the northern side, while *columbaria* 1 and 2 were erected on top of the back wall during the first half of the second century AD.

Columbarium 22 was also built to the north of *columbarium* 21 and aligned in the same way. However, whilst built of brick and bearing a square form, it is slightly smaller than *columbarium* 21.[156] Very little of its elevation is preserved having been levelled and built over by other tombs. In particular, its back wall was built over by the façades of *columbaria* 2 and 3. *Columbarium* 22 has a structure similar to 21 with rows of niches that hold two bricked in cinerary urns inside and a similar geometric floor pattern made up of black and white mosaic tiles of squares overlaid by lozenges.[157]

This utilisation of these small *columbaria* must have lasted for relatively little time given that a few years after their construction (although prior to the middle of the second century AD), they were covered by another series of *columbaria* at a slightly higher level which invaded the back part of the burial chambers. The rest of the structures were levelled to make way for a pathway that passed in front of the new tombs. The first two – *columbaria* 1 and 2 – seem to have been built in a single block, realised in brick during the first half of the second century AD. In *columbaria* 1, we only have the northern wall with its two rows of superimposed niches.[158] The walls, which are covered in white plaster, seem to have been decorated with frescoed plant motifs. *Columbarium* 2, of a rectangular layout, is rather better conserved and still exists under the Annona warehouse.[159] It contains niches on all four walls which are positioned on a number of levels (even if only the first order remains). A niche with larger dimensions can be found at the centre of the back wall and the lateral walls: it has two shelves which were meant to support small columns of a sort of *aedicula* (plate 53).[160] The space in front of the threshold was raised, perhaps following landslides, and a sort of rough *cupa*, a small masonry structure destined to contain and protect a terracotta sarcophagus, was built on top of it.[161]

Columbarium 4, which has only been partially excavated, was built slightly to the north.[162] One can distinguish the presence of at least one row of niches for cinerary urns in a decorative context rather carefully taken care of, consisting of probably red plaster (the photos preserved are in black and white) and decorated by stucco-work that frame the niches. At the time of the excavations, a part of the mosaic floor was also preserved. It bears a motif of white squares on a black background[163], cut off on one side to probably make way for a grave (plate 56).

Columbarium 3 was inserted in between *columbaria* 2 and 4. An external *forma* was later also realised under its façade.[164] The tomb, which is of an almost square layout[165] was made by perfectly aligning the brick walls of the façade and the back wall with those of *columbarium* 2. A flight of steps can be found along the left-hand side which lead to an upper level where we would probably find a *solarium* (a sort of terrace) where libations and ceremonies took place in honour of the deceased. The burial chamber, covered in light plaster with frescoed floral motifs, once counted at least two rows of niches with two cinerary urns each. The floor, however, was constructed of a mosaic "rug" comprising of white mosaic tiles and a black border (plate 55). The excavation carried out under the mosaic floor is of noteworthy interest: here, two small wells connected to the pavement by means of two libation tubes were discovered. The tube at the centre of the mosaic floor in particular led to a marble urn of Greek production from the late sixth – early fifth century BC. The urn is made up of a small container and its lid (pierced by the tube) with *acroteria* at the corners (plate 57).[166] The chronological difference between the realisation of the Greek urn and the tomb's construction is at least six centuries and poses an issue that is difficult to resolve[167]: does it concern the purchase of a antiquarian luxury which was destined for the ashes of the deceased who had a particularly refined taste or, what is probably more likely, the fortuitous discovery of an ancient tomb of which its most precious handiwork was reused?

Columbarium 12 belongs to the same period, the first half of the second century AD, although it occupies a central area of the plateau which is located about 10 metres further east than the tombs described thus far.[168] The tomb, which was made of brick, must have found itself at the crossing of two pathways. It was destroyed by the construction of Tomb 11 built a few decades afterwards, which invaded its western part. Inside, the *columbarium* contains the habitual rows of niches for cinerary urns; other cremations were placed inside several wine *amphorae* of the Dressel 2-4 type[169] located under the floor level made of marble slabs, most of which was then removed during ancient times.

Tomb 23 also belongs to the same building phase although it is only generically linked to the north-east area of the excavation site.[170] This structure, which was the first to be discovered in the 1930s, was constructed with a facing of brick, whilst the small wells, found under the floor and linked to the surface by means of tubes, was realised using small blocks of tuff and covered with a lid of *bipedales* placed gable-wise.[171] Inside, the burnt bones of cremated bodies were discovered; a terracotta sarcophagus and the remains of more buried people were found in another larger grave located at the centre of the floor. The tomb also contained a fragment of a marble sarcophagus portraying a ploughing scene of unknown pertinence.

Previous pages:
51. *Annona area area, overview from the northern side.*
52. *Annona area, overview of the central area.*

53. *Annona area,* columbarium 2.

54. Annona area, columbarium *21.*

55. *Annona area,* columbarium 3.

56. *Annona area,* columbarium 4.
57. *Annona area, cinerary urn in Greek marble.*
58. *Annona area,* columbarium 14 *with "Dressel 20"*
type amphorae *under the floor.*

59. Annona area, statuette of Venus and Priapus.

60. Annona area, funerary building 11.

61. *Annona area, building 10.*

In close vicinity to the centre of the piazza two funerary structures were soon built against *Columbarium* 12. The first could have been a small *columbarium* with cremations placed inside two *amphorae* affixed under the floor, whilst the second tomb, situated behind it, was set in front of its entrance and, as a result, also abutted Tomb 11. Despite being located on a slightly lower level compared to that of *columbarium* 12, the fact that Tomb 11 occupied structures, partly demolishing them, demonstrates that it is a later tomb. Tomb 11, which is of a rectangular layout made of *opus listatum* in tuff and brick, is in fact dated to the middle of the second century AD.[172] There is an *arcosolium* on every lateral wall protecting the *forma* containing the buried dead. On the back wall, however, we see the construction of a large niche containing three cinerary urns decorated by a fresco depicting an acanthus branch. Similar pictorial decorations must have also ornated the *arcosolia*. The floor is made up of a black and white mosaic bearing a series of quatrefoils which frame a large tuft of acanthus. This was a plant motif that was fairly well diffused during the course of the second century AD and repeated here in a rather cursive style (plate 60).[173] Nine cremations were found below the floor level, as attested by the small pierced marble slabs. The holes in the slabs correspond to the tubes' openings and appear between one quatrefoil and another.

Along the southern edge of the piazza, which is cut on the other side by a road in east-western direction, tomb 19 was built dating back to the second half of the second century AD. It is a large rectangular tomb[174] with an entrance that opens onto the road in the north[175], and was intended to hold burials in *formae* placed along the walls. The floor is made up of a black and white mosaic, which repeats a scheme of isidomo masonry. This ornamental motif was known until the first century AD, but remained fashionable even during the second century AD, appearing in numerous variants[176], including the mosaic found in *columbarium* 1, close to the Santa Rosa area (dated mid second century AD).

Tomb 15 belongs to the same building phase. Located along the piazza's eastern side, it is not too far away from the *Via Triumphalis*. The tomb's trapezoid layout is owed to the condition of a pre-existing structure, perhaps the road itself or a more ancient tomb that was orientated towards it.[177] The entrance to the tomb, which is built of brick, appears on the southern side, presumably upon a side lane which led from the *Via Triumphalis* to the large open space. A photograph of the tomb taken in the 1930s shows that it had at least one *forma* for burials on one side; the mosaic floor appears broken, perhaps caused by the construction of a *hypogaeum* as is the case in the second phase of Tomb 2 of the Galea. The mosaic "rug" consists of a white background with a figurative motif, perhaps a tuft of acanthus, which is almost completely destroyed.

The subject is placed in the inside of two black squares whilst the side of the oblique wall bore a triangular field. Tomb 15 was still used when, some time afterwards, Tomb 16 was built, abutting the left side of the former's façade but leaving its entrance unobstructed.[178] The tomb of a rectangular plan[179] is constructed in *opus listatum* with external walls made of bricks and internal walls made of small blocks of tuff, like the *formae*.[180] The razing of the walls prevents us from checking whether there were niches for cremations, while there are *formae* along the lateral north and south walls and one could hypothesise that the entrance to the tomb was westwards, towards the piazza.

Tomb 17 can be attributed to the same phase and is only identifiable through some panoramic photographs. Built of brick next to the tomb discussed previously, it is of large dimensions and probably has an entrance that opens onto the same direction as Tomb 16.[181] The southern side of the piazza was also occupied by new tombs between the end of the second and the first half of the third century AD. Tomb 18, constructed *opus listatum*, abuts Tomb 19's eastern side in a slightly withdrawn position.[182] Tomb 20, on the other hand, is built against the opposite side, in perfect alignment with its façade facing towards the large open space, partially built on top of *columbarium* 21.[183] What is rather curious is the discovery of the lower part of a statue of Venus next to a young Priapus (dated mid second century AD) just beyond the threshold. It is a subject that traditionally alludes to prosperity and fertility, and was apparently more appropriate for the decoration of villas and gardens rather than a funerary context[184] unless, that is, it was the portrait of a deceased dressed as the goddess, which is a well-documented custom in the necropolis during this period (plate 59). Continuing with the Severan Period, the northern side of the piazza was occupied by at least four large tombs belonging to an overall complex which perfectly opposes the series on the southern side. Only three of these tombs, Tombs 6, 7 and 8, were completely uncovered during the 1930s.[185] The building, in *opus listatum* of brick and small blocks of tuff, comprises of a series of burial chambers which opens to the south onto the piazza by means of small flights of stairs. Inside, the burials were positioned on several levels in *formae* underneath *arcosolia* placed along the walls. These terraced tombs repeat the structure, internal layout and building technique of contemporary tombs found in the area, but one can also draw parallels with other tombs from the end of the second century AD or of the early third century AD of nearby zones, such as the series of Tombs 2, 6, 7 and 8 of the Galea area, Building 5 of the Autoparco area, and the series of Tombs IX, XXIX and XII of the Santa Rosa area. Tomb 13 was built just a few metres eastwards, beyond an alley. It is also built in *opus listatum*, of

*62. Overview of the Santa
Rosa area*

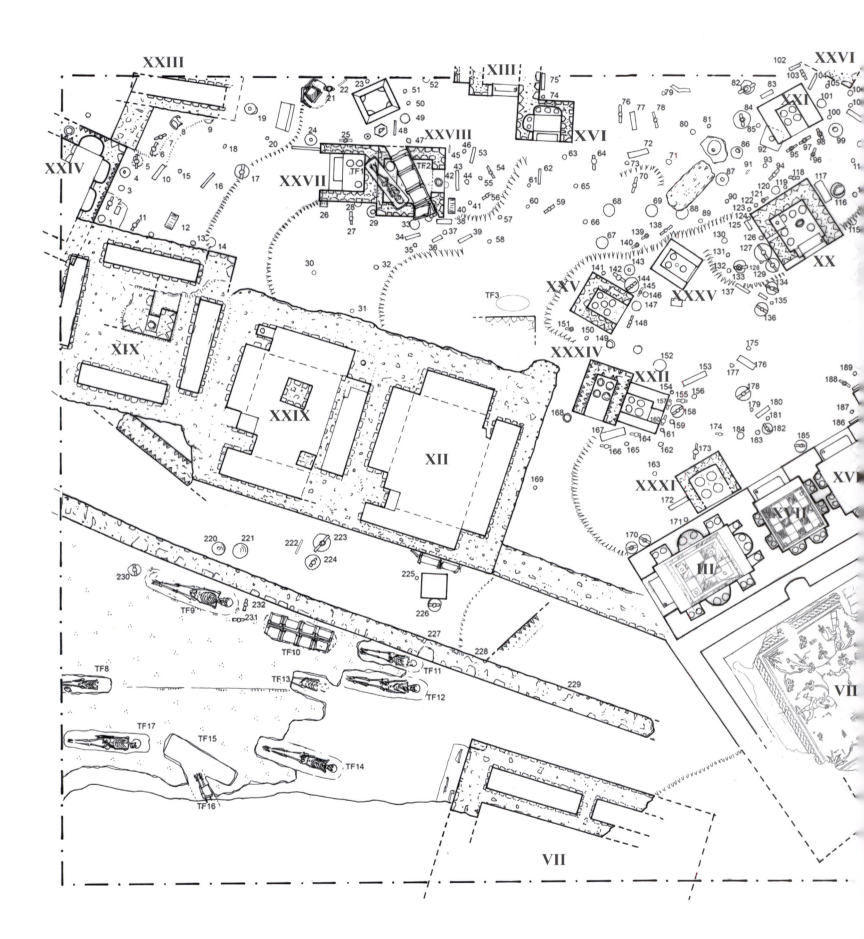

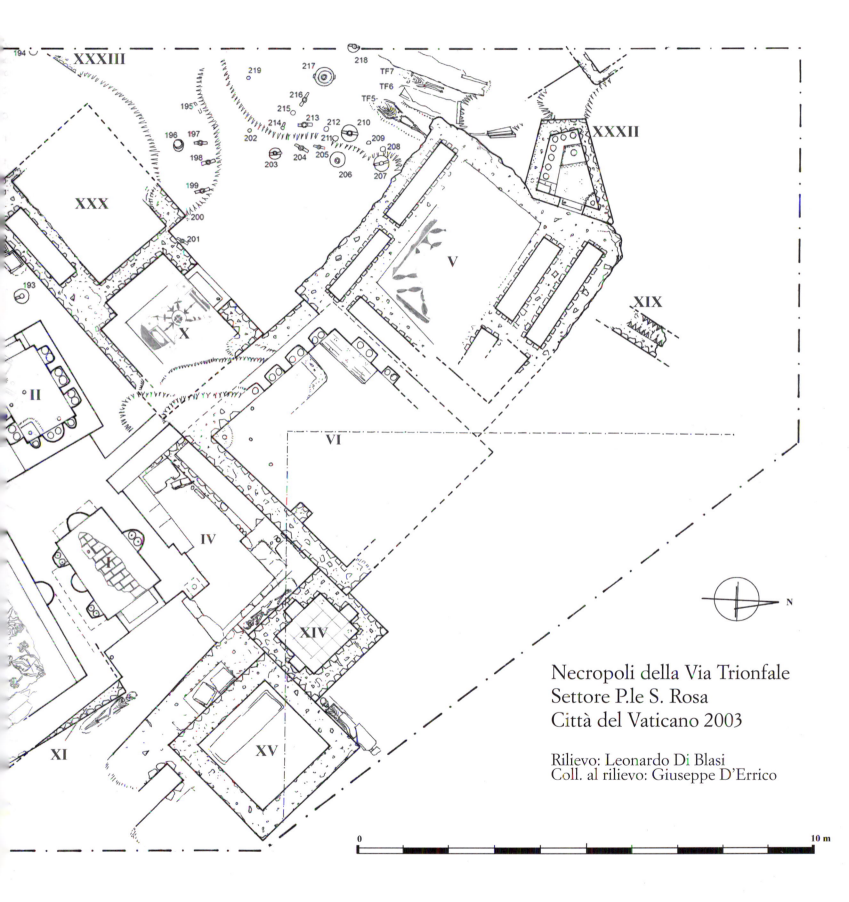

Necropoli della Via Trionfale
Settore P.le S. Rosa
Città del Vaticano 2003

Rilievo: Leonardo Di Blasi
Coll. al rilievo: Giuseppe D'Errico

0   10 m

64. Santa Rosa area, hypothetical reconstruction of the area (Di Blasi).

65. Santa Rosa area, hypothetical reconstruction of the upper level (Di Blasi).

which, however, only a few remains have been found. Its construction invaded a part of *columbarium* 14 which, at the time, had been abandoned for more than a century.[186] After a few years, two small tombs were built against the complex of Tombs 6, 7 and 8 without, however, putting them out of use. Tomb 5, which is made in *opus listatum*, appears at the corner between the first tomb of the (unnumbered) series, Tomb 6 and *columbarium* 4. It was a tomb that was intended for a mixed funerary rite: at the back wall, there is a *forma* for the burials whilst on the lateral walls there are two niches for housing cinerary urns. Under the floor level, other spaces had been created for additional cremations.[187] *Columbarium* 9 is located further towards the east. It is made of brick and abuts the façade and staircase of Tomb 8. Inside, its lateral walls contain two niches for two cinerary urns whilst there is a larger niche, containing three cinerary urns, in the back wall.[188] The construction of a *columbarium* this late in time certainly represents an anomaly: in the first half of the third century AD, the practice of burial was by far the most preferred funerary rite. Perhaps only this very small space was at the disposal for creating tombs specifically for the cremated or, alternatively, this tomb used by a particularly traditionalist family.

Tomb 10 is dated even later: it is positioned at the centre of the piazza, in front of the flights of stairs for the series of Tombs 6, 7 and 8, thus incorporating and destroying a large number of previous tombs. It is probably the latest and biggest tomb of the entire Annona area (plate 61).[189] The building, which is made in *opus listatum*, is of a rectangular layout[190] with its entrance facing south, that is, towards the piazza which was still vacant. Inside, there are two *arcosolia* along the lateral walls and just one *arcosolium* on the back wall. Even though its internal structure repeats that of tombs dating to the early third century AD, the tomb demonstrates that it is later: it abuts the building but does not obstruct the entrances. Consequently, one can hypothesise a date of the central decades of the third century AD. The Annona area was also certainly occupied by new tombs later on, at least until the start of the fourth AD, but these should be understood as being less monumental and located at a higher level. Subsequent historical events in this area, however, must have removed all trace of them.

The Santa Rosa Area

The Santa Rosa area is the part of the necropolis along the ancient *Via Triumphalis* that has been excavated most recently. The excavations started in February 2003 and finished in June of that same year. Therefore, after a break of nearly three years, during the Spring and Summer of 2006, a campaign of surveys, restorations and preparations to set up an on-site museum took place and from October 2006, the area has been made accessible to the general public (plate 62).[191] The project for the new car park came about as a result of the necessity to speed up the traffic inside of Vatican City. It was for this reason that the area of the Santa Rosa piazza was chosen inside the Vatican walls (it corresponds to the last stretch of *Via Leone IV* which bends in order to reach Piazza Risorgimento). The archaeological excavation began only after a few months of work at the construction site, as soon as the first irrefutable signs of an archaeological presence emerged. Unfortunately, however, this happened when some tombs had already been destroyed and archaeological material removed. At a later stage, attempts have been made to re-contextualise these losses.[192]

Dealing with an area that measures about 500 square metres, the archaeological investigations brought to light over 40 group funerary structures of different sizes and about 250 individual tombs (of which more than 230 were for cremations and about 20 for burials) that were placed on different terraces (plate 63). A project regarding the continuation of the excavations towards the south is currently ongoing in order to link this section of the necropolis to the area found near the Autoparco area and to create one large underground archaeological area.[193] The opportunity of investigating a site that has been left practically unchanged by subsequent interventions with modern techniques and scientific methodologies has produced an exceptional accumulation of new data for the study of tombs and funerary rituals of the less affluent classes of Rome.

In this area of the necropolis, the terrain spreads out into a small valley which, at a slight slope, runs transversally across to the area, to then sharply re-descend with a small increase in height, until it reaches another shallow plane. The *Via Triumphalis* must have crossed just beyond (at least 50 metres away and about 5 metres lower). The slope, at least at the beginning, was very uneven and disconnected, with various natural cuts in the terrain created by streams of rain water which flowed down from the hill's summit converging into one, avoiding small bumps, uneven areas and other obstacles. The first tombs were built with a certain liberty and irregularity, exploiting the

available spaces which seemed most suitable. One notes how several masonry tombs, contemporary and adjacent to one another, were orientated differently: the presence of a tree or a big bush apparently influenced the positioning of their respective entrances.

Between the end of the first century AD and the middle of the following century, these tombs adjusted their positioning to the orography of the hills. Their distribution on the terrain almost seems to repeat the course of the contour lines of the slope. If we accept the theory that the zone was still located within the boundaries of the Imperial property, the considerable presence of imperial slaves and freedmen of the Julio-Claudian family amongst the deceased could lead one to believe that these people were favoured by granting them the funereal use of the Vatican Hill.

During the second half of the first century AD until the early decades of the second century AD, the beginning of some kind of planned type of occupation in the area can be observed: larger tombs were built and some of them record the extent of the tomb plot in their respective inscriptions, evidence of a first parcelling out of the available space. Various shallow artificial terraces were created by cutting into the slope and immediately removing the excess earth to the valley, levelling the areas around the small funerary buildings and, presumably, cutting down the trees in the areas around natural clearings. This series of human interventions helped make way for the construction of new tombs but, at the same time, reduced the slope's stability. The landslides, which had always occurred in the small valleys between the ridges of the hill, were less restrained at this point and heavy rainfall provided a constant threat for the area. Shortly before the middle of the second century AD, a large landslide, which was bigger than previous ones, took place in the small valley, hitting against the walls of a series of *columbaria* (III, XVII, XVIII and II) which covered them before slightly increasing in height. These terraced tombs constituted a barrier which stopped the landslide's natural outlet of going towards the valley. They produced an increase of the terrain of more than 2 metres, sealing all the tombs beyond the barrier with a thick layer of and gravel and clay.

The relatives of the deceased in this part of the necropolis gave up unearthing the tombs of their loved ones. Only a shortly afterwards, towards the middle of the second century AD, the funerary function of the area was resumed. The accrued negative experience contributed to the decision to construct more stable and reliable terraces in brick, created by digging their foundations right into the landslide. On top, tombs more imposing than the previous ones were built and among them, in the gaps that remained, poorer tombs were added. One can follow the construction of the tombs until the early decades of the third century AD and the funerary practices until the start of the fourth century AD, after which the tombs were slowly abandoned and buried or used for other things (plates 64, 65).

In brief, the Santa Rosa area can be chronologically analysed in two important phases. The first, which was characterised almost exclusively by the rite of cremation, started at the end of the first century AD (even if one cannot exclude the existence of a previous phase which is still buried) and finished with the large landslide of AD 130-140. The second phase, which was mainly connoted by the rite of burial, started shortly after the landslide and finished at the start of the fourth century AD, perhaps with the construction of the Basilica over St. Peter's tomb (towards AD 320). These two large phases are further articulated from within but only local sequences of the area appear identifiable. For he who was wealthy he was able to organise the place of his tomb in a dignified way, reserving a space inside a masonry tomb. For he who was poorer, he found a plot wherever he could there (plate 66). On the other hand, solutions were chosen from time to time. For the less affluent, one rarely notices a real overall planning of the occupation of spaces: death cannot be planned and, in their case, could not even be factored into long term plans. One dug a grave in a place, throwing away the excess earth to the side, thus covering previous tombs. As such, the stratigraphies were often confused with one another and their dating must therefore be reached based on other considerations, in particular by the uncertain relationship shared between relevant dates on one side (which were determined by the physical relationship amongst tombs) and definite dates on another (obtained by analysing intrinsic elements bearing dates that were found in several tombs).[194] The most ancient tombs of the Santa Rosa area are found on the side of the small valley, in the part beyond the excavation site. They are recognisable thanks to several cremations that are marked out by travertine *stelae* bearing inscriptions that paleographically appear to be dated between the last decades of first century AD and the early decades of the following century (plate 67). Amongst these, one recalls two *tabellarii* (the *tabellarius* did a job that was

V. Vatican Museums, Lapidario Profano ex
Lateranense, marble funerary urn in the form of a
basket (inv. 9237).

67. Santa Rosa area, view of the tombs
on the upper level.

similar to the modern-day postman)[195] of the first half of the first century AD: one was *Primus* who organised his tomb plot during his lifetime and the other was *Herennia Secunda*[196], and a second imperial slave *Priscus*, buried by someone who was most likely his partner *contubernalis* (lived together) *Claudia Stacte* (a freedman), together with *Successus*, *conservus* (in this case, a fellow ex-slave) of *Claudia Stacte*.[197] As aforementioned, there are many tombs here that belong to servants of the Emperor's *familia*. For example, there is the tomb of *Fulcinia Nereidis* buried by the *conserva Heraclida*[198] which is located at the top of the small valley. The oldest tomb relates to a freedwoman called *Lucina*[199] whilst the other, however, relates to a slave by the name of *Grathus*.[200] The latter was an imperial slave *ex Nemore Cai et Luci*, commemorated by *Abascantus*, another slave who worked as an *aquarius* (a general indication that refers to a subordinate for the administering of Rome's public waters)[201] probably in the same place. *Nemus Cai et Luci* corresponds to *Nemus Caesarum*, known of through various sources.[202] It was only refered to as this by Cassius Dio (as on the discussed stele but in Greek).[203] It concerns a monumental garden created in Julius Caesar's *horti* located near Augustus' *Naumachia* in Trastevere in memory of Lucius and Caius Caesar, the two sons of Giulia and Agrippa who were meant to inherit the reins of the Empire from Augustus but instead died prematurely in AD 2 and AD 4 respectively.[204] The *Naumachia Augusti*, which was opened on AD 2, and was intended for naval battles, was built using a large basin containing *aqua Alsietina* that came from the Lake of Martignano (*Alsietinus*), close to the Lake of Bracciano. At the centre of the reflective water was an artificial island (measuring around 60 x 40 metres) where Caius and Lucius Caesar were commemorated. This island was linked to the *Nemus Caesarum* on the neighbouring shore by a small wooden bridge.[205]

In the lower terrace there is a travertine altar, dating to the first half of the first century AD which *Cominia Optata* dedicated to her husband, the sculptor *Tiberius Claudius Thesmus*.[206] The work of the deceased is not declared in the inscribed text but in the low-relief representation on the front: in fact, *Thesmus* is represented seated upon a stool in front of his dog whilst he is busy working on a bust using his mallet and chisel (plate 68). The sculptor's craft was rarely portrayed during the Roman Period: one remembers the famous sepulchral slab of *Eutropos* (which is chronologically much later) in the Museo Archeologico di Urbino.[207] But if we confine ourselves to Rome, the only possible comparison comprises of an altar that does not bear an inscription but contains a subject matter that is very similar to that of *Thesmus*, even if it was realised about a century later (AD 110-120). Housed in the Vatican Museums[208], the anonymous sculptor portrays a woman here, who is perhaps his wife, within a *clipeus*, placing her in pose (frontal standing up position). The lady sports an elegant hair-style with a large *toupet* of curls that was fashionable at the time.

Slowly but surely, numerous *amphorae* that were partly buried appeared along the slope. These were originally intended to cover the funerary urns underneath as well as supply them with a cavity for libations. However, their sheer number does not always mean that they were directly related to surrounding altars and inscriptions. For the entire second half of the first century AD, one can note how the so-called "Spello" *amphorae* (mid first century AD – mid second century AD)[209] are far more prevalent in number than the "Dressel 2-4" type *amphorae* (beginning of the first century AD – first half of second century AD)[210] – a peculiarity that one can also

68. *Santa Rosa area, altar of the sculptor Tiberius Claudius Thesmus.*

69. *Santa Rosa area, statuette of a* servus lanternarius.

clearly see in the area near to the Autoparco. The ratio between the two (estimated at about 90% of "Spello" *amphorae* and 10% "Dressel 2-4" type *amphorae*) is in inverse proportion to the numbers found in the archaeological sites of contemporary urban settlements. Both *amphorae* types were used for the transportation of wine and their shapes were therefore rather similar. However, the "Spello" *amphorae* have a wider shoulder and the body is more ovoid in shape whilst the "Dressel 2-4" type has a narrower and more angular shoulder with a more elongated body. It is evident that the former type (the least common) was more sought after due to its shape. Its upper part was normally cut off and reused in order to protect the tomb. As such, an amphora that could best incorporate the cinerary urns below was required.

A small marble sculpture placed directly over cremated remains was found underneath one of these "Spello" amphora in the plateau area. The statuette, which bears traces of colour, portrays a man of prominent features dressed in a short tunic (plate 69).[211] The person, who lies on his left side in a tucked up position, leans against a large oil lamp and a turned over jug; the handle of a big bag (which is held onto tightly for fear of someone being able to steal him of his supplies) is slipped over his right arm that is bent so that it can support his cheek. The person portrayed is a *servus lanternarius* (or *lampadarius*) who has fallen asleep[212] whilst waiting for his master who would have returned during the night in order to open the door of his home to him, safe-guarding him from possible ill-intentioned people. The subject matter is certainly not common – another example is conserved in the Vatican's Museo Chiaramonti[213] – and until now, it was thought to have been suitable for the decoration of villas and gardens. However, this case logically assumes a funerary association due to the fact that, up until now, it is the only example whose context of discovery is known of.[214] At this point, we remain in doubt as to whether the sculptural representation relates directly to a poor person and anonymous slave's job who is buried there or it contains an allegorical reading and therefore portrays a reassuring presence, ideally meant to illuminate the obscure journey undertaken by the deceased towards the final resting place.

Several grooves filled with combusted bones and sometimes carbon fragments with traces of pivots and nails have also been found on the terrain. These elements relate to the necropolis' most humble types of cremation: the combusted bones of several cremated deceased peo-

ple must have been placed into baskets, wicker baskets or wooden boxes – organic materials that have dissolved away over time due to the acidity of the land. A rather more costly form can be seen with the discovery of several marble cinerary urns which reproduce these latter types of containers but despite being more luxurious, wanted to remain part of this traditional and popular sepulchral practice (fig. V).[215] At this point, it is permissible to suppose the existence of many funerary handicrafts and, perhaps even, small sepulchral buildings made of wood or another perishable material. The vast number of anonymous burials in cinerary urns, or burials in graves, perhaps originally stated their identity on painted or engraved wooden *stelae*. Some of these could have survived for eternity inside of tombs in the form of simple little huts, boxes or small oven-forms or indeed enclosures with structures made up of planks and boards. This hypothesis, which has yet to be physically proven, is only hinted at by the presence of aggregations of contemporary individual tombs in the surrounding areas.[216]

One can attribute the start of construction of the most ancient masonry tombs to the early decades of the first century AD. These tombs were first made in *opus reticulatum*, later on in brick or *opus mixtum*. They have a cubic form covered by a barrel vault, containing terracotta cinerary urns equipped with a masonry lid that was

71. Santa Rosa area, tomb XXV.

Following pages:
72. Santa Rosa area, aedicula of the youth Tiberius
Natronius Venustus.
73. Santa Rosa area, small terracotta female bust form the
Flavian-Trajanic period.

built into the floor. Their reduced dimensions did not actually permit access into it but only to face it from the outside for funerary rituals. The structure of these tombs, which are comparable with similar tombs in the necropolis of the *Via Ostiense* (close to St. Peter's Basilica) and Portus (near to Fiumicino), resemble the shape of small ovens. As a result, these will be referred to as oven-type tombs. Amongst the most ancient of these, is Tomb XXXIV which is probably of the Augustan Period and is located on the small plane in the lower part of the valley. It contains four large urns which are inserted into the floor. The choice of facing used for covering the cement core of the walls is both anomalous and curious. It was covered by tuff *cubilia* (pyramidal small blocks with a square base) positioned into horizontal rows[217], rather than apply a sort of diagonal chessboard design as would have been normal for *opus reticulatum* (plate 70). A travertine stele dedicated by *Poppidia Musa* to her husband *Crescens* (who died at 30 years of age) and their son *Quintus Poppidius Thesmus* (who died at 16 years of age) can be found in front of this tomb: they should be related to one another or perhaps (but less likely) related to the similar-looking Tomb XXII which, after some time, was built against it, exploiting the left wall of the former tomb and using it as its back wall.[218] Nevertheless, one cannot exclude anything even if it was pertinent to some cremations nearby.[219] However, thanks to their close physical relationship shared between the tombs, this group of cremations could constitute the only family environment represented in several generations.

Another tomb of the same type, Tomb XXXI, is located two metres north-easterly and has an exterior facing of *opus reticulatum* plastered over in red. Four cinerary urns are affixed to the floor plane and are placed in front of the small niche at the back.[220] Later on, during the course of the second half of the first century AD, the cremation of *Artoria Prima* was placed next to this tomb (perhaps due to some kind of relationship between the deceased inside of the tomb), as shown by the tube for libations and an inscribed stele.[221] The dedication to this woman, who died at 26 years old, was organised by her husband *Clemens* who defines himself as *hortator fact(ionis) Venetae*. Even if the term *hortator* is not completely clear, he must have been a skillful circus rider who participated in racing competitions in the circus. His job appears to have been to help the charioteer of the *factio Veneta* (the Blues) to release the horses and improve the trajectory of the curves, mounting a horse bareback next to the *biga*

(or *quadriga*).[222] Certainly, it is not by chance that another stele of a *hortator* of the *factio Veneta*, *Titus Albanus* comes from the same area of Santa Rosa. The written text contains a dedication from the wet nurse *Quintilia Tyche* to the deceased and his wife *Quintilia Albana*.[223] During the years when theses dedications were written, the Blue-Shirts, that is the *factio Veneta*, had won the sympathy of the Emperor (fig. VI). In particular, it is noted in *De Vita Caesarum* by Suetonius (AD 69) that he was their fierce protector and even brought their denigrators to justice.[224] Other inscriptions mentioning charioteers have been found in areas nearby and presumably can be related to the Circus of Caligula and Nero at the Vatican.[225]

Two other small oven-type tombs, Tomb XXV and Tomb XXXV are located to the west, on the edge of the slope close to the plateau. Tomb XXXV is definitely the oldest of the two. It contains a slab (in the form of a *tabula ansata*) which is placed at the bottom of its front. It contains a dedication to the young girl *Erotis,* who died at 14 years of age, by her husband *Onesimus* and father *Glaucia*.[226] On the inside, which is plastered and decorated by red squares on a white background and has a masonry plane, one sees three funerary urns and a tube at the centre. The walls and background are instead cursively frescoed with floral racemes. We should not be surprised by the tender age of the deceased bride as it was a rather habitual practice to get married during a period of life that we consider adolescence. *Erotis'* tomb, which was constructed during the reign of Tiberius (AD 14-37) was probably then used by *Glaucia* and *Onesimus*. During a later period, it was filled in with earth and damaged by a subsequent cremation tomb. All of these tombs of a very reduced size still conserve a layer of red plaster which covered the external walls. This colour, which was fairly common for covering Roman walls, must have been detectable in the overall panaroma of these specific areas of the necropolis. Only Tomb XXV is frescoed on top of the red plaster- with an elegant design of plant tufts and long green and yellow leaves (plate 71).[227] This small *columbarium* is constructed of brick with its entrance opening onto the valley (north-east). Underneath the oven-type tomb's mouth are four cinerary urns affixed to the floor as well as a large terracotta tube for libations.[228]

The tiny *columbarium* XIV, which was built around AD 20, is located on a plane close to the *Via Triumphalis* that is slightly higher up. Its entrance is orientated towards the pathway that ran parallel to the *Via Triumphalis* (north-west) and served the contemporary tombs of the

74. Santa Rosa area, infant burial with
ceramic grave goods and an egg.

plateau.[229] The tomb contains a niche for cinerary urns on the two lateral walls and back wall and its floor is made in *opus sectile* of small white marble tiles.[230]

A tomb of large dimensions, Tomb IV (of the *Natronii*) was built behind it. This belonged to a family of freedmen who had clearly enjoyed discrete economic means.[231] The tomb is dated between AD 20 and 40, even if its structures are partially covered by successive phases. Its layout was conditioned by the presence of *columbarium* XIV which sets the opening of its entrance towards the south-east, looking out onto a small piazza. It consists of a short anti-chamber upon which the small main burial chamber (a sort of narrow rectangular enclosure) was grafted onto to, widthways and in an irregular fashion. However, its entire perimetre is not completely definable as its walls were levelled and covered over by ensuing constructions pertaining to Tomb VI (of the *Passieni*) and, above all, Tomb 1. Instead, almost the whole lower area has been conserved due to the sealing off caused by a filling in of earth which resulted from the subsequent rising of the floor. The burial chamber opens up shortly after the anti-chamber which contains a second small oven and a masonry bench along the left side. An *aedicula*, built with small terracotta columns and capitals was constructed on top of this bench. Towards the back wall of this sort of room-corridor, one notes the presence of several tombs marked by a series of underground tubes for libations, a stele dedicated by *Natronia Sinphyle* to their son who died at 20 years of age *Tiberius Natronius Zmaracdis* and the *aedicula* of *Tiberius Natronius Venustus* who died at the age of 4 years, 4 months and 10 days. This marble *aedicula* is positioned in front of a large chest made of brick which is covered by a slab of pierced travertine close to the bottom of the tomb. A beautiful portrait of the young boy appears at the centre of the aedicule, framed by Corinthian columns. Below his eardrum one sees the inscription *hic situs est* ("here is buried"); at the bottom there is a relief which instead bears the name and life duration of the young deceased boy (plate 72).

The procedure for making the *aedicula* is rather curious: this was not created to hold the bust as made clear by its re-working with the type of chiselling practiced for inserting the head. Even the head, which was produced by a high-quality workshop belonging to the Julio-Claudian Period, must have originally had a different positioning as clearly demonstrated by the work done on all sides including the back of the head and the showy optical corrections to the face. The lifting and greater relief applied to the right eye and cheekbone of the face, accompanied by a subsequent change to the mouth area, prove that the head must have originally been placed to the left of the spectator (and preferably seen from that side). Consequently, it must have been part of a family

group statue, probably conceived for a domestic setting which perhaps included the presence of other figures (the parents?) to the left-hand side of the young boy.[232]

During the course of the second half of the first century AD, Tomb IV underwent an early reworking. In the anti-chamber located at the side of the entrance, a small oven for cremations was built using brick that saw the addition of four oil lamps during the first decades of the second century AD which were placed there to provide light during funerary ceremonies.[233] A small bust made of terracotta that portrays a woman sporting a high hair-style (the so-called *Schildtoupet*) that was fashionable during the late Flavian and the early Trajanic Period (about AD 90-110) was found along the left side, covered over above the bench belonging to the first phase.[234] This type of small terracotta bust is often associated with infant tombs throughout the Roman world. Nearly all of them were *crepundia*, empty rattles with small clappers or little stones placed around them. Many of them reproduced (and seems to be the case) the features of the mother (plate73).[235] According to another interpretation, they might have been identified with *sigilla*, statuettes which were donated to children during the *Sigillaria*, the festivities of the *Saturnalia*.[236].

Another infant tomb of great interest which came to light following a survey consists of a small grave covered by just one *sesquipedalis* (a brick that measures one foot and a half or about 45 cm per side) (plate 74).[237] The tomb was dug out next to *columbarium* XXV which dates to the middle of the second century AD The skeleton suggests that the tomb belonged to a baby who was less than a year old (as further attested by the missing seepage of milk teeth) who was accompanied by a small number of grave goods. This comprised of a series of small colourless and very fine vases and a hen's egg placed in his right hand. As is the case here, one must remember the function of *crepundia* (rattles) which were frequently made from eggs: once pierced and filled with seeds, they served as a children's game. This egg, however, appears empty and intact. As a consequence, one should place a different type of value to it. Rather than seeing it as an unusual food for the young deceased baby (seeing as one usually offered liquid foods such as milk, honey and wine by means of the tubes), it is appropriate to interpret it as an allegorical element held tightly in his hand, a symbol of rebirth, a new life which counters his unjust premature end.

Other small oven-type tombs (dating to the middle of the first century AD and constructed in brick) can be found just a little bit beyond. Unfortunately, however, nearly all of them have been levelled during successive sepulchral building phases.[238] The first to have been built was Tomb XXVIII with its entrance turned towards the north, orientated to the lower part of the small valley. Several terracotta urns and a tube are affixed to the floor. However,

75. Santa Rosa area, amphorae *that cover some cremation burials.*

76. Santa Rosa area, "small oven"
tomb XXI.

ALCIMO
NERONIS CLAVDI
CAESARIS AVG SER
CVSTODI DE THEATRO
POMPEIANO DE SCAENA
FECI REABIA FHITATE
CONIVGI CARISSIMO
NFR PIMII IVAGR T V

77. *Santa Rosa area, stele of Alcinus.*

78. *Santa Rosa area, Tomb XX, the tomb of Alcinus.*

79. Santa Rosa area, glass cinerary urn from Tomb XX, the tomb of Alcinus.

VII. Santa Rosa area, travertine floor block with cavities for cinerary containers and a large central hole.

Following pages:
80. Santa Rosa area, altar of Passiena Prima.
81. Santa Rosa area, altar of Tiberius Claudius Optatus.

the floor was later cut by two tombs *a cappuccina* dating to the third century AD which changed its state of conservation.[239] Tomb XXVII was then built at a higher level and abuts the back wall of the former tomb, exploiting the back of Tomb XXVIII as its back wall. As a consequence, Tomb XXVII's entrance opens out towards the south, on the most elevated side of the slope. It still conserves its travertine threshold whilst one sees five terracotta cinerary urns built into the internal floor in which various grave goods were added once again (following the restoration). These included two oil-lamps and a glass balsam holder. This was done so that the tomb's appearance returned to how it once appeared during the excavation. Little remains of the two tombs that are located even higher up, in correspondence with the south-west corner of the excavation area. Tomb XXIII has been completely destroyed due to modern piling whilst *columbarium* XXIV, characterised by niches for cinerary urns on the walls, is traversed by two reinforced concrete posts inside but the planned expansion of the excavation area might bring the best part of it to light.[240]

Tombs XXVI, XXXIII and XXI were built at the same time, during the middle of the first century AD and are typologically similar to one another. They are located close to each other on the western border of the excavation area. As is the case here as well, practically nothing remains of the first two tombs, having been cut down by modern piling whilst the third one has been left intact.[241] Tomb XXI is a cubic structure built using brick. It is a oven-type tomb with a barrel vault and looks towards the north-east on the lower level (plate 76). On the outside, it is covered by red canonical plaster whilst a marble slab is built into the front's lower part. This is incised with the dedication to *Faenia Lyris* who died at just four years old, placed there by her parents *Publius Aledius Priscus* and *Faenia Favor*.[242] It is remarkable how many grave goods are still found inside: four oil-lamps and a bowl for making food offerings, found in their original positions, above four funerary urns affixed to the floor plane. The vault and back wall's yellow floral frescoed motifs on the white plaster are particularly delicate.

Shortly afterwards (around AD 60), Tomb XX of *Alcimus* was built in front of it. It consists of a cubic form structure made of brick with a covering of red plaster on the external walls and white plaster on the inside (plate 78).[243] Seven terracotta cinerary urns as well as a lid made from a slab pierced by tiny holes for libations were found built into the floor. An eighth cinerary urn (made of glass

with a double-handle and covered by two lids placed one on top of the other) was placed at the corner of the tomb and is still full of combusted bones of the deceased (it is currently exhibited in a glass show case, plate 79). A wide tube that leads to an underground space (which is slightly smaller than that of the tomb) is located at the centre of the floor. Several oil-lamps that were placed next to the urns and date to between the end of the first century AD and the second century AD, attest to the continuity of funerary practices for various decades.[244]

A large stele made of travertine which has been placed to the side of the threshold as if it were a left jamb to the entrance of the tomb, is of exceptional interest (plate 77). One detects an inscription in the lower part which is dedicated by *Fabia* to her husband *Alcimus*, one of Nero's servants, stating that he was "*custos de Theatro Pompeiano de scaena*", thus he worked as a guard and custodian of the stage at the Theatre of Pompey.[245] In the upper panel of the stele, *Alcimus* is sculpted in low-relief, standing and dressed in a short tunic. He holds a scalpel and a hatchet in his hand with which he must have materially made the theatre sets and scenery machines whilst next to him are sculpted the other tools of his trade, connected to the planning and execution phases: a set-square, a compass, a level (a mason's level) and a sort of

DIS MANIBVS
PASSIENAE PRIMAE
SANCTISSIMAE ET
INDVLGENTISSIMAE
ERGA ME SVOSQVE
EVARISTVS LIB BENE
MERENTI

L PASSIENO EVARISTO PATR OPTIMO
ET CONIVG INDVLG ET PASSIENAE PRIM MET SIBI

OPTATVS·NERONIS·CLAVDI
CAESARIS·AVG·L·TABVLAR
A·PATRIMON·ET·PASSIENA
PRIMA
DIS·MANIBVS
FLORAE·FILIAE·SVAE
DEDERVNT·ET
TI·CLAVDIO   TI·FOVI
PROCLO   FIL
ET·L·PASSIENO·LIB
OPTATO·FRATRI

82. *Santa Rosa area, detail of the altar of Passiena Prima, with maenads, a satyr and the infant Dionysus.*

83. *Santa Rosa area, detail of the altar of Tiberius Claudius Optatus with the head of Medusa.*

groma or measuring rod.[246] The tools and inscription record a profession that is documented here for the first time, carried out at one of the most famous monuments of Rome: the Theatre of Pompey, the biggest in the city and the first to be constructed in stone in AD 55.[247] Julius Caesar was killed in the Curia of the Theatre of Pompey a century earlier. The building then underwent various changes and was subjected to noteworthy building works amongst which we remember the large restoration intervention started by Tiberius and finished by Caligula or Claudius.[248] It is likely that *Alcimus* was involved in these restorations and perhaps was still even still alive, during works for the set ups for Tiridate. In fact, in AD 66, on occasion of Tiridate's coronation in Rome as the King of Armenia, the historian Cassius Dio describes the great apparatus that Nero wanted: "not only the theatre stage but also the entire internal area of the building is to be covered with gold, just as the rest of the mobile structures which were introduced were adorned with gold, the reason for which they attribute the epithet of 'golden' to that same day. The large curtains that had been drawn over as protection from the sun's rays were purple coloured. An image of Nero was embroidered in the middle leading a chariot with resplendent golden stars around him."[249] A few years later, with the great fire of AD 80, the theatre scenery was completely destroyed and all of *Alcimus'* work would certainly have gone up in flames.[250] It should not surprise us that such a fascinating activity was entrusted to a simple imperial servant as his abilities would have led him to such a role and he, conscious of his role, clearly expresses his pride in his job in the epigraphic text, as with the punctual notation of the tools that accompany his portrayal.

The presence of a tube at the centre of the tomb floor is a characteristic found in many small sepulchral buildings in the area during the first century AD. Its function should definitely be placed in relation to the ritual libations that were carried out in memory of the deceased but, being different from the other cavities that directed into the cinerary urns, one must search deeper for a more defined use. In the case of Tomb XX of *Alcimus*, such a cavity was created with two bowls facing one another which led to a small space under the floor built of brick. Next to this was a small tube orientated towards the same small well. It has been hypothesised that this could perhaps represent the consecrated area of the *Manes* (the spirits of the deceased relatives) who were entrusted with the guardianship and protection of the tomb. If this was true, they would have received direct offerings of food, above all liquid ones (milk, wine and honey) with a propitiatory objective in mind[251]. However, what is even more likely is that this space was used for burial, employing a large common-use cinerary urn that held the remains of deceased of minor importance. With concern

to this, one can also recall the finding of a large block of travertine (inv. 52461) amongst the washed away soil of the Santa Rosa area. This acted as the floor of a sepulchral structure with three rectangular grooves for small (wooden?) cinerary urns and a large central loop hole which must have permitted it to first place the ashes and then the libations in this underground space (VII).

Columbarium VI (of the *Passieni*) was built level beneath, which shares the same orientation as Tomb XX (of *Alcimus*), with it being parallel to the *Via Triumphalis* although closer to it. This *columbarium* is much bigger compared to the former structure.[252] The *columbarium*, which is made of brick, has been subjected to various damage caused by modern building works just as the other two contemporary tombs located immediately to the north (amongst which Tomb XIX). Only the high up structures positioned closest to the west corner have survived. The large burial chamber (of a square layout with its entrances facing the north-east) contains between four and six niches with two cinerary urns placed along a single row on each of the walls. In particular, there is also a large *aedicula* on the right lateral wall which produced a beautiful glass cinerary urn next to the affixed clay urns.[253] Two burial tombs can be found in the lower part of the walls: one *cupa* built on the floor close to the *columbarium*'s west corner and a sort of tub covered in red plaster which holds a terracotta infant's sarcophagus inside of it.[254] Two altars that almost certainly come from this tomb and were removed at the start of building works prior to the archeological intervention are of a very high quality and of great interest (plate 80, 81). The first altar is decorated on the front by protomes of a ram which are linked by a garland with two eagles underneath and a *gorgoneion* at the centre (the head of Medusa was needed to chase away the evil eye (plate 83). The top of the altar consists of two acantiform shoots that burst out of a large crater and fold back in correspondence with the pulvins.[255] Typologically and iconographically, the altar can be aligned with production of the early Flavian Period but one can find previous examples even dating to the Neronian Period.[256] In fact, the inscription with the dedication to a daughter by the name of *Flora* by her parents *Passiena Prima* and *Tiberius Claudius Optatus* dates to this period. Later on, a mention of the son *Tiberius Claudius Proclus* was also added and, below the wreath, *Lucius Passienus Optatus*, freed by a woman and brother *Passiena Prima*. What is of great interest is the specification of *Optatus'* job: he was a freedman of Nero whose work was that of a *tabularius a patrimoniis*. He was therefore an administrative archivist of the Emperor's private patrimony. To declare yourself a freedman by Nero himself, as well as even specify a very delicate job and one of trust, would have been seen as inopportune after the Emperor's death and consequent *damnatio memoriae* (the removal of his images and name from public monuments). This implies that the text must have been chiselled whilst Nero was still alive, that is before AD 68.

The second altar is dedicated to the memory of *Passiena Prima* who was probably the woman mentioned in the other altar as the mother of *Flora* and the wife of *Optatus* (whose bust is portrayed in a half-shell between two dolphins at the centre of the decorative top). Her freedman *Lucius Passienus Evaristus* shares this dedication. Following the latter's death, he was added as a dedicator on behalf of his wife and freedwoman who shared the same surname, *Prima*, in honour of his mistress. In the portrait of *Passiena Prima*, we see her sporting a hair-style that was typical of the late Julio-Claudian Period which followed a fashion seen in many portraits of Agrippina the Younger, Nero's mother. On the altar's body, one sees garlands held up by two cupids at the corners of the front or linked to the horns of two ram protomes on the sides. On each of the sides we see a swan with two small birds who argue over a worm, with a dolphin under the wreath. At the feet of the cupids are two eagles whose heads are turned towards the inscription. On the front between the inscribed tablet and the garland, one sees a Dionysian scene which is carried out in front of a curtain that is held up by two winged Victories: a satyr, seated on a feline fur with a bunch of grapes in his outstretched right hand supports an infant Dionysus on his left thigh, who leans towards the bunch of grapes. A maenad appears in front of them, covered by drapery and a *nebris*[257], who places a branch of vine leaves upon the satyr's head (plate 82).

The two altars, which are both of high quality, are roughly contemporary of one another even if the second one must be slightly later than the first due to its prosopographical motifs. The people commemorated are freedmen who were all linked, directly or indirectly, to the *familia Caesaris*, something that, as aforementioned, was common in many tombs of the deceased in this area of the *Via Triumphalis* during the Julio-Claudian Period[258]. A forthcoming prosographic study might be able to better clarify the possible connection between these freedmen and the historical figure *Gaius Sallustius Crispus Passienus*[259], the second husband of Agrippina the Younger, Nero's mother. His properties and therefore also his slaves and freedmen, were inherited by Agrippina and when she died in AD 59, they became part of the imperial estate.[260]

Tomb XXXII is more or less contemporary to the tomb of the *Passieni*. Built of brick close to the north-west corner of the excavation area, it is located between two almost completely destroyed tombs that are roughly contemporary to it (amongst which Tomb XIX). Tomb XXXII is a structural anomaly with its trapezoid layout, a plan that clearly had to adapt to pre-existing conditions with the presence of several previous tombs as well as to

its particular position close to a junction. Indeed, it was bound to a ramp of large steps which linked two *necropoleis'* terraces along its northern side and by an ascending pathway (to the east) that it opened its entrance onto.[261] On the outside, it was completely covered in red plaster whilst inside, underneath a curious irregular vault, one sees floral and geometric motifs (almost all of which are evanescent) painted onto light coloured plaster. The cinerary urns are placed on two levels: one is a high up bench made of masonry that contains seven built-in terracotta urns which went round the left side and back wall whilst another two small chests for holding new cremations were constructed at a later date and placed at the corners of the floor. A small stucco column bearing a Corinthian capital that is painted red and yellow is found in the corner located between the door and the bench. This divided a deep rectangular niche from a small well which was used for cult practices (plate 84). Part of the iron frame of the small wooden door has survived. Located in correspondence with the entrance, between piers and the travertine architrave, it is affixed to the concrete of the foundation belonging to the subsequent Tomb 5 (dated to the end of the second century AD – beginning of the third century AD). This demonstrates that the tomb was covered and well conserved and therefore perhaps still used and frequented at the moment of the great landslide of AD 130-140.

Tomb XIII was also constructed during the second half of the first century AD on the western border of the excavation. It is a small building of brick of semi-cylindrical form (plate 85). Only the tomb's façade is visible whilst the rest has been removed due to modern piling. In any case, its depth is retrievable using the property's measurements that were engraved on the travertine architrave of the small entrance door: five feet (about 1.5 metres).[262] The iron frame and hinges of this wooden door, whilst supported by modern-day cement, have been conserved and left in their original position. They indicated that this tomb was also perfectly closed up at the moment it was filled up with earth.[263] A marble altar-cinerary urn has been placed above the architrave, built into the barrel vault[264], on whose front is sculpted the dedication by *Vivia Anthiocis* to her husband *Aulus Cocceius Hilarus*, whose combusted bones are still preserved today inside of the urn. This particular positioning of the altar-cinerary urn by the tomb's owner leads one to believe that this altar originally had another location and that it was only in a later moment that the masonry tomb was built with the aim of giving greater prestige to the deceased and allow for the burial of his relatives. A small cube-like tomb (presumably a tomb for cremations of people belonging to *Hilarus'* actual family) is found next to the tomb on the left-hand side. Another two cremation tombs, which are individual ones this time, abut the

84. Santa Rosa area, Tomb XXXII.

85. Santa Rosa area, Tomb XIII and XVI.

86. Santa Rosa area, columbaria II, XVIII and XVII.
87. Santa Rosa area, altar of the legatus *Caius Vibius Marcellus.*

88. Santa Rosa area, columbarium II.
89. Santa Rosa area, Tomb III.

248

Following pages:
98. Santa Rosa area, Tomb III, rear niche featuring Aeneas,
Avernus (?) and Cerberus at the entrance of Hades.
99. Santa Rosa area, Tomb III, left-hand niche featuring Pelias,
Medea and the Peliades at the cauldron.

right-hand side of the tomb and behind *columbarium* XVI.[265] Indeed *columbarium* XVI, which is built of brick covered in red plaster and dated to the end of the first century AD and the beginning of the second century AD) appears to be a sort of appendix to the former tomb. In fact, it was built by abutting the right jamb of Tomb XIII, with its front brought further forward towards the valley.[266] This tomb was also found almost intact, thus conserving a travertine threshold, a balanced hinge and part of the iron frame of the door, as well as the grave goods for the funerary ceremonies carefully set down on the floor, comprising of three *urceoli* (small jugs for libations) and several oil lamps and balsam holders. Two niches appear on the internal walls which are decorated by pink plant shoots on a white background. Two cinerary urns are found on the plane of the left wall whilst the back wall contains a good three of them. Two marble *stelae*, that had almost certainly been reused, are affixed to the floor which bear sepulchral texts: the first is dedicated by *Larcius Hermeros* to his wife *Victoria* and their young children *Asinoinis* and *Victorina*, whilst in the second stele, *Rubellia Augustalis* commemorates her husband *Cerialis*.

Other cremation tombs soon started to be placed inside these masonry tombs.[267] Amongst these are a small trunk-like tomb with marble slabs inserted sharply into the ground and a marble altar of *Marcus Vibius Marcellus* (dated to the end of the first century AD – end of the second century AD) which sealed the persons cremated ashes in the base underneath. Both are situated a few metres onwards (towards the south).[268] The front of the altar bears a dedication by the wife *Maria Quinta* and daughter *Vibia Marcella* which specifies the job *Legatus Coloniae Augustae Firmae* undertaken by the deceased man. One can therefore deduce that he was a representative, a sort of ambassador[269], sent by the central authorities by a city of the province of *Baetica* in Spain, *Augusta Firma Astigi* (today's Écija near Seville). Various cremations are found around the altar of *Marcellus*.[270] In particular, a small and curious hexagonal slab was found in the area in front of the altar with a *patera* in low-relief which contains holes at the centre for libation. An inscription appears on top of this, *D(is) M(anibus) / MA . FE*, with the last four letters being carved back-to-front.

Between the last years of the first century AD and the first years of the following century, the lower part of the area also underwent an initial structural reorganisation, orientated in alignment with the *Via Triumphalis* network. A terrace was created at the back of the small valley with the construction of a series of three tombs (Tombs III, XVII and XVIII) which was then followed by a fourth (Tomb II), that was made a few years later (plate 86).

Tomb III, the most southern one, is a chamber tomb and is the richest and best conserved tomb of the series. It is the only one that contains an entrance that is orientated to the south-east whilst the tombs that follow open onto the south-west plane. One can define it as a *columbarium* as it contains just one *arcosolium* on the back wall with a canonic *forma* for the buried underneath whilst the lateral walls are articulated into two rows of niches with terracotta urns affixed to the floor, framed by pilasters, small columns, cornices, small vaults with half-shells and small pediments made of stucco (plate 89).[271] A large part of the grave goods have been found in some of the niches and above the corresponding shelves. They consisted of various incense burners, oil lamps, balsam holders and small vases for offerings. The coffers of the barrel vaults are also made in stucco and are framed by two series of ionic *kymatia* between listels and flues with floral motifs and mythological subjects inside whilst in the circular spaces human protomes have been identified (plates 90-97).[272] The mosaic floor, comprises of a curious asymmetric decorative motif with black and white mosaic tiles within a series of square panels. Two rectangles of different colour are found at the sides of the entrance, at the centre of which follows an oblong hexagon placed diagonally within a square that was once inscribed within a crown of another four squares. A change of colour takes place in the intersecting and overlying areas.[273] Four tubes directed towards as many underfloor cremations are positioned in correspondence of the mosaic "rug's" corners.[274]

The stucco scenes found in the three main niches merit particular attention. These niches are of a semi-circular layout with a half-shell vault and are located at the centre of the lateral walls and the back wall. All of these representations, which still conserve some traces of colour, seem to deal with Greek myths linked to death. These had filtered down through versions by the great Latin poets such as Ovid and Virgil.

The two episodes refigured on the lateral niches once had a curtain placed behind the figures, a sort of framing that could suggest a representation in a theatrical setting. In the niche at the back, of which only the lower part of the scene has remained, a bearded figure stands out who is dressed in a tunic and wrapped up in a heavy mantle.

100. *Santa Rosa area, Tomb III, right-hand niche featuring a scene that possibly depicts Achilles sitting in front of Priam.*

101. *Santa Rosa area, the front of columbarium II.*

Whilst seated, he holds a branch in his left hand, which is resting on his arm (plate 98). His Phrygian cap attests that he is originally from Asia Minor. Cerberus, the monstrous dog with three heads who guards the Hereafter lies at his feet. Another bearded figure is seen in the background, this time depicted nude and standing. He leans on a branch or a rush which he tightly holds in his left hand. The scene can be interpreted as portraying Aneas who is about to enter Hades with the golden branch in hand (which one must reconstruct in the missing part) after the Sibyl has made the ferocious Cerberus fall asleep with soporific bread. There is a river personification of the Hereafter behind, perhaps the River Acheron or perhaps the River Styx[275], upon whose shores the Virgilian journey of the Aeneid brings about the meeting with Cerberus (VERG., *Aen.*, VI, 410-425).[276] In the niche's missing left-hand side, one could suppose that it once depicted the representation of the Charon's small boat and the same Sibyl. Other ancient depictions of this particular episode do not appear to exist and so this therefore appears to constitute a fresh piece of iconography both in Greek and Roman art.[277]

In the central niche of the left wall, one sees a scene containing five figures placed in front of a curtain: four young women accompany a male figure (who is depicted bigger) towards a great receptacle under which burns a flame and to whose right there appears to be part of a ram (plate 99). The first of the young women (to the right), pushes the man by the arm with an unsteady pose whilst the others seems to indicate the receptacle to him with arm gestures. Without a doubt, this scene recounts the mythical story of King Pelias who was led by his daughters towards the boiling cauldron next to which one can perhaps recognise Medea. The event is an epic episode of the Argonauts which is worth being told here. Pelias usurped the throne of Iolcos from his brother Aeson, who keeps him prisoner in the palazzo. Jason, the son of Aeson, after conquering the Golden Fleece at Colchis, planned by Pelias, takes the legitimate throne. At this point, he needs Medea, the deceitful witch who asserted that she had a potion that resulted in rejuvenation. In order to try that which she proclaimed, he took an old ram, cut it up into pieces and boiled it with the potion. A lamb then emerged from the cauldron: the operation seemed to have succeeded with this stratagem. Therefore, he convinced first Pelias and then his daughters Evadne and Anfinome (but not Alcestis) to undergo the same fatal procedure. The daughters of Pelias cut their father into pieces and threw them into the cauldron. At the same time, the Argonauts entered Iolcos and conquered it. This stucco representation seems to be a version taken from Ovid's *Metamorphoses*[278], of which numerous depictions exist. In particular, two appear iconographically rather similar: one is a fresco of a *domus* at Pompei

(*Regio* IX, 2, 16)[279] and the other is found on the left side of a sarcophagus portraying the myth of the Argonauts, located in the catacombs of Pretestatus.[280]

The third scene, which appears in the central niche of the right wall, is more difficult to interpret (plate 100). Here, the loss of the majority of the stucco prevents a proper reading of the subject depicted. One can only briefly describe the three figures with a curtain behind them. To the left, there is a seated figure, wrapped up in rich drapery with a shield placed behind him on the ground and a diagonally placed sword. He seems to cross his legs and have his arms folded over his chest or towards his face. Behind him, in the background, one sees a pilaster bearing an Ionic capital from which two garlands hang whilst in front there is another standing figure (who has almost completely disappeared) who turns to the first figure. One could hazard a guess that he also wears heavy clothing, a long mantle that reaches his legs, under which he might have worn Oriental trousers that almost fell down to his knees and perhaps a Phrygian cap on his head. A figure dressed in military clothes appears behind the first two figures who are of smaller proportions: he wears an anatomical armour plate (*lorica*) with *pteryges* (a sort of short skirt made up of leather strips) under his mantle (*paludamentum*) and typically high boots (*mullei*). He seems to tightly grasp a sword in his left hand whilst his right hand is drawn up to this chest. With these uncertain foundations, it is difficult to interpret the iconography. One might think of one of the numerous scenes of leave-taking with the warrior's departure, with the velarium behind him and the funerary context possibly referring to the theatrical representation of a tragic mythological subject. Amongst mythological themes, it is, however, possible to propose two episodes which bear iconographies which are similar to the present one discussed in which Achilles is the protagonist: in the first one, Achilles is seated (slightly bent forwards and with his hand lifted up to his head) who, overcome, has received the news of Patroclus' death[281]; in the second episode, Achilles remains seated and with his weapons next to him, receives the old Trojan King Priam who beseeches him for having the body of his son Hector.[282]

On occasion of the great landslide of AD 130-140, *columbarium* III was partially filled in with earth and inside the fill a grave was laterdug that also damaged the floor.[283] From then until shortly afterwards, towards the end of the second century AD, the tomb was sealed by a great terrace wall for the realisation of a series of tombs at a higher level which resulted in definitively closing its entrance. At the time, this wall was pierced by a plunder tunnel of the XVI-XVII century which removed piers and the tomb's architrave and also destroyed part of the niche in the back wall.

As aforementioned, contemporary to *columbarium* III's construction, the other two *columbaria* of the series were also erected: Tomb XVII and Tomb XVIII. These tombs were also affected by pillaging by means of the tunnel: as well as jambs and the door's travertine architrave, the plunderers were also interested in wall material, removing bricks from the facings in order to reuse them. *Columbarium* XVII[284] and *columbarium* XVIII[285] are like two burial chambers with a square layout. They face onto the piazza to the south-west. At least two rows of niches are found on the walls, each one of them meant to hold two affixed cinerary urns.[286]

Only the mosaic floor of *columbarium* XVII has survived which bears a motif of black squares placed in diagonal rows.[287] Tubes which link up to the underground cremations were inserted along the left side and the far side of the mosaic. These two tombs also must have enjoyed a precious decoration of applied stucco both on the walls and on the vault. This was unfortunately destroyed by the plundering that occurred in the 16th and 17th centuries, leaving only fragments of it to be discovered in the surrounding earth. *Columbarium* II, which is the biggest and the oldest of the row (even if just by a few years), is built against the side of *columbarium* XVIII and once upon time had the back of *columbarium* I of the lower terrace lean onto it.[288] It also faces onto the piazza to the south-west but its front is located further forwards compared to the others (plate 101).[289] The jambs and the entrance's architrave were discovered out of place, ready to be taken away using the habitual tunnel for such plunders. A panel was placed above the door, delineated by brick listels which accommodated a marble slab that contained the inscription for the tomb. This was removed during the 16th-17th century. On each of the walls, including the back wall, one sees three rows bearing three niches each. A larger niche is found at the centre of the back wall which is decorated by a stucco half-shell applied to the small vault and by a red frescoed curtain in the vault.[290] The walls of the room, which is rectangular in form, are also frescoed. Subtle racemes, with brown and small leaves emerge from a light background from which linear tendrils hang with red apples tied to them and small birds in flight. The pictorial decorations which follow the architectural partitions, are stylistically linked to the others of the same period, which can be placed in the so-called late fourth style. The names of the deceased belonging to this tomb have not been conserved. These must have been painted onto small marble slabs that were inserted into the wall under the niches. Only one dedication (which is engraved this time) can be seen on a small masonry slab in a concrete chest, built in a corner of the *columbarium* during a second phase when the original mosaic floor was demolished in order to create space for further cremations. The name of the deceased, *Signa*

Felicula, is written on the small slab, after the consecration to the *Manes*.

The precautions taken with the aim of protecting the tombs from being buried due to subsidence from the summit areas (such as placing barriers made of slabs or bricks at an angle in front of entrances) did not come into use until AD 130-140 when the large landslide rocked the small valley. As has already been mentioned, it got blocked when it hit against the front of *columbaria* XVII, XVIII and II and the left side of *columbarium* III. At that point, the mass of earth filled up the entire small valley and was raised so high that it even submerged the tombs located further downhill, exceeding the vault of Tomb XII by almost half a metre. The whole Santa Rosa area was sealed off by the landslide and the tombs were not brought to light again. Occasionally, burial graves were created by reusing those old tombs which had only partially been filled in but for several years, no structure was built *ex novo*.

Later on, around AD 150-160, a new sepulchral occupation first began to pop up in the more northern area with a series of tombs placed in a "V" shape: Tombs XXX, X, V and the room (which was demolished) above Tomb VI (of the *Passieni*). Contemporary, Tomb I was built immediately downhill and next to it, a second tomb above Tomb IV (of the *Natronii*). After another two or three decades, the southern area was also built on with the terraced pathway which separated the series of Tombs XII, XXIX and IX placed above, from Tomb VII in the lower terrace. At this point, the building interventions could no longer avoid a consistent regularisation of the slope. The first tombs of this new arrangement to follow the subsidence were erected on a small peak in the northern area which spread out around the unoccupied triangular area[291] where we find Tomb XXX, Tomb X and the tomb placed above *columbarium* VI (of the *Passieni*) which faced one another. Only Tomb V and the adjacent tomb, to the north-east (but now completely destroyed) had entrances that opened towards the north-west onto the pathway or a ramp which linked the lower terrace to the small triangular piazza.[292] These tombs bear noteworthy analogies with a sepulchral system found in the necropolis of the Galea fountain – that of Tombs 2, 6, 7 and 8 (dated to AD 180-190) which would be slightly earlier (AD 150-160). In fact, the proportional ratio between cremations and burials also changed. In this case, it was more or less an equal relationship whilst at the Galea Necropolis it already saw about 30% cremations to 70% burials. Their structure comprises of a quadrangular burial chamber built of brick on the outside and small blocks of Cappellaccio tuff in the internal *arcosolia*. The latter were located along the lateral walls and contain a *forma* below. The niches for the cinerary urns were instead dug close to the room's corners and presumably above the

*102. Santa Rosa area, mosaic floor of
Tomb X.*

*103. Santa Rosa area, mosaic floor of
Tomb V.*

arcosolia. Other cremations must have been found under the floor as the tubes inserted into the mosaic floor[293] through which libations could be poured tend to indicate. Only two tombs of the series have been conserved in a recognisable manner, even if the majority of the walls have been levelled: Tomb X, the smaller tomb, and Tomb V, the larger one. One can appreciate the mosaic floors in both which bear a geometric decoration of black and white mosaic tiles. The mosaic motif of Tomb X occurs inside of a central white square panel framed by a black stripe that is decorated with elongated hexagons (plate 102). There is a cross-shaped flower at the centre with four heart-shaped petals inscribed in a circle from which eight stylised plant candelabra come off from, bearing lanceolate leaves and covered chalices. These ornamental elements are articulated in different compositions in numerous other mosaics, created over a long chronological spectrum from the middle of the second century to the start of the third century AD.[294]

The decorative motif of the mosaic found in Tomb V was even more diffused. It is characterised by diagonal rows of black lanceolate leaves which come off black triangles from concave and convex sides (plate 103). The mosaic can be inserted in the series characterised by illusionary composed geometric motifs which mark a large part of the production during the second half of the second century AD and the first half of the third century AD; we have already seen several examples of this typology in Tombs 6, 7 and 8 in the Galea area (see above) but even more stringent comparisons can be found in various contemporary mosaics from Ostia[295].

As aforementioned, Tomb IV was rebuilt during the middle of the second century AD immediately further downhill. It covered the Tomb of the *Natronii* and Tomb I was built next to it. The latter was erected on a plot which must have already been occupied by previous tombs[296] but of which no traces can be found, using the same building firm that built the adjacent tomb above Tomb IV (of the *Natronii*).[297] These two tombs next to one another are notable for the identification of the technical solutions used, with the walls made of brick whilst the *arcosolia*, with their underlying *formae* for burials, had facings of small blocks of Cappellaccio tuff. In the case of Tomb I, the *arcosolia* were only distributed along the back wall and the left wall whilst they are missing from the right due to a lack of space. There are niches for cinerary urns on all internal sides and on the back wall there is a small window which opens onto the rear even higher up. The *columbarium*'s walls were decorated with linear red motifs on a white background whilst the vault's intrados was articulated by applied stucco lacunars. Unfortunately, this decoration is only partially conserved. However, a good amount of the mosaic floor remains which consists of black and white mosaic tiles, a motif

that recalls the structure of isodome masonry.[298] This decoration is above all attested to during the first half of the second century AD and must have been realized during the tomb's first phase.[299]

Tomb I opens out onto the north-east by means of a step and a travertine threshold, towards a small closed off piazza, a sort of cul-de-sac where the entrances to *columbarium* XIV, Tomb XI (upon which Tomb VIII of the Sarcophagi was erected), Tomb IV (of the *Natronii*) previously also looked onto even during the second phase. Next to it, Tomb IV was filled in with earth by just under a metre's worth and that which emerged above it, was levelled off. On the same occasion, a series of *arcosolia* made of small blocks of Cappellaccio tuff (a poor-quality tuff extracted from the layer surfaces of this rock) which were meant for overlying burials were built along the back and the north-west side at a higher level. Furthermore, a mosaic floor was made, nearly almost all of which was removed by the graves of subsequent burials.

A new regularisation of the southern area of the zone was started around AD 180-190. The earth that had been placed there by the landslide was removed and two long parallel support walls (made of *opus listatum* with alternating rows of small blocks of tuff and courses in brick covered by a layer of red plaster-) were built (plate 104).[300] As a result, three terraces were created: a series of tombs already mentioned (IX, XXIX and XII) was placed on the highest terrace; an ascending pathway going from the north towards the south was laid out on the intermediate level; and below was an area allocated for poorer individual burials and another masonry tomb. The pathway, which was narrow due to the two long walls, diagonally linked the lower terrace with the upper one towards the area of the Autoparco. It was built mainly using recycled materials such as many bricks and even two previous bases: the one on which the long-lived *Lucius Sutorius Abascantus*, who died at 90 years of age, was commemorated[301], as well as that which supported the statue of a woman by the name of *Iulia Prima*.[302] Its construction resulted in the sealing off of several older cremations: the floor plane was in fact located at a level that coincided with the upper part of the altar of the sculptor *Thesmus* (see above), so much so that its pulvin was consumed by the passageway. The wall of the upper terrace coincides with the south-east and north-east perimetre walls of the new series of tombs of the upper terrace (IX, XXIX and XII). It was therefore linked to the path with the upper level by means of a short and wide horizontal ramp that passed between the north-east wall of Tomb XII and the front of *columbarium* III (partially filled in).[303]

An open area allocated for the burials of the poor (buried in simple graves which often lacked even a cover *a cappuccina* made of brick) was located just below the pathway.[304]

*104. Santa Rosa area, alleyway between
Tombs IX, XXIX , XII and the lower area
with graves.*

*105. Santa Rosa area, Tomb XXIX.
106. Santa Rosa area, Tomb IX,
sarcophagus of Ulpia Marcella.*

107. *Santa Rosa area, burials - dated to after the landslide - which cut through Tomb XXVII.*

VIII (p. 262) - *Cuma, tomb from the Severan Period with frescoed* arcosolia.
IX (p. 262) – *Cuma, tomb from the Severan Period with frescoed* arcosolia.

Considering the skeleton's position, one can deduce that the deceased were tightly wrapped in a sheath and were buried with a wooden box but perhaps with just the protection of a wooden plank as a type of cover.

The series of tombs on the upper terrace (Tombs XII, XXIX and Tomb IX that is further backwards) and Tombs VII and Tomb XV of the lower terrace are organised as rooms built in *opus listatum* in small blocks of Cappellaccio tuff and courses in brick. *Arcosolia* and *formae* were placed along the walls which, undoubtedly in at least two cases (Tombs XV and XXIX) contain four cinerary urns affixed in correspondence to the corners. The gradual moving away of using the cremation rite in favour of the burial rite is clearly expressed here in the form of percentages which seem to allocate the first 25% to the former and 75% to the latter. These percentages correlate with the contemporary Tombs 2, 6, 7 and 8 of the Galea area which are also very similar in structure. Equally close in their articulation are also the other sepulchral series in the areas of the necropolis along the *Via Triumphalis*, particularly in reference to Tombs 6, 7 and 8 of the Annona and Building 5 of the Autoparco.[305] Inside one of Tomb IX's *forma*, fragments of a sarcophagus of *Ulpia Marcella*, dating to the first half of the third century AD, were found. The *imago clipeata* (half bust portrait depicted within a shield) of a young woman of an unrefined face stands out from the front of the tomb which is decorated with strigil-style elements and framed by small columns (plate 106).[306] These tombs, placed in series, seem to have been built with the funding of a *collegium funeraticium* but occasionally one can pick out deceased figures who had greater financial means.

Tomb VII can be found on the lower terrace. It bears larger dimensions than the others and is placed parallel to the upper terrace about a metre further downhill (towards the east) of the alley.[307] Tomb XV was built about 8 metres more northerly on the same level but ori-

entated on the stretch that is close to the *Via Triumphalis*. This tomb, which consists of a small square room (of almost 3 metres long each side), was erected in a blind alley, closed off by Tomb XI, I, IV and XIV and it must have opened towards the north-east close to the *Via Triumphalis*.[308] Inside, it is structured like the others with the walls articulated by an *arcosolium* with an underlying *forma*. Two cubic masonry structures containing a mouth to receive ashes are found at the corners. The discovery of several burials within terracotta sarcophagi with a cover made of tiles and *bipedales* (square bricks that measure 2 feet or 60 cm per side) is of noteworthy interest. These, in their turn, were closed over by large marble slabs of which two are inscribed. The more considerable text, also due to its quality, regards the dedication made in remembrance of and to the *sanctitas* of a young *honesta femina*, *Cocceia Marciana*, who died at 16 years and 11 months old, by her mother *Marcia Successa* (around the middle of the third century AD). Her title leads one to believe that this young woman probably belonged to the Equestrian Order[309], a social level that constituted somewhat of a novelty in the sociological panorama of the area but not a *unicum* (unique) with the presence of another tomb, Tomb VIII, of a deceased person belonging to a similar class, which is one of the wealthiest tomb's amongst those discovered in the necropolis.

During the third century AD, various individual burial tombs appeared not just in the area below the alley but also in other areas of the necropolis that were free of masonry tombs in use.[310] Amongst these, one recalls a series of Tombs IX, XXIX and XII to the west, two tombs of which were *a cappuccina* whose graves cut through the subsidence and the structures of the old Tomb XXVIII (see above; plate 107).[311] It is also worth mentioning the contemporary *cupa*, which is fairly poorly conserved, behind Tomb XX (of *Alcimus*).[312] Equally worthy of mention is the discovery of several burials that

108. *Santa Rosa area, Tomb VIII.*

present the deceased with a bronze coin in his mouth. This relates to Charon's obol which the ancient sources identify as the price for the transport to Hades.[313] As already mentioned, next to these poorer deceased figures in the necropolis, were also members of the more affluent Equestrian Order as demonstrated with the tomb of *Cocceia Marciana* and, above all, with *Publius Caesilius Victorinus* in Tomb VIII. This tomb belongs to the last building phase of the necropolis and can be dated to the first two decades of the third century AD.

Therefore, towards AD 200-220, the brick walls of Tomb XI (which had been built about a century beforehand and by now had been abandoned) were partially levelled and Tomb VIII was built on top of it. This new tomb was constructed in *opus listatum* of bricks and small blocks of Cappellaccio tuff, abutting the walls of Tombs III, XVII, XVIII and I. The stopping up of the small ramp was physically tied to the southern corner of these walls that horizontally linked the alley to the upper terrace. This stopping up, which aligned itself as a prolongation of the upper wall of the alley[314], also definitively closed off the entrance to *columbarium* III beyond the ramp. They had continued to bury (adding interred graves until the quota of the mosaic floor was complete) in this *columbarium*, which had been partly covered over during the subsidence of AD 130-140, up until the end of the second century AD. With the construction of Tomb VIII, the width of the alley's lower access point between the terraces of AD 180-190 was further reduced, bending into a bottle-top pathway at that particular point.

Tomb VIII was once a large square burial chamber (measuring about 5.60 metres per side) and made of *opus listatum* in tuff and brick with two *arcosolia* and underlying *formae* on each side (see figs. VIII, IX). Only the entrance side, which opened up to the northeast, contains just one *arcosolia* as it had to leave the other half free for the tomb's threshold.[315] One can compare both the tomb's articulation and structure to Mausoleum Z (of the Egyptians) in the necropolis underneath St. Peter's Basilica, dated to the end of the second century AD. Thanks to its integrity and state of conservation, it constitutes a valid tool for reconstructing the incomplete parts of the tomb discussed (plate 108).[316] In this case, one must imagine that there were high niches (which one sees some parts of) at the centre of the upper parts of the walls, and therefore sarcophagi (at least eight of them that were discovered in the tomb were partly intact and partly in fragments). Furthermore, one can also presumably link four of them that were built under *arcosolia* and others above the mosaic floor only in the lower part of the tomb.[317]

The tomb contains a noteworthy decorative scheme which has only partly survived. Indeed, nearly of the wall frescoes are been lost[318] whilst one can only see two subjects inside of the *arcosolia* on the back wall: placed between flowering garlands, one sees a peacock on the left and a basket full of fruit on the right.[319] The mosaic floor is of greater interest: made up of black and white mosaic tiles, it contains a figurative subject that turns within a plaited motif and a linear square. Vine tufts rise from the four corners from which long tendrils fall that frame the central scene, forming a pergola. Several musical instruments hang from the tendrils: cymbals, a horn, a simple flute, pan pipes and others that are not easily identifiable. Four cupids are placed at the centre of each side, along the border. They are busy at work and celebrating on occasion of the grape harvest. The first one (starting at the entrance in a clockwise direction) carries a torch and a ladder, the second busily picks a bunch of grapes with the use of a sickle, the third is depicted at the top of a ladder and is about to place a lamp onto a pergola, and the last cupid is bent over placing a bunch of grapes in a basket with a sickle in his hand. The central figurative theme, which is directed towards the entrance, consists of two figures of larger dimensions: in the foreground one sees Dionysus with his right arm stretched out and his left presumably placed on the shoulder of the young satyr. The latter, who holds a *pedum* in hand (a shepherd's staff), is next to him, trying to hold up the drunken god of wine. This was a common subject matter during the mid and late Imperial Period, above all on sarcophagi but also reworked in various mosaic works.[320] In particular, it can be considered as being on the same wavelength to the mosaic style produced during the Severan Period as well as even finding good iconographic similarities with mosaics of several decades later.[321]

After the first sepulchres in *formae*, Tomb VIII began to be occupied by a good number of sarcophagi. During the first half of the third century AD, a sarcophagus bearing two winged Victories and a sarcophagus with the Calydonian Boar hunt were placed along the south-east wall whilst another two or three marble chests were added, perhaps incased in the *arcosolia*. Their positioning is difficult to pinpoint as they were reconstructed by recuperating fragments which were thrown into peripheral *formae*. The first sarcophagus mentioned bears two winged Victories on the front of the chest which hold the bust of the deceased in a *clipeus* with a sketched face only (plates 109-111); two cupids in a boat appear underneath the *clipeus* amongst idle figures of the Earth and Sea: *Tellus* (Terra Mater) and *Okeanos*.[322] Two Season Spirits appear at the corners holding a *pedum* (the shepherd's staff) and game in their hands and a small panther sits between their legs. Two winged griffins appear at the sides, sculpted in low-relief. It is likely that a raised part of a lid, bearing angular grotesque masks and decorated on the front with a hunting scene (on the left) and a banquet (on the right) belongs to this chest[323]; the *tabula* appears at the centre with an inscription dedicated by a

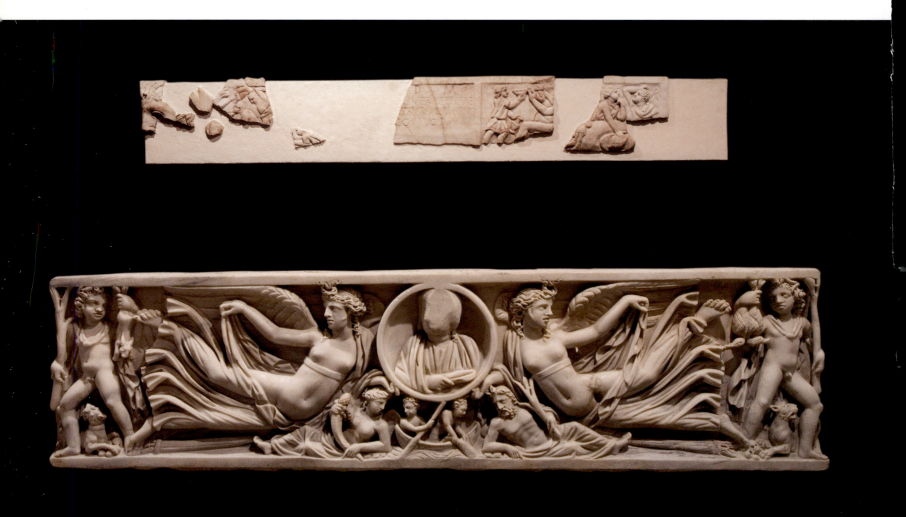

*109. Santa Rosa area, sarcophagus
with winged Victories.
110. Santa Rosa area, sarcophagus
with winged Victories, detail of a
Spirit of the Season*

*111. Santa Rosa area, sarcophagus with
winged Victories, detail of the Victory on the
left-hand side with* Tellus *below.*

112. *Santa Rosa area, sarcophagus*
featuring the Caledonian boar hunt.

113.-114. *Santa Rosa area, sarcophagus*
featuring the Caledonian boar hunt, details.

man to his daughter *[F]l(avia?) Vera* and his wife *Aur(elia) Agrippina*. Both the chest and the raised part contain traces of polychromy: several lines of red colour highlight the details of the representation[324], with a graphic stylistic taste that was suitable for the semidarkness of a tomb where colours were difficult to distinguish and it was deemed necessary to reinforce the scene's legibility by enhancing the borders.[325] The second sarcophaghus, a work of noteworthy quality of the late Severan Period, bears the sculpted scene of Calydonian Boar hunt on the chest's front (plates 112-114).[326] This dealt with the mythological hunt of a fierce wild boar who infested the Calydonian countryside. It was sent by Artemis in order to punish Oeneus, the king of that city, for having not honoured the goddess as he should have. Meleager, Oeneus' daughter, summoned the greatest Greek heroes to kill the ferocious beast who was first wounded by the arrows of the heroine Atalanta and then killed by Meleager's spear. All of the main characters of the myth appear in the sarcophagus' representation. The cover, which is associated to the chest with regard to size and the use of marble, depicts cupids busying away with agricultural activities including the harvest and grape picking.[327]

Only fragments of another three sarcophagi which are more or less contemporary to one another, survive. Part of the pictorial representation can be depicted in two of these. On the right-hand corner of a chest (dated around AD 220-230), it depicts the passionate kiss between Cupid and Psyche (plate 115), with a winged Victory in flight next to them which must have held the portrait of the deceased (just as with the first sarcophagus) whilst the side is sculpted with a winged griffin in a shallower type of relief.[328] Part of the cover can perhaps be linked to a fragment of the chest. Grape-picking cupids and an angular grotesque mask can be seen on the raised part.[329] An almost contemporary Season Spirit with a raised left hand whose right arm leans upon a *pedum* is found on the left-hand corner. On the right, one realises that there was once a mantle belonging to a figure in flight (a cupid?) under which there is a reversed quiver whilst on the left side is the usual winged griffin[330], a permanent feature of this repertoire. The family who owned the tomb therefore appears to have been financially well-off and seems to have wanted to bury their own family members in the expensive marble cinerary urns.[331] Therefore, for the entire third century AD, they continued to add new sarcophagi to the tomb. The left-hand corner of the other

chest appears to be slightly later than the previous ones mentioned (it is roughly attributable to the middle of the third century AD). It depicts a cupid above a hare's warren next to a winged Victory in flight above a peacock.[332] During the second half of the third century AD, two deceased people were buried in sarcophagi of great interest. The first one, which contains a virile portrait inserted into the traditional *clipeus*, was placed in front of the two *arcosolia* of the back wall where fragments were found. The second one, which belongs to a certain *Publius Caesilius Victorinus*, was placed so that it closed off the first *arcosolium* of the tomb's north-west side. Following these two late arrivals, the sarcophagus with the Victories was also moved in order to leave space near to the entrance, pushing it over so that it was positioned in front of the *Victorinus* urn at the centre of the tomb. This episode caused serious damage to the mosaic floor[333], which inwardly collapsed by about 30 cm under the weight of the sarcophagus with the winged Victories and the virile portrait in the *clipeus*. At this point, the mosaic's central scene which contains the figures of a drunken Dionysus and a young satyr, which are partially incomplete in the lower area, were integrated by means of a crude type of restoration that filled in the gap(s) with replacement mosaic tiles without reconstructing the figurative parts. A style that one could almost define as impressionistic was employed. A kind of dotting of black and white mosaic tiles was inserted in the gaps found in the figures whilst only white mosaic tiles were positioned in the other missing parts.[334] During the same period, the tomb seems to have also undergone structural repairs which were perhaps necessary due to some subsidence of the cover.[335] The oldest of the last two sarcophagi discussed, which dates to around AD 260-280, contains a chest that is decorated with semi-gadroons (plates 116-117). Two lions sculpted in low-relief on the lateral sides drink from two large craters (vases for mixing water and wine). The beasts appear to emerge out of the chest's front and move around the side, progressively becoming more plastic with a relief that increases in thickness on the chest's front. There is a male portrait inside a *clipeus* – a man with a stern glance, a short beard and close-fitting hair to his head who holds a strip of his clothing in his right hand (plate 118). A ploughing scene appears under the *clipeus*, and contains two oxen pulling a plough, driven by a peasant with a whip, whilst another peasant throws seeds gathered in a basket in front of him. The sarcophagus finds many close comparisons with

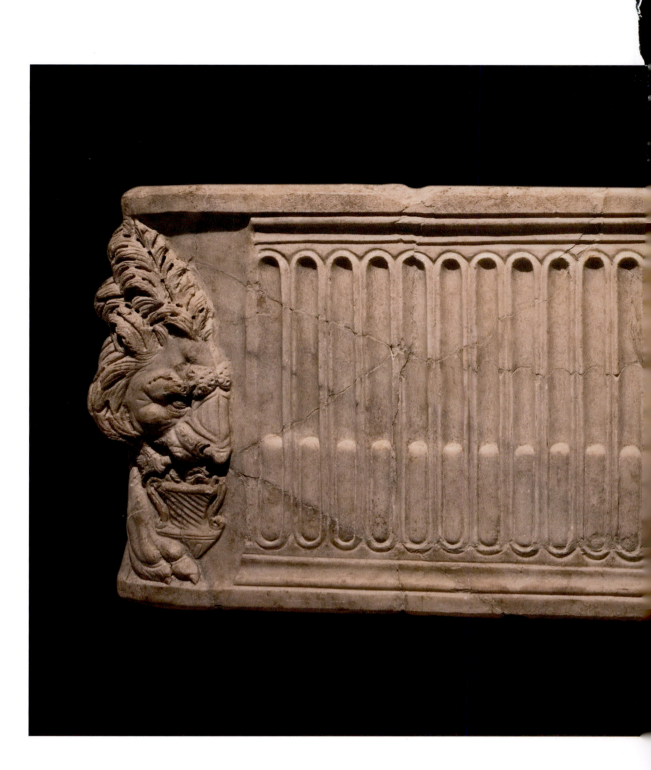

116. *Santa Rosa area, sarcophagus with a male bust in a* clipeus.

117-118. Santa Rosa area, sarcophagus with a virile bust in a clipeus, *details of the lion who drinks from a large* crater, *and of the* imago clipeata *with ploughing scene below.*

119. *Santa Rosa area, sarcophagus of Publius Caesilius Victorinus.*

120. *Santa Rosa area, sarcophagus of Publius Caesilius Victorinus, detail.*

121. *Santa Rosa area, glass* balsamaria
(balsam holders).

122. *Santa Rosa area, bone and ivory
needles, hairpins and disk.
Following pages:*
123. *Santa Rosa area, ceramic fragments,
coins and oil lamps.*

regard to the subject and sometimes also with concern to the portrait in analogous marble urns which are attributable to the second half of the third century AD.[336]

The latter sarcophagus (a strigil-style oval basin) was placed in Tomb VIII towards the end of the third century AD. As indicated by the inscription found on the engraved *tabula* in the raised part of the cover[337], it belonged to a youth of the Equestrian Order, *Publius Caesilius Victorinus*, that is *Eques Romanus*, who died at just 17 years and 27 days old (plate 119). The front elements converge towards the almond-shaped centre which is decorated with a stylised amphora.[338] There are two figurative areas in the corners which host two standing figures. There is a bearded philosopher to the right in front of a curtain whose clothes leave his right shoulder bare. Two fingers of his right hand (in the gesture of the word) touch a *volumen* (scroll) that he tightly holds onto in his left hand. There is a basket full of scrolls to the right of his feet. However, there is a veiled woman to the left who sports a wavy hair-style with both her arms raised up in an Orante-like position (plate 120). There are two small trees with a bird perched at the top of the right-hand one who faces the woman.[339]. The lid, which is made up of various reused fragments, is decorated with two pairs of dolphins amongst waves[340] that converge towards the centre which contain the tablet with the name of the deceased on it.

This sarcophagus has posed the question regarding Christianity of or at least the identity of the young horseman called *Victorinus*. The figure of the Orante woman contains details, such as the presence of a bird on a tree to her left which was a common and indeed explicit part of successive early Christian iconography. As it portrays a female figure, we are unable to identify "her" with *Victorinus* but rather with a Spirit in prayer. At the same time, her association with the figure of the philosopher, who appears in the opposite corner of the chest, is disclosed. At this point, one could identify him as a reader of the Sacred Scriptures and the dolphins (on the raised area) might belong to one of the common "neutral" themes that may be found in the Crypto-Christian iconographic repertoire of the pre-Constantinian Period. Other elements, however, cause us to doubt the Christian faith of the deceased person. First of all, there is the tomb's same context which, since its construction, is marked by various pagan references as documented by the Dionysian theme of the mosaic floor. Continuing along these lines during the course of the third century AD, we see the presence of mythological subjects in other sarcophagi. But the element that most distances itself from the Christian sphere is the actual inscription with the dedication to *Victorinus*: this starts with the consecration to the *Manes* which, as is well known, appear on more than a hundred of the earliest Christian sepulchral inscriptions. This has been explained as being a form of traditionalism such as a predisposed element added by the workshop of sculptors for such series or for its juridical value which sanctioned the tomb's sacredness.[341] In such cases, the formula *D(is) M(anibus)* was followed by the name of the deceased person in the nominative case whilst here the deceased's name is given in the genitive case. Therefore, it specifies that it deals with the *Manes* of *Victorinus*, a detail that creates a presumably unsurmountable obstacle in attributing a Christian reading to the scenes represented on the chest. At this point, it would therefore appear more logical to retain that the Orante woman is a generic depiction of *Pietas* and the philosopher who reads is an allusion to the deceased youth's philosophical-literary erudite culture.

After about a century of use, the tomb was abandoned and was gradually filled in with earth. In reality, all of the areas of the Vatican Necropolis facing the *Via Triumphalis* seem to have stopped hosting sepulchral use and funerary practices during this period. Perhaps it was actually the construction of the Constantinian Basilica over the tomb of the First among the Apostles in AD 320 (about 30 metres to the south) which demotivated the funerary destination of this area in favour of areas closer to St. Peter's tomb. Indeed, it was only there that burials continued to take place.

Pilgrims who entered from the north and visited the Basilica and the Apostle's tomb started to pass along the *Via Triumphalis*. It is likely that during the Early Medieval Period, the tombs closest to the pathway must have been used as shelters for travellers and animals alike. Some traces of such uses are found in the area of the Santa Rosa Necropolis. For example, nearly all of the sarcophagi in Tomb VIII were destroyed and their fragments thrown into *formae* in order to create more space. Only *Victorinus'* sarcophagus and that of the winged Victories (even if deprived of their covers) were left almost intact in their places, and were perhaps reused as mangers.[342]

A long period of total abandonment therefore followed, during which the entire area was subjected to a noteworthy yet gradual covering over of earth. One needed to wait until the 16th and 17th centuries before finding new signs of human presence in the area when, in order to find construction materials and retrieve valuables, a series of tunnels, wells and shafts were built along the entire eastern slope of the Vatican hill (plates 121-124).

124. *Santa Rosa area, marble cinerary*
urn of Stiaccia Helpidis.

CHAPTER FIVE
THE NECROPOLIS UNDERNEATH ST. PETER'S BASILICA
CONSERVATION AND RESTORATION

Pietro Zander[*]

On the eve of the Jubilee Year of 1950, the difficult explorations underneath the Confession of St. Peter in the Vatican that had led to the discovery of the first Pope's tomb and the retrieval of twenty-two sepulchral structures (built during the course of the 2nd century AD and subsequently buried to make way for the construction of the Constantinian Basilica) came to an end. With the gradual carrying out of excavations, which were concentrated during the tormented years of the Second World War, the Roman necropolis unveiled itself before the eyes of these early archeologists just as Constantine's workers had seen it for the last time. Underneath the ancient Church's floor, was a place where time dating back to the end of the 4th century AD appeared to have stood still and now began to reemerge – a time when the sun ceased to illuminate the tombs, streets, and alleyways which crossed the burial ground forever. Having removed the earth originally added in Constantinian times, discoveries were made of brick walls, stucco and mosaic decorations, inscriptions, cinerary urns, sarcophagi and splendid frescoes whose original colours had been preserved in almost unaltered form for one thousand six hundred years. After many centuries, the earth offered Man an archeological site that had remained practically intact and untouched. At the same time, he was faced with the rather difficult job of preserving a place of extraordinary religious, historical and archeological importance for future generations to enjoy as well as rendering it accessible.

As if coming out of a long hibernation, the necropolis was thus met with important building work at its awake, works which were sometimes daring, but nonetheless necessary in order to be able to proceed with the explorations. In fact, the opening up of passages in the ancient and new Church foundations proved necessary in order to deviate and insure the flow of water-bearing strata. It was indispensable to reinforce and buttress the shafts of the overhanging structures which had been deprived of the earth that had once supported them. Still today, along the necropolis' streets and inside of the sepulchral buildings, one notices pillars of reinforced concrete, powerful modern masonry structures as well as a passageway situated in front of Tomb L, the tomb of "the Caetennii *minores*" which had been laboriously opened up through the solid foundations of the triumphal arch of the Constantinian Basilica. During the carrying out of the excavations, unforeseen and noteworthy difficulties were overcome thanks to the determination and professionalism of the Fabric of St. Peter's technicians and, in particular, that of Giuseppe Nicolosi (1889-1967), a professor of Building Science and architect of the same building site from 1934 onwards. With regard to this great undertaking, it is sufficient to recall the hasty creation of stable foundations for the column located south-west of Bernini's baldachin when, during the summer of 1942, this basement was found to be resting upon a small vault that had been seriously damaged by a Roman tomb.[1] If, as is the case, the aforementioned works conditioned the ensuing recovery work, it was above-all the realisation of a floor made of reinforced concrete which determined the choice of subsequent precautionary measures for the site's conservation. Indeed, with the construction of such a floor, which started in July 1948, the necropolis was permanently confined to an underground environment, under the Vatican Grottoes in correspondence with the Basilica's central nave above.[2]

As such, the conclusion of such works in 1949 marked the start of various problems that are typical of every

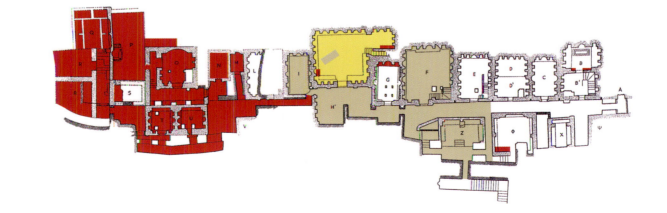

1
2
3

underground environment. These essentially refer to unstable microclimatic conditions and problems of a microbiological nature. Raised temperatures and levels of humidity, linked to high levels of carbon dioxide and uncontrolled air currents, determine early yet unmistakable signs of progressive deterioration detectable in the work through superficial formations of salt (chlorides, sulphates and nitrates), algae and microorganisms which, with the passing of time, tend to conceal the walls' facings and pictorial decorations. Numerous visitors can also be added to this list of deterioration phenomena. They act as unconscious vehicles of spores and bacteria and are responsible for damaging microclimatic variations.

With regard to the necropolis' problems, one attempted to remedy them with a series of interventions which were mainly carried out according to a criteria of urgency, above and beyond a general plan in order to understand the entire excavation area until, from 1998 (fig. 4) onwards (nearly fifty years on since the conclusion of the first excavations), the Fabric of St. Peter's arranged to embark upon a well-constructed program of works. Following careful preliminary investigations, this program allowed for the implementation of a series of conservative interventions in order to stop or reduce the causes of deterioration, and thus be able to take care of the restoration of structures and important decorations.[3] This difficult and all-consuming undertaking, which has now been concluded for the most part, required the synergic commitment of different professional figures. One recalls, for example, the work of the chemist regarding the analysis of materials and salifications present in works, the biologist dealing with the study of damaging microorganisms (algae, fungi, bacteria and actinobacteria), the physicist with the monitoring of environmental parameters (temperature, relative humidity, carbon dioxide, oxygen), the lighting technician who deals with a suitable system of illumination and, naturally, the work of the restorer, architect and archaeologist.

On the whole, the work's articulation has established the application of a method that has resulted in interventions of restoration and the definition of a maintenance plan that is deemed indispensable for the site's conservation. This has been based upon a preliminary investigation of discovery through the analysis of its state of conservation and specific causes of deterioration.

In the following pages, the main interventions adopted by the Fabric of St. Peter's will be discussed to further knowledge and provide details regarding the conservation of the necropolis' underground environments. With concern to this, one recalls with pleasure the effective collaboration with Dr. Nazzareno Gabrielli, ex-director of the Gabinetto di Ricerche Scientifiche dei Musei Vaticani (Institute of Scientific Research of the Vatican Museums) and consultant to the Fabric of St. Peter's.[4]

People who are involved in the field of conservation and restoration nearly always compare their work to that of a doctor. Therefore, the restoration of the necropolis was preceded by a preliminary acquaintance with the patient. As such, every tomb was studied and the existing documentation was collected: bibliography, photographs, graphic surveys, reports and technical notes regarding previous works and conservative interventions. What proved to be particularly useful was the analysis of numerous black and white photographs held at the Fabric of St. Peter's. In fact, a thorough photographic campaign was carried out during the excavations in order to document not only structures, decorations and archeological finds but also completed works so that one could proceed with archeological research to safeguard the structures of the overlying Basilica. A large number of these photographs, which were mostly taken by Renato Sansaini, have been published in the official report of *Esplorazioni sotto la Confessione di San Pietro in Vaticano* (*Explorations under the Confession of St. Peter in the Vatican*): two great tomes were presented to Pope Pius XII on 19 December 1951 by Monsignor Ludwig Kaas, the Fabric of St. Peter's's bursar[5] (figs. 5, 6). Further photographs were taken during the research undertaken between 1952 and 1958 by Adriano Prandi and Margherita Guarducci in the sepulchral area of St. Peter's and the "Tomb of the *Valerii*".[6] New photographs were taken in 1980 of the interiors of tombs located in the eastern part of the necropolis[7] and subsequently, before, during and after the recent restoration work (1998-2000 and 2007) of every single sepulchral building situated in the central and western area of the excavation site[8] (fig. 7).

Parallel to the photographic documentation, one recalls the pictorial reproductions executed on the inside of some tombs during the course of the explorations and the years immediately following the conclusion of the excavations. The first six watercolours, painted between 1945 and 1946 by A. Levi, reproduce particular illustrations found in Tomb M (vault and north and east walls, fig. 8, 10) and Tomb Φ (upper *arcosolia* of the west, north and east walls, fig. 1, 2) In 1950, another four watercolours were executed of the inside of Tomb F by G. Alessio (vault and details of the west wall, figs. 11-14).

As well as the aforementioned pictorial reproductions on paper, another ten paintings on canvas which were executed between 1951 and 1955 by the Norwegian F. Fjürgenson are conserved at the Fabric of St. Peter's. These precious paintings were donated to the Pope and, in 1975, were entrusted to the Fabric of St. Peter's.[9] They portray the interior views of the *Clivus* and the following sepulchral structures: Z, Φ, B, E, F, H, I, M, T[10] (figs. 15-18). The interior representation of every single tomb, with inscriptions, sarcophagi and cinerary urns as they were initially arranged, precisely correspond to the photographs held at the Fabric of St. Peter's. Amongst Fjürgenson's paintings, the view of Tomb H is of particular interest as it faithfully reproduces the stucco decorations' state of conservation prior to the restoration interventions of 1958 which, amongst else, resulted in the relocation of different fragments that had fallen off the walls or that were recovered during the excavations. With meticulous realism, the same painting (fig. 19) shows an extensive formation of condensated humidity in the form of numerous drops of water on the modern concrete ceiling. It is clear that already by the middle of the last century the environment contained a high quantity of water in the form of vapour which condensed on the ceiling's cold surface, thus causing the process of dehumidification and changing the thermo hygrometric equilibrium found inside of the tomb.

With regard to the graphic documentation, one recalls the campaign of architectonic survey carried out before and during the famous archaeological explorations of last century (1939-1949). At the time, Professor Giovanni Cicconetti (1872-1953) and Professor Carmelo Aquilina of the University of Rome's School of Engineering, produced an exact topographical survey which, for the first time, placed the Basilica's structures in direct correspondence with those of the grottoes below.[11] Once the excavations of the necropolis were underway, Professor Bruno Maria Apollonj Ghetti (1905-1989) was given the task of documenting the structures and monuments which had been discovered during the investigations carried out under the Confession of St. Peter. As such, the first general map of the excavations came into being, surveys of the sepulchral buildings in the necropolis' western area were undertaken, as well as plans and sections of existing structures located at the Apostolic Memorial. These drawings, which were partly re-elaborated by the engineer Francesco Vacchini (1915-1993), ex-manager of the Fabric of St. Peter's's Technical Office, were published in the two cited volumes of "Esplorazioni".[12] Furthermore, in 1944, Professor Giuseppe Zander (1920-1990), the technical manager of the Fabric of St. Peter's from 1980 to 1990, carried out a survey of Tomb H or the tomb "of the *Valerii*" which, at the time, was still being excavated, together with the architect Franco Sansonetti.[13] Didactic drawings and graphics were then

5. Vatican Necropolis, tomb H, the tomb "of the Valerii", view of the interior west wall during the excavations.
6. Vatican Necropolis, tomb φ, the tomb "of the Marcii", detail of the interior west wall immediately after the excavations.

7. *Vatican Necropolis, tomb N , the tomb "of the Aebutii and of the Volusii", photographic documentation from before and after the restoration (1998-2000).*
8.-10. *Fabric of St. Peter's, tomb M, the tomb "of the Iulii", watercolours on paper by A. Levi from between 1945-1946:*
a. *Vault with figure of Christ-the Sun;*
b. *Interior north wall with fisherman;*
c. *Interior east wall depicting Jonah swallowed by the marine monster.*

a.

11-14. Fabric of St. Peter's, tomb F,
the tomb "of the Tullii and of the
Cactenni", watercolours on paper
by G. Alessio (1950). a. View of
the interior west wall; b. Detail of
the decoration of the vault;
c. Interior west wall, Aries;
d. Interior west wall, Taurus.

b.

c.

d.

15. *Fabric of St. Peter's, tomb B, the tomb "of the Fannia Redempta".*
16. *Fabric of St. Peter's, tomb T, the tomb "of Trebellena Flaccilla".*

elaborated upon by the engineer Adriano Prandi (1900-1979) at St. Peter's tomb.[14]

In relation to a careful study conducted in the necropolis' eastern part, the Germanic Archaeological Institute of Rome was given the opportunity in 1980 of carrying out a new and scrupulous architectonic study of this area which lacked graphic documentation[15] (fig. 20).

And finally, following the completion of the previous campaign of architectural drawings, the Fabric of St. Peter's gave Giuseppe Tilia's Studio 3R the task between 1998 and 1999 of undertaking a new digital drawing of the decorations and existing structures found in the western area of the excavations. As such, a more complete documentation regarding the necropolis zone surrounding St. Peter's tomb was acquired, with the production of maps of the different levels and sections on a ratio of 1:25 and 1:10 as well as drawings of the most important decorative details on a ratio of 1:5[16] (fig. 21).

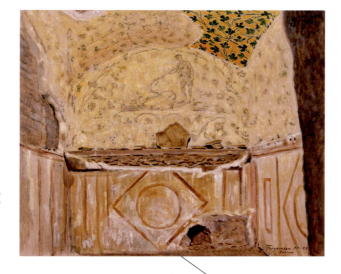

17. *Plan of the Vatican Necropolis, indicating the tombs reproduced in the paintings on canvas by F. Fjürgenson between 1951-1955: tomb Z, the tomb "of the Egyptians" (67 x 82 cm); tomb φ, the tomb "of the Marci" (61 x 74 cm); tomb B, the tomb "of Fannia Redempta" (61 x 74 cm); tomb E, the tomb "of the Aelii" (74 x 61 cm); tomb F, the tomb "of the Tullii and of the Caetenni" (67 x 82 cm); tomb H, the tomb "of the Valerii"(67 x 82 cm); tomb I, the tomb "of the Quadriga" (74 x 61 cm); tomb M, the tomb "of the Iulii" (52 x 63 cm); tomb T, the tomb "of Trebellena Flaccilla" (67 x 55 cm); Clivus (67 x 82 cm).*

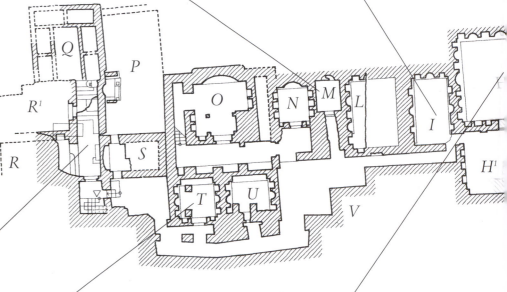

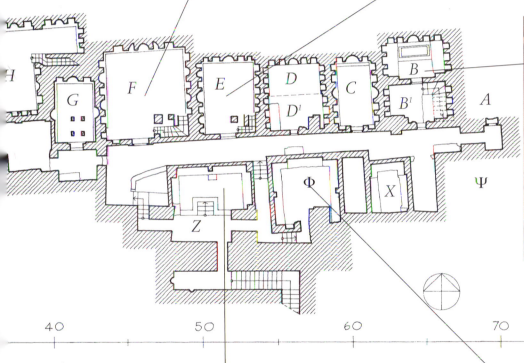

H

G

F

E

D

D^1

C

B

B^1

A

Z

Φ

X

Ψ

40   50   60   70   80 M

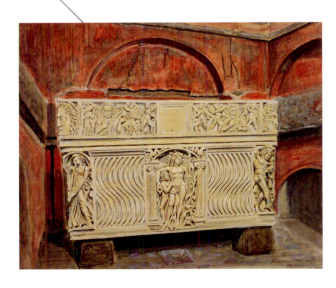

18. *Fabric of St. Peter's, interior view of tomb F,*
the tomb "of the Tullii and of the Caetennii",
watercolour by F. Fjürgenson (1953).

*19. Fabric of St. Peter's, interior view of tomb H,
the tomb "of the Valerii", watercolour by F.
Fjürgenson (1953).*

If we return to the comparison between "restoration" and "medicine" in order to "make sense of the patient's clinical notes", it was also necessary to conduct new laboratory research and more profound analyses. On the basis of such investigations, carried out with sophisticated instruments and utilising the most modern types of technology, the necropolis' state of conservation, as a whole and of every single component (wall paintings, stuccoes, stone surfaces, facings in brick etc.) was charted. This enormous undertaking, which did not leave perceptible traces on the works, represented the initial moment of every restoration and, in particular, assumed fundamental importance for an archaeological site confined to an underground environment with specific conservation problems. It is not by chance that the famous architect Leon Battista Alberti (1404-1472) resolutely asserted that "the efficiency of remedies, for the majority of cases, depends upon the knowledge that one has of the illness" (*De aedificatoria* 10, 1).

Thanks to the autopsic examination, instrumental investigations and laboratory analyses, it was therefore possible to formulate a "diagnosis", or rather the "illnesses" which affected the necropolis were diagnosed as well as the root causes. The ensuing "medical prescription" was articulated by way of a series of precautions aimed at eliminating or reducing the causes of deterioration, some interventions of emergency aid, and restoration (in the strictest sense of the term) which is comparable to that of a surgical operation.

The preliminary studies of restoration, which are summarised in the following paragraphs, can be defined as a type of "prudent therapy", with the administration of "pharmaceuticals" that have been carefully considered with regard to "undesirable effects". This course of treatment was chosen in order that, after one thousand eight hundred years, the archaeological site could naturally rediscover its own equilibrium without the need of traumatic interventions (such as "insulation" from embankments and "artificial air conditioning") – interventions that would have irreparably compromised its conservation.

EVALUATION OF THE THERMO-HYDROMETREIC CONDITION

The study of thermo-hydrometric parameters in an underground environment that is accessed by the general public, places fundamental importance on the evaluation of the archaeological site's state of conservation and the definition of consequent works as well as restoration and maintenance work.

This is the case for the necropolis of St. Peter's, a place that is characterised by different types of humidity problems (from embankments, rises and condensation): it has been indispensable to prepare a stable system in the whole excavation area that allows for the continuous monitoring and computerised acquisition of relative humidity (RH) and temperature (T) levels. To this end, sensors have been positioned that constantly survey the microclimatic parameters along the entire visitor's path (*iter*) and inside of each sepulchral structure. Furthermore, some temperature detectors have been placed on the plastered surfaces whilst monitor and environmental control devices have been positioned in the Vatican Grottoes and on the Basilica's external surfaces.[17]

The information obtained through the microclimatic monitoring and the subsequent study of acquired data has established that the temperature was subjected to normal seasonal changes (even if delayed due to the site's particular location below the imposing Basilica) and that relative levels of humidity nevertheless remained high inside of the sepulchral structures and along the visitor's path. On the basis of such presuppositions, it needed to be established whether one should carry out the important project of insulating the necropolis structures from their surrounding embankments in an attempt to sensibly bring down or reduce the level of humidity. Alternatively, one should leave such humidity as long as it was stabilised, thus distancing all of those problems connected to and derived from reaching the dew-point.[18]

Numerous laboratory analyses done on substance samples extracted from the plaster of wall paintings and stucco of architectonic and figurative decorations have contributed to a better understanding of the issue.[19] Such

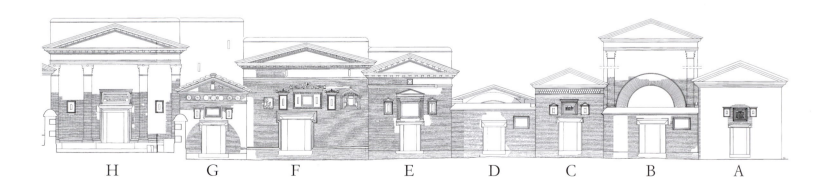

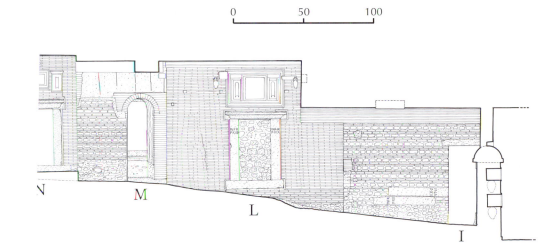

Errata

THE VATICAN NECROPOLES

Page 303

| Fig. 20 reads | 0 | 50 | 100 |
| | 0 | 50 | 100cm |

| Fig. 21 reads | 0 | 50 | 100 |
| | 0 | 1,5 | 3m |

0   50   100

N   M   L   I

20. Graphic reconstruction of the sequence of the tombs H-A along the iter of the Vatican Necropolis. From Mielsch-Hesberg-Gaertner, 1986 and 1995.

21. North and south sections of tomb N, the tomb "of the Aebutii and of the Volusii" and longitudinal section of the sequence of the tombs I-O in the Vatican Necropolis (drawings by G. Tilia-Studio 3R).

investigations demonstrated that the material components of those decorations presented substantial changes compared to its original nature. It was therefore believed too risky to extract the water from such materials when, paradoxically, the water itself could be considered a precious cohesive element of the altered component materials. Thus if, on the one hand, water could not be removed due to the risk of material decohesion, on the other it was the main reason behind the damaging salifications which disfigured and damaged the works. In fact, the water contained in the walls and especially those in contact with the ground (which evaporated due to unstable environmental conditions) left its salt content on the surface. It therefore acted as the root problem of damaging deterioration phenomena.

As such, the study of microclimatic parameters in relation to material components and different signs of deterioration, allowed one to class the intervention criteria as "prudent" and "minimal", aimed at creating a thermo-hydrometric balance between the inside of structures and their surrounding environment.

In consideration of the quantities and qualities of salifications present in the works[20] and the marked alteration of frescoed plasters and stuccoes (which demonstrated noteworthy changes in the carbonate background due to an appreciable water content), the decision was taken to not carry out traumatic interventions with the aim of reducing relative levels of humidity. The following measures were carried out instead:

1) the elimination of the stack effect with the installation of a containing "inner door" placed at the stairs which allows access to the excavations;
2) the interruption of ventilation along the visitor's path within the excavations with built-in devices that allow the doors to open automatically;
3) the closure of trap doors located in the reinforced concrete ceiling situated between the necropolis and the Grottoes;
4) the predisposition of each tomb being placed behind closed doors.

PRECAUTIONARY MEASURES FOR THE REDUCTION OF AIR FLOWS ALONG THE VISITOR'S PATH AND FOR THE IMPROVEMENT OF THE THERMO-HYDROMETRIC STATUS FOUND INSIDE OF THE TOMBS

In order to be able to stabilise the necropolis' levels of temperature and relative humidity, a containing "inner door" was prepared near to the stairs which accessed the excavations. In this way, an insulated place equipped with sequential automatic doors was set up. Furthermore, this intervention allowed for the reduction of preferential currents owing to the difference in amounts found at the entrance and exit of the necropolis ("the stack effect").[21] In order to increase the positive results achieved through the installation of the "inner door", a series of automatic doors were also positioned along the visitor's path which, as well as containing the aforementioned currents, needed to fulfill their main objective of eliminating "the stack effect"[22] caused by the movement of air produced by the repetitive flow of visitors. The effects of their presence were seen through the salifications which appeared on the screens that border the passage areas but also in the pictorial and stucco decorations inside of the tombs.[23] In fact, it is well-known that evaporation phenomena that determined the leakage of salts, originate not only from unstable microclimatic conditions but also from rather accentuated air turbulences (fig. I).

Furthermore, the circular openings (with a diameter of about 1 metre) that exist in the ceiling of reinforced concrete (which acts as the roof of the necropolis and the floor of the Grottoes) were closed up.[24] These trap doors, which are positioned on the Grottoes' floor in the form of artistic gratings made of bronze and adorned with papal coats of arms, had been executed following the conclusion of the excavations to "aerate" the necropolis' hydrogean environments. This solution would later prove inappropriate as it tended to contribute in altering the necropolis' thermo-hydrometric equilibrium, increase "the stack effect" and introduce unfiltered and unpurified dry air into the excavation area.

It was finally decided that the single sepulchral structures would be closed off with doors and insulating panels so that they did not submit to the effects of the inevitable microclimatic changes owed to the presence of the general public (the thermal contribution of a man of medium height corresponds to about the same amount of heat emitted from a 80 watt light-bulb). The latter precautionary measure would have brought about a noteworthy reduction in levels of salification found in the decorative works: this would have been generated by the established equilibrium shared between the tension of vapour found in the environment and that of the embankments, which form the substratum of the said decorative works. The creation of such an equilibrium, through elevated gradients of relative humidity, would have furthermore inhibited the movement of water from the embankments towards the surface of the plaster and therefore have hindered the migration of salt-rich solutions with the subsequent formation of damaging salifications (figs. II, III). The sepulchral structures' closed doors are made up of insulating glass with crystals mounted onto stainless steel frames and fortified by appropriate anti-condensation devices (fig. IV).[25]

The closure of the individual tombs and the barriers of automatic openings along the visitor's path determined the following beneficial effects:

1) the normalisation of temperature and relative humidity parameters;

2) the equilibrium between the tension of the embankments' vapour and that of the environment;

3) the subsequent halt in salt-rich solutions migrating from the inside of embankments onto the surfaces of pictorial and stucco decorations.

In contradiction to the precautionary measures described above, the following undesired effects were produced:

1) the proliferation of microorganisms inside of the sepulchral structures due to a confined increase in temperature and for the absence of the ventilation;

2) the formation of condensed humidity owed to the presence of dew forming on the cold surface of the reinforced concrete roof;

3) the reduction of cubic air capacity along the visitor's path within the excavations, with an increase in CO_2 brought about by the presence of visitors.

In order to stop or reduce "undesirable effects", the following measures were carried out:

1) the typification of microorganisms and setting up of antibiograms for the selection of efficient biocidal products. Further precautions to combat the proliferation of microorganism biodeterioration;

2) the addition of insulating panels to the cold reinforced concrete roof in order to prevent the formation of condensed humidity;

3) the reduction in the concentration of CO_2 through an

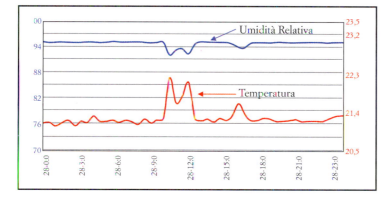

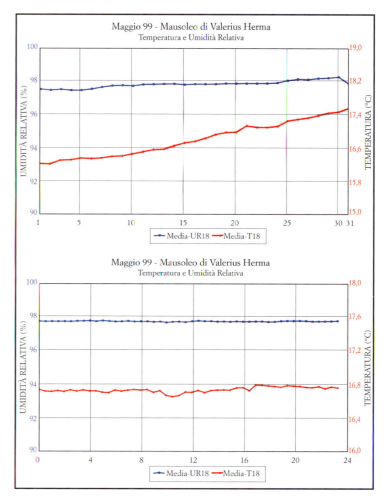

I. Stabilisation of the relative temperature and humidity after the installation of the automatic doors along the Necropolis' visitor path. The graph highlights the change in microclimatic parameters (rise in temperature and consequent decrease in relative humidity), in the periods of the Necropolis' general public opening hours.
II. III. Thermogrometric progress detected inside tomb H, the tomb "of the Valerii", after adding a glass door to the room; above, the monthly graph; below, the daily graph.

22. Vatican Necropolis, tomb O, the tomb "of the Matucci", spread-out salifications on the interior north wall.
23. Next page: Vatican Necropolis, door placed at the entrance of tomb F, the tomb "of the Tullii and of the Caetennii"; here below the same image, indicating the main technical characteristics (fig. IV)

Crystal doors of the mausolea;

doorframe of stainless steel reinforced on both sides;

Glass chamber sealed by packing and silica gel.
visarm glass on the outside, temperato glass on the inside;

Valve for the inflow of nitrogen. At the top, the emission valve;

Exit cable of the electric resistance connected to the anti-condensation system consisting of: 1 power unit, 2 transformator, 3 timer.

*24.-26 – Vatican Necropolis, tomb H, the
tomb "of the Valerii", head of a stucco
figure of the central niche of the east wall,
before and after the biocide treatment.
The intervention made it possible to
control the clear microbiological
deterioration. Below, the same head after
the restoration carried out in 2007.*

27. *Vatican Necropolis, tomb A, the tomb "of Popilius Heracla"; marble inscription above the entrance-way with clear green-coloured algae formations.*

THE NECROPOLIS UNDERNEATH ST PETER'S BASILICA.
CONSERVATION AND RESTORATION

"integrated system" equipped with adequate devices that withdraw of clean air (opportunely filtered and conditioned) and instruments suitable for purifying the internal air from particulars and CO_2;
4) the control of the flow of visitors.

AEROBIOTIC AND PHYTOSOCIOLOGICAL
STUDY AND MEASURES TO COMBAT
THE PROLIFERATION OF MICROORGANISM
BIODETERIORATION

The microbiological study of an archaeological site confined to an underground environment bears great importance not only for the definition of conservative interventions and restoration but also for determining and activating a suitable and necessary plan of maintenance. With the excavations at St. Peter's, the proliferation of microorganisms is particularly favoured inside of the sepulchral buildings – structures that are enclosed by doors made of crystal, devoid of ventilation and heightened levels of temperature. In addition, the temperature rises along the visitor's path due to the continual flow of people who, unbeknownst to them, act as vehicles for spores and bacteria and are carriers of heat. Furthermore, prior to the restoration work, the predisposition of unsuitable artificial lighting systems resulted in the formation of algae on the humid surfaces of the necropolis. This created undesired chromatic effects and, as such, the phenomena of micro-exfoliation which effected the stone, tomb-stones and frescoed stucco and plaster-work. The effects of this attack by algae, actinobacteria, funghi and bacteria populations, was noticeable on the necropolis' surfaces in the form of extensive green marks found at close proximity to the light sources, in diffused encrustations and blackish or whiteish marks, in polychromatic dust, in greenish patinas etc (figs 24-26). Such clear manifestations of deterioration as well as the site's environmental characteristics which prompted a heightened anthropic impact, together with the negative effects of precautionary measures used for the improvement of the microclimatic conditions already discussed, rendered a preliminary study of the epilithic development of all biodeteriorant components (on the surfaces) or suspended in the air (aerosol) absolutely necessary. Thus, with the intention of activating aspiring conservative strategies, a careful aerobiotic and phytosociological study was already embarked upon by 1998. The study's aim was to identify suitable biocidal products and eradicate different

forms of microorganisms present in the necropolis which were harmful for the monument and the place's state of well-being.[26] Therefore, it was deemed necessary to carry out sample testing for microorganisms present in the air and on the works; set up cultures and sub-cultures for the typing of such forms and, consequently, antibiograms for the evaluation and selection of efficient biocidal products[27] (fig. 28).

Following the typification of autotroph forms (algae) and saprophagous forms (bacteria, actinobacteria and microfungi), antibiograms were set up in order to observe the efficiency of main biocidal products which were commercially available at the time.[28] Amongst the different products tested and in varying levels of concentration, *Troysan 174* (5% concentrate formula) proved to be the most effective in attacking bacteria, algae and actinobacteria whilst *Metatin 70/40* (3% concentrate formula) was the most effective in beating bacteria and micro-fungi. Nevertheless, it is important to mention that the efficiency of such biocides is pertinent to the product with which they are diluted and applied with on the surfaces.[29]

Some biocides, such as *Metatin 70/40*, have today been

replaced with alternative products. It is necessary to know the ins-and-outs of previously-used products before using new ones (fig. V). In particular, one must carefully observe the formulation of each in order to evaluate the composition's gradient of polarity or, alternatively, determine whether the composition is not completely polar. On the basis of such evaluations, water-based solutions can be used, or better still, alcohol-based ones containing at least three carbon atoms (the increase in the number of carbon atoms ups the substratum's level of permanency) for polar products. Alternatively, non-polar products or partially polar products can be turned into solutions using pure alkane solvents (n-octane or its isomers) if the biocide has to be applied directly to the paintings or alternatively white spirit for other disinfestations of less delicate substrata.

Accurate microbiological studies correlated with the necropolis' chemical physical parameters (microclimatic conditions, CO_2 levels, the hydration of structures, soluble salts, light, temperature etc.) have allowed for the elaboration of a meditated plan of maintenance which initially planned two cycles of disinfestation each year. These were to be carried out during the spring and autumn months, depending on days when the excavation site was closed to members of the general public. Furthermore, having established the efficiency of the biocidal treatments of the sepulchral buildings which, along with the new closures, were insulated from anthropic contamination, it was possible to reduce the number of times the inside of tombs were disinfected overall. Instead, preference was given to the application of bioci-

dal products on the ground, walls and modern structures and for those areas of decoration which were considered more at risk due to their location (exposure to light) or where, more accentuated signs of biodeterioration had previously been registered.

With the desire of avoiding a sort of "therapeutic tenacity" in the administration of biocidal products, together or as an alternative to the treatments already discussed, suitable air purification systems were installed in strategic points along the visitor's path. These systems continuously cleansed the flow of air in order to carry out an opportune environmental disinfestation against spores and bacteria. In proportion to the cubic air capacity that they have to cover, such equipment is supplied by extractor fans, filters and ultraviolet germicide lamps.

Following such studies and careful experiments, the Fabric of St. Peter's also evaluated the possibility of using UV germicide lamps during nocturnal hours and during the absence of the general public.[30] Such lamps, equipped with moveable blades in order to position and direct the ultraviolet radiations, could be used according to specific time programs. They could also be used during certain periods and specific places in order to hinder the diffusion of microorganisms along the visitor's path and, above-all, inside of the sepulchral structures adorned with delicate pictorial and stucco decorations. Finally, as will be explained later on, further measures to deter the proliferation of algae were adopted by the Fabric of St. Peter's by supplying lamps with suitable filters in order to inhibit the process of photosynthesis

BYOCID	%	Bacteria	Actinomjcet.	Microfunghi	Algae	
Preventol R80	1% 2% 3%	• ••	 • ••	• • •		
Nipacide DFF	1% 2% 3%			• • •		
Nipacide DFX	1% 2% 3%	 • 		• • •		
Troysan 174	1% 2% 3%	• • ••	• •• •••	 • 	• •••	
Troysan 1AF3	1% 2% 3%		• ••		• •	
Traetax 225	1% 2% 3%			• • ••		
Metatin 470/40	1% 2% 3%	••• ••• •••	• • ••	• •• •••	•• ••• •••	
Metatin 5810	1% 2% 3%	 • 	• •• 		 • 	

28. Vatican Necropolis, tomb B, the tomb "of Fannia Redempta", biodeteriorant formations of autotrophic nature on the vault's pictorial decorations.

V. Table with values of different biocide products (available in 1998), tested with the setting up of the microfungi antibiograms, actinomycetes, algae and bacteria.

Application of Insulating Panels on the Reinforced Concrete Roof in order to Prevent the Formation of Condensed Humidity

As seen in chemistry when two products are supposed to react with one another and give rise to calculated effects of reaction, so certain solutions which are opted for in order to avoid or reduce some causes of deterioration can bring about new and damaging phenomena for the works. These consequences have to be predicted and evaluated in order to be able to weigh up the validity of the planning criteria, prior to embarking on restoration interventions. As such, whilst the closing of the sepulchral buildings may have benefited the microclimate, deterioration problems of a microbiological nature followed. Such consequential effects had been predicted and stemmed according to the various courses of action described in the previous paragraph. Above all, as has already been mentioned, an additional negative consequence of closing off the tombs was the resulting formation of dew which forms on the cold surface of the concrete roof that lays over each funerary room. This second "undesirable effect" was nevertheless also predictable. In fact, the quantity of water in the form of vapour, which at a certain temperature saturates the chamber room without turning into dew, could not retain the same status when it came into contact with the cold surface of the roof. Thus, the reinforced concrete roof of the inside of the building behaved like a kind of natural dehumidifier, reducing a significant percentage of water (present in the form of vapour in the surroundings) with consequential changes regarding the delicate microclimatic balance inside of the structure as well as with the formation and dripping of water [drops] onto the works themselves. Therefore, in order to prevent problems of dehumidification created by the condensation of water on the cold concrete surface, it was deemed necessary "to rise the temperature" of the aforementioned surface. To this end, the roof was "heated up" by means of affixing 5 cm thick "cadorite" or "termanto" panels made of expanded polyvinyl chloride to the concrete roof. These panels were separated from one another by a distance of 2 cm using the same material in order to create a perfectly closed cavity wall on each panel. Such a precautionary measure was adopted after two years of testing. During this period, no problem occurred with the use of a similar cadorite panel, plastered over with lime and pozzolana which was especially positioned onto the reinforced concrete roof of Tomb C, the Tomb of Tullius Zethus[31] (figs. 29, 30).

Ways for Cutting CO$_2$ Levels and Making the Air inside the Necropolis Healthier

Unfortunately, the desired temperature and humidity lev-

els needed in order to create optimum microclimatic parameters required for the site's decent conservation clash with the need for making the necropolis easily accessible to a large number of visitors.

In fact, many people have expressed their discomfort due to the specific microclimatic conditions of the St. Peter's excavation site where levels of relative humidity are particularly high. This disturbance is felt particularly during the summer months when the temperature is much higher. For some people, this level of discomfort is increased by the fact that they find themselves in an underground environment (situated between three and eight metres below the Basilica floor) and being forced to move about in confined spaces which are illuminated by a suffused light.

The Fabric of St. Peter's has always dedicated particular attention to this aspect, especially following the closing off of the single sepulchral structures and the positioning

29. The creation of "dew-point" in the form of condensated water-drops on the cold surface of the reinforced concrete roof inside tomb C, the tomb "of Tullius Zethus".

30. Vatican Necropolis, tomb C, the tomb "of Tullius Zethus", experimental panel of "Cadorite" or "Termanto" (expanded PVC), plastered over with lime and pozzolana in order to avoid condensation of water vapour on the reinforced concrete roof.

of automatic opening doors along the visitor's path. Indeed, the problem with the healthiness of the air (caused by airborne chemical and biological pollutants) is a particularly important factor for an underground site surrounded by the clay-based soil of the Vatican hill and overlaid by the Basilica's imposing structure; a site, moreover, that is subjected to a high frequency of visitors (there were over 60,000 registered visitors in 2008 alone). Let us not forget that the arrangement of suitable equipment for air disinfection and the continual monitoring of oxygen levels present in the necropolis is linked to the problem of visitors. By means of sensors which have been opportunely distributed along the visitor's path, it is actually possible to control CO_2 levels which are constantly kept below levels that would cause alarm.

In order to improve and facilitate the accessibility of the excavation site, the possibility of installing a system that pumps different air in and along the visitor's path is currently being evaluated: a system integrated with ionizing equipment and suitable devices in order to purify the air from both CO_2 and particulars.

In relation to this, a main working plan foresaw the placement of a special apparatus that controlled the admission and emission of air in some of the trap doors which link the necropolis to the Grottoes. These exhaust fans were opportunely studied with filters in order to cut down particulars and chemical and biological pollutants, and ultrasound devices in order to humidify the air. This proposed air replacement system should have been activated during certain nocturnal hours when the air found in the Grottoes is cleaner and/or during excavation visits when special sensors, placed in strategic points in the necropolis, signaled a significant increase in the presence of pollutants. Naturally, the air that was pumped into the excavation site had to be introduced with the same levels of relative humidity found in the necropolis. It also had to be introduced very slowly and in a way that was suitably positioned, so as to prevent direct contact with pictorial works and tomb walls. Furthermore, the addition of suitable equipment for the negative ionization of the air would have improved Man's absorption of oxygen.[32]

Such a project has nonetheless experienced a setback due to the changed environmental conditions found in the Grottoes where the air should have been tested. In fact, from April 2005 onwards, the number of presences in such surroundings has noticeably increased due to the pilgrimage to Pope John Paul II's tomb. Such presences have changed the site's microclimatic and microbiological conditions. However, in the absence of the abovementioned air removal and treatment set-up, a device that reduces the level of CO_2 (using soda lime and/or activated carbon) is currently being tested.[33]

Whilst awaiting the integration and activation of planned ways of reducing CO_2 levels and making the necropolis' air healthier, and, [in addition], considering the rise visitor numbers to the excavation site and the Grottoes above where the papal tombs are located, the following solutions were put forward:
– Reduce the amount of time visitors spend in the necropolis;
– Extend the waiting time between one visitor group and the next in the excavation site:
– Limit the number of visitors.

Such precautionary measures are necessary since, as has been illustrated, Man's presence in the St. Peter necropolis' underground environments, constitutes one of the main reasons for it's deterioration. In fact, Man contributes in changing the delicate microclimatic equilibrium which has been studied in depth: he is an unknowing vehicle of spores and bacteria and, what is more, is responsible for the production of carbon dioxide.

The importance of the anthropic impact on the site's conservation was made evident by the annually documented visitor numbers in *L'Attività della Santa Sede* (*The Activity of the Holy See*).[34] These meticulous reports have charted how, from 1970 to today, more than 1.2 million people have visited the necropolis of St. Peter's. With regard to the progressive rise in the number of visitors (which reflects a growing interest in this site of fundamental religious and historical importance), it should be noted that in 1970 there were 7,784 visitors, in 1980 there were 23,016 visitors and in 1990, there were 29,723 visitors. Numbers continued to grow: in the Year 2000, 37,670 visitors were registered, 45,345 in 2003 and 61,529 in 2008.

In order to guarantee the maximum accessibility to the necropolis without, above all, neglecting the necessary attention required in maintaining the site's level of conservation as well as wanting to limit the discomforts encountered during the visit in an underground place with the environmental characteristics already described, it therefore seemed sensible to reduce the amount of visiting time in the excavation area. As such, preliminary visitor explanations took precedence in the so-called "Archaeological Rooms" of the Grottoes and prolonged stays in the "Clementine Chapel" and "Apostolic Memorial". Furthermore, different groups of visitors were spaced out in a more opportune fashion with the use of different opening hours to the public for visiting the excavation site. Finally, the issue of limiting the number of visitors is currently been worked on. Compared to other archaeological sites, the carrying out of the latter objective is more complex because a visit to the necropolis does not merely constitute an interesting historical-cultural itinerary but also an actual pilgrimage.

Going back up the Vatican Hill and passing through the ancient beaten track of the necropolis' pre-Constantinian tombs, one reaches St. Peter's rather humble tomb which is situated at the centre and origin of the majestic Basilica which is the beating heart of Christianity.

For reasons described above, it is not always possible to admit, in short amounts of time, the growing number of visitors who want to access the excavation site. In order to cope, in part, with this difficulty, the Holy See's Internet Department has recently made a virtual tour of St. Peter's necropolis available. Furthermore, one notes that the Fabric of St. Peter's Excavation Site Department deals with the organisation of guided visits on a reservation booking basis only.[35]

THE ILLUMINATION OF THE ST. PETER'S NECROPOLIS

The installation of the first fixed electric system in the necropolis dates back to 1951. At the time, great care was taken by the Fabric of St. Peter's technicians in positioning supply cables which could not cause any visual disturbance and, above all, had to follow the ancient walls "bearing in mind at the same time the difficult environmental conditions, especially humidity."[36] Much work was subsequently carried out in the necropolis' underground environments but it has only been in recent years that traditional electric lamps have been replaced with neon lamps. The latter are considered less damaging for the structures, safer and more resistant to humidity. With the use of such light, which is at times

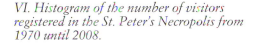

VI. Histogram of the number of visitors registered in the St. Peter's Necropolis from 1970 until 2008.

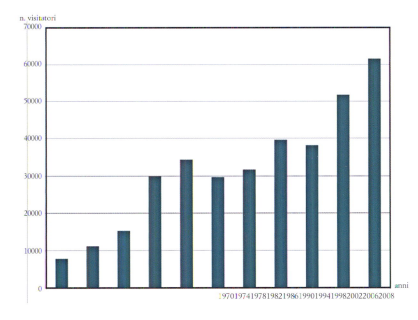

placed in close proximity to stuccoes, paintings and mosaics, the whole area of the excavation site was illuminated without distinguishing ancient and modern structures from one another. Furthermore, in 1998, during the planning of further restorative actions and interventions that would enhance the necropolis, the planning of a new lighting system was reevaluated as one of the most urgent, difficult and important projects to carry out.[37] Indeed, the lighting needed to emphasise the elegant brick buildings and valuable decorations kept within them without altering, in any way, the delicate microclimatic balance nor encouraging the growth of damaging microorganisms.

The main planning constraint was therefore that of illuminating the excavation site with cold luminous sources or rather with lamps that emitted the smallest amount of heat into the [surrounding] environment. As such, it was decided to keep nominal electric power at a level of circa 5Kw and illuminate the necropolis with fiber optic and halogen mounted on technical apparatus equipped with suitable filters. With the use of such equipment, it was possible to reduce heat dispersion to a maximum, the amount of light produced by the single luminous sources and the emission of UV radiation. The light sources were generally placed on the outside of the sepulchral structures as well as at a sensible distance away from the stuccoes, brick facings and pictorial works.

A second constraint linked to the new system consisted in the need for inalterability with regard to the materials and all the system components which needed to be arranged in the necropolis' underground environment - an environment which, as previously discussed, is characterised by particularly high levels of humidity.

And finally, in order to significantly cut back the proliferation of algae formations, those involved sought to inhibit, at least in part, the process of photosynthesis[38], or rather the absorption of luminous radiations by means of chlorophyll which triggers photosynthesis. There are essentially two types of radiation: the first is visible between 400 and 500 nm and is more active; the second is visibly perceptible between 700 and 770 nm. This latter type of radiation was culled through the predisposition of filters which were especially made for the necropolis' conservative needs (fig. VII).

Different levels of illumination were adopted in order to distinguish the inside of sepulchral rooms from the outside of structures which were originally placed in the open. Through the choice of opportune lighting tones, the value of works, inscriptions and most important decorative details was increased. Furthermore, appropriate structures were planned and realised in order to reduce the visibility of the lighting apparatus, electric auxiliary components and power cables to a minimum (fig. 31). In particular, along the *iter* that runs between Tomb B and

VII. Graph which highlights the abatement of the spectral fraction between 700 and 770 nm.
31. Vatican Necropolis, view from the iter, *with a track in steel and aluminum containing 200 fiber optic terminals. The system is directed in a way that reduces the visibility of the roof and the modern walls to a minimum, producing a homogeneous and suggestive lighting that falls on the tombs' facing in* opus latericium *with spotlights that are directed onto sarcophagi, inscriptions, doorways and brick decorations.*

32. Vatican Necropolis, small piazza between tombs M, N, U and V, view of the fiber optic illumination on the false ceiling, realized with panels of alveolar aluminum in order to hide the cables of the electric and monitoring system.

Tomb F, the fiber optic generators were placed on a steel platform which was fixed to the reinforced concrete ceiling; a support that manages to both dissipate and transmit heat onto the cold concrete surface, thus preventing the damaging formation of water condensation which has already been discussed.

Thanks to such solutions, the necropolis is illuminated today by a discrete lighting (fig. 32) that leaves the modern structures in semidarkness whilst highlighting the ancient works. As thus, it helps guide the visitor through the suggestive route which gradually accompanies them in their rediscovery of the Basilica and the Catholic Church's most ancient and deepest roots.[39]

RESTORATION

Having eliminated or reduced the causes of deterioration, it was still necessary to intervene on the brick facings and tomb decorations which clearly showed signs of wear and tear as well as previous interventions of restoration that had used unsuitable materials. Professionals of well-established experience in underground environment restoration, who used the most modern type of technology, were therefore called in.[40] The numerous laboratory studies have consented a choice of products that are more suitable for the cleaning of surfaces, consolidation and stucco work. Non-organic products were used due to their resistance to biodeterioration attacks as well as the fact that superficial protective layers could be avoided.

After the first emergency or "first aid" interventions to stop the loss of painted plaster and, above all, fragments of stucco decorations, work was subdivided into different phases of intervention. This was worked out on the basis of the state of conservation and spatial dislocation of sepulchral buildings. As such, every single tomb was transformed in an "operating theatre" where restorers worked after having carried out careful "mapping outs" of the materials, the state of conservation and restoration. The cleaning of the brick facings and Constantinian walls with recurring horizontal small blocks of tuff alternated with courses of brick proved to be particularly laborious due to the widespread presence of efflorescence and saline carbonatisation, sedimentary earth residues and the formation of biological attacks of various natures. Interventions made on resolving problems of disintegra-

tion, alveolisation and exfoliation of bricks proved to be equally time-consuming (figs 33, 34).

The impressive restoration work has therefore allowed one to appreciate the elegance of the façades, which consist of ordered rows of brick, carefully polished and connected by thin layers of coloured mortar (mixture of slaked lime and brick dust) with joins between the recurring bricks which are highlighted by a low-relief white joint sealing (fig. 36).

The restoration of the sepulchral building façades also permitted the recovery of valuable terracotta decoration that was occasionally decorated with insets made of pumice and yellow and red bricks, finely worked and carved by hand (Tombs E, F, G and L, fig. 35). Furthermore, painted plasterwork (Tombs G and V), holes left by nails for the fixing of votives (Tomb V) and traces of black smoke on top of bricks (with clear signs of ancient deterioration and therefore traceable to fires lit at the beginning of the IV century AD when the necropolis was buried, making way for the construction of the Constantinian Basilica) have been found on the wall surfaces.

With regard to the mosaics, various types of techniques of great importance surfaced during the restoration of Tomb M, the tomb "of the *Julii*"[41]. Indeed, one identified a homogeneous layer of plaster and painted yellow-ochre fresco (upon which have been found traces of sinopites which must have acted as a guide for the insertion of mosaic *tesserae*) on all of the interior surfaces including

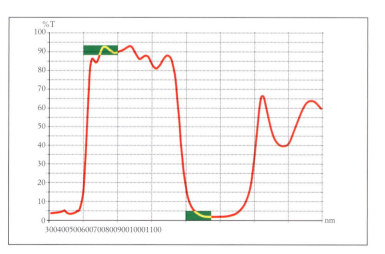

the upper area and vault designed with mosaic decoration (figs. 39, 40).

The spectrum of pigments used for such preparatory drawings is faithfully reproduced by the single tonalities found in the mosaic *tesserae*. In fact, in the gaps between the *tesserae*, where only the impression of *tesserae* once prepared and painted remain (Jonah on the east wall, Christ-Sun on the vault), one can clearly see direct traces of different colours (black, grey and red) on the inside of the painted figures which overlap ordered mosaic rows of equal tonality even if a greater variety of shades sometimes appears.

As such, it has been possible to verify the use of polychrome *tesserae* made of a transparent vitreous paste which, in the areola and clothes of Christ-Sun, are at times covered by thin gold leaf protected by a glassy cover which is similarly transparent.

There are at least two different tonal gradations present in the chalky stone and white-grey marble mosaic *tesserae* belonging to the figures of Christ-Sun and the horses. The other parts of the mosaic are mainly made up of vitreous-based pastes that are rich in chromatic shading (four gradations of yellow, five of green, three of blue, two of red etc.). The *tesserae* used in the backgrounds are bigger and more regular in size (a maximum of 5 x 7 mm) compared to those smaller and irregular tiles used for the figurative parts (a minimum of 3 x 3 mm): in both cases the thickness is about 10 mm.

Even the restoration of the pictorial decorations, which was mainly carried out in the open in the most ancient tombs of the north row and overlies dry paint-work in the tombs of the south row, gave excellent results. Indeed, brightly coloured decorations were discovered once the unsightly concrete stucco work, thick and widespread salt incrustations and earth residues were removed from the pictorial surfaces – decorations of painted figures that no one knew the existence of which, during the passing of years, had become vanishing shadows that were only partly legible. The conservative interventions undertaken at the necropolis have brought about not only a deeper knowledge concerning the iconography of single tombs but have also prompted the acquisition of greater information regarding ancient techniques of execution and about the materials used.

Even the restoration of tombstone elements has brought about unexpected results. Clear traces of colour have been found on ancient marble sarcophagi and on the marble floor of the ancient Basilica's presbytery (figs. 47-

37. Vatican Necropolis, tomb F, the tomb "of the Tullii and of the Caetenni", exterior view of the south, detail of the polychrome terracotta decoration with architectural prospect.

50). Indeed, with regard to the latter, the important inscription AT (!) PETRU(M) (which marked the block of marble used by Constantine in St. Peter's) was found in the exact same spot where the south-west column of the ciborium was erected during the IV century A.D. in the "Constantinian Memorial".[42]

For the restoration of the stucco decorations, a special mention should be made regarding the intervention carried out inside of Tomb H or the tomb "of the *Valerii*" during the course of 2007.[43] After preliminary diagnostic investigations, and early consolidations in this tomb, where partial conservative interventions had been carried out between 1957 and 1958, the removal of cemented plastering (which was carried out during last century in order to stop the loss of plaster work and fill in numerous gaps found in the stucco decorations) proved especially laborious.[44] The restoration of the *hermae* by means of inserting a glass resin support into the internal cavity was particularly difficult. In ancient times, a wooden axis covered by a spiral made of rope had been placed inside of the cavity where a copper framework (flattened down by mortar made up of travertine dust and gesso) had been inappropriately added during previous interventions[45] (fig. 40-41). Furthermore, the study of stucco fragments held in the Fabric of St. Peter's warehouses has resulted in piecing three magnificent *hermae* back together again and returning them to the Tomb "of the *Valerii*" (one on the west wall and two on the north wall, figs. 43-46).

Finally, it has been possible to reunite some erratic fragments of low-reliefs with Dionysian figures, architectonic decorations and the image *Hypnos*. The patient work needed for cleaning was carried out using scalpels, tiny

drills and, for the most delicate areas, sophisticated laser equipment. Furthermore, the restoration has provided the opportunity for rediscovering unknown sepulchral graffiti and interesting traces of hand-crafted work (mould imprints for the execution of repetitive decorative marks, preparatory incisions for the realisation of low-reliefs, the use of ochre pigment found in the lime and marble dust stucco mixture[46] (figs 38, 53). Replica polychrome marble decorations were restored near to the *arcosolia*, whilst polychrome traces were detected amongst clothing folds of some statues made of stucco.

Lastly, in order to not compromise possible future research, limited sections of plaster-work bearing fleeting inscriptions in charcoal and pictorial drawings (located on the east and north walls) were intentionally excluded from being cleaned. Indeed, it is well known that in the central niche of the north wall, opposite the entrance door, drawings bearing two virile busts were discovered during previous excavations which, at the time, were referred to depicting Christ or St. Paul (in the upper part) and St. Peter (in the lower part, fig. 51). Some inscriptions were found next to these images, inscriptions which were already illegible during the years that immediately followed the excavations. In particular, in October 1952, Margherita Guarducci thought she could read a prayer directed to St. Peter for the Christians buried near to his body in the surviving and unclear signs at the sides of the lower figure.[47]

Today, doubt still remains over the inscription's true meaning and established concerns, from many parts, continue to be offered regarding the interpretation of the presumed text and the reading of the many hypothetical

41. Vatican Necropolis, tomb H, the tomb "of the Valerii", central hole of a Herm inside of which a support beam was originally fixed, covered by a spiral rope of which the imprint is still visible.

42. Vatican Necropolis, tomb H, the tomb "of the Valerii", restoration of a Herm of the west wall by inserting a new glass resin support inside the central hole.
43.-46. Vatican Necropolis, tomb H, the tomb "of the Valerii", interior west and north walls, details of the Herms.

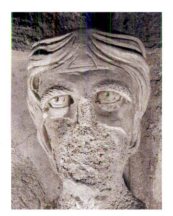

*47-48. Vatican Necropolis, tomb F, the tomb
"of the Tullii and of the Caetennii", interior east wall,
before and after the restoration.*

49-50. Vatican Necropolis, tomb T, the tomb "of Trebellena Flaccilla", interior east wall, before and after the restoration.

51. *Vatican Necropolis, tomb H, the tomb "of the Valerii", north wall, view of the central niche which has been partly excavated (1944) showing two virile busts bearing overlying traces of black pigment on white plaster.*
Over the right shoulder of the figure are recognizable the letters "P T R" related to the apostle Peter's name.

52. *Vatican Necropolis, tomb H, the tomb "of the Valerii", central niche of the north wall, multispectral colour image in visible light. One can just about make out the profile of a lower virile bust in the image (elaboration Art-Test s.n.c.).*

53. *Vatican Necropolis, tomb H, the tomb "of the Valerii", central niche of the north wall, image in fluorescent UV light in a narrow band with a peak at 750 nm and width of 50 nm. One can clearly see the profile of a lower virile bust in the image. The different vision of the upper drawing is due to the fact that in this second case, the organic adhesive used as a binding agent contains a good amount of pigment which makes a large part of the marks discovered at the time of the excavations still visible (elaboration Art-Test s.n.c.).*

54. Vatican Necropolis, tomb H, the tomb "of the Valerii", north wall, detail of the stucco decoration using an ochre-coloured impasto above the figure of Hypnos.

and lost writings written close to the upper figure. Regardless of this issue, the inscriptions are not any more legible today whilst drawings, most likely traced before works carried out by Constantine, are now much more faded and are just about visible but perfectly legible when seen under ultraviolet light.

With regard to the works carried out inside of Tomb H, the Fabric of St. Peter's actually deemed it necessary to undertake multispectral investigations using visible UV (ultraviolet) fluorescence and IR (infrared) reflectography.[48] The analysis and comparison of acquired information and, above all, the study of images using UV fluorescent light (with a narrow band peaking at 750 nm with a width of 50 nm) allowed one to establish with the upmost certainty that the drawings and lost inscriptions were executed at different times and in different ways. The two virile busts were actually realised through the use of an organic adhesive pigment detected through the use of UV light. It was also ascertained that the inscriptions were probably carried out using black smoke, a process which determined the loss of colour which was made soluble and faded away due to the strong humidity present in the tomb (figs 52, 53). However, the aforementioned investigations have not revealed even a minimum trace of their presumed colour. Furthermore, the UV fluorescent photographs of the lower bust have unveiled previously unknown details of the figure (left shoulder, clothing drapery). According to Professor Margherita Guarducci, it has also been possible to ascertain that certain signs belong to the inscription (the first three letters of the word HOM[INI]BUS) actually form part of the overall design due to the discovery that their pigment, as already mentioned, is different from that of the inscription's.[49]

At the conclusion of the works, a crystal casket was made in order to observe the Tomb "of the *Valerii*" from the outside without altering its delicate microclimatic equilibrium. This balance is constantly controlled by a high precision computerised monitoring system.

Whilst awaiting the start of restoration work in the eastern part of the excavation site, the Fabric of St. Peter's is busy carrying on with planned maintenance works.

MAINTENANCE WORK

Once the restoration work had ended, the "maintenance therapy" began, or rather the implementation of a meditated maintenance program carried out by means of a continuous monitoring of environmental parameters, frequent checks on the works' state of conservation, periodic biocide treatments and systematic and specific care. A certain sensitive promptness is not only necessary but indispensable for an excavation site confined to an underground environment which hosts a number of environmental characteristics already described as well as for a place that is subjected to a high affluence of the general public. Therefore, constant maintenance works by qualified personnel is required in those parts of the St. Peter's necropolis that are exposed to the continual passing of pilgrims and visitors. As already described, they are the main culprits behind the damaging microclimatic and microbiological changes. If one was to use judicial language, one could affirm that "the sentence must fit the crime". Indeed, it is well-known that the everyday maintenance works must be in direct proportion to the site's accessibility.

It is for these precise reasons that with the carrying out of a maintenance plan in the necropolis, great care is required when removing salts from the wall hangings (placed along the visitor's path). As such, they are subject to inevitable thermohydrometric changes and air movements caused by the presence and movement of people.[51] The removal of salts at the first signs of their appearance on brick facings as well as other maintenance interventions already discussed are carried out by the Fabric of St. Peter's in order to prevent, or at least postpone difficult, expensive and heroic surgical interventions later on. Indeed, the saying "maintain so as not to restore" is very dear to specialists in conservation.

NOTES

CHAPTER ONE

[1] Plin., *Nat. Hist.* 3.53: *Tyberis (...) Veientem agrum a Crustumino, dein Fidenatem Latinumque a Vaticano dirimens (...).* "The Tiber (...) separates the territory of Veii from that of Crustumerium, and afterwards that of Fidenae and Latium from Vaticanum." (transl. Loeb)

[2] Hor., *Carm.* 1.20.3-8.

[3] *Nat. Hist.* 18.20.

[4] Liv., 3.26.8.

[5] F. Coarelli, *QuadTopAnt* 1968, pp. 31-32; Id., *MEFRA* 89, 1977, p. 823; L. Quilici, in *Tevere, un'antica via per il Mediterraneo*, Roma 1986, p. 227; F. Coarelli, entry *Navalia*, in *Lexicon Topographicum Urbis Romae* III, Roma 1996, pp. 339-400; Id., *Il Campo Marzio*, Roma 1997, pp. 345-361.

[6] L. Cozza, P.L. Tucci, *Navalia*, *Archeologia Classica* 57, 2006, pp. 175-201.

[7] LIVERANI 1999, pp. 13-19; Id., entry *Vaticanus ager*, *LTUR Sub* V, 2008, pp. 235-236.

[8] For a discussion of the ancient sources see LIVERANI 1999, pp. 19-21; Id., entry *Vaticanum*, LTUR *Sub* V, 2008, pp. 233-234.

[9] *AE* 1945, 136; F. De Visscher, *A propos d'une inscription nouvellement découverte sous la basilique de Saint Pierre*, *L'Antiquité Classique* XV, 1946, pp. 117-126.

[10] Ps.-Acro, in Hor. *Epod.* 9.25. B.M. Peebles, *La «Meta Romuli» e una lettera di Michele Fermo*, *RendPontAcc* XII, 1936, pp. 21-63; G. Gatti, *Fasti Archeologici* IV, 1949, pp. 359-360, n. 3771; M. Demus-Quatember, *Est et alia Pyramis*, Rom 1974; P. Liverani, entry *Pyramis in Vaticano*, in LTUR *Sub* IV, pp. 275-276.

[11] Tac., *Hist.* 2.93.1.

[12] Mart. 1.18.1-2; 6.92.3; 10.45.5; 12.48.13-14.

[13] P. Liverani, entry *Pons Neronianus*, in LTUR IV, 1999, p. 111.

[14] Cfr. B. D'Overbeke, *Les restes de l'ancienne Rome* III, Amsterdam 1709, table before p. 11; G. Vasi, *Delle magnificenze di Roma antica e moderna* V, Roma 1754, p. XIX, table 87, n. 2.

[15] F. De Caprariis, entry *Pons Aelius*, in LTUR IV (1999), pp. 105-106.

[16] Cic., *ad Att.* 13.33.1: "*a ponte Mulvio Tiberim perduci secundum montes Vaticanos, campum Martium coaedificari, illum autem campum Vaticanum fieri quasi Martium campum.*" (transl. Loeb); cfr. 13.35.1.

[17] W. Eck, entry *Horti Scapulani*, in LTUR III, 1996, p. 83; E. Papi, entry *Horti: Otho*, *Ibid.*, p. 76.

[18] *Il giardino antico da Babilonia a Roma. Scienza, arte e natura* (cat. of the exhibition, Firenze 8.5-28.10.2007), Firenze 2007, pp. 86-88.

[19] G. Alföldy, *Der Obelisk auf dem Petersplatz in Rom*, *SBHeidelberg*, 1990, 2. Useful, but only for the modern position of the obelisk, C. D'Onofrio, *Gli obelischi di Roma*, Roma 1992 (III ed.), pp. 108-121; on the Circus: Liverani 1999, pp. 21-28; Id., entry *Gai et Neronis Circus*, in LTUR *Sub* III, 2005, pp. 11-12.

[20] P. Liverani, entry *Aelii Hadriani Sepulcrum*, in LTUR *Sub* I, 2001, pp. 15-19.

[21] The evidence for this is the inscription on a lead pipe (*CIL* XV 7508) which was found during the excavations for the foundation of the Palace of Justice containing the name of Passienus Crispus; P. Baccini Leotardi, entry *C. Crispi Passieni praedium*, in LTUR *Sub* II, 2004, pp. 169-170; *Carta* 2005, n. 177.

[22] An honorary inscription dedicated to her supports this interpretation (*CIL* VI 16983, cfr. 34105c). The inscription was identified by Achilles Statius in a vineyard behind the Castel Sant'Angelo at the end of the sixteenth century; *Carta* 2005, Appendix I, n. 4.

[23] I thank François Chausson for his suggestions and discussions on this topic.

[24] G. Di Vita-Évrard, *Des Calvisii Rusones à Licinius Sura*, 99, 1987, pp. 281-338; Ead., *Sur les charges africaines des frères Cn. Domitii Afri Titii Marcelli Curvii Lucanus et Tullus*, in A. Mastino (editor), *L'Africa Romana*, IV, Sassari 1987, pp. 509-529; Ead., *Le testament dit «de Dasumius»: testateur et bénéficiaires*, in C. Castillo (editor), *Epigrafía jurídica romana* (Actas del Coloquio internacional AIEGL, Pamplona 9-11.4.1987), Pampelune 1989, pp. 159-174; Ead., *La famille de l'empereur: pour de nouveaux 'Mémoires d'Hadrien'*, in J. Charles-Gaffiot, H. Lavagne (editors), *Hadrien. Trésors d'une villa impériale* (cat. of the exhibition, Paris 22.9-19.12.1999), Milano 1999, pp. 27-36; F. Chausson, in G. Bonamente, H. Brand editors), *Historiae Augustae Colloquium Bambergense*, Bari 2007, pp. 131-133.

[25] F. Chausson, *Devil dynastique et topographie urbaine dans la Rome antonine*, in N. Belayche (editors), *Rome, les Césars et la Ville aux deux premiers siècles de notre ère*, Rennes 2001, pp. 293-342 (specialmente 314-315; Liverani, in *Il giardino antico*, cit. *supra*, note 18, pp. 88-90; J.-C. Grenier, *L'Osiris ANTINOOS* (Cahiers de l'ENIM I), Montpellier 2008, p. 44 (available on-line: http://recherche.univ-montp3.fr/egyptologie/enim/index.php?page=cenim&n=1); more cautious: F. Chausson, *Annuaire – EPHE, SHP*, 139, 2006-2007, pp. 96-97 (available on-line: http://ashp.revues.org/index220.html).

[26] Grenier, *L'Osiris ANTINOOS*, cit. in the previous note. For the modern history only see D'Onofrio, *Gli obelischi*, cit. *supra*, note 19, pp. 304-305, 435-445.

[27] Cfr. J.-C. Grenier, MEFRA 98, 1986, pp. 222-225; Grenier, *L'Osiris ANTINOOS*, cit., pp. 8, 37-45.

[28] K. Lehmann Hartleben – J. Lindros, *Il Palazzo degli Horti Sallustiani*, *Acta Instituti Romani Regni Sueciae* 4, 1935, pp. 196-227; F. Castagnoli, *Gli Horti Sallustiani*, in Gaio Sallustio Crispo, *Opere* (ed. Mariotti), Roma 1972, pp. 383-396; G. Cipriani, *Horti Sallustiani*, Roma 1982 (II ed.); B. Ferrini – S. Festuccia, *Quirinale. Horti Sallustiani*, *BollArch* 28-30, 1994 (1999), pp. 85-108; P. Innocenti – M.C. Leotta, s.v. *Horti Sallustiani*, in LTUR III, 1996, pp. 79-81; E. Talamo, *Gli horti di Sallustio a Porta Collina*, in Cima – La Rocca 1998, pp. 113-169; P. Innocenti – M.C. Leotta, *Horti Sallustiani: le evidenze archeologiche e la topografia*, *BullCom* CV, 2004, pp. 149-196; Liverani, in *Il giardino antico*, cit. *supra*, note 18, pp. 91-92.

[29] G. Botti – P. Romanelli, *Le sculture del Museo Gregoriano Egizio*, Città del Vaticano 1951, nn. 28, 31-33; J.-C. Grenier, *Bollettino dei Monumenti, Musei e Gallerie Pontificie* IX.1, 1989, pp. 21-33; Talamo, *Gli Horti*, cit. *supra*, note 30, pp. 130, 142-143.

[30] M. de Vos, in P.C. Bol (editors), *Forschungen zur Villa Albani. Katalog der antiken Bildwerke* IV, Berlin 1994, pp. 462-465, n. 546, tavv. 274-275; P. Liverani, *Aegyptus* 79.1-2, 1999, p. 58.

[31] F. Poulsen, *Catalogue of Ancient Sculpture in the Ny Carlsberg Glyptotek*, Kjøbenhavn 1951, n. 187; J. Lund, in M. De Nuccio – L. Ungaro, *I Marmi colorati dell'antica Roma* (cat. of the exhibition, Rome 28.9.2002-19.1.2003), Venezia 2002, pp. 361-364, n. 65.

[32] D'Onofrio, *Gli obelischi*, cit. *supra*, note 19, pp. 355-368; J.-C. Grenier, s.v. *Obeliscus: horti Sallustiani*, in LTUR III, 1996, p. 358.

[33] Innocenti – Leotta, *Horti Sallustiani: le evidenze*, cit. *supra*, note 28, pp. 181-183.

[34] J.C. Grenier – F. Coarelli, *La tombe d'Antinoüs à Rome*, MEFRA 98, 1986, pp. 217-253.

[35] M. Royo, entry *Adonaea*, in LTUR I, 1993, pp. 14-16; F. Chausson, MEFRA 107, 1995, 706-718.

[36] For a vast bibliography on the *pomerium* question, see M. Andreussi's synthesis *Roma. Il Pomerio*, *Scienze dell'Antichità* 2, 1988, pp. 219-234; for the Imperial period, P. Liverani, Porta Triumphalis, arcus Domitiani, templum Fortunae Reducis, *arco di Portogallo*, *Atlante tematico di topografia antica* 14, 2005, pp. 53-65; Id., Templa duo nova Spei et Fortunae *in Campo Marzio*, *RendPontAcc* LXXIX, 2006-2007, pp. 291-314; differently, F. Coarelli, in *Divus Vespasianus. Il bimillenario dei Flavi* (cat. of the exhibition, Rome 27.3.2009-10.1.2010), Roma 2009, pp. 69-71, fig. 5 it considerably modifies, however, its previous reconstructions, including monuments that could hardly have been located inside the *pomerium*, such as the *Saepta* and the Iseo Campense.

[37] Explicitly attested by Eutropio 8.5.2: *Traianus (...) solus omnium intra urbem sepultus est* ("Only Trajan, among all, was buried inside the city."). Recently B. Gesemann, *Zum Standort der Traianssäule*, in *Jahrbuch des Römisch-Germanischen Zentralmuseums Mainz* 50, 2003, pp. 307-28 contested this source, but without strong arguments, cfr. P. Liverani, *RendPontAcc* LXXIX, 2006-2007, p. 291, note 2.

[38] C. Paterna, entry *Circus Varianus*, in LTUR V, 1999, pp. 237-238.

[39] Based on scarce evidence it has been attempted to identify this as the tomb of the *gens* Cornelia (M. Castelli, *Dedica onoraria di età tiberiana a due membri della famiglia degli Scipioni*, MEFRA 104, 1992, pp. 177-208; cfr. L. Chioffi, *BullCom* C, 1999, p. 52), that is, the cenotaph of Cornelius Gallus (M. Verzar-Bass, in M. Cima – E. La Rocca (editors), *Horti romani* (Atti del convegno internazionale, Roma 4-6 maggio 1995), *BullCom Suppl.* 6, 1998, pp. 422-424. Doubts regarding the first identification stem from the accidental nature of the discovery, which makes it impossible to exclude a re-use – very common for the marble in the Vatican area due to the construction of the Renaissance basilica.

[40] P. Liverani, entry *Terebintus – Tiburtinum Neronis (nelle fonti medioevali)*, in LTUR *Sub* V, 2008, pp. 137-138. The basic text on which all the others depend is that of the *Mirabilia* (§ 20: R. Valentini – G. Zucchetti, *Codice topografico della città di Roma* III, Roma 1946, pp. 45-46).

[41] Ps.-Marcellus, edition A, 63 (ed. Lipsius, p. 172); edition B, 84a (ed. Lipsius, p. 216); Latin version 63 (ed. Lipsius, p. 173).

[42] *Ordo* by Benedetto Canonico: processions *in vigilia Nativitatis Domini* (Valentini – Zucchetti III, cit., p. 212) and *in secunda feria* (*Ibid.*, p. 218). It should not be confused with the obelisk of the Circus of Caligula and Nero, which at the time carried the name *Agulia* or was interpreted as the tomb of Julius Caesar.

[43] For the theatre cfr. P. Liverani, *Due note di topografia vaticana: il* theatrum Neronis *e i toponimi legati alla tomba di S. Pietro*, *RendPontAcc* LXXIII, 2000-01, pp. 129-146; Id., entry *Neronis theatrum*, in LTUR *Sub* V, 2006, pp. 91-92.

[44] F. Magi, *Il Circo Vaticano in base alle sue più recenti scoperte, il suo obelisco e i suoi «carceres»*, *RendPontAcc* XLV, 1972-73, pp. 37-73.

[45] Regarding the problems F. Castagnoli, *Il Vaticano nell'età classica*, Città del Vaticano 1992, pp. 37-64, 153-154; LIVERANI 1999, pp. 21-28, 131 table 57; Id., entry *Gai et Neronis Circus*, in LTUR *Sub* III, 2005, pp. 11-12.

[46] LIVERANI 1999, table 76; for a different interpretation M. Cecchelli, *S. Stefano Maggiore cata galla patricia, poi degli Abissini: appunti per una revisione del monumento*, *BullCom* LXXXVIII, 1997, pp. 283-300.

[47] Tomb Θ: Liverani 1999, table 19.

[48] F. Castagnoli, *Il Circo di Nerone in Vaticano*, *RendPontAcc* XXXII, 1959-60, pp. 97-121 (reprinted in F. Castagnoli, *Topografia antica. Un metodo di studio* I, Roma, Roma 1993, pp. 549-571).

[49] P. Liverani, *La basilica di S. Pietro e l'orografia del colle Vaticano*, in R. Harraither – Ph. Pergola – R. Pilliger – A. Pülz (a cura di), *Frühes Christentum zwischen Rom und Konstantinopel* (Akten des XIV. internationalen Kongresses für Christliche Archäologie – Wien 19.-26. 9. 1999), Wien-Città del Vaticano 2006, pp. 501-508; J. Niebaum, *Die spätantiken Rotunden an Alt-St.-Peter in Rom*, *Marburger Jahrbuch für Kunstwissenschaft* 34, 2007, pp. 101-161.

[50] *CIL* XIII 1751.

[51] *CIL* XIII 7281.

[52] M.J. Vermaseren, *Cybele and Attis, the Myths and the Cult*, London 1977, pp. 45-51; LIVERANI 1999, pp. 28-32, 127-128, n. 51, 149, n. 72; Id., *Il Phrygianum Vaticano*, in B. Palma (editors), *Testimonianze di culti orientali tra scavo e collezionismo* (Atti del Convegno: Roma, 23-24 marzo 2006), Roma 2008, pp. 40-48.
[53] *Perist.*10.1006-50; R. Duthoy, *The Taurobolium. Its evolution and terminology*, Leiden 1969; Vermaseren, cit. in the previous footnote, pp. 101-107.
[54] N. McLynn, *The Fourth-Century «taurobolium»*, *Phoenix* 50.3-4, 1996, pp. 312-330.
[55] LIVERANI 1999, pp. 20-21.
[56] P. Liverani, *L'agro Vaticano*, in Ph. Pergola – R. Santangeli Valenzani – R. Volpe (editors), *Suburbium. Dalla crisi del sistema delle ville a Gregorio Magno* (Atti del convegno, École Française de Rome, 16-18 March 2000), Rome 2003, pp. 399-413.
[57] LIVERANI 1999, table 75; *ICUR* II 4251, 4248, 4241, 4229, 4244, 4252, 4253, 4243.
[58] F.W. Deichmann (editor), *Repertorium der christlich-antiken Sarkophage* I, Wiesbaden 1967, n. 52, 53.
[59] J.F. Dölger, *Römische Quartalschrift* XXIV, 1910, pp. 57ss. with ample bibliography; *ICUR* II, 4246; C. Wessel, *Inscriptiones grecae christianae veteres Occidentis*, Bari 1989, 390; G. Filippi, in *Le iscrizioni dei cristiani in Vaticano*, Città del Vaticano 1997, pp. 218-220, n. 3.2.2.
[6] C. Carletti, χθυσ ζωντων. *Chiose a ICUR II 4246*, *Vetera Christianorum* 36, 1999, pp. 15-30; for a more balance discussion D. Mazzoleni, in *Petros eni – Pietro è qui. 500 anni della Basilica di S. Pietro* (cat. of the exhibition, Città del Vaticano 11.10.2006-8.3.2007), Roma 2006, pp. 190-193, IV.8.
[61] *CIL* VI 41341=32004, *add.* p. 3814 = *ICUR* 4164; *AE* 1953, 239; Deichmann, *Repertorium*, cit. *supra*, note 58, pp. 279-283, n. 680, table. 104-105; B.M. Apolloni Ghetti – A. Ferrua – E. Josi – E. Kirschbaum, *Esplorazioni sotto la confessione di San Pietro in Vaticano*, Città del Vaticano 1951, pp. 220ss.; E. Josi, *RendPontAcc* XX, 1943-44, p. 9; G. Daltrop, *Anpassung eines Reliefragmentes an den Deckel des Iunius Bassus Sarkophags*, *RendPontAcc* LI-LII, 1978-80, pp. 157-170; E. Struthers Malbon, *The Iconography of the Sarcophagus of Junius Bassus*, Princeton 1990.
[62] LIVERANI 1999, table n. 68.
[63] LIVERANI 1999, table n. 60; M.J. Johnson, *On the Burial Places of the Theodosian Dynasty*, *Byzantion* 61, 1991, 334-339; F. Paolucci, *La tomba dell'imperatrice Maria e altre sepolture di rango di età tardoantica a S. Pietro*, *Temporis Signa* 3, 2008, pp. 225-252.

CHAPTER TWO

[1] R.F. Jones, *Cremation and Inhumation-Change in the Third Century*, in *The Roman West and the Third Century*, *British Archaeological Reports* 109, Oxford 1981, pp. 15-19; Koch, Sichtermann 1982, 27-30; *Incinérations et inhumations dans l'Occident romain aux trois premiers siècles de notre ère* (Colloque international Tolouse-Montréjeau 7-10 octobre 1987), *Archeologia Paris* 231, 1988.
[2] In percentages, 87% would be cremations and13% inhumations.
[3] There were spaces provided for approximately 52 cremations and 17 inhumations.
[4] Approximately 10 cremations and 20 inhumations have been preserved.
[5] In tomb 6 there were 8 *ollae* for cremations, 5 *formae* and an *arcosolium* for inhumations, reaching a total of 21 burials. In percentages, 28% versus 72%; in tomb 7 4 cinerary urns were found, 3 *formae* and 2 *arcosolia* , inside which two coffins were located with a total of 14 inhumations (29% versus 71%).
[6] It should be noted, however, that the western wall is not preserved high enough to exclude the presence of niches for cremations. In addition, only a small stretch of the back wall remains and of the walls near the entrance and on the east side little more than the outline is left.
[7] Cfr. *infra* pp. 124-126.
[8] Cfr. the synthesis of PELLEGRINO 1999.
[9] J. Scheid, *Quand faire, c'est croire. Les rites sacrificiels des Romains*, Aubier 2005, pp. 161-209.
[10] Cicero, *De Legibus* 2.55, 57; Fest., (ed. Lindsay 1913) p. 296, r. 37 *porca (...) Cereri immolatur.*
[11] Virgil, *Aeneis* III, vv. 67, poetically talks about 'blood' at the funeral of Anchises.
[12] Tibullus, I, 3, 5; III, 2, 9.
[13] N. Belayche, *La neuvaine funéraire à Rome, ou «la mort impossible»*, in L. Deschamps, in F. Hinard (ed.), *La mort au quotidien dans le monde romain* (Actes du colloque, Paris 7-9 octobre 1993), Paris 1995, pp. 155-169.
[14] Varro, fragm. 105 (ed. Riposati 1939; 1972^2); Nonius Marcellus 549M defined the *ricinum*: "*quod nunc mafurtium dicitur palliolum femineum breve*". Cfr. L. Deschamps, in F. Hinard (ed.), *La mort au quotidien dans le monde romain* (Actes du colloque, Paris 7-9 octobre 1993), Paris 1995, pp. 171-174.
[15] Virgil, *Aeneis* V vv. 42-105.
[16] Ovid, *Fasti* II, vv. 533-638.
[17] J. D'Arms, *Journal of Roman Studies* 90, 2000, pp. 135-141.
[18] Cfr. the regulations preserved in *CIL* VI 10248: *Quodannis die natalis sui et / rosationis et violae et parentalib(us) / memoriam sui sacrifici(i)s quater in an/num factis celebrent* ("every year on his birthday, during the festivals of the roses and the violets, and the *parentalia* his memory should be celebrated by making sacrifices four times a year.").
[19] "*In triclin(i)o quod est super sepulchrum.*"
[20] C. Pietri, Roma Christiana. Recherches sur l'Eglise de Rome, son organisation, sa politique, son idéologie de Miltiades à Sixte II (311-440), I, Paris 1976, pp. 381-389; R. Raccanelli, Cara Cognatio: la tradizione di una festa tra propinqui, Quaderni urbinati di cultura classica n.s. 53, 1996, pp. 27-57.
[21] I. Bragantini, in ANGELUCCI *ET ALII* 1990, pp. 62-70.
[22] In the necropolis under St Peter's basilica: tombs O, T, U; in the Galea necropolis: tombs 2 and 11; in the Santa Rosa necropolis, *columbaria* II, XVI e XXXV.
[23] Cfr. *supra* note 18.
[24] Cfr. *infra* p. 240. See also the cinerary altar no. 4 of *Marcus Oppius Receptus* in the Autoparco Necropolis.
[25] PELLEGRINO 1999, pp. 18-19.
[26] G. Sena Chiesa, *Angera romana. Scavi nella necropoli 1970-1979*, Roma 1985, II, pp. 487-518.
[27] G. Parmeggiani, *Voghenza, necropoli. Analisi di alcuni aspetti del rituale funerario*, in *Voghenza. Una necropoli di età romana nel territorio ferrarese*, Ferrara 1985 (II ed.), pp. 203-219.
[28] *CIL* II 2102: "*Rogamus ut.. lucerna quotidiana (...) poni*".
[29] *CIL* VI 30102: it should be noted, however, that it concerns an inscription in verse, in which the literary aspect may be predominant.
[30] *CIL* VI 10248: "*Omnib(us) K(alendis) / Nonis Idibus suis quibusq(ue) mensib(us) lucerna / lucens sibi ponatur incenso inposito*".
[31] It concerned the first, fifth and eleventh day of the month, or the first, seventh and thirteenth in March, May, July and October.
[32] *Digestae* XL.4.44.
[33] Cfr. *infra* p. 187.
[34] Cfr. *infra* p. 173.
[35] Cfr. *infra* p. 101.
[36] Cfr. *infra* p. 225.
[37] Cfr. *infra* p. 173.
[38] Cfr. *infra* p. 103.
[39] H. Wrede, *Consecratio in formam deorum*, Mainz 1981; P. Zanker, *Un'arte per l'impero. Funzione e intenzione delle immagini nel mondo romano*, Milano 2002; P. Liverani, *Tradurre in immagini*, in F. e T. Hölscher (eds), *Römische Bilderwelten. Von der Wirklichkeit zum Bild und zurück* (Kolloquium der Gerda Henkel Stiftung am Deutschen Archäologischen Institut Rom 15.-17. März 2004), Heidelberg 2007, pp. 13-26.
[40] Cfr. *infra* p. 103.
[41] Cfr. infra p. 265.
[42] H.A. Marrou, *Les portraits inachevés des sarcophages romains*, *Revue archéologique* s. VI, XIV, luglio-sett.1939, pp. 200-202; G. Bovini, *I sarcofagi paleocristiani. Determinazione della loro cronologia mediante l'analisi dei ritratti*, Città del Vaticano1949, pp. 78-79; J. Engemann, *Untersuchungen zur Sepulkralsymbolik der späteren römischen Kaiserzeit*, *Jahrbuch für Antike und Christentum. Ergänzungsbände* 2, 1973, pp. 76-78; Koch, Sichtermann 1982, pp. 610-614; B. Andreae, *Bossierte Porträts auf römischen Sarkophagen*, *Wissenschaftliche Zeitschrift der Humboldt-Universität zu Berlin. Gesellschafts- und sprachwissenschaftliche Reihe* 31, 1982, pp. 137-138; Id., *Bossierte Porträts auf römischen Sarkophagen. Ein ungelöstes Problem*, *Marburger Winckelmannsprogramm* 1984, pp. 109-128; J. Deckers, *Vom Denker zum Diener. Bemerkungen zu den Folgen der konstantinischen Wende im Spiegel der Sarkophagplastik*, in B. Brenk (ed.), *Innovation in der Spätantike* (Kolloquium Basel 6. und 7. Mai 1994), Wiesbaden 1996, pp. 137ss., especially 143 with note 15; J. Huskinson, *Unfinished portrait heads on later Roman sarcophagi. Some new perspectives*, *Papers of the British School at Rome* 66, 1998, pp. 129-158.
[43] DEICHMANN 1967, p. 39, n. 43. For the Christian production in the Constantinian period see the observations of G. Koch, *Produktion auf Vorrat oder Anfertigung auf besonderen Auftrag? Überlegungen zu stadtrömischen frühchristlichen Sarkophagen der vorkonstantinischen und konstantinischen Zeit*, in *Antike Porträts. Zum Gedächtnis von Helga von Heintze*, Möhnesee 1999, pp. 303-316.
[44] S. Walker, *The Sarcophagus of Maconiana Severiana*, *Roman Funerary Monuments in the J. Paul Getty Museum* (*Occasional Papers on Antiquities*, 6), Malibu 1990, pp. 83-94.
[45] Matthew 22.20-21: "Τίνος ἡ εἰκὼν αὕτη καὶ ἡ ἐπιγραφὴ"; (in the Vulgate *imago et suprascriptio*).
[46] Paulinus of Nola, Letter XXXII, 2-3.
[47] Paulinus of Nola, Letter XXX.
[48] Paulinus of Nola, Letter XXXII, 3 *Martinum veneranda viri testatur imago / altera Paulinum forma refert humilem*.
[49] H. Belting, *Il culto delle immagini. Storia dell'icona dall'età imperiale al tardo Medioevo*, Roma 2001, p. 122 seems to misunderstand the significance of the passage when it interprets the opposition *homo coelestis / terrestris* of Paulinus as a neoplatonic relfection, rather than as an echo of Saint Paul, *I Lettera ai Corinzi*, 15.49.
[50] B. Andreae, in *Opus Nobile. Festschrift zum 60. Geburtstag von Ulf Jantzen*, Wiesbaden 1969, p. 6.
[51] DEICHMANN 1967, p. 72, n. 87, table 28 (from the cemetery of Pretestato); the inscription also only mentioned the name of the name, leaving out the identity of the woman: *ICUR* V, 13901, "*Depos(itus) <F>l(avius) Faustinus iii idus aug(stas) Const/an<t>io Aug(usto) G <et> C<o>nstantio ii con/ss(ulibus) in pace*".
[52] DEICHMANN 1967, pp. 319-320, n. 772, tav. 12.2; first third of the fourth century AD.
[53] *CIL* VI 3558: "*L Pullio Peregrino C(enturioni) legion(is) / deputato qui vix(it) ann(is) xxviiii / mens(ibus) iii die(bus) i hor(is) i S(emis) / eq(uiti) rom(ani)*". M. Wegner, *Die Musensarkophage* (Die antiken Sarkophagreliefs V, 3), Berlin 1966, p. 133, table 60; K. Fittschen, *Gnomon* 44, 1972, p. 493; Koch, Sichtermann 1982, pp. 200, 204, fig. 264; G. Koch, *Sarkophage der römischen Kaiserzeit*, Darmstadt 1993, fig. 50.
[54] Cfr. *infra* p. 217.
[55] For Italy, cfr. PELLEGRINO 1999, pp. 20-21; Id., in HEINZELMANN, ORTALLI, WITTERER 2001, p. 125; F. Ceci. *L'interpretazione di monete e chiodi in contesti funerari: esempi dal suburbio romano*, *Ibid.*, pp. 87-97; J. Ortalli, *Ibid.*, pp. 236-237; L. Passi Pitcher (ed.), Sub ascia. *Una necropoli romana a Nave*, Modena 1987, p. 25; F. Taglietti, in ANGELUCCI ET ALII 1990, pp. 74-75; cfr. also J. Prieur, *La mort dans l'antiquité romaine*, Paris 1986, pp. 29-35.
[56] For the Roman world cfr. Sinn 1978, p. 95, nn. 17 e 18; in Spain P. Rodriguez Oliva, *Talleres locales de urnas cinerarias de sarcofagos en la Provincia Hispania Ulterior Baetica*, in D. Vaquerizo (ed.), *Espacio y usos funerarios en el Occidente Romano* I, Córdoba 2002, pp. 259-285.
[57] M. Harari, in G. Sena Chiesa (ed.), *Angera romana. Scavi nella necropoli 1970-1979*, Roma 1985, I, p. 34; C. Morselli, in ANGELUCCI ET ALII 1990, pp. 55, 57; F. Taglietti, *Ibid.*, p. 85.
[58] SINN 1978, pp. 62-63, 175, nn. 341-344.
[59] M. Buora, *Urne e pseudourne a cista aquileiesi*, *Aquileia Nostra* 53, 1982, pp. 189-216; L. Bertacchi, *Urna cineraria di recente rinvenimento*, *Aquileia Nostra* 53, 1982, pp. 217-228. Già G. Brusin, *Aquileia, guida storica e artistica*, Udine 1929, p. 57 hypothesized that such examples presupposed real wicker baskets.
[60] B. Päffgen, *Die Ausgrabungen in St. Severin zu Köln*, Mainz a. Rh. 1992, *Kölner Forschungen* 5, I, pp. 36, 45, 72 and note 8; p. 112; G.R. Burleigh, *Some aspects of burial types in the cemeteries of the Romano-British set-*

tlement at Baldock Herfordshire, Engl., in M. Struck (ed.), *Römerzeitliche Gräber als Quellen zu Religion, Bevölkerungsstruktur und Sozialgeschichte*, *Archäologische Schriften / Universität Mainz* 3, 1993, p. 43; M. Feugère, *L'évolution du mobilier non céramique dans les sépultures antiques de Gaule méridionale*, *Ibid.*, p. 126.
[61] Cfr. also Päffgen, cit. in the previous note, II, pp. 29, 79.

CHAPTER THREE

[1] A.A. De Marco, *The Tomb of St. Peter. A Representative and Annotated Bibliography of the Excavations*, Leiden 1964.
[2] Cfr. previous chapter, *supra* p. 18.
[3] F. Magi, *Un nuovo mausoleo presso il Circo Neroniano e altri minori scoperte*, *Rivista di Archeologia Cristiana* 42, 1966, pp. 207-226; Liverani 1999, pp. 111-113, figure 39.
[4] *CIL* VI 14897, *add.* p. 3516; LIVERANI 1999, p. 110, figure 38.
[5] Cfr. previous chapter, *supra* p. 13.
[6] Cfr. previous chapter, *supra* p. 18.
[7] Liverani 1999, p. 41.
[8] Tacitus, *Annales* 15.44.4-5: "Accordingly, an arrest was first made of all who pleaded guilty; then, upon their information, an immense multitude was convicted, not so much of the crime of firing the city, as of hatred against mankind. Mockery of every sort was added to their deaths. Covered with the skins of beasts, they were torn by dogs and perished, or were nailed to crosses, or were doomed to the flames and burnt, to serve as a nightly illumination, when daylight had expired. Nero offered his gardens for the spectacle, and was exhibiting a show in the circus, while he mingled with the people in the dress of a charioteer or stood aloft on a car. Hence, even for criminals who deserved extreme and exemplary punishment, there arose a feeling of compassion; for it was not, as it seemed, for the public good, but to satisfy one man's cruelty, that they were being destroyed."
[9] The crucifixion was already outlined in the Gospel of John 21, 18-19 when Christ predicts to Peter: "when you were young, you girded yourself and walked where you wanted; but when you are old, you will stretch out your hands, and another will gird you and carry you where you do not wish to go. This he said to show by what death he was to glorify God." Tertullian, Scorpiace 15,3 interpreted the fragment as such: that the allusion to the type of death he underwent is clearly indicated in the Gospel and the extension of the hands in this passage must allude to his position at the cross. The death of Peter during the Neronian persecution is also testified by the First Letter of Clemens 5,3-6,2 where at the martyrdom of Peter and Paul is "there is to be added a great multitude of the elect, who, having through envy endured many indignities and tortures, furnished us with a most excellent example", an expression that becomes more understandable if one bears in mind that Clemens wrote in Rome around AD 96. For a complete analysis of the texts that allude to the death of Peter in Rome, see recently R. Pesch, Simon Pietro. Storia e importanza storica del primo discepolo di Gesù Cristo, Brescia 2008, pp. 195-229 (original ed.: Simon-Petrus. Geschichte und geschichtliche Bedeutung des ersten Jüngers Jesu Christi, Stuttgart 1980); J. Gnilka, Pietro e Roma. La figura di Pietro nei primi due secoli, Brescia 2003, pp. 103-130 with bibliography (original ed.: Petrus und Rom. Das Petrusbild in den ersten zwei Jahrhunderten, Freiburg i.B. 2002).
[10] *De viri illustribus* V.
[11] *Historia Ecclesiastica* 2.25.7: "I am able to show you the tombs of the apostles; for if you go to the Vatican or along the Via Ostiense, you will find the tombs of those who founded this church."
[12] *Esplorazioni* 1951, pp. 107-131; Prandi 1963, pp. 380-447.
[13] Five examples of brick stamp *CIL* XV 401, datable to AD 146-161, were found on *bipedales* of a drain cover below the street: *Esplorazioni* 1951, pp. 102-104; Prandi 1963, p. 361.
[14] *CIL* XVI 1237: Prandi 1963, pp. 428-431 (tomb 8).
[15] *CIL* XV 1120a: Prandi 1963, pp. 348-353 (tomb 3), fig. 60 (with a print error in the legend).
[16] M. Guarducci, *I graffiti sotto la confessione di S. Pietro in Vaticano*, Città del Vaticano 1958; Guarducci 1959; Ead., *La tomba di S. Pietro*, Roma 1989.
[17] The easiest integration is: Πέτρ[ος]/ἔνι "Peter (rests) in peace" as has been suggested by J. Carcopino, *Étude d'histoire chrétienne: le christianisme secret du carré magique: les fouilles de Saint-Pierre et la tradition*, Paris 1953, p. 300, and A. Ferrua, *La Tomba di San Pietro*, in: *La Civiltà Cattolica* 141, issue 3353, 1990, p. 465, note 7 (reprinted in *Scritti vari di epigrafia e antichità cristiana*, Bari 1991, p. 357, n. 7). Cfr. also D. Mazzoleni, in Petros eni – *Pietro è qui. 500 anni della Basilica di S. Pietro* (cat. of the exhibition, Città del Vaticano 11.10.2006-8.3.2007), Roma 2006, pp. 236, table VI.6.
[18] P. Silvan, *From the Tomb to the Dome. The Architectural Evolution of the «Memorial» to the Apostle Peter*, in *Vatican Treasures. 2000 Years of Art and Culture in the Vatican and Italy* (cat. of the exhibition, Denver 1993), Milano 1993, pp. 27-31; Id., *Le radici della chiesa romana. L'evoluzione della Memoria Petrina*, in G. Rocchi Coopmans de Yoldi (ed.), *San Pietro. Arte e Storia nella Basilica Vaticana*, Bergamo 1996, pp. 17-29.
[19] G. Filippi, *La tomba di S. Paolo e le fasi della Basilica tra il* IV *e il* VII *secolo. Primi risultati di indagini archeologiche e ricerche d'archivio*, *Bollettino dei Monumenti, Musei e Gallerie Pontificie* 24, 2004, pp. 187-224; H. Brandenburg, *Die Architektur der Basilika San Paolo fuori le mura. Das Apostelgrab als Zentrum der Liturgie und des Märtyrerkultes*, *Mitteilungen des Deutschen Archäologischen Instituts, Römische Abteilung* 112, 2005-2006, pp. 237-275; G. Filippi, *Die Ergebnisse der neuen Ausgrabungen am Grab des Apostels Paulus. Reliquienkult und Eucharistie im Presbyterium der Paulsbasilika*, *Ibid.*, pp. 277-292; Id., *La tomba di San Paolo alla luce delle recenti scoperte*, in G. Azzopardi (ed.), *Il culto di San Paolo nelle chiese cristiane e nella tradizione maltese*, Acts of Int. symposium. Malta 26-27.6.2006, s.l. 2006, pp. 3-12, tables on pp. 99-106; Id., *Recenti ricerche nella Basilica di San Paolo fuori le mura*, in M. De Matteis – A. Trinchese (eds), *Il complesso basilicale di Cimitile. Patrimonio culturale dell'umanità? Der basilikale Komplex in Cimitile. Ein Weltkulturerbe?*, Oberhausen 2007, pp. 123-137; Id., *Nuovi documenti sui lavori del 1838 nella vecchia confessione*, *BMusPont* 25, 2006, pp. 87-95; Id., *La tomba di San Paolo. I dati archeologici del 2006 e il taccuino Moreschi del 1850*, *BMusPont* 26, 2007-2008, pp. 321-352; H. Brandenburg, *La basilica teodosiana di S. Paolo fuori le mura: articolazione, decorazione, funzione*, in U. Utro (ed.), *San Paolo in Vaticano. La figura e la parola dell'Apostolo delle Genti nelle raccolte pontificie* (cat. of the exhibition, Città del Vaticano 26.6-27.9.2009), Todi 2009, pp. 13-27; G. Filippi, *Un decennio di ricerche e studi nella basilica ostiense*, *Ibid.*, pp. 29-43.
[20] Announcement by Pope Benedict XVI on 29 June 2009; cfr. G. De Rosa S.J., *Il sarcofago di S. Paolo e la sua più antica immagine*, in *La Civiltà Cattolica*, 160, n. 3822, pp. 522-525. The remains have been dated to the first-second century AD through radio-carbon dating.
[21] *Esplorazioni* 1951; J. Ruysschaert, *Réflexions sur le fouilles vaticanes, le rapport officiel e la critique. Données archéologiques*, *Revue d'histoire ecclésiastique*, XLVIII, 1953, pp. 573-631; Id., *Réflexions sur le fouilles vaticanes, le rapport officiel e la critique. Données épigraphiques et littéraires*, *Revue d'histoire ecclésiastique*, XLIX, 1954, pp. 5-58; Guarducci 1953; Toynbee – Ward Perkins 1956; T. Klauser, *Die römische Petrustradition im Lichte der neuen Ausgrabungen unter der Peterskirche*, Köln-Opladen 1956; E. Kirschbaum, *Die Gräber der Apostelfürsten*, Frankfurt a.M. 1957 (III ed. 1974); J. Ruysschaert, *Recherches et études autour de la confession de la basilique vaticane 1940-1958. État de la question et bibliographie*, in *Triplice omaggio a Pio XII*, II, Città del Vaticano 1958, pp. 3-47; Guarducci, *I graffiti*, cit. *supra*, note 16; Guarducci 1959; Prandi 1963; J. Ruysschaert, *La tomba di Pietro. Considerazioni archeologiche e storiche*, *Studi Romani* 15, 1967, pp. 268-276; D. O'Connor, *Peter in Rome. The Literary, Liturgical and Archaeological Evidence*, New York-London 1969; J. Ruysschaert, *La tomba di Pietro. Nuove considerazioni archeologiche e storiche*, *Studi Romani* 24, 1976, pp. 322-330; M. Guarducci, *La tomba di S. Pietro*, Roma 1989; A. Ferrua, *La tomba di S. Pietro*, in *Scritti vari di epigrafia e antichità cristiane*, Bari 1991, pp. 352-359; L. Reekmans, *Bemerkungen zum Petrusgrab unter der Konstantinischen Basilika am Vatikan*, *Boreas* 20, 1997, pp. 49-82; Thümmel 1999. It is interesting and important to note that the different opinions of the scholars are not related to their religious backgrounds.
[22] The most recent monograph dedicated to this topic (Thümmel 1999) compiles a very detailed examination of the excavation report (*Esplorazioni* 1951; Prandi 1963) and comes up with differences between the drawings, photographic documentation and the field notes of Courtyard P and the "Trophy of Gaius", inferring its unreliability and considering them as a posterior compilation. Although the execution of the excavations has not always been completely clear and consistent, these observations have to be verified by means of an outmost punctual examination of the conserved remains, something which the author considers a priori impossible. Moreover, the author could not accomplish this in person for at the time of his research he did not have the opportunity to leave the former German Democratic Republic. Thümmel proposes a completely hypothetical reconstruction, therefore not better founded than the one he opposes, which does not exclude the possibility of the apostle being buried in this area even if not right underneath the "trophy of Gaius". Others have proposed that the "trophy" would have marked the location of the Martyr and not the burial (Cullmann 1965, pp. 207, 212-213), but these hypotheses seem hard to defend.
[23] The cult of the two apostles *ad catacumbas* is attested by the *Depositio Martyrum*, *Monumenta Germaniae Historica, Auctores Antiquissimi* IX.1 (1892), p. 71, lines 14-16: *Mense Iunio: III Kal. Jul. Petri in catacumbas et Pauli Ostense, Tusco et Basso cons.*, or "the 29th of June: [the festival] of Peter at the Catacombs and of Paul at the Via Ostiense. Under the consulate of Tuscus and Bassus (AD 258)." One has to observe that the *Depositio Martyrum* is generally dated to AD 336 (L. Duchesne, *Le Liber Pontificalis. Texte, introduction et commentaire*, I, Rome 1886, pp. VI-VII; H. Stern, *Le calendrier de 354*, Paris 1961, p. 44) because it is considered complementary to the *Depositio episcoporum*, together with which it was diffused in the miscellany of texts that constitute the Codex-Calendar of AD 354 and that can be dated to this period. Altogether the *Depositio Martyrum* taken on its own has no elements that would obstruct an earlier dating, for example the first quarter of the IVth century: cfr. R. Krautheimer, in *Römisches Jahrbuch für Kunstgeschichte* 25, 1989, pp. 18-20.
[24] P. Styger, *Gli Apostoli Pietro e Paolo in Catacumbas*, *Römische Quartalschrift* 29, 1915, pp. 149-205; A. Prandi, *La Memoria Apostolorum in Catacumbas*, Città del Vaticano 1936; A. Ferrua, *Rileggendo i graffiti di S. Sebastiano*, *La Civiltà Cattolica* 116.3, 1965, pp. 428-437: 116.4, pp. 134-141 (reprinted in *Scritti vari di epigrafia e antichità cristiane*, Bari 1990, pp. 297-314); M. Guarducci, *Pietro e Paolo sulla via Appia e la tomba di Pietro in Vaticano*, Città del Vaticano 1983; A. Ferrua, *La Basilica e la catacomba di San Sebastiano*, Città del Vaticano 1990; Thümmel 1999, pp. 73-95. Two more elements can be added: an inscription (*ICUR* V 13273) of Pope Damasus (AD 336-384) claiming that in earlier times Peter and Paul would have "dwelled" near the sanctuary on the Via Appia; this claim has been interpreted as a figurative allusion of their temporary burial. Furthermore, following a late tradition, attested in the VI century by the apocryphal writings of "pseudo-Marcellus" 66 (ed. Lipsius, pp. 174-176), for a short while the bodies of the apostles would have been buried here. The hypothesis of a translation was favoured after H. Lietzmann (*Petrus und Paulus in Rom: liturgische und archäologische Studien*, Bonn 1915), but more recently is generally abandoned, due to the fact that the excavations of the area – finally completed – have not identified any structure that could be interpreted as a tomb and therefore one has to consider only the transfer of the cult due to the persecutions of Valerian. See also the considerations at the end of this chapter.
[25] Reekmans, *Bemerkungen zum Petrusgrab*, cit. *supra*, note 21.
[26] S. Heid, *The Romaness of Roman Christianity*, in J. Rüpke, *A Companion of Roman Religion*, Oxford

2007, pp. 406-426, in specific pp. 410-411. I would like to thank the author for kindly keeping me up to date with new developments of his research and of his still unpublished work.

[27] Ignatius of Antioch, *Letter to the Romans*.

[28] Cfr. as already marked by Cullmann 1965, p. 190.

[29] Cullmann 1965, pp. 91-213; Pesch, *Simon Pietro*, cit. *supra*, note 9; Gnilka, Pietro e Roma, cit. supra, note 9. The exception consists in the radical and prejudgementally negative position on the subject that is taken by O. Zwierlein, *Petrus in Rom. Die literarischen Zeugnisse* (Untersuchungen zur antiken Literatur und Geschichte 96), Berlin – New York 2009, this is not the place to discuss this view since it would request a thorough section of its own. In so far as it may concern, one should observe that the author in question dedicates little or no more than three pages (of 476 in total) to the archaeological excavations without referring once to the original site publications and only using secondary literature, solely in German and of no more recent date than the fifties of the last century.

[30] H. von Hesberg – S. Panciera, *Das Mausoleum des Augustus. Der Bau und seine Inschriften*, Bayerische Akademie der Wissenschaften. Philosophisch-Historische Klasse. Abhandlungen. Neue Folge, 108, München, 1994; H. von Hesberg, *Mausoleum Augusti: das Monument*, in *LTUR* III, 1996, pp. 234-237.

[31] P. Liverani, *Aelii Hadriani Sepulcrum*, in *LTUR* I, 2001, pp. 15-19.

[32] Liverani 1999, pp. 142-143, note 2.

[33] Liverani 1999, pp. 139-140.

[34] *Esplorazioni* 1951, pp. 221-222; *CIL* VI 32004=41341, *add.* p. 3814; F.W. Deichmann (ed), *Repertorium der christlich-antiken Sarkophage* I, Wiesbaden 1967, pp. 279-283, n. 680, tavv. 104-105. Other fragments of the lid were found in 1940-43 and were recognized by the editors of *Esplorazioni* 1951 (pp. 220ss.; E. Josi, *Sul coperchio del sarcofago di Giunio Basso, Rendiconti della Pontificia Accademia Romana di Archeologia* XX, 1943-44, p. 9) and by G. Daltrop (*Anpassung eines Relieffragmentes an den Deckel des Iunius Bassus Sarkophags, Rendiconti della Pontificia Accademia Romana di Archeologia* LI-LII, 1978-80, pp. 157-170); E. Struthers Malbon, *The Iconography of the Sarcophagus of Junius Bassus*, Princeton 1990; J. Dresken-Weiland, *Sarkophagbestattungen des 4.-6. Jahrhunderts im Westen des römischen Reiches*, *Römische Quartalschrift*, 55. Supplementband, 2003, p. 372, Kat. E 5. Nowadays, the sarcophagus is exhibited at the entrance to the necropolis of the Vatican Grottoes, while other pieces can be found in the Pio-Clemente Museum in the Vatican Museums and the Museum of Roman Civilization.

[35] A.H.M. Jones – J.R. Martindale – J. Morris, *The prosopography of the later Roman Empire*, 1, *A.D. 260-395*, Cambridge 1971, p. 155 *Iunius Bassus signo Theotecnius* 15.

[36] B. Nobiloni, *Le colonne vitinee della basilica di S. Pietro a Roma*, *Xenia antiqua* 6, 1997, pp. 81-142.

[37] P. Liverani, *Costantino offre il modello della basilica sull'arco trionfale*, in M. Andaloro (ed.), *La pittura medievale a Roma. 312-1431. L'Orizzonte tardoantico e le nuove immagini, 312-468. Corpus I*, Milano 2006, pp. 90-91, n. 2b; F.R. Moretti, *La traditio legis nell'abside*, *Ibid.*, pp. 87-90; P. Liverani, *Saint Peter's, Leo the Great and the leprosy of Constantine*, *Papers of the British School at Rome* LXXVI, 2008, pp. 155-172.

[38] T.F. Mathews, *The Clash of Gods. A Reinterpretation of Early Christian Art*, Princeton 1993, pp. 12-22; J.-M. Spieser, *The Representation of Christ in the Apses of Early Christian Churches*, *Gesta* 37.1, 1998, pp. 63-73 (especially p. 66).

[39] Mielsch – von Hesberg 1986, pp. 9-10, tav. 1.

[40] Eck 1996, p. 257.

[41] Mielsch – von Hesberg 1996, p. 275.

[42] Toynbee – Ward Perkins, pp. 37-44; Mielsch – von Hesberg 1986, pp. 11-38, tables 1b-4; Feraudi-Gruénais 2001b, pp. 46-48, K 13.

[43] Papi 2000-2001, pp. 250-252, n. 5.

[44] Mielsch – von Hesberg 1996, pp. 259-274, tables 33-35; Feraudi-Gruénais 2001b, p. 62, K 25.

[45] P. Liverani, in A. Donati (ed.), *Romana Pictura. La pittura romana dalle origini all'età bizantina* (catalogue of the exhibition, Rimini 28.3-30.8.1998; Genova 16.10.1998-10.1.1999), Milano 1998, p. 289, n. 60, fig. 60.

[46] R. Santolini Giordani, *Ibid.*, p. 290, n. 63, fig. 63; Feraudi-Gruénais 2001b, pp. 63-65, K 26.

[47] M. De Vos, in *Gli Orti farnesiani sul Palatino* (Conv. Int., Roma 28-30 November 1985), Roma 1990 (Roma antica, 2), pp. 173-176, fig. 9; S. Miranda, *Francesco Bianchini e lo scavo farnesiano del Palatino (1720-1729)*, Milano 2000, pp. 225-226, n. 18.4; figg. 96, 110.

[48] H. Mielsch, *Römische Wandmalerei*, Darmstadt 2001, p. 159 fig. 186.

[49] Mielsch – von Hesberg 1986, pp. 39-59, tavv. 5-6a; Feraudi-Gruénais 2001b, p. 48, K 14.

[50] *AE* 1987, 154.

[51] Feraudi-Gruénais 2001b, p. 48, note 272, n. 2.

[52] *D(is) M(anibus) / Tullia Secunda / filia hic sita / est / Passulenae Secu/ndinae mater / cessit*, Feraudi-Gruénais 2001b, p. 48, nota 272, n. 1.

[53] *AE* 1987, 148; Eck 1996, p. 253.

[54] See, for example, the inscription of Quintus Marcius Hermes on his sarcophagus in tomb Φ. One might suggest that the inscription could have been integrated with a painted element, specifying the conditions of those living.

[55] Mielsch – von Hesberg 1986, pp. 61-66, tables 6b-7.

[56] *CIL* XV 192.

[57] Mielsch – von Hesberg 1996, pp. 235-255; Feraudi-Gruénais 2001b, pp. 59-62, K 24.

[58] H.P. L'Orange, *Likeness and Icon. Selected Studies in Classical and Early Mediaeval Art*, Odense 1973, 178-180; Toynbee – Ward Perkins, pp. 71-72; K. Werner, *Mosaiken aus Rom. Polychrome Mosaikpavimente und Emblemata aus Rom und Umgebung*, (diss.) Würzburg 1994, pp. 172-173 K 73.

[59] A. Ahlqvist, *Cristo e l'imperatore romano. I valori simbolici del nimbo*, *Acta ad archaeologiam et artium historiam pertinentia* 15, 2001, pp. 207-227.

[60] *AE* 1987, 160; F. Matz, *Die antiken Sarkophagreliefs* 4. *Die dionysischen Sarkophage*, IV.4, Berlin 1975, p. 479, n. 306, tables. 320-321, 323: reign of Alexander Severus (222-235).

[61] M.C. Parra, in *Mélanges de l'École française de Rome. Antiquité* 90, 1978, pp. 822-825.

[62] Mielsch – von Hesberg 1996, pp. 71-91; Feraudi-Gruénais 2001b, p. 49, K 15.

[63] *AE* 1945, 134; Eck 1996, p. 233; Feraudi-Gruénais 2001a, p. 205, K 15, fig. 2.

[64] On parrots in funerary contexts see. J.S. Østergaard, *Avium Gloria – parakitter på et byromersk askealter*, in M.S. Christensen (ed), *Hvad tales her om? – 46 artikler om græske-romersk kultur. Festskrift til Johnny Christensen*, København 1996, pp. 159-168.

[65] Stat., *Silv.* 2.6.92. Other sources can not be attributed with certainty to funerary: cfr. *CIL* VI, 5306: *hydriam onychinam*; SHA, *Heliog.* 32.2: *Onichina vasa*.

[66] Toynbee – Ward Perkins, pp. 44-51; Mielsch – von Hesberg 1996, pp. 93-121; Feraudi-Gruénais 2001b, pp. 49-50, K 16; Zander 2007, pp. 66-73.

[67] G. Koch – H. Sichtermann, *Römische Sarkophage*, München 1982, p. 196.

[68] *CIL* XV 1684.

[69] *AE* 1987, 148; Eck 1996, p. 232.

[70] Cfr. *supra* note 52.

[71] *AE* 1987, 149; Sinn 1987, p. 222, n. 537, table 80b.

[72] *AE* 1987, 150.

[73] *AE* 1987, 151; Sinn 1987, p. 220, n. 533.

[74] *AE* 1987, 108; Papi 2000-2001, pp. 252-256, n. 6.I.

[75] *AE* 1987, 109.

[76] *AE* 1987, 155; Papi 2000-2001, pp. 252-256, n. 6.II.

[77] *AE* 1987, 153; Feraudi-Gruénais 2001a, p. 205, K 16, fig. 3.

[78] Eck 1986, 233, 236, 248-251, n. 4; Feraudi-Gruénais 2001a, p. 205, K 16, fig. 4.

[79] *AE* 1987, 156; Papi 2000-2001, pp. 256-257, n. 7, fig. 10: *Anima dulcis / Gorgonia // Mire ispecie et castitati / eius, Aemili(a)e Gorgoniae, qu(a)e / vixit ann(is) xxviii, mens(ibus) ii, d(iebus) xxviii // Dormit in pace. / Coniugi dulcissim(ae) / feci.*

[80] Toynbee – Ward Perkins 1956, pp. 51-57; Mielsch – von Hesberg 1996, pp. 225-233, tables 26b-28, 39; Feraudi-Gruénais 2001b, pp. 58-59, K 23; Zander 2007, pp. 36-38.

[81] The front wall did not have enough space for *arcosolia* because of the opening for the doorway.

[82] M. De Vos, *L'egittomania in pitture e mosaici romano-campani della prima età imperiale* (EPRO 84), Leiden 1980, 9-12, n. 4, table B; 15-21, n. 9, tables XII-XIII.

[83] R. Paris, *Le tarsie di Giunio Basso*, in M.R. Di Mino – M. Bertinetti (eds), *Archeologia a Roma. La materia e la tecnica nell'arte antica* (catalogue of the exhibition, Rome Aprile-December 1990), Rome 1990, 147-150, nn. 122-123, fig. 122, table XVII.

[84] F. Matz, *Die antiken Sarkophagreliefs*, *Die dionysischen Sarkophage*, IV.2, Berlin 1968, pp. 298-300, n. 159 (170-180 d.C.); P. Kranz, in *Bullettino della Commissione archeologica comunale di Roma* 84, 1974-75, p. 191 (beginning of the third century AD). For another Dionysian sarcophagus found in the tomb, see Matz., *Die antiken Sarkophagreliefs*, cit., IV.4 (1975), p. 481, n. 306, tables 322.1, 324.3, 325.

[85] A. Ferrua, in *Bullettino della Commissione archeologica comunale di Roma*, 70, 1942, p. 104; Toynbee – Ward Perkins 1956, p. 57; Zander 2007, p. 38.

[86] Mielsch – von Hesberg 1996, pp. 123-142, tables 17-20; Feraudi-Gruénais 2001b, pp. 50-51, K 17.

[87] *CIL* XV, 293: H. Mielsch, *Rendiconti della Pontificia Accademia Romana di Archeologia* XLVI, 1973-74, pp. 79-82; H. Mielsch, *Römische Stuckreliefs*, *RM* 21. Ergh. 1975, pp. 164-165, K 101; Mielsch – von Hesberg 1996, pp. 123-142; Eck 1996, p. 254.

[88] Guarducci 1953; Toynbee – Ward Perkins 1956, pp. 14-17, 78-79, 82-88; Eck 1986; Id., *Iscrizioni sepolcrali romane. Intenzione e capacità di messaggio nel contesto funerario*, in Eck 1996, pp. 233-234; Mielsch – von Hesberg 1996, pp. 143-208; Papi 2000-2001, pp. 239-245, nn. 1-2; Feraudi-Gruénais 2001b, pp. 51-53, K 18; Caliò 2007; Zander 2007, pp. 76-92.

[89] *C(aius) Valerius Herma fecit [sibi] et / Flaviae T(iti) f(iliae) Olympiadi coniugi et / Valeriae Maximae filiae et C(aio) Valerio / Olympiano filio et suis libertis / libertabusque posteriq(ue) eorum.*

[90] Toynbee – Ward Perkins 1956, p. 40, interpreted these stairs rather as an access to a higher terrace that abutted the aligned tombs to the north.

[91] *CIL* XV 780; Guarducci 1953, p. 82 note 22; Eck 1996, p. 254.

[92] The cover slab of the burial niche was dismantled by the Constantinian workers when constructing the wall that cut the burial, and was reused in Courtyard P for the burial coffer. ε (*Esplorazioni* 1951, pp. 113-114, fig. 83; Toynbee – Ward Perkins 1956, p. 101, note 59).

[93] Eck 1996, pp. 254-256.

[94] On the dating of the basilica, see R. Krautheimer, *The Building Inscriptions and the Dates of Construction of Old St. Peter's. A Reconsideration*, *Römisches Jahrbuch für Kunstgeschichte* 25, 1989, pp. 3-22; P. Liverani, *Saint Peter's, Leo the Great and the leprosy of Constantine*, *Papers of the British School Rome* 76, 2008, pp. 155-172.

[95] P. Zanker, *Die Maske des Sokrates. Das Bild des intellektuellen in der antiken Kunst*, München 1995, pp. 240-242 fig. 139.

[96] It would not be coherent to consider a sacrificial *patera* and a magical wand, as is retained by Caliò 2007, p. 295. One should think of the shell shaped cup that was found in the scribe's box in the Autoparco Necropolis: Steinby 2003, pp. 106-108, table. 22. Cfr. the chapter on the Autoparco Necropolis.

[97] Guarducci 1953, p. 5, thought of Hermes as a forefather, which would be problematic since the owner of the tomb could not, as a freedman, have had a father in a strictly legal sense. Furthermore, the character wears a toga and is therefore a free citizen; Toynbee – Ward Perkins 1956, p. 84, are thinking of Hermes as well, but this would cause a conflict with the interpretation of the central character on the west wall. Moreover, furthermore the head in high relief is not considered which, as we will see later on, belongs to the owner of the tomb

[98] Cfr. H.R. Goette, *Studien zu römischen Togadarstellungen*, Mainz 1990, p. 28, 113 A d 8, table 4.6.

[99] Guarducci 1953, pp. 11-12.

[100] The term *lararium* is used here metaphorically, however one should at least refer to the classical example handed down by the *Historia Augusta*, a collection of imperial biographies of the late IV century, that combines well documented stories with pieces of fantasy or tendentious reinterpretation. In particular a piece on the life of Alexander Severus (29.2), according to which the emperor "in the early hours of the morning paid homage in his *lararium*, in which he held (the images of) the divined emperors, of whom he had picked the best, and of the most holy souls,

among which Apollonius (of Tyana) and, according to a contemporary writer, Christ, Abraham and Orpheus and others of this kind and the ancestral portraits." In the same *lararium* he "kept (also an image of) Alexander the Great" (31,5). The same emperor allegedly had a secondary *lararium* where he kept the image of Virgil "together with a statue of Cicero (..), where there were also those of Achilles and of great men"(31,4). Independent of their historic value, these stories reveal a mentality. Already Irenaus, (*Contra Haer.* 1, 25, 6), mentions how in the second century AD, the Gnostic sect of Carpocrates assembled characters, in our modern view rather heterogeneous, like Christ, Pythagoras, Plato and Aristoteles, or according to Augustine (*De Haeres.* 7), Christ, Paul, Homer and Pythagoras.

[101] MIELSCH – VON HESBERG 1996, pp. 186-192, nn. 1-3, figs 230-234.

[102] MIELSCH – VON HESBERG 1996, pp. 192-193, n. 4 figs 235-236.

[103] MIELSCH – VON HESBERG 1996, pp. 193-196, nn. 5-6, figs 237-242.

[104] H.R. Goette, *Römische Kinderbildnisse mit Jugend-Locken, Mitteilungen des Deutschen Archäologischen Instituts, Athenische Abteilung* 104, 1989, pp. 203-217.

[105] For the same period, one can mention two private female portraits and one attributed to Faustina the elder, found by Fauvel at Athens in the Dipylon necropolis excavations of the late eighteenth and early nineteenth century. Nowadays, these are missing or destroyed: Ph.-E. Legrand, *RA* s. III, XXX, 1897, p. 393.

[106] MIELSCH – VON HESBERG 1996, pp. 196-198, nn. 10-12, figg. 246-253.

[107] H. Drerup, *Totenmaske und Ahnenbild bei den Römern*, *RM* 87, 1980, pp. 81-129.

[108] Oxford, cod. Bodleian. fol. 139: R. Lanciani, *Storia degli Scavi di Roma*, II, Roma 1903, p. 102 (II ed. edited by L. Malvezzi Campeggi, Roma 1990, p. 108); CASTAGNOLI 1992, table LXXVIII, fig. 159; LIVERANI 1999, pp. 45-46, n. 2.

[109] L. Chioffi, *Mummificazione e imbalsamazione a Roma e in altri luoghi del mondo romano, Opuscula Epigraphica* 8, Roma 1998.

[110] GUARDUCCI 1953, pp. 8-10; cfr. CALIÒ 2007, p. 315.

[111] As we have seen, the head of Selene is not the original one; the curls of the young Olympianus refer generally to a devotion of mystery cults, which can not be specified more closely; the relationship between Minerva-Isis does not explain – at least in this case – the proposed interpretation; mummification and funerary masks are common in various regions of the empire and therefore do not necessarily imply a link to Egyptian religion. Lastly, the Dionysian repertoire is the most common of all Roman funerary art and therefore the least characteristic.

[112] B. Andreae, *Sarkophage mit Darstellungen aus dem Menschenleben. Die römischen Jagdsarkophage, Die Antiken Sarkophagreliefs* 1, 2, Berlin 1980, pp. 77-79, 183, n. 240, tables 44,2, 45,4-5, 46,1-6, 47,1-6, 50,1, 115,3, 121,4.

[113] On this aspect, see *supra* pp. 32-35.

[114] GUARDUCCI 1953, p. 22, figs 9-10: *D(is) M(anibus). / Valerinus / Vasatulus / vixit annis xxxi, m(ensibus) iii, d(iebus) x, / h(oris) iii. Valeria Flo/rentia coius / fecit marito / suo animo benemerenti; d(e)p(ositio) eius vii idus s(e)pt(embres).*

[115] M.L. Caldelli, *Nota su* D(is) M(anibus) *e* D(is) M(anibus) S(acrum) *nelle iscrizioni cristiane di Roma*, in I. Di Stefano Manzella (ed.), *Le iscrizioni dei cristiani in Vaticano*, Inscriptiones Sanctae Sedis, 2, Città del Vaticano 1997, pp. 185-187 (with earlier bibliography).

[116] GUARDUCCI 1953, pp. 22-25; TOYNBEE – WARD PERKINS 1956, pp. 91-92.

[117] C. Carletti, *Dies mortis-depositio: un modulo 'profano' nell'epigrafia tardoantica, Vetera Christianorum* 41, 2004, pp. 21-48, especially 29-37.

[118] ECK 1986, p. 277, n. 28: *Flavius Istatilius Olympus χρ / qui vixit annos xxxv et mensis / decem dies xvii fratri bene/merenti fecit. Cum omnes / iocatus est numquam rixatus / est.*

[119] TOYNBEE – WARD PERKINS 1956, p. 271; ECK 1986, p. 277, n. 28.

[120] D. Mazzoleni, *Origine e cronologia dei monogrammi: riflessi nelle iscrizioni dei Musei Vaticani*, in I. Di Stefano Manzella (ed.), *Le iscrizioni dei cristiani in Vaticano*, Inscriptiones Sanctae Sedis, 2, Città del Vaticano 1997, pp. 165-171.

[121] Cfr. *supra*, note 94.

[122] GUARDUCCI 1953.

[123] GUARDUCCI 1953, p. 18: "*Petrus roga Christus Iesus pro sanctis hominibus Chrestianis ad corpus tuum sepultis*".

[124] ZANDER 2007, p. 87.

[125] GUARDUCCI 1953, pp. 70-72: the author spreads the manufacture of the various inscriptions over different moments until the period following the Edict of Milan in AD 313.

[126] TOYNBEE – WARD PERKINS 1956, pp. 14-17.

[127] MIELSCH – VON HESBERG 1996, pp. 209-221, tables 25-26a; FERAUDI-GRUÉNAIS 2001b, pp. 53-56, K 19; ZANDER 2007, pp. 93-96.

[128] *Esplorazioni* 1951, p. 30, note 2.

[129] R. Lindner, *Der Raub der Persephone in der antiken Kunst* (Beiträge zur Archäologie 16), Würzburg 1984.

[130] *Ibid.*, table 19.3.

[131] A. Ferrua, in *Rendiconti della Pontificia Accademia Romana di Archeologia* XXIII-XXIV, 1947, p. 222, followed by M. Schmidt, s.v. *Alkestis*, in *LIMC* I (1981) p. 536, n. 14; Feraudi-Gruénais 2001b, p. 55.

[132] MIELSCH – VON HESBERG 1996, pp. 214, 221.

[133] MIELSCH – VON HESBERG 1996, p. 214, on the excavation photos these authors recognised an object in the figure's hand as a cornucopia. Recent restorations, however, forced the abandonment of this idea. An identification of Victory has been proposed by FERAUDI-GRUÉNAIS 2001b, p. 55.

[134] B. Andreae, *Studien zur römischen Grabkunst*, *Mitteilungen des Deutschen Archäologischen Instituts. Römische Abteilung, Ergänzungsheft* 9, 1963, p. 44.

[135] Ferrua, in *Rendiconti*, cit. *supra*, note 131, p. 217, folowed by M. Schmidt, s.v. *Admetos I*, in *LIMC* I (1981) p. 221, n. 20; FERAUDI-GRUÉNAIS 2001b, p. 55.

[136] L. Curtius, in *Mitteilungen des Deutschen Archäologischen Instituts* 4, 1951, p. 31; Andreae, cit. *supra*, note 134; F. Canciani, s.v. *Protesilaos*, in *LIMC* VII (1994), p. 559, n. 29.

[137] *Esplorazioni* 1951, pp. 29-37.

[138] A. Ferrua, *Esedra sepolcrale nel sepolcreto vaticano, Rendiconti della Pontificia Accademia Romana di archeologia* LVIII, 1985-86, pp. 181-187 (republished in *Saggi in on. di G. De Angelis D'Ossat* I, Roma 1987, pp. 40-42). The exedra was built later than both L and M, to which it must have abutted for a short while. Its date should therefore go up to the early fourth century AD.

[139] *CIL* XV 1065; *Esplorazioni* 1951, p. 30.

[140] PAPI 2000-2001, pp. 257-259, n. 8, fig. 12.

[141] *Esplorazioni* 1951, pp. 38-42; FERAUDI-GRUÉNAIS 2001b, pp. 56, K 20.

[142] T. Alpharani, *De Basilicae Vaticanae antica et nova structura*, ed. Cerrati, Roma 1914, n. 8 on the plan.

[143] *Ibid.*, p. 154, appendix n. 6; cfr. also p. 168, appendix n. 31; *Esplorazioni* 1951, pp. 39-40; *CAR* I, G24, A.XVII; Castagnoli 1992, pp. 84-85; Liverani, in M.A. Tomei – P. Liverani (eds), *Lexicon Topographicum Urbis Romae, Supplementum* I.1. *Carta Archeologica di Roma. Primo quadrante*, Roma 2005, p. 239.

[144] *CIL* VI 20293. The inscription was "kept in store by the Fabric of Saint Peter", but one generation later, Giacomo Grimaldi drew it in a private house: *in horto Sabuntianorum transtiberim*, after which we loose track of it.

[145] This is the reading suggested by F.W. Deichmann, *Zur Frage der Gesamtschau der frühchristlichen und frühbyzantinischen Kunst, Byzantinische Zeitschrift* 63, 1970, p. 56, and B. Brenk, *Spätantike und frühes Christentum*, in *Propyläen Kunstgeschichte*, Supplementband 1, Berlin 1977, p. 51.

[146] *Esplorazioni* 1951, pp. 38-42, tables X-XII; O. Perler, *Die Mosaiken der Juliergruft in Vatikan*, Freiburg 1953; TOYNBEE – WARD PERKINS 1956, pp. 72-74; T. Klauser, *JACh* 10, 1967, p. 100, n. 5, pp. 102-103; B. Sear, *Roman Wall and Vault Mosaics, Mitteilungen des Deutschen Archäologischen Instituts, Römische Abteilung.* Supplementband 23, 1977, pp. 127-128, n. 135, table 53.2.3; J. Miziołek, *Apotheosis, ascensio o resurrectio. Osservazioni sull'Helios del Mausoleo dei Giulii sotto la basilica Vaticana di S. Pietro, Arte Cristiana* 85, 1997, pp. 83-98; L. De Maria, P. Zander, in A. Sperandio – P. Zander (eds), *La tomba di S. Pietro, Restauro e illuminazione della Necropoli Vaticana*, Milano 1999, 75-77; L. De Maria, *Spunti di riflessione sul programma iconografico del mausoleo dei Giulii nella necropoli vaticana*, Atti del VI Colloquio dell'Associazione italiana per lo studio e la conservazione del mosaico (Venezia 20-23 gennaio 1999), Ravenna 2000, pp. 385-396; FERAUDI-GRUÉNAIS 2001b, p. 56, K20; M. R. Menna, *Il mosaico con Cristo-Helios nel sepolcro dei Giulii nella necropoli vaticana*, in M. Andaloro (ed.), *La pittura medievale a Roma. 312-1431. L'Orizzonte tardoantico e le nuove immagini, 312-468. Corpus I*, Milano 2006, table 9, 126-130; ZANDER 2007, pp. 99-100.

[147] Miziołek, *Apotheosis*, cit. previous note, tends to lower the date to the early fourth century AD.

[14] Still valid is the classic: E. Auerbach, *Literary Language and Its Public in Late Latin Antiquity and in the Middle Ages*, Princeton 1965 (1st German edition: Bern 1958).

[149] S. MacCormack, *Art and Ceremony in Late Antiquity*, Berkeley 1981, fig. 37; M. Perraymond, in F. Bisconti (ed.), *Temi di iconografia paleocristiana*, Città del Vaticano 2000, s.v. *Elia*, pp. 170-171.

[150] C. Ihm, *Die Programme der christlichen Apsismalerei vom vierten Jahrhundert bis zur Mitte des achten Jahrhunderts*, Wiesbaden 1960, pp. 58-59, XX, table I.1; G. Bovini, *I mosaici del S. Aquilino di Milano, Corsi di cultura sull'arte ravennate e bizantina* 17, 1970, pp. 61-82; D. Kinney, *Capella Reginae. S. Aquilino in Milano, Marsyas* 15, 1970-71, pp. 13-35; C. Bertelli, *I mosaici di Sant'Aquilino*, in G.A. Dell'Acqua (ed.), *La basilica di San Lorenzo in Milano*, Milano 1985, pp. 145-169; P.J. Nordhagen, *The mosaics of the Cappella di S. Aquilino in Milan. Evidence of restoration, Acta ad archaeologiam et artium historiam pertinentia* 2, 1982, pp. 77-94.

[151] Tomb F, the tomb of Aemilia Gorgonia; tomb H, the tomb of Flavius Istatilius Olympius (?); tomb Z, anonymous terracotta sarcophagus. The situation for the area closer to St. Peters tomb is slightly different but certainly more complex.

[152] *Esplorazioni*, pp. 37-38; M. Guarducci, *L'urnetta cineraria di* C. Clodius Romanus *nella Necropoli Vaticana, Archeologia Classica* XLIV, 1992, pp. 185-191; Zander 2007, pp. 102-103.

[153] *Esplorazioni* 1951, p. 37, table VIb; PAPI 2000-2001, pp. 259-261, n. 9.

[154] M. Basso, *Simbologia escatologica nella necropoli vaticana*, Città del Vaticano 1981, pp. 159-160; Guarducci, *L'urnetta cineraria*, cit. *supra*, note 152, p. 186; *AE* 1992, 185.

[155] P. MENCACCI-M. ZECCHINI, *Lucca romana*, Lucca 1981, pp. 120, 438, tables 59-60.

[156] SINN 1987, n. 421, table 66a.

[157] The date is proposed by the first editor (Basso, cit. *supra*, note 154), but should be verified and specified as the coin has not been published yet.

[158] Tombs B, C, D, E, H, I.

[159] *Esplorazioni* 1951, pp. 37-38, tavv. VII-VIII; F.W. Deichman (ed.), *Repertorium der christlich-antiken Sarkophage* I, Wiesbaden 1967, pp. 271-272, n. 674, table 102.

[160] *Esplorazioni* 1951, p. 63; TOYNBEE – WARD PERKINS 1956, pp. 25, 34; ZANDER 2007, p. 106.

[161] G.B. De Rossi, *Bullettino di Archeologia Cristiana* 1864, p. 50, n. 4; *Esplorazioni* 1951, pp. 46, 52-53.

[162] *Esplorazioni*, pp. 43-53; PRANDI 1963, pp. 306-312; ZANDER 2007, pp. 104-105.

[163] Cfr. the topographic introduction.

[164] *CIL* XV 123 datable to AD 123; *Esplorazioni* 1951, p. 48. The brick stamp is now hidden by a cement pillar that was constructed for stability reasons.

[165] *Esplorazioni* 1951, p. 43, tav. IXb.

[166] *Esplorazioni* 1951, pp. 48-49. Cfr. anche PAPI 2000-2001, pp. 246-248, n. 3.

[167] *Esplorazioni* 1951, pp. 55-60; FERAUDI-GRUÉNAIS 2001b, pp. 56-58, K 21; ZANDER 2007, pp. 108-110.

[168] M. Guarducci, *Una moneta nella necropoli vaticana, Rendiconti della Pontificia Accademia Romana di Archeologia* XXXIX, 1966-67, pp. 135-143; C. Pietri, in *Mélanges W. Seston*, Paris 1974, p. 414; SINN 1987, pp. 53, 265-266, n. 714, tav. 104f; P. Liverani, in: Petros eni – *Pietro è qui. 500 anni della Basilica di S. Pietro* (catalogue of the exhibition, Città del Vaticano 11.10.2006-8.3.2007), Roma 2006, p. 182, IV.2.

[169] PAPI 2000-2001, pp. 248-250, n. 4: unfortunately we do not know the circumstances of the discovery and we can therefore not exclude a case of reuse. From burials lowered from the basilica's pavement,

originates a recycled slab with the dedication of Cn. Coelius Masculus (*Ibid.*, pp. 261-265, n. 10, fig. 10): this tomb was covered by a tile containing a rare brick stamp of Constantius, son of Constantine CIL XV 1657; *Esplorazioni* 1951, p. 50

170 H. Mielsch, in *Aufstieg und Niedergang der römischen Welt* II.12.2 (1981), p. 205 holds it possible to lower the date to the beginning of the third century AD.

171 *Esplorazioni* 1951, pp. 60-62; FERAUDI-GRUÉNAIS 2001b, p. 58, K 22; ZANDER 2007, p. 107.

172 *Esplorazioni* 1951, pp. 69-77; PRANDI 1963, pp. 312-314.

173 LIVERANI 1999, pp. 139-140; on this subject see also D'AMELIO 2005.

174 There are references to excavations for making a drain in front of the main altar in 1536 (the new St. Peter was under construction and open air during that period); in 1540, a sarcophagus came to light, in 1544 mediaeval burials were found near the Confession,and again in 1592. In 1597, the sarcophagus of Junius Bassus (cfr. note 34) was found, and above all, the works of Pope Paul V in 1615 around the main altar discovered numerous burials, marked on the map by Benedetto Drei of 1635. Regarding these matters, see. P. Liverani in *Il Cortile delle Statue. Der Statuenhof des Belvedere im Vatikan.* (Atti Conv. Int. Rome 21-23 Oct. 1992), Mainz 1998, pp. 352-353; LIVERANI 1999.

175 One by Ugo Ubaldi, canon of Saint Peter, later author of one of the excavation reports: Archivio Capitolare di San Pietro, cod. H 55, foll. 181-181v, 183-184v; a second one was written by N. Alemanni, *Risposta ad alcuni motivi fatti circa la fabrica della Confissione di S. Pietro*, cod. Ferraioli 961, foll. 98-101v; on the reception of Ubaldi's work, see note 179.

176 *Risposta ad alcuni vani sospetti circa la Confessione di S. Pietro*, Archivio Capitolare di San Pietro, cod. H 55, foll. 173-176, with an accurate plan of the Confession (fol. 172) and a drawing that explains the distance from the Confession to where the excavations for the foundation were carried out (fol. 171), now published by D'AMELIO 2005, p. 133, figs. 10-11. Three other copies are kept in the same codex (foll. 177-178, 186-188, 189-90) and another one in codex H 61, foll. 275ss.

177 Michel Lonigo, *Breve relazione del sito, qualità et forma antica della Confessione di S. Pietro*, dedicated to Urbano VIII (cod. barb. lat. 4516; cod. Ferraioli 691, fasc. 5); F.M. Torrigio, *Discorso dei corpi trovati intorno al sepolcro di S. Pietro*, cod. barb. lat. 4344, foll. 1-4.

178 H. Lietzmann, *Petrus und Paulus in Rom*, Berlin-Leipzig 1927 (II ed.), pp. 304-310. The text, incomplete, is preserved in the already mentioned codex of the Archivio Capitolare di San Pietro, H 55, foll. 169b-169g.

179 U. Ubaldi, *Relazione di quanto è occorso per cavare i fondamenti delle quattro colonne di bronzo*, Archivio Capitolare di San Pietro, H 55, foll. 141-166 (copy in the Archive of the Fabric of Saint Peter, Arm. 12, ripiano D, vol. 3, foll. 1200-1215), edited by M. Armellini, *Le chiese di Roma*, Roma 1887 (2nd ed.) pp. 697-718.

180 G.M. Torrigio, *Diarium anni MDCLXXVI sedente S.D.N. Urbano VIII*, cod. barb. lat. 2324, published in LIVERANI 1999, pp. 159-160, appendix, n. 1. Unfortunately, the excavation drawings that, according to the documentation of the archive, were done by Giovanni Battista Calandra, supervisor of the Fabric of Saint Peter and mosaicist, are no longer to be found.

181 Archivio Capitolare di San Pietro, cod. H 55, fol. 191, letter from 26.8.1626.

182 D'AMELIO 2005.

183 The identification of the tomb is by CASTAGNOLI 1992, p. 87 who has corrected the inversion of tombs R and S, as can also be found in *Esplorazioni* 1951, pp. 86-88; TOYNBEE – WARD PERKINS 1956, p. 30; GUARDUCCI 1959, p. 74. The statue was drawn by Cassiano dal Pozzo: C.C. Vermeule, in *Transactions of the American Philological Association* n.s. 56.2, 1966, p. 37, n. 8548, figs 136-136a; A. Claridge – N. Turner, in *Quaderni Puteani* 4, 1993, p. 46, n. 7, fig. 7. Cfr. also the account by the same Dal Pozzo, in *Miscellanea di storia italiana* XV, Torino 1876, pp. 175-176. It was already part of the Barberini collection, successively passed on to commercial antiquarians (P. Arndt – W. Amelung, *Photographische Einzelaufnahmen antiker Sculpturen*, n. 5092) and is now in the Indianapolis Museum of Arts: G. Pucci, *L'epitaffio di Flavio Agricola e un disegno della collezione Dal Pozzo-Albani*, *Bullettino della Commissione archeologica comunale di Roma* LXXXI, 1968-69, pp. 173-177; H. Wrede, in *Archäologischer Anzeiger* 1981, pp. 101-109, c, with bibliography. Cfr. anche H. Häusle, *Das Denkmal als Garant des Nachruhms*, *Zetemata* 75, 1980, pp. 98ss. n. 32; P. Zanker, *I sarcofagi mitologici e i loro osservatori*, in *Un'arte per l'impero. Funzione e intenzione delle immagini nel mondo romano*, Milano 2002, p. 162, fig. 126, p. 181, n. 15 (original edition *Die mythologische Sarkophagreliefs und ihre Betrachter, Bayerische Akademie der Wissenschaften. Philosophisch-Historische Klasse. Sitzungsberichte* 2000, 2); K.M.D. Dunbabin, *The Roman Banquet. Images of Conviviality*, Cambridge 2003, pp. 103-104; M. Koortbojian, *Classical Antiquity* 24.2, 2005, p. 301; P. Zanker – B.C. Ewald, *Mit Mythen Leben. Die Bilderwelt der römischen Sarkophage*, München 2004, pp. 158-159, fig. 143; G. Davies, in Z. Newby – R. Leader Newby, *Art and Inscriptions in the Ancient World*, Cambridge 2007, 46-49, fig. 2.3; Zander 2007, pp. 112-113, fig. 204.

184 CIL VI 17985a = 34112; F. Buecheler, *Carmina Latina Epigraphica* I^2 (1930), n. 856; L. Vidman, *Sylloge inscriptionum Isiacae et Serapiacae*, Berlin 1969, p. 217, n. 451; M. Malaise, *Inventaire préliminaire des documents égyptiens découverts en Italie*, *EPRO* 21, Leiden 1972, pp. 127-128, n. 51: "*Tibur mihi patria, Agricola sum vocitatus / Flavius, idem ego sum discumbens, ut me videtis, / sic et aput superos annis, quibus fata dedere, / animulam colui nec defuit umqua Lyaeus. / Praecessitque prior Primitiva gratissima coniuncxs / Flavia et ipsa, cultrix deae Phariaes casta, / sedulaque et forma decore repleta, / cum qua ter denos dulcissimos egerim annos. / Solaciumque sui generis Aurelium Primitivum / tradidit, qui pietate sua coleret fastigia nostra, / hospitiumque mihi secura servavit in aevum. / Amici qui legitis moneo miscete Lyaeum / et potate procul redimiti tempora flore / et venereos coitus formosis ne denegate puellis; / cetera post obitum terra consumit et ignis*".

185 *Esplorazioni* 1951, p. 69: a *poliandrion* was found at the foundation of each column: they were marked by an inscription in a lead plate with letters in relief that, in the case of tomb S, stated: "*Corpora santor(um) / [p]rope sepulcrum S. / Petri reperta cu[m] / fundamenta effode/rentur aeneis col[u]mnis ab Urbano viii su/per hoc forni[ce] erec/t[i]s hic [s]imul collec[t]a / et re[po]sita a(nno) 1626 / 2[8] iul[i]i.*" ("The bodies of the Saints found near the sepulchre of St. Peter were collected here and deposited on July 28, 1626, when the foundations were dug for the bronze columns of Urbanus VIII above this arch"). Cfr. *Esplorazioni* 1951, p. 69.

186 *Esplorazioni* 1951, pp. 69-88; PRANDI 1963, pp. 314-321.

187 *Esplorazioni* 1951, p. 229, nn. 16-17.

188 G. Koch, *Die Mythologischen Sarkophage* 6, *Meleager* (*Die Antiken Sarkophagreliefs* XII.6), Berlin 1975, 54-57, 131, n. 146, tables 120c, 121.

189 *Esplorazioni* 1951, pp. 88-93; Prandi 1963, pp. 316-321, 338-344; Castagnoli 1992, p. 103.

190 CIL XV 401; Prandi 1963, p. 341.

191 CIL XV 426 and 1220 respectively; Prandi 1963, p. 342.

192 CIL VI 721; Prandi 1963, p. 333.

193 Deichmann, *Repertorium*, cit. *supra*, note 34, n. 681.

194 *Esplorazioni* 1951, pp. 96-107; Prandi 1963, pp. 371-380; Castagnoli 1992, p. 102.

195 Cfr. *supra* note 23.

CHAPTER FOUR

1 See J.R. PATTERSON, in *LTUR*, V, Rome 1999, pp. 147-148, see entry "*Via Triumphalis (1)*"; L. BIANCHI, *Ad limina Petri. Spazio e memoria della Roma cristiana*, Rome 1999, pp. 39-44; LIVERANI 1999, pp. 34-40; STEINBY 2003, pp. 13-21.

2 See F. COARELLI, in *LTUR*, V, Rome 1999, p. 148, see entry "*Via Triumphalis (2)*"; M. MAIURO, in *LTUR*, *Suburbium*, V, Rome 2008, pp. 202-207, see entry "*Via Triumphalis*".

3 L. BOSIO, *La Tabula Peutingeriana, una descrizione pittorica del mondo antico*, Rimini 1983.

4 LIVERANI 1999, pp. 13-43; P. LIVERANI, in *LTUR*, *Suburbium*, V, Rome 2008, pp. 233-234, see entry "*Vaticanum*", and pp. 235-236, see entry "*Vaticanus ager*".

5 As well as imperial properties (which, amongst other things, are deducible through mentions in tomb inscriptions belonging to many of the deceased in this area), one should remember *Vaticanum rus*, a suburban property belonging to *Quintus Aurelius Symmachus*, the great pagan orator and politician. He mentioned this place in a few of his letters dated AD 398 as well as another property, defined as a *praedium*, which belonged to his daughter and son-in-law *Nicomachus Flavianus* (see LIVERANI 1999, pp. 20-21; ID., in *LTUR*, *Suburbium*, IV, Rome 2006, p. 94, see entry "*Nicomachi Flaviani praedium*"; D. DE FRANCESCO, in *LTUR*, *Suburbium* V, Rome 2008, pp. 234-235, see entry "*Vaticanum rus*").

6 P. LIVERANI, in *LTUR Suburbium*, IV, Rome 2006, see entry *"Pyramis in Vaticano"*.

7 P. LIVERANI, A. TOMEI, in *LTUR Suburbium*, I, Rome 2001, see entry *"P. Aelii Hadriani Sepulcrum"*, pp. 15-22.

8 E. JOSI, *Scoperta d'un tratto dell'antica via Trionfale in Vaticano*, in *IllVat*, 3, 17, 1932, p. 842; *CAR*, D 13; STEINBY 1987, p. 86; CASTAGNOLI 1992, pp. 30 and 115; LIVERANI 1999, pp. 52-53; STEINBY 2003, pp. 16-17 and 94; *Carta* I, n. 88.

9 *Rapporti mensili* (*Monthly Reports*) mentions how objects (inscriptions, marble and clay fragments) discovered in the gardens during building work were given to the Vatican Museums (ASMV, *Rapporti mensili*, 1920-30, 11/4/1928, p. 734; ASMV, *Rapporti mensili*, 1931-34, 21/4/1931, p. 986 and 18/7/1931, pp. 998-999; LIVERANI 1999, p. 46). R. Venuti (R. VENUTI, *Accurata e succinta descrizione delle antichità di Roma*, Rome 1763 [1ª ed.], p. 108) recalls how "sepulchral urns were discovered when the Great Courtyard of this palazzo was built" (see CASTAGNOLI 1992, pp. 115-117; LIVERANI 1999, p. 57, n. 6). This (not necessarily trustworthy) piece of information refers to a stretch of the necropolis site positioned underneath the original location of the Belvedere court yard (the enormous and monumental Renaissance and Baroque court yard) which is currently stressed in the court yard of the "Pigna", the library and the Belvedere. From the heights of the Vatican, it once sloped down towards the south. For a general overview, see CASTAGNOLI 1992, pp. 114-115; LIVERANI, SPINOLA 1999, p. 219 and ss.; LIVERANI 1999, pp. 46-52.

10 CASTAGNOLI 1992, pp. 115-116; *CAR*, G 5; STEINBY 1987, p. 88; LIVERANI 1999, pp. 58-60, n. 7; *Carta* I, n. 123.

11 S.P., *IllVat* III.8, 1932, p. 379; LIVERANI 1999, p. 91, n. 10.

12 R. KRAUTHEIMER, W. FRANKL, *Corpus Basilicarum Christianarum Romae* III, Vatican City 1967, p. 177, plate VII; LIVERANI 1999, p. 61, n. 8.

13 LIVERANI 1999, p. 92, n. 13.

14 JOSI, in *IllVat* 1932, *cit.* footnote 8, p. 842; B. M. APOLLONI GHETTI, A. FERRUA, E. JOSI, E. KIRSCHBAUM, *Esplorazioni sotto la confessione di San Pietro in Vaticano*, Vatican City 1951, p. 12; *CAR*, D 15; F. MAGI, in *EAA* VI (1965), see entry Rome, p. 869; STEINBY 1987, p. 86; CASTAGNOLI 1992, pp. 30, 115; LIVERANI 1999, pp. 52-53, n. 4; *Carta* I, n. 89.

15 See STEINBY 1987; P. LIVERANI, *L'Agro Vaticano*, in PH. PERGOLA, R. SANTANGELI VALENZANI, R. VOLPE, *Suburbium*, Rome 2003, pp. 399-413.

16 A detailed publication regarding this second campaign of excavations, which was headed by Paolo Liverani and Giandomenico Spinola with the supervision of the then Director General of the Vatican Museums, Professor Carlo Pietrangeli, is imminent.

17 A scientific publication about this Necropolis is also being currently prepared. The excavation was directed by Paolo Liverani and Giandomenico Spinola under the supervision of the then Director of the Vatican Museums, Francesco Buranelli.

18 See BURANELLI, LIVERANI, SPINOLA 2005-2006, p. 464; SPINOLA 2006, p. 49. It is certainly not by chance that Pope Leo III founded the Church of St. Pellegrino around the year 1800 on this very road, and that this stretch of *via Triumphalis* should take the name of *via di S. Pellegrino* or *via del Pellegrino*, a toponym which is still used to this day (see S. DELLI, *Strade in Vaticano*, Rome 1982, pp. 110-111).

[19] Josi 1931; see also B. Nogara, in *RendPontAcc*, VI, 1927-29, p. 132; *BullCom*, LXI, 1933, p. 285; Liverani 1999, pp. 160-161, nn. 1-2.
[20] E. Josi, *Scoperta d'un tratto dell'antica via Trionfale in Vaticano*, cit. footnote 8 in the present essay, p. 842; *CAR*, D 13; Steinby 1987, p. 86; Castagnoli 1992, pp. 30 e 115; Liverani 1999, pp. 52-53; Steinby 2003, pp. 16-17 and 94; Liverani, Spinola 2006, pp. 12-29.
[21] See footnote 16 in the present essay.
[22] Some restoration interventions were carried out by the Vatican Museum's Restoration of Tombstone Materials Laboratory under the direction of Maestro Luciano Ermo. Other works were entrusted to external collaborators such as Giuseppe Mantella, Chiara Scioscia Santoro, Paola Minoja and Giovanna Prestipino. The relief plan and graphic documentation was done by Dr. Angela Napoletano.
[23] Inv. 54989. Italic white fine marble. It measures: height 10.5 cm, width 39.5 cm and depth 28.3 cm.
[24] During the building works for the realisation of the new entrance and the new entrance spaces for the Jubilee Year of 2000, numerous excavations and the creation of terraces were carried out on the north slopes of the Vatican Hill. On this occasion, the Marble Restoration Laboratory rediscovered traces of destroyed tomb walls containing four sealed tombstones (invv. 57100-57103) and two inscribed marble tomb fragments: "[—]*E HED. D.* / [—*con*]*tuber(nal-)* / [—]*ssimae*" (inv. 57104; 23.3 x 14 x 3 cm); "[—] / *hoc mon(umentum) her(edes) non [sequetur] / in f(ronte) p(edes) VIII in agr(o) [p(edes)* —]" (inv. 57105; 16 x 94.2 x 25 cm). In 1998, a complete inscription with a sepulchral dedication to *Quintus Codicarius Florentinus* (inv. 54978; 61 x 78 x 12 cm) was discovered underneath the Courtyard of the "Corazze" (Armour); P. Liverani, in *Carta* 2005, n. 77.
[25] An inscribed slab (51 x 47 x 2.5 cm; inv. 57108) was discovered in the slope [leading to] the new restaurant bar in its recycled form as a sewer lid. It bears several lines of a long medieval inscription: "*[———] / [—]CVIV[—] / et pos[t—] / ER[—] / tabulae con[—] / ccinerary urnscta L[—] / summum consilium[—] / obsequii GI[—] / anno Christi[—]*".
[26] Burial tomb 28, which is a tomb *a semicappuccina* contains three *bipedales* that are obliquely placed over the south foundation of room tomb 26. Two of these bear the stamp (*CIL* XV 824) – *Apol(lonius?) Ant(oni) L(uci) s(ervus)* – which is dated to the beginning of the first century AD. We are also able to roughly attribute chamber tomb 26 (whose burial is rested upon) to this period. See Liverani, Spinola 1999, p. 219; Liverani, Spinola 2006, p. 13. However, Steinby (Steinby 2003, pp. 17 and 29) is of the opinion that the two brick stamps could belong to the Augustan Period and therefore would not be contemporary to the other burial tomb. This first terrace is no longer visible due to the fact that it has been covered by the modern-day warehouse's structure.
[27] Josi, in Liverani 1999, p. 51, n. 5; Liverani, Spinola 2006, p. 14.
[28] Josi 1931, p. 27, fig. 5; Id., in *BullCom*, 1933, p. 285; *CAR*, D 13.a; F. Magi, in *ActaInstRomFin*, VI, 1973, p. 15, plate IV.1; Castagnoli 1992, p. 114; Liverani 1999, p. 46, figs. 10, 13-14; Steinby 2003, p. 30; Liverani, Spinola 2006, p. 22. Underneath the cobbledstones which are known as "*sampietrini*", reduced foundations (perhaps levelled off as a result of the insertion of subsequent infrastructures underneath the road) are probably still conserved.
[29] The measurements are approximately 3.5 x 5 metres.
[30] Liverani, Spinola 2006, pp. 22-23, figs. 12, 14 and 15.
[31] Liverani 1999, pp. 46 and 48; Steinby 2003, p. 16; Liverani, Spinola 2006, p. 21, fig. 13.
[32] See Steinby 2003, p. 30; Liverani, Spinola 2006, p. 21.
[33] *CIL* XV 265. Liverani, Spinola 1999, pp. 219-220; Liverani, Spinola 2006, pp. 21 and 29, footnote 30.
[34] *CIL* XV 265.
[35] Liverani, Spinola 2006, pp. 22-25, fig. 17. Inv. 54980. Italic fine white marble. It measures: height 57.5 cm, width 24.5 cm, depth 5.3 cm. With regard to the style of the portrait and hair-style, several comparisons can be made, for example: G. Kaschnitz Weinberg, *Sculture del magazzino del Museo Vaticano*, Vatican City 1937, p. 275, n. 654, plate CIV; A. Giuliano, *Catalogo dei ritratti romani del Museo Profano Lateranense*, Vatican City 1957, p. 44, n. 48, plate 30; L. Martelli, in A. Giuliano (ed.), *Museo Nazionale Romano. Le sculture*, I/9,1, Rome 1987, pp. 228-229, n. R172; B. Andreae [ed.], *Bildkatalog der Skulpturen des Vatikanischen Museum. Museo Chiaramonti*, Berlin-New York 1995, p. 22*, plates 200-201; B. Andreae [ed.], *Bildkatalog der Skulpturen des Vatikanischen Museum. Museo Pio Clementino. Cortile Ottagono*, Berlin-New York 1998, p. 15*, plate 172.
[36] Liverani, Spinola 2006, pp. 25-26, figs. 16 and 18.
[37] Steinby 2003, p. 115; Liverani, Spinola 2006, p. 26, fig. 19.
[38] Liverani, Spinola 1999, p. 223.
[39] See M.R. Picuti, *Il contributo dell'Epigrafia latina allo scavo delle necropoli antiche*, in Aa.Vv., *Pour une archéologie du rite. Nouvelles perspectives de l'archéologie funérarie (études réunies par John Scheid)*, Collection de l'École Française de Rome, 407, Rome 2008, pp. 49-50 (with reference bibliography).
[40] Liverani, Spinola 2006, pp. 14, 25 and 28, figs. 16 and 20.
[41]As the Latin name implies, these are square bricks that measure 1.5 ft (equivalent of 45 cm) each side.
[42] This is a stamp relating to a certain *Aprilis* (see *CIL* XV, 1109 and 1110).
[43] Cappellaccio is a type of tuff that geologically forms "a hat" over other volcanic rocks. This type of tuff, which is rather crumbly, is found in great abundance in the Lazio area. As such, it was frequently used as a construction material.
[44] Josi 1931, p. 27; Castagnoli 1992, p. 115; Liverani 1999, p. 51, figs. 21-23; Steinby 2003, pp. 16-17 and 30.
[45] Inside, a fragmentary sepulchral inscription was discovered: *[Dis] Manibus. / [— T]rophimes / [—] Amandus / [uxori* (o *coniugi*) *c]arissimae / [—] fecit / [— vix(it) a]nnis XXX*. See I. Di Stefano Manzella, in Castagnoli 1992, pp. 115 and 138-139, n. 25; *AE* 1993, n. 399; Liverani 1999, p. 51.
[46] Josi 1931, p. 27; Castagnoli 1992, p. 115; Liverani 1999, p. 50, figs. 19 and 20; Steinby 2003, pp. 16 and 30.
[47] See Liverani, Spinola 1999, p. 221; Liverani, Spinola 2006, p. 21. These clay frames find much collation, for example, with those found *in situ* in the numerous tombs of the second century AD in the necropolis of Portus (Isola Sacra, near Fiumicino) and on the front of public buildings such as the monumental "*protiri*" porticoes of the Ostienese *Horrea Epagathiana* (see G. Becatti, *Horrea Epagathiana et Epaphroditiana*, in *NSc*, 1940, p. 32 and ss.; G. Rickman, *Roman Granaries and Store Buildings*, Cambridge 1971, *passim*), mid-second century AD and of the Trasteverian *Excubitorium* at the end of the same century (see A.M. Ramieri, in *LTUR*, I, Rome 1993, pp. 292-294, see entry "*Cohortium Vigilum Stationes*").
[48] Josi 1931, p. 27, fig. 14 (reverse photography); Id., in *BullCom*, 1933, p. 285; *CAR*, D 13.b; Castagnoli 1992, p. 114, plate LXXVII, figs.155-157; Liverani 1999, pp. 48-50, figs. 15-17; Liverani, Spinola 1999, pp. 222-223, fig. 6; Steinby 2003, pp. 24, 36 and 39; Liverani, Spinola 2006, pp. 15-17, figs. 4-8.
[49] The internal measurements are 3.68 metres (length) and 2.10 metres (width), excluding the spaces located under the *arcosolia*.
[50] See Liverani, Spinola 1999, pp. 222-223, fig. 6; Steinby 2003, p. 30; Liverani, Spinola 2006, pp. 15-16.
[51] See Steinby 2003, pp. 104-105; Liverani, Spinola 2006, p. 16, fig. 5.
[52] For example see M. Borda, *La pittura romana*, Milan 1958, pp. 314-322 and 332-333; H. Joyce, *The Decoration of Walls, Ceilings, and Floors in Italy in the Second and Third Centuries AD*, Rome 1981, pp. 40-67; R. Ling, *Roman Painting*, Cambridge 1991, pp. 186-197.
[53] See Borda, *op. cit.* footnote 52, pp. 314-315.
[54] See Joyce, *op. cit.* footnote 52, pp. 44, 81 and 109, figs. 38, 39 and 94.
[55] See Borda, *op. cit.* footnote 52, p. 320 and ss.; F. Astolfi, in *LTUR*, II, Rome 1995, pp. 117-118, see entry "*Domus SS. Iohannis et Pauli*".
[56] See Joyce, *op. cit.* footnote 52, p. 25, figs. 7and 8.
[57] B. Andreae (ed.), *Bildkatalog der Skulpturen des Vatikanischen Museums, I, Museo Chiaramonti*, III, Berlin - New York 1995, plate 886, p. 85* (with previous bibliography); Liverani 1999, p. 50, fig. 18; Steinby 2003, p. 115. The most up-to-date analysis can be found in P. Liverani, *Sarcofago infantile con scena nilotica*, in A. Donati (ed.), *Pietro e Paolo. La storia, il culto, la memoria nei primi secoli*, Milan 2000, p. 205, n. 40.
[58] In reality, the theme that is known as the "Island of the Blessed" alludes to Nilotic surroundings. In antiquity, they told stories about life in Paradise which took place in an Alessandrian setting at the mouth of the River Nile. They imagined parties and banquets in the delta region and, above all, ideally hoped to reach it during the Afterlife.
[59] In 1940 the floor was removed, restored and replaced with a slab and borders made of cement.
[60] See G. Becatti, *Scavi di Ostia*, IV, *Mosaici e pavimenti marmorei*, Rome 1961, pp. 149-150, n. 287, plate LXXIX; M.L. Morricone Matini, *Roma: Reg. X Palatium*, *Mosaici Antichi in Italia, Regione I*, Rome 1967, pp. 92-93, plates XVIII-XIX; P. Chini, "Mosaici inediti di Roma dall'archivio disegni della Sovraintendenza BB.CC. del Comune di Roma", in *Atti del V Colloquio AISCOM 1997*, Tivoli 1999, pp. 200-201, fig. 3.
[61] M.E. Blake, in *MAAR*, XIII, 1936, plate 39, n. 1; Becatti, 1961, pp. 195-196, n. 373, fig. 69, plate LXXXVII.
[62] C.C. van Essen, in *MededRome*, s. III, VIII, 1954, p. 115 (he dates it to the fourth century AD); Becatti, 1961, pp. 199-201, n. 379, plate LXXXVIII (who, however, attributes it to the Severan Period). See also the contemporary mosaics edited in M.E. Blake, in *MAAR*, XVII, 1940, plate II, n. 1 and p. 91 (National Roman Museum).
[63] G. Calza, *La necropoli del Porto di Roma nell'Isola Sacra*, Rome 1940, p. 175, fig. 87; Becatti, 1961, p. 335, plate LXXVIII; I. Baldassarre, in *Studi in memoria di Lucia Guerrini*, Rome 1993, pp. 305-308 and 321-322, fig. 1.
[64] Two inscriptions are also found in the tomb: a dedication to *[C]neus Asinius* and the sepulchral epigraph to *[Volussia] Maxima* (see I. Di Stefano Manzella, in Castagnoli 1992, nn. 24 and 23; *AE* 1993, 398; Steinby 2003, p. 16).
[65] Excluding the spaces underneath the *arcosolia*, the length measures 3.30 metres and the width 2.48 metres.
[66] Liverani, Spinola 1999, pp. 221-222, fig. 5; Steinby 2003, pp. 36 and 39; Liverani, Spinola 2006, p. 18, fig. 9.
[67] A slab fragment with the funerary inscription"[—]*us e Gavia* [—] / [—] / [— *fec*]*erunt vod*[—] / *vix ann*[—]" was found in the grounds enclosure in front of the tomb as was a little marble window with a rectangular opening which had perhaps been inserted at the front of the tomb (invv. 54984 and 54988).
[68] Becatti, 1961, p. 182, n. 336.
[69] Becatti, 1961, pp. 199-201, n. 379.
[70] *CIL* XV 429; H. Bloch, *I bolli laterizi e la storia edilizia romana*, Rome 1938, pp. 79, 298 and 339; T. Helen, *Organisation of Roman brick production in the first and second centuries AD*, Helsinki 1975, pp. 50-52. The stamp contains the winged victory with a crown in hand within the orbiculus.
[71] The filling up of *formae* inside of the tomb does not contain material dating after the end of the second century AD Amongst these, there is also a funerary urn lid which dates back to the first century AD, although this is to be considered residual (inv. 54983).
[72] See Liverani, Spinola 1999, p. 221, fig. 4; Steinby 2003, pp. 36 and 39; Liverani Spinola 2006, p. 19, fig. 10.
[73] The internal measurements are: height 2.36 metres (excluding the *arcosolium* and the niches), width 2.16 metres (excluding the benches and the *arcosolia*).
[74] See M.L. Morricone Matini, see entry "Mosaico", in *EAA*, Supplement, Rome 1970, pp. 518-520.
[75] The space is also known as the "common room" or "HS2 mortuary chapel". See S. Aurigemma, *Villa Adriana*, Rome 1961, p. 177, fig. 182.
[76] R. Paribeni, in *NS*, 1920, p. 161; Becatti, 1961, pp. 44 and 280, n. 66, plate XL. Another comparison can be made with a mosaic found in Rome which is cited in M.E. Blake, in *MAAR*, XIII, 1936, plate 10, n. 3. See Steinby 2003, p. 36.
[77] N. Cassieri, mosaic floors of the archaeological site

Tres Tabernae nell'Agro Pontino, in Atti del VI Colloquio AISCOM, Tivoli 2000, p. 244, fig. 7.

[78] This deals with the *stelae* of *Marcus Ulpius Cuntianus* (perhaps of numidian origin judging by his surname) and two other slab fragments bearing sepulchral inscriptions "[—-] *fecit* [—-] / [—-] *coniugi* [—-]" e "[—-*On*]*omaste emit s*[*ibi et suis?*—-]" (invv. 54981, 54982, 54986).

[79] LIVERANI, SPINOLA 1999, pp. 220-221, fig. 3; LIVERANI, SPINOLA 2006, pp. 20-21, fig. 11.

[80] The walls feature mirror borders made up of listels in brick and made up of red bricks and tiles which are joined by a very low bed of mortar. A great slab of bardiglio (at the front of Tomb 7) on an analogous travertine slab (in front of Tomb 8) is supported by a corner, placed at a right-angle. This slab might once have had a painted inscription on it which has since disappeared.

[81] The stamp refers to a Domitian brick production site: "*Cn*(*ei*) *Domit*(*i*) *Arignot*(*i*) / *fec*(*it*)"; *CIL* XV, 1094d.

[82] The measurements are about 3.60 metres in length and 1.84 metres in width.

[83] G. GHINI, residential systems at Lanuvio and their mosaic decoration, in Atti del II Colloquio AISCOM, Bordighera 1995, Tivoli 1997, pp. 492-493, fig. 12.

[84] L. QUILICI, "I mosaici delle case di via San Paolo alla Regola in Roma. Scavi e restauri 1993-1995", in *Atti del III Colloquio AISCOM 1996*, Tivoli 1998, pp. 516-517, fig. 3.

[85] M.L. MORRICONE MATINI, *Roma: Reg. X* Palatium, *Mosaici Antichi in Italia, Regione I*, Rome 1967, pp. 100-102, plates XXI-XXII.

[86] G. BECATTI, 1961, p. 87, n. 144, plate XLIX. There are another three very similar ones which are conserved in the warehouses at Ostia but are of unknown provenance (BECATTI, 1961, p. 241, nn. 440-442, plate XLIX).

[87] P. LOPREATO, "Le grandi terme di Aquileia. I mosaici del frigidarium", in *La Mosaïque gréco-romaine*, IV, Trèves 8-14 August 1984, Paris 1994, p. 96, plate XLIX, 2. Another similar mosaic, which was found in 1889 in the area of Policlinico in Rome, is recorded through a drawing that is reproduced in P. CHINI, "Mosaici inediti di Roma dall'archivio disegni della Sovraintendenza BB.CC. del Comune di Roma", in *Atti del V Colloquio AISCOM 1997*, Tivoli 1999, pp. 201-202, fig. 5.

[88] With regard to this complex and fascinating epitaph, one refers to the definitive opinion regarding the writing's correct definition and the precise significance of the words.

[89] MAGI 1958, pp. 87-115; AA.VV. 1973; STEINBY 1987 pp. 85-110; CASTAGNOLI 1992 pp. 112-114, plates LXXV-LXXVI, figs. 151-153; LIVERANI 1999, pp. 54-57; STEINBY 2003; LIVERANI, SPINOLA 2006, pp. 30-55.

[90] AA.VV. 1973, pp. 28-29, n. 5, plate VI, 2; BOSCHUNG 1987, p. 79, n. 29; STEINBY 2003, p. 45; LIVERANI, SPINOLA 2006, pp. 43-44, fig. 39.

[91] AA.VV. 1973, pp. 27-28, n. 4, plate VI, 1; BOSCHUNG 1987, p. 103, n. 770; STEINBY 2003, pp. 46-47; LIVERANI, SPINOLA 2006, pp. 43-44, fig. 39.

[92] MAGI 1958, p. 92, plate II a; STEINBY 1987, pp. 98-99; STEINBY 2003, pp. 96-98, plates 18.4 e 19.1; LIVERANI, SPINOLA 2006, p. 43, fig. 38.

[93] STEINBY 2003, pp. 82-83, plate 11.1-2; LIVERANI, SPINOLA 2006, pp. 47 and 49-51, fig. 46.

[94] STEINBY 1987, p. 98; STEINBY 2003, pp. 82-83, plate 11.1-2.

[95] MAGI 1958, p. 92 and plate III; STEINBY 1987, p. 99; STEINBY 2003, pp. 85-88, plates 13.1-2 and 14.1-3; LIVERANI, SPINOLA 2006, pp. 47-49, figs. 44-45.

[96] STEINBY 2003, pp. 86-87, footnotes 40-44. As well as these comparisons, one can also cite tomb XXV of Santa Rosa (see *infra* and LIVERANI, SPINOLA 2006, pp. 66-67, fig. 66).

[97] The voluntary knocking down of the vault leads one to believe that the underground tomb was reused in order to realise some interment graves.

[98] MAGI 1958, p. 96; STEINBY 1987, pp. 99-100; STEINBY 2003, pp. 90-95, plates 16.1-5 and 17.1; LIVERANI, SPINOLA 2006, pp. 44-47, figs. 41-42.

[99] With regard to this type of college see footnote 39. On the back wall, two niches belonging to the upper level contain at least three inscribed small slabs: the first on the left is dedicated by *Lucius Pontius Hermeros* to himself and his wife *Atalante*; the other two on the right refer to *Eros*, *servus atriensis* (a sort of porter) of the *Horti Serviliani* to his wife *Claudia Tiberia Venusta* and *Manius Servilius Romanus*, a soldier of the first court, to his wife *Betiliena Euryale*. On the left wall is an inscribed small slab which related to the largest niche and attributes the ownership of the cinerary urns to *Tiberius Claudius Onesimus*, freed slave of *Menophilus*, and to his wife *Claudia Prisca*, freed slave of *Iliades*; the latter tomb features the addition of a later dedication relating to the premature death of their son. See AA.VV. 1973, pp. 56-58, nn. 52-57, plate XXVIII, 4, plate XXIX, 1 and 2, plate XXX, 1 and 2, and plate XXXI, 1.

[100] AA.VV. 1973, p. 57, n. 55. Various other inscriptions mention the discussed *Horti* (*CIL* VI 8673; *AE* 1958, 278; AA.VV. 1973, pp. 41-42, n. 28, p. 64, n. 70, p. 68, n. 79 and pp. 158-160). These include a stele which was found in the same Vatican area and is conserved in the ex-Lateran Profane Lapidary (inv. 26593). It bears a dedication from *Sextilia Secunda* to her convivial partner, imperial slave of the *Horti Serviliani* which was "found during the month of June 1840 in some ancient burial grounds discovered in the Belvedere piazza during the new building works carried out here by order of the house-steward, Mr Massimi,[Emiliano Sarti]" (*CIL* VI 8674). On the *Horti Serviliani* see L. CHIOFFI, in *LTUR*, III, Rome 1996, p. 84, see entry "*Horti Serviliani*"; STEINBY 2003, pp. 20-21, 26.

[101] The finding of this stele prompted the start of an archaeological dig undertaken by Magi. F. MAGI, in *RendPontAcc*, 29, 1956-57, p. 10; *AE* 1959, 299; AA.VV. 1973, pp. 43-45, n. 32, plate XX; STEINBY 2003, pp. 58-59, plate 6.2; LIVERANI, SPINOLA 2006, pp. 39-40, fig. 34. One can hypothesise that the *saltus* in question was connected to the previously mentioned *Horti Serviliani*.

[102] *AE* 1959, 300 (B); F. MAGI, *Il Titolo di Verecunda Veneria*, in *RömQSchr*, 57, 1962, pp. 287-291; AA.VV. 1973, pp. 41-42, n. 28, plate XVIII, 1; STEINBY 2003, p. 56; LIVERANI, SPINOLA 2006, p. 42 (see the previous footnotes 100 and 101 in the present essay). There are two other *stelae* next to the *Verecunda* one – stele 27 of *Hordonia* and *Ptolemaeus*, and stele 29 which refers to a freedman called *Anpennius Felix*. These *stelae* are chronologically later than stele 28 and *columbarium* 1 which they rest upon (AA.VV. 1973, pp. 40-41, n. 27, plate XVII, 2, and p. 42, n. 29, plate XVIII, 2).

[103] SUET., *Nero*, 6, 47; CASS. DIO, 63, 27, 3.

[104] MAGI 1958, p. 95, plate 8; AA.VV. 1973, pp. 38-40, nn. 24-26, plate XVI, 1 and 2, and plate XVII, 1; STEINBY 1987, p. 108; BOSCHUNG 1987, p. 79, n. 33; STEINBY 2003, pp. 45-46; LIVERANI, SPINOLA 2006, p. 42, fig. 37.

[105] MAGI 1958, pp. 94-95, plate 7; STEINBY 1987, pp. 100-101; STEINBY 2003, pp. 75-78, plates 7.1-2 and 8.1-2; LIVERANI, SPINOLA 2006, pp. 41-42, fig. 36.

[106] AA.VV. 1973, p. 43, n. 31, plate XIX, 2.

[107] Other "Charon obols" have been found in the car park area close to tunnel 66 (see STEINBY 2003, p. 134, n. 40, and p. 137, n. 71) and numerous coins discovered during the dig can also be considered [as having been used for this function] (see STEINBY 2003, pp. 126-140) including those found inside two *formae* and a sarcophagus of Tomb 4 (see *infra*). On the general subject matter, see F. SINN HENNINGER, in G. KOCH, H. SICHTERMANN, *Römische Sarkophage*, Munich 1982, p. 41; G. BERGONZI, P. PIANA AGOSTINETTI, *"L'obolo di Caronte", "aes rude" e monete nelle tombe: la pianura padana tra mondo classico e ambito transalpino nella seconda età del ferro*, in *ScAnt*, 1987, 1, pp. 161-223; F. CECI, *L'interpretazione di monete e chiodi in contesti funerari. Esempi dal suburbio romano*, in M. Heinzelmann, J. Ortalli, P. Fasold (eds), *Römischer Bestattungsbrauch und Beigabensitten in Rom, Norditalien und den Nordwestprovinzen von der späten Republik bis in die Kaiserzeit* (Internationales Kolloquium, Rome 1-3. April 1998), *Palilia*, 8, Wiesbaden 2001, pp. 87-97; STEINBY 2003, pp. 127-128. Many reports have been published in *Trouvailles monétaires de tombes*. Actes du deuxième Colloque International du Groupe Suisse pour l'étude des trouvailles monétaires (Neuchâtel, 3-4 March 1995), Lausanne 1999. See also *Caronte. Un obolo per l'aldilà*, Giornate di Studio, 20 (Salerno, 20-22 February 1995) in *PP*, 50, 1995, pp. 161-535; M.P. DEL MORO, *L'utilizzo della monete in corso e l'utilizzo delle monete fuori corso nelle catacombe romane*, report in Atti del XIII Congresso Internazionale di Numismatica di Madrid (15-10 September 2003).

[108] MAGI 1958, p. 95, plate IV; STEINBY 1987, p. 101; STEINBY 2003, pp. 79-80, plate 9.1-2; LIVERANI, SPINOLA 2006, p. 37, fig. 31.

[109] AA.VV. 1973, pp. 45-47, nn. 33, 34 and 35, plate XXI, 1 and 2, and plate XXII, 1; STEINBY 2003, pp. 59-60, plate 6.3; LIVERANI, SPINOLA 2006, p. 37.

[110] STEINBY 2003, pp. 28 and 103-104, n. S1, plate 20.5; LIVERANI, SPINOLA 2006, p. 37, fig. 30. The stamp is the same sort as that of *CIL* XV 1293 = Suppl. 530, found in Pompei (therefore prior to the eruption of Mount Vesuvius in AD 79). The basin is covered by three *bipedales*, two of which bear the stamp *CIL* XV 981 and mention *Cneus Domitius Afer*, perhaps the suffect consul of AD 39 who then died in AD 59.

[111] AA.VV. 1973, pp. 50-51, nn. 40-43, plates XXIV and XXV, and p. 77, n. 95, plate XLVI, 2.

[112] AA.VV. 1973, p. 49, n. 39, plate XXIII, 2; STEINBY 2003, pp. 47 and 100; LIVERANI, SPINOLA 2006, p. 54.

[113] STEINBY 2003, pp. 62-63 and 100; LIVERANI, SPINOLA 2006, p. 54, fig. 52.

[114] STEINBY 1987, p. 102; STEINBY 2003, p. 99, plate 19.2 and 4; LIVERANI, SPINOLA 2006, p. 52, fig. 49.

[115] See STEINBY 2003, p. 99, footnote 93.

[116] STEINBY 1987, p. 102; STEINBY 2003, pp. 95-96, plates 17.3-4 and 18.3; LIVERANI, SPINOLA 2006, p. 52, fig. 50.

[117] U. SANSONI, *Il nodo di Salomone. Simbolo e archetipo d'alleanza*, Milan 1998; see also the article by P. LIVERANI, in *ArchCl*, LI, 1999-2000, pp. 513-515.

[118] STEINBY 1987, p. 102; STEINBY 2003, pp. 98-99, plate 19.2-3; LIVERANI, SPINOLA 2006, pp. 51-52, fig. 48.

[119] AA.VV. 1973, pp. 72-73, n. 87, plate XLIII, 2.

[120] STEINBY 2003, pp. 98, 118-119, n. 3, plate 24.1-2; LIVERANI, SPINOLA 2006, pp. 35-37, fig. 28.

[121] STEINBY 1987, p. 102; STEINBY 2003, pp. 88-89, plate 15.2-5; LIVERANI, SPINOLA 2006, p. 51, fig. 47.

[122] AA.VV. 1973, pp. 52-53, n. 46, plate XXVI, 3.

[123] A certain *Apuleia Felix* is buried in a funerary urn found on the inside of the contemporary *columbarium* 9. It is possible that this deceased person had some kind of blood relationship with the first owners of this small sepulchral area (see AA.VV. 1973, pp. 77-78, n. 96, plate XLVII, 2; STEINBY 2003, p. 89).

[124] STEINBY 2003, p. 89.

[125] STEINBY 2003, pp. 101-104. Amongst the sarcophagi, one recalls a clay basin, dated to the first century AD but reused during the Severan Period (see STEINBY 2003, p. 104, n. S2).

[126] The most common type consists of covered interments or a simple grave (see STEINBY 2003, pp. 108-114; LIVERANI, SPINOLA 2006, pp. 44 and 47, fig. 40)

[127] STEINBY 2003, p. 111, plate 62.

[128] STEINBY 2003, p. 158, plate 41, figs. 1 and 2, and plate 66; LIVERANI, SPINOLA 2006, p. 31, fig. 24.

[129] MAGI 1958, p. 92; STEINBY 1987, p. 103; STEINBY 2003, pp. 78-79, plate 8.3; LIVERANI, SPINOLA 2006, pp. 40-41, fig. 35.

[130] STEINBY 2003, pp. 104-105, n. C 1.

[131] For example see T. NOGALES BASARRATE, J. MARQUEZ PÉREZ, *Espacios y tipos funerarios en* Augusta Emerita, in D. VAQUERIZO (edited by), *Espacio y usos funerarios en el Occidente Romano*, I, Córdoba 2002, pp. 130-133.

[132] STEINBY 2003, pp. 106-108, plate 22.

[133] MAGI 1958, p. 92, plate IV; STEINBY 1987, p. 103; STEINBY 2003, pp. 80-82, plates 9.2 and 10.1-2; LIVERANI, SPINOLA 2006, pp. 37-39, figs. 32-33.

[134] AA.VV. 1973, pp. 47-48, n. 36, plate XXII, 2; STEINBY 2003, pp. 60-61. The entrance of *Columbarium* 4 is decentralised out of respect for the *stelae*. Consequently, one can deduce that the latter was built and used earlier than the tomb mentioned.

[135] For comparisons see STEINBY 2003, p. 81, footnote 24.

[136] In reality, the *oscilla* were marble elements of circular, semilunar or pelta form which were hung from the arcades or portico architraves in order to decorate them with their movement in the wind.

[137] AA.VV. 1973, pp. 48-49, n. 38; STEINBY 2003, pp. 49-50, n. 1, and p. 82, plate 3.1.

[138] MAGI 1958, p. 96, plate II b; STEINBY 1987, pp. 103-104; STEINBY 2003, pp. 83-85, plate 12.1-2; LIVERANI, SPINOLA 2006, p. 37, figs. 29 and 30.

[139] For this type of college see footnote 39.
[140] STEINBY 2003, pp. 23 and 84-85. An "as" coin, dedicated to *Diva Faustina* (141-161 AD) was found in a *forma*. It is a more ancient type of coin assigned to the tomb but this coin might have circulated for many decades.
[141] STEINBY 2003, p. 162.
[142] AA.VV. 1973, pp. 76-77, n. 94, plate XLVII.
[143] AA.VV. 1973, p. 66, n. 74, plate XXXVI.
[144] The treaty between the Holy See and the Italian State was signed on 11 February 1929.
[145] The numbering of the burial chambers follows the one established by Josi 1931 and Liverani 1999.
[146] JOSI 1931; E. JOSI, in *RendPontAcc*, VII, 1929-31, p. 195; G. GATTI, in *BullCom*, 1933, p. 285; P. STYGER, *Römische Katakomben*, Berlin 1933, pp. 348-349; ID., *Römische Märtyrergrüfte*, Berlin 1935, pp. 48 and ss., plates 37-40; L. CASTELLI, *Quel tanto di territorio*, Rome 1940, pp. 78, 80; B.M. APOLLONI GHETTI - A. FERRUA - E. JOSI - E. KIRSCHBAUM, *Esplorazioni sotto la confessione di San Pietro in Vaticano*, Vatican City 1951, p. 20, fig. 7; A. VON GERKAN, *Von antiker Architektur und Topographie*, Stuttgart 1959, p. 361; *CAR*, G 3; F. MAGI, in *EAA* VI (1965), s.v. Roma, p. 868-869; ID., *ActaInstRomFin* VI, 1973, pp. 15-16, plate III; S. DELLI, *Strade in Vaticano*, Rome 1982, pp. 110-111; STEINBY 1987, pp. 87-88; CASTAGNOLI 1992, pp. 108-112; LIVERANI, SPINOLA 1999, pp. 223-225; LIVERANI 1999, pp. 61-90; *Carta* I, n. 124; LIVERANI, SPINOLA 2006, pp. 96-115.
[147] The general schematic plan put forth by LIVERANI 1999, fig. 47 was realised, for the most part, using photographs and only partly using the tombs' direct sculptural reliefs that were still visible.
[148] JOSI 1931, fig. 10; LIVERANI 1999, pp. 78-79, n. 14, figs. 78-81; LIVERANI, SPINOLA 2006, pp. 109-110, figs. 125-126.
[149] It must have measured around 2.5 metres on each side.
[150] The amphora form known as "Dressel 20" is, without doubt, the most common form found in the Mediterranean Area between the middle of the first century and the middle of the second century AD. It was produced over a long period, dating from the beginning of the first century AD to the middle of the third century AD.
[151] LIVERANI 1999, p. 79, figs. 81-83. The *amphorae* were moved to the Vatican Museums' warehouses where they are still conserved today.
[152] CASTAGNOLI 1992, p. 110, n. p; LIVERANI 1999, pp. 79 and 81, figs. 89-90; LIVERANI, SPINOLA 2006, pp. 106-107, fig. 123. Part of a sarcophagus bearing a horse, part of a marble gadrooned vase and several fragments of inscriptions were found in the area of this funerary monument.
[153] It measures about 2.8 metres on each side; JOSI 1931, fig. 11; CASTAGNOLI 1992, p. 110, n. g; LIVERANI 1999, p. 83, n. 21, figs. 93-96; LIVERANI, SPINOLA 2006, pp. 112-113, fig. 132.
[154] LIVERANI, SPINOLA 1999, p. 224. See BECATTI 1961, p. 97, n. 170, fig. 29, p. 102, n. 184, plate XXXVI, p. 106, n. 195, fig. 39, plate XXXVIII, p. 132, n. 265, plate XXXIV).
[155] As is also the case here, see the following paragraph regarding the area of Santa Rosa for the description of *columbarium* III.
[156] It measures about 2.5 metres on each side. JOSI 1931, fig. 16; CASTAGNOLI 1992, p. 110, n. i; LIVERANI 1999, p. 83, n. 22, fig. 97; LIVERANI, SPINOLA 2006, pp. 113-114, fig. 131.
[157] LIVERANI, SPINOLA 1999, p. 224.
[158] CASTAGNOLI 1992, p. 109, n. h, plate LXVIII, fig. 136; LIVERANI 1999, p. 61, n. 1, figs. 48-49; LIVERANI, SPINOLA 2006, p. 100, fig. 112.
[159] It measures about 4 x 3.2 metres.
[160] JOSI 1931, figs. 4 and 18; CASTAGNOLI 1992, p. 109, n. c, plate LXX, fig. 140; LIVERANI 1999, p. 61, n. 2, fig. 50; LIVERANI, SPINOLA 2006, pp. 100-101, fig. 113.
[161] JOSI 1931, p. 29, figs. 17-18; CASTAGNOLI 1992, p. 110, n. h; LIVERANI 1999, p. 61, figs. 51-53; LIVERANI, SPINOLA 2006, p. 101, fig. 114.
[162] JOSI 1931, fig. 7; CASTAGNOLI 1992, p. 110, n. and; LIVERANI 1999, pp. 67-68, n. 4, fig. 59; LIVERANI, SPINOLA 2006, p. 102, fig. 4.
[163] LIVERANI 1999, p. 68, fig. 59; LIVERANI, SPINOLA 1999, p. 224. The floor of *columbarium* 1 of the Santa Rosa Necropolis is not dissimilar (see *infra*) as are several mosaics found in Ostia (see BECATTI 1961, p. 17, n. 16, plate XIV and pp. 42-44, n. 64, plate XV). All of these date to the early decades of second century AD
[164] JOSI 1931, p. 29, figs. 3, 4, 6, 15 and 18; CASTAGNOLI 1992, p. 109, n. d, plate LXX, fig. 140; LIVERANI 1999, pp. 61 and 67, n. 3, figs. 54-56; LIVERANI, SPINOLA 2006, pp. 101-102, figs. 115-116.
[165] It measures about 3.9 x 3.5 metres.
[166] Inv. 38847. JOSI 1931, fig. 6; CASTAGNOLI 1992, plate LXXI, fig. 142; LIVERANI 1999, pp. 61 and 67, figs. 57-58.
[167] For similar exportations, see D.U. SCHILARDI, *Paros and the Export of Marble Sarcophagi to Rome and Etruria*, in D.U. SCHILARDI, D. KATSONOPOLOU (ed.), *Paria lithos*, Athens 2000, pp. 537-557.
[168] LIVERANI 1999, pp. 75-77, n. 12, figs. 76-77; LIVERANI, SPINOLA 2006, p. 109, fig. 125.
[169] End of the first century AD – beginning of second century AD
[170] JOSI 1931, p. 27, fig. 8; CASTAGNOLI 1992, p. 109, a, plate LXX, figs. 138-139; LIVERANI 1999, pp. 84-85, figs. 98-105; LIVERANI, SPINOLA 2006, p. 114.
[171] The *bipedales* take their name from the measurement of two feet which equates to 60 cm. Some bear the brick stamp *CIL* XV 811d of the Trajanic Period. See LIVERANI 1999, p. 85, footnote 55.
[172] P. STYGER, *Römische Katakomben*, Berlin 1933, plate 54; JOSI, *IllVat* 1932, *cit.* footnote 8, fig. 9; CASTAGNOLI 1992, plate LXXIII, fig. 146; LIVERANI 1999, pp. 73-75, figs. 71-74; LIVERANI, SPINOLA 1999, p. 224, fig. 7; LIVERANI, SPINOLA 2006, pp. 73 and 75, figs. 71-74.
[173] For example, see BECATTI 1961, p. 84, n. 136 and p. 89, n. 150, plate LXXXI, pp. 149-150, n. 287, plate LXXIX, p. 197 n. 377 and pp. 197-198, n. 378, plate LXXXIII. The mosaic was removed in 1930 and transferred to the Vatican Museums (inv. 45776).
[174] It measures about 4 x 3 metres.
[175] CASTAGNOLI 1992, p. 110, n. p; LIVERANI 1999, pp. 79-82, n. 19, figs. 41, 87-89; LIVERANI, SPINOLA 2006, p. 112, fig. 129.
[176] For example, see some mosaics found in Ostia in BECATTI 1961, p. 17, n. 16, plate XIV, pp. 42-44, n. 64, plate XV, pp. 133-134, n. 267, p. 208, n. 394, p. 212, n. 394, plate XIII.
[177] LIVERANI 1999, p. 79, n. 15, fig. 84; LIVERANI, SPINOLA 2006, p. 110, fig. 127.
[178] At this point, it becomes a blind alley and Tomb 15 consequently faces onto a small piazza that is only connected to the neighbouring *via Triumphalis* area.
[179] It measures around 3.5 x 3 metres.
[180] LIVERANI 1999, p. 79, n. 16, fig. 85; LIVERANI, SPINOLA 2006, p. 110, fig. 128.
[181] LIVERANI 1999, p. 79, n. 17; LIVERANI, SPINOLA 2006, p. 110.
[182] LIVERANI 1999, p. 79, n. 18, fig. 86; LIVERANI, SPINOLA 2006, p. 112.
[183] CASTAGNOLI 1992, p. 110, n. l; LIVERANI 1999, pp. 82-83, n. 20; LIVERANI, SPINOLA 2006, p. 112.
[184] JOSI 1931, p. 27, n. 3; CASTAGNOLI 1992, p. 111; LIVERANI 1999, p. 83, fig. 92; LIVERANI, SPINOLA 2006, p. 112, fig. 130. The statuette is now conserved in the Magazzino delle Corazze (The Armour Warehouse) in the Vatican Museums (Inv. 4739; G. VON KASCHNITZ WEINBERG, *Le sculture del magazzino del Museo Vaticano*, Vatican City 1936-37, pp. 126-127, n. 269, plate LVII; E. SCHMIDT, in *LIMC*, VIII, Zurich-Munich 1997, s.v. *Venus*, p. 203, n. 94).
[185] JOSI 1931, fig. 12; CASTAGNOLI 1992, p. 111, nn. r, s; LIVERANI 1999, pp. 68-71, nn. 6, 7, 8, fig. 61-63; LIVERANI, SPINOLA 2006, p. 104, figs. 119-121.
[186] LIVERANI 1999, p. 78, n. 13, figs. 41 and 42 (upper illustration); LIVERANI, SPINOLA 2006, p. 109.
[187] CASTAGNOLI 1992, p. 110, n. f; LIVERANI 1999, p. 68, n. 5, fig. 60; LIVERANI, SPINOLA 2006, p. 102, fig. 118.
[188] JOSI 1931, fig. 13; CASTAGNOLI 1992, p. 110, n. q, plate LXXIV, fig. 149; LIVERANI 1999, p. 71, n. 9, fig. 64; LIVERANI, SPINOLA 2006, pp. 104-106, fig. 122.
[189] CASTAGNOLI 1992, p. 110, n. n; LIVERANI 1999, pp. 71-73, n. 10, figs. 65-70; LIVERANI, SPINOLA 2006, pp. 106-107, fig. 123.
[190] It measures about 4.1 x 4.9 metres.
[191] The excavation was carried out under the supervision of Francesco Buranelli (the then director of the Vatican Museums), Paolo Liverani, Giandomenico Spinola and Leonardo Di Blasi who also looked after, with the help of Giuseppe D'Errico, the graphical part of the project. Amongst the archaeologists of various qualifications, I would like to thank Giorgio Filippi, Alessia Amenta, Daniele Battistoni, Claudia Valeri, Eleonora Ferrazza and Daniele Borgonovo. Furthermore, lest we not forget the restorers of the Vatican Museums who worked in the building sites and laboratories: for marble restoration: Luciano Ermo and Guy Devreux, Massimo Bernacchi, Stefano Spada, Andrea Felice, Patrizia Rossi; for mosaic restoration: Roberto Cassio and Paolo Monaldi; for terracotta, glass and metal restoration: Flavia Callori, Henriette Schokking, Fabiana Francescangeli, Angelica Mazzucato, Alice Baltera, Massimiliana Landi, Giulia Barella, Eva Mentelli; for the restoration of frescoes and stucco: Alessandra Zarelli, Fabio Piacentini, Simone Virdia, Vittoria Cimino, Maria Pustka, Francesco Prantera, Paola Guidi, Marco Innocenzi and Bruno Marocchini, which was coordinated by Maestro Maurizio De Luca. Precious assistance was given by the Laboratorio di Ricerche Scientifiche (The Laboratory of Scientific Research) with Ulderico Santamaria and Fabio Morresi. Finally, one must mention the Laboratorio di Materie Plastiche (The Laboratory of Plastic Materials) with Fabio Mastrolorenzi and Alessandro Bartomioli, the maintenance team directed by Antonio Maura, the General Inventory that was coordinated by Alessandra Uncini and the entire Archivio Fotografico (The Photographic Archive) which curated the realization of photographic documentation of the excavations and its materials. Particular thanks goes to Rosanna Di Pinto, Filippo Petrignani, Daniela Valci, Luigi Giordano, Pietro Zigrossi and, above all, Alessandro Bracchetti, who was responsible for the last photographic campaign. A separate mention goes to Giovanni Lattanzi's valuable work, the man responsible for having taken numerous photographs of the excavation during 2006 on occasion of an article that appeared in the magazine *Archeo*. The majority of the evocative images that are reproduced here are accredited to these last two photographers.
[192] The first details were published in *L'attività della Santa Sede* 2003, pp. 1294-1295; *ibid.*, 2004, p. 1308; F. BURANELLI, L. ERMINI PANI, *MemPontAcc* XVII, 2003, pp. 2-3; STEINBY 2003, pp. 1-3. A more complete picture of the excavation was published in F. BURANELLI, P. LIVERANI, G. SPINOLA, *I nuovi scavi della necropoli della via Trionfale in Vaticano*, in *RendPontAcc*, LXXVIII, 2005-06, pp. 369-390, in SPINOLA 2006 and, above all, in LIVERANI, SPINOLA 2006, pp. 56-95. Individual tombs (cremation and burial) were recorded thanks to the work of Isabella Bucci whom I would like to take the opportunity to thank.
[193] The project was mostly funded by a group of generous supporters of the Vatican Museums, the *Canadian Chapter of the Patrons of the Arts in the Vatican Museums*. The work, which also includes a layout review of the two archeological areas that adjoin one another should finish in the Autumn of 2010.
[194] On the subject, see also J. ORTALLI, *Scavo stratigrafico e contesti sepolcrali. Una questione aperta*, in AA.VV., *Pour une archéologie du rite. Nouvelles perspectives de l'archéologie funéraire (études réunies par John Scheid)*, Collection de l'École Française de Rome, 407, Rome 2008, pp. 137-159 (with updated bibliography).
[195] See H. SCHROFF, in PAULY – WISSOWA, *Real-Encyclopädie der classischen Altertumswissenschaft*, see entry *Tabellarius*, IV, A, 2, Stuttgart 1932, coll. 1844-1847.
[196] TC 26; inv. 52374. See LIVERANI, SPINOLA 2006, p. 59.
[197] TC 72; inv. 52393. With regard to union relationships between freed women slaves and slaves as well as the law which sometimes controlled them, one can see the synthesis in DI STEFANO MANZELLA, Felix Q. Canusi Praenestini libertus *in un'epigrafe inedita*, in *BMonMusPont*, XIV, 1994, pp. 90-92.
[198] TC 12; inv. 52215.
[199] TC 176; inv. 52424. The text can only be generally attributed to the second half of the first century AD
[200] TC 153; inv. 52423. BURANELLI, LIVERANI, SPINOLA 2005-2006, p. 467, fig. 17; LIVERANI, SPINOLA 2006, p. 69, fig. 70.
[201] P. HABEL, in PAULY – WISSOWA, *Real-Encyclopädie der classischen Altertumswissenschaft*, see entry

Aquarii, II,1, Stuttgart 1895, coll. 311-312; E. De Ruggiero, *Dizionario epigrafico di antichità romane*, I, voce *Aqua* I.B *Familia publica a) Aquarius*, pp. 554-555, with numerous epigraphic comparisons. With slaves in a private setting, the task of *aquarii* was that of transporting water in earthenware pots which was necessary for all private homes as it also was in many public places and offices: Juvenal in *Satirae* (VI, 332) speaks about *aquarii* as the most humble of slaves. In this case, it is likely that work regarding the particular topographical context of *Nemus Cai et Luci* was connected to the place's numerous water basins and relative adductions, presumably carried out during the years immediately after its opening.

[202] *Res gestae divi Augusti*, app. 2; Suet., *Aug.*, 43, 2; *CIL* VI 31566 = XI 3772; see also Tac., *Ann.* 14, 15, 2.

[203] Dio Cass., 66.25.3-4: "ἐν τῷ ἄλσει τῷ τοῦ Γαΐου τοῦ τε Λουκίου."

[20] *PIR* I 222 and 216.

[20] See A.M. Liberati, *LTUR* III, Rome 1996, p. 337, see entry "*Naumachia Augusti*"; E. Papi, *ibid.*, p. 340, see entry "*Nemus Caesarum*". Some believe that this complex was located in the current area of Piazza S. Cosimato. Others (F. Coarelli, in *Ostraka*, 1.1, 1992, pp. 39-54) believe that it was beyond Porta Portese.

[206] P. Liverani, in Aa.Vv., *Vixerunt Omnes. Romani ex imaginibus. Ritratti romani dai Musei Vaticani,* (exhibition catalogue in Japanese) Tokyo 2004 (Italian edition, Tokyo 2005), p. 26, fig. 10; Buranelli, Liverani, Spinola 2005-2006, p. 471, fig. 18; Liverani, Spinola 2006, p. 60, fig. 56; Spinola 2006, pp. 44-45.

[207] Inv. 40674. The sculptor, assisted by his helper, executes the decoration of a tub sarcophagus with lion protomes with the current drill (see J. Stroszeck, *Die antiken Sarkophagreliefs*, VI,1, *Löwen-Sarkophage*, Berlin 1998, pp. 19, 23, 72, 90, 95, footnote 771, plate 94, fig. 8; K. Eichner, *Technische Voraussetzungen für die Massenproduktion von Sarkophagen in konstantinischer Zeit*, in G. Koch (ed.), *Sarkophag-Studien*, 2, Akten des Symposiums "Frühchristliche Sarkophage", Marburg, 30.6 – 4.7. 1999, Mainz am Rhein 2002, pp. 75-77, plate 26).

[208] Galleria dei Candelabri, inv. 2671; G. Lippold, *Die Skulpturen des Vaticanischen Museums*, Berlin 1956, pp. 317-318, n. 52, plate 142; G. Zimmer, *Römische Berufsdarstellungen*, Berlin 1982, pp. 157-158, n. 80; P. Liverani, in *Vixerunt omnes* (see footnote 206) Tokyo 2004, pp. 110-112, n. 14 (Italian edition, Tokyo 2005, pp. 62-63); G. Spinola, *Il Museo Pio Clementino. 3*, Vatican City 2004, pp. 255-256, n. 52 (with the previous bibliography).

[209] This is a container that was produced in the [surrounding] high valley of the Tiber river between Umbria and Etruria for the transport of good wine in central Italy. The so-called "Spello" container seems to have been used in clearly definable chronological period – between 50 - 150 AD, even if there are sporadic examples of its use slightly later on. The exported wine could be the product of those vineyard hills mentioned by Pliny such as *hirtiola* (or *irtiola*), which comes from *gens Hirtia* (Hirtia people) and the small dimensions might indicate that such a wine was considered one of good quality. Gradually, from the end of the first century AD, the "Spello" amphora (even if it was reduced in size) replaced part of the market covered by the "Dressel 2-4" amphora which was used for the transport of wine throughout the entire peninsula but above all in Lazio and Campagna (see *Ostia I*, p. 108, fig. 544; *Ostia II*, pp. 105-106, figs. 521-523; *Ostia III*, pp. 206 and 624, fig. 369; A. Tchernia, *Le vin dans l'Italie romaine*, Rome 1976, *passim*).

[210] It is a series of *amphorae* which derive from a Greek-insular (Cos) prototype but of Italian or provincial fabrication (often Spanish). In Italy, the container was mainly used for the transport of Campagna and Lazio wines, from the end of the first century AD until the beginning of the second century AD (see *Ostia II*, pp. 119-124, 127-136, 143-146, nn. 16-46; *Ostia III*, pp. 497-504; C. Panella, M. Fano, *Le anfore con anse bifide conservate a Pompei: contributo ad una loro classificazione*, in *Méthodes classiques et méthodes formelles dans l'étude des amphores*, in *MEFRA*, suppl. 32, 1977, pp. 133-177; L. Fariña del Cerro, W. Fernandez de la Vega, A. Hesnard, *Contribution à l'établissement d'une typologie des amphores dites "Dressel 2-4"*, *ibidem*, pp. 179-206; M. Sciallano, P. Sibella, *Amphores. Comment les identifier?*, Barcelona 1994, p. 38). In some rare cases, the "Dressel 2-4" amphora also shows several later signs (see A. Desbat, H. Savay Guerraz, in *Gallia*, 47, 1990, pp. 203-213).

[211] Buranelli, Liverani, Spinola 2005-2006, p. 471, fig. 20; Liverani, Spinola 2006, pp. 79-80, fig. 84; Spinola 2006, p. 45.

[212] *Servi lanternarii* were generally used for night-time illumination. For example, they illuminated the work of those artists who did the inscriptions (see A. Hug, in Pauly – Wissowa, *Real-Encyclopädie der classischen Altertumswissenschaft*, see entry *Lanterna*, XII,1, Stuttgart 1921, coll. 693-694; *AE* 1915, 62). However, some of these were also *ostiari*, thus resided near the entrance of their homes (see Cic., *Pis.*, 20). A very similar lantern to that found in the present statuette was sculpted into the altar of *Marcus Hordonius Philargurus Labeo*. Known as a *lanternarius*, which in this case should be understood as a lantern-maker, he was a freedman (*CIL* X 3970; G. Zimmer, *Römische Berufsdarstellungen*, Berlin 1982, pp. 203-204, n. 149). The altar was discovered at Herculaneum and then moved to the Church of St. Michael in Capua but has since gone missing. An engraving of it can be found at Plate XXVII of "*Antiquités d'Herculanum*". Gravées par Th. Piroli avec une explication par S.-Ph. Chaudé et publiées par F. et P. Piranesi, frères. Tome VI. *Lampes et Candelabras*, Paris 1806 (*Antichità di Ercolano*, tome VIII, p. 265).

[213] B. Andreae (ed.), *Bildkatalog der Skulpturen des Vatikanischen Museums*, I, *Museo Chiaramonti*, Berlin-New York 1995, p. 101*, n. 340, plate 1068 (with previous bibliography). In this case, the statuette was once part of a small fountain. Indeed, a hole that let a gush of water through can be found on the earthenware pot.

[214] The statuette is missing part of its right leg and also contains several small gaps. The fractured parts were not found underneath the amphora. As a result, one is of the opinion that the small sculpture was buried in the same imperfect state of conservation as when it was rediscovered. Therefore, this constitutes the recycling of a damaged handicraft that was originally intended for another destination.

[215] Buranelli, Liverani, Spinola 2005-2006, pp. 471-472, fig. 21; Liverani, Spinola 2006, p. 59; Spinola 2006, p. 42. Amongst these tombs, one recalls the cremated Tomb TC 15. One can compare, for example, several cinerary urns in the shape of a box with four brackets (see those published in F. Sinn, *Stadrömische Marmorurnen*, Mainz 1978, p. 95, nn. 17 and 18; P. Rodriguez Oliva, *Talleres locales de urnas cinerarias de sarcofagos en la* Provincia Hispania Ulterior Baetica, in D. Vaquerizo (edited by), *Espacio y usos funerarios en el Occidente Romano*, I, Córdoba 2002, pp. 259-285) or other cinerary urns in the form of a basket (see Sinn, *ibid.*, pp. 62-63, 175, nn. 341-344).

[216] On the subject of creating funerary spaces and enclosures (also with the use of perishable materials), see D. Vaquerizo, *Recintos y Acotados funerarios en* Colonia Patricia Corduba, in *Madrider Mitteilungen*, 43, 2001, pp. 168-205; Id., *Espacio y usos funerarios en Corduba*, in D. Vaquerizo (edited by), *Espacio y usos funerarios en el Occidente Romano*, II, Córdoba 2002, p. 168 and ss.; A.B. Ruiz Osuna, *La monumentalización de los espacios funerarios en* Colonia Patricia Corduba *(Ss. I a.C. – II d.C.)*, *Arqueologia Cordobesa*, 16, 2007, p. 56 and ss.; M.R. Picuti, *Il contributo dell'Epigrafia latina allo scavo delle necropoli antiche*, in Aa.Vv., *Pour une archéologie du rite. Nouvelles perspectives de l'archéologie funéraire (études réunies par John Scheid)*, Collection de l'École Française de Rome, 407, Rome 2008, pp. 47-49 (with reference bibliography).

[217] Liverani, Spinola 2006, pp. 67-69, fig. 68. The tomb's raised parts had already been all but levelled during ancient times. The cinerary urns, which are bigger than usual, are of particular interest. They were a type of urn that was, above all, used during the early Augustan Period.

[218] Liverani, Spinola 2006, p. 69, fig. 69. Tomb XXII is built of brick. Its box cover still exists and is missing only the extrados. A panel made of brick is found on the front which originally would have contained a marble slab with a dedication to the owners of the tomb. This inscription would render the stele pleonastic.

[219] The front of the stele, which is identified by the abbreviation TC 167, contains a tube for libations that led to a funerary urn (TC 165) and an amphora (TC 166) belonging to another cremation tomb.

[220] Liverani, Spinola 2006, pp. 69-70, fig. 71. The tomb's entrance is orientated towards the east, to the valleys, but after more than half a century, it was closed off by the western wall of Tomb III.

[221] Tube: TC 171; stele: TC 172. An oil lamp was found in front of the stele (inv. 52306). It bears a crow, a palm branch and perhaps a Bailey Piii-type "fareta", dated between the second half of the first century AD and the first half of the second century AD

[222] E. De Ruggiero, *Dizionario epigrafico di antichità romane*, III, word *Hortator*, p. 992; Liverani, Spinola 2006, p. 70, fig. 72; Spinola 2006, p. 45. Two other *hortatores* of the *factio veneta* (*CIL* VI 10074, 10076, both found at Villa Doria Pamphilj) are known of in Rome.

[223] The stele, which measures 98 cm in height, 45 cm in width and 25 cm in depth, is dated to around the middle of the first century AD It is part of a lot of handicrafts that were illegally exported from the archeological area of Santa Rosa in December 2002. These objects are currently being held in a judicial deposit at the barracks of the Guardia di Finanza (a military body responsible for enforcing the law on income tax and monopolies) at Fiumicino. What is of particular importance in the text of this travertine stele is the mention of *Titus Albanus Hortator* who was a member of the *factio veneta*, one of the four factions that competed in circus races and enjoyed noteworthy social standing (see A. Cameron, *Circus Factions. Blues and Greens at Rome and Byzantium*, Oxford 1976). Amongst the confiscated materials, there are also three inscribed altars dating to the middle of the first century AD The first is dedicated by *Titus Occius Euschemus* to his parents *Pinnia Heureusi* and *Titus Occius Telesphorus*; the second was dedicated by the freedman *Censorinus* to the imperial freedman *Callistus Abascantus* and to the freedman *Creticianus*; the third is dedicated by *Lucius Sempronius Urbanus* to her sister and freedwoman *Sempronia Genice*, which is followed by *Sempronia Thallusa*, the wife of *Urbanus*, as well as to *Ulvius Numerius Apollonius* and his brother *Marcus Aponius Sabbio*.

[224] Suet., *Vit.* 14.3: "*Quosdam et de plebe ob id ipsum, quod Venetae factioni clare male dixerant, interemit contemptu sui et noua spe id ausos opinatus*". "Bring simple plebeians also to justice only because they manifested against the *factio* Veneta (the Blues) in a loud voice, thinking that they had dared to scorn him, in the hope of a revolution."

[225] There are numerous testimonies of burials linked to the circus environment in the Vatican area although, realistically, this is due to the presence of the nearby Circus of Caligula and Nero. Indeed, as is well-known, this circus was located in an area to the left of the Vatican Basilica and was the most important and characteristic monumental structure of the pre-Christian Vatican area. In fact, one notes the large inscription of the charioteer *Publius Avilius Teres* (*CIL* VI 37834), fragments of which have been found on different occasions between Castel Sant'Angelo and the Vatican; the charioteer's funerary inscription *Pompeius* (*CIL* VI 33953) which came from the same area; inscriptions *CIL* VI 10056 from the Vatican Basilica; and *CIL* VI 10067 which was seen in the St. Petronilla rotunda before it was destroyed. Objects found in the same Vatican area that belong to various periods include the charioteer inscription *Appuleius Diocles* (*CIL* VI 10048) as well as others that no longer bear their name but are always related to circus games (*CIL* VI 10052, 10057). A funerary stele of *Theseus* (Aa.Vv. 1973, p. 69, n. 81, plate XL), a charioteer belonging to the Green-shirts team ("*agitator*" of the *factio Prasina*), and a small bust of a charioteer have been found in the car park area. Lastly, one should mention the horse *Volucer* that once belonged to the same faction and was buried in the Vatican by Emperor Lucius Verus (*SHA*, *Verus* 6. 3-4). See also Liverani 1999, pp. 21-28 e 32-34; Id., in *LTUR*, *Supplementum*, III, Rome 2005, pp. 11-12, see entry "*Gai et Neronis Circus*"; M.A. Tomei, *ibidem*, pp. 12-13, see entry "*Gaianum*".

[226] Liverani, Spinola 2006, p. 67, figs. 67a and 67b.

227 LIVERANI, SPINOLA 2006, pp. 66-67, fig. 66.
228 With regard to the function of this larger tube, one can also consider parallel examples found in tombs located at the nearby Annona Necropolis: photographs of the archaeological dig show that small wells (which were seemingly used during cremation ceremonies) contain similar tubes (LIVERANI 1999, pp. 84-85, n. 23, figs. 103-104; furthermore see pp. 61-67, n. 3, fig. 58 and above p. 199 and *infra* p. 235).
229 LIVERANI, SPINOLA 2006, p. 89.
230 Unfortunately, nearly the entire tomb is currently covered over by a large slab of reinforced concrete.
231 BURANELLI, LIVERANI, SPINOLA 2005-2006, pp. 457-459, figs. 5-6; LIVERANI, SPINOLA 2006, pp. 88-89, figs. 98-100; SPINOLA 2006, pp. 42 and 44
232 SPINOLA 2006, p. 42. Several infant portraits belonging to the Tiberian-Claudian Period are rather similar: see, for example B. DI LEO, in A. GIULIANO (edited by), *Museo Nazionale Romano. Le sculture*, I/9,1, pp. 172-174, n. R132; B. ANDREAE (edited by), *Bildkatalog der Skulpturen des Vatikanischen Museums*, I, *Museo Chiaramonti*, Berlin-New York 1995, p. 17*, nn. 193 and 194, plates 131 and 132-133.
233 The sealed context allows one to date the life of this tomb's second phase with certainty. In fact, "round beaked" oil lamps with the factory stamp *MVN-TREPT* (Bailey "Pi" type; *CIL* XV, 2, 6565) date to the end of the first century AD and the middle of the second century AD
234 For example, see A.A. AMADIO, in A. GIULIANO (edited by), *Museo Nazionale Romano. Le sculture*, I/9, Rome 1987, pp. 202-203, n. R158.
235 The head of a similar small bust had already been discovered in the car park area but outside the stratum (see STEINBY 2003, p. 121, n. 6, plate 25.2). With regard to making comparisons, one recalls other similar handicrafts in AA.VV., *Mostra Augustea della Romanità*, catalogue, Rome 1938 (IV ed.), p. 920, n. 1c; V.F. CECI, *Ermetta fittile dalla via Nomentana: un nuovo tipo di sonaglio di età romana*, in *ArchClass* 42, 1990, pp. 441-448; G. MESSINEO, in *RivStPomp* 5, 1991-92, 130, figs. 25-26; E. SALZA PRINA RICOTTI, *Museo della Civiltà Romana. Vita e costumi dei Romani antichi*, 18, *Giochi e giocattoli*, Rome 1995, pp. 18-24.
236 D. VAQUERIZO GIL, *Immaturi et innupti*, Barcelona 2004, *passim* (with previous complete bibliography).
237 TF 3. LIVERANI, SPINOLA 2006, p. 66, fig. 65; SPINOLA 2006, p. 46.
238 LIVERANI, SPINOLA 2006, p. 63.
239 Several sepulchral structures lean against this tomb which are marked by *stelae*: at the front can be found the tomb that *Avillius Felix* built for his mother *Avillia Soractina* (TC 40; inv. 52390) – it is in direct contact with the left jamb of Tomb XXVIII which was constructed by *Gratina* for his servants *Syrus* and *Roman[us?]* (TC 53; inv. 52380); *Auctinus* and his wife *Anthidis* (TC 45; inv. 52379); as well as *Cestia Eutychia, Iucundus* and *Alexander* (TC 48; inv. 52377), all three of whom are located on the other side. The tomb dedicated by *Zelothos* to his convivial partner *Aestiva* (TC 43; inv. 52378) obliterates the entrance of the same tomb whilst along the left wall (the eastern wall) one instead finds three anepigraphic *stelae* TC 34 (inv. 52386), TC 36 (inv. 52387) and TC 39 (inv. 52389).
240 LIVERANI, SPINOLA 2006, pp. 61-63. Part of this *columbarium*'s northern wall, which dates to the middle of the first century AD is visible. It contains two niches with double cinerary urns. There also remains part of the western wall which contains a bigger niche. The walls are plastered over and painted in red whilst the floor once contained a frame made up of marble listels.
241 Numerous cremations are located between Tombs XXI and XXVI, some of which are marked out by *stelae*. Many dedications bear names that were probably imperial freedmen of the Julian-Claudian Dynasty. Of these, one recalls the stele dedicated to *Caius Iulius Anchinus* (TC 83; inv. 52434), that with the dedication to *patronus Severus* (TC 102; inv. 52433), that of *Claudia Nice* to her son *Tiberius Claudius Vitalis* (TC 104; inv. 52432) as well as that of *Tiberius Pyramus* and *Faenia Favor* to their children *Ianuarius* and *Restitutus* (TC 108; inv. 52431).
242 BURANELLI, LIVERANI, SPINOLA 2005-2006, pp. 464-467, fig. 14; LIVERANI, SPINOLA 2006, pp. 81-82, figs. 88 and 89. A "Spello" amphora (50-150 AD),

which was used for a subsequent cremation, is inserted in the ground in front of the slab.
243 BURANELLI, LIVERANI, SPINOLA 2005-2006, p. 467, fig. 15; LIVERANI, SPINOLA 2006, pp. 80-81, figs. 86 and 87; SPINOLA 2006, p. 43. Later on, a large number of individual cremation tombs crowded around the tomb. Amongst these, one notes those that bear the name of the deceased which is chiselled into the stele. An example of this is seen with TC 117 (inv. 52429), a fragment bearing the inscription *r[—]onius dulgentissimus*, TC 125 (inv. 52410) with the dedication of a freedman called *Agathangelus* to his master *Matius Martialis*, and TC 137 (inv. 52422) by *Attia Eutychia* to her husband *Titus Senius Abascantus*.
244 During a subsequent phase when the tomb of Alcimus had been abandoned, a long stele bearing a dedication from *Lucius Marcus Valerius Onesimus* to his wife *Clodia Elpidiva* was discovered on top of the tomb although it does not belong to it. It is likely that the stele slid down from another tomb which was located higher up during one of the large landslides that occurred on the hill's terrain around 130-140 AD
245 In light of the instruments depicted near the figure of *Alcimus, t*he term "*custos*" (custodian, guard, protector) can alo be understood with the more generic meaning of "curator" (see, for example, the different readings in *CIL* VI 130, 1585, 3962, 6226, 8431).
246 These tools are documented in numerous altars, basements and *stelae*: see G. ZIMMER, *Römische Berufsdarstellungen*, Berlin 1982, pp. 161-179, nn. 84-111. During the Imperial Period, the existence of various structures [that specifically] put on shows is well-known: machinery scenes such as *proscenium*, the part of the scene closest to the orchestra upon which the theatrical setting was depicted (a street, piazza square or something else), the *scaenae frons*, an architectonic backdrop that was often integrated with painted panels called *periaktoi*, triangular moveable prisms (derived from the Greek theatre) with three sides painted with a tragic scene, a comedy and a satyric drama, and an *auleum*, a sort of curtain which was let down or raised on occasion of the set changes or at the end of the show.
247 See P. GROS, in *LTUR*, V, Rome 1999, pp. 35-38, see entry "*Theatrum Pompei*" (with previous bibliography).
248 TAC., *Ann.*, 3, 72, 4 and 6, 45, 2; VELL., 2, 130; SEN., *Dial.*, 6, 22, 4; SUET., *Tib.*, 47, 1, *Cal.*, 21, 1 and *Claud.*, 21, 3; CASS. DIO, 57, 21, 3 and 60, 6, 8).
249 CASS. DIO, 63, 6, 1-2; see also PLIN., *Nat. Hist.*, 33, 54.
250 CASS. DIO, 66, 24, 2.
251 See pp. 199 and 235.
252 BURANELLI, LIVERANI, SPINOLA 2005-2006, pp. 455-457, figs. 3 and 4; LIVERANI, SPINOLA 2006, pp. 86-88, figs. 95-97. The perimetre wall of the *columbarium* (about 5 metres per side) partially "cuts" through the structures of *columbarium* XIV and Tomb IV (of the *Natronii*) without, however, destroying them. These more ancient tombs must presumably have already been in a state of abandon.
253 A small marble slab bearing the dedication by *Lucius Granius Restitutus* to his son *Restitutus* is inserted into the wall of the back wall underneath one of the niches and next to a cavity hole for a larger slab. Another large niche can be found in the upper part of the same back wall. A rectangular cavity for a large slab is found underneath it. This niche, which has a reliefwork frame and two cinerary urns affixed to it, was probably destined for the owners of the mausoleum and the slab (which is unfortunately lost) bore the main inscription with a dedication to the monumental tomb.
254 The *columbarium*, which was built towards AD 60, must have held depositions at least until the end of the first century AD.
255 Two small nails must have affixed a plant above the marble garland.
256 See D. BOSCHUNG, *Antike Grabaltäre aus den Nekropolen Roms*, Bern 1987, pp. 96-97, nn. 643, 644, 649, 651, 656.
257 The female figure places her left hand on a vat. The interpretation of the scene results in margins of uncertainty as it could represent instead infantile games of the god, guest of the nymphs of Nysa.
258 See P. CASTRÉN, *Acta Instituti Romani Finlandiae* VI, 1973, pp. 158-161; STEINBY 2003, pp. 20-21, 26.

259 R. HANSLIK, *RE* XVIII (1949), see entry *Passienus*, cc. 2097-2098, n. 2; *PIR* VI² (1998) *Passienus* 146. We thank Claudia Lega and Ivan Di Stefano for having discussed the prosopographic aspects with us.
260 SCHOL. AD IUV., 4.81; HIER., *Chron.* ad a. 38 (p. 178 Helm). With regard to his estates on the right bank of the Tiber river, see P. BACCINI LEOTARDI, in *LTUR, Suburbium*, II, Rome 2004, pp. 169-170, see entry "C. Crispi Passieni Praediorum".
261 LIVERANI, SPINOLA 2006, pp. 85-86, figs. 93-94. The tomb is generally dated to the second half of the first century AD.
262 LIVERANI, SPINOLA 2006, pp. 63-64, figs. 61-62; SPINOLA 2006, p. 43.
263 The tomb must have been subjected to frequent small landslides and filling in [of earth] given that an open area that is outlined by cut bricks in order to preserve the tomb from infiltrations of earth as well as its access from other tombs.
264 The vault wall covers the lateral sides of the funerary altar where two canonical sacrificial elements are sculpted, the *urceus* and the *patera*.
265 The tomb (TC 75; inv. 52385) is furnished with a stele that bears a dedication to *Seria Fortunata* by her husband *Lucius Serius Secundus*, under which there is a pierced slab for libations. Part of an amphora (TC 74) belonging to another cremation is found to the side.
266 BURANELLI, LIVERANI, SPINOLA 2005-2006, p. 471, fig. 19; LIVERANI, SPINOLA 2006, pp. 64-65, figs. 63-64; SPINOLA 2006, p. 43.
267 There were a great number of cremations amongst which the aforementioned stele TC 75 (inv. 52385; see above), the stele fragment TC 62 (inv. 52420) and many cinerary urns marked out by tubes and *amphorae*. Furthermore, a little towards the north and positioned between *columbarium* XVI and Tomb XXI, is the stele dedicated by *Marcus Eulutus Proculus* to his son *Primus* and his wife and freedman *Pyramidis* (TC 77; inv. 52394). An altar-cinerary urn bearing a dedication from *Rutilia Sunthyche* to her son *Publius Rutilius Felix*, who died at just 5 years old, comes from an indefinable part of the necropolis in that it was discovered without a setting. On the stele's front, the young boy is dressed in a toga with a container of coils at his feet. Another altar-cinerary urn was found without a context and shows clear traces of its recycling: the cavity for ashes on the back was filled in with masonry whilst the front bears the inscribed dedication "*D(onum) D(edit)*" of *Sextus Aonius Barronius*, freed by *Aonius Thophimus* (see *CIL* VI 4731), added by *Sancto Silvano*. Perhaps its reuse with the new votive dedication should be placed in relation to a cult place of Silvanus *dendrophoros* inside the great sanctuary of *Magna Mater* (Cybele) found close to the Vatican area. Various dedications by *dendrophoroi* (members of a professional college of tradesmen and wood craftsmen) exist to Silvanus and *Magna Mater*. For example, in the *Basilica Hilariana,* Rome, several dedications by *dendrophoroi* to Silvanus were discovered (*CIL* VI 637 e 641; see also *CIL* VI 642) whilst at Ostia one knows of the dedication by the *apparator* (the priest in charge of sacrifices and ceremonies), *Caius Atilius*, of *Magna Mater* of a statue portraying Silvanus to the Ostian *dendrophoroi* (*CIL* XIV 53). Another direct and very interesting connection with Attis and *Magna Mater* can be found in the inscription of a column (*CIL* IX 3375) of *Aufinum* (Ofena). In the *Basilica Hilariana*, the *dendrophoroi* participated in ceremonies in which they cut the pine tree of Attis (*arbor sancta*) and transported it in a procession.
268 BURANELLI, LIVERANI, SPINOLA 2005-2006, p. 467, fig. 16; LIVERANI, SPINOLA 2006, p. 63, fig. 60; SPINOLA 2006, pp. 44-45.
269 We do not know any more precise details regarding which mandate *legatus* might have been involved in and if his ambassadorship was answerable to the Emperor, Senate or some important administrative official. The justifications for having municipal and colonial legions is attested by literary or epigraphic sources collected together in G. IACOPI, s.v. *Legatus* n. 5, in E. DE RUGGIERO, *Dizionario epigrafico di antichità romane*, IV, 512-521.
270 Stele TC 22 (inv. 52370) was found next to it that bears a dedication from *Glaucinus* to his wife *Iunia Cryso*. It caved in due to a tomb located a bit further beyond.

341

[271] BURANELLI, LIVERANI, SPINOLA 2005-2006, p. 464, figs. 12 and 13; LIVERANI, SPINOLA 2006, pp. 70-74, figs. 73-77; SPINOLA 2006, pp. 45-46.

[272] See H. JOYCE, *The Decoration of Walls, Ceilings, and Floors in Italy in the Second and Third Centuries AD*, Rome 1981, pp. 72-78, figs. 69, 70, 71, 73-79.

[273] This illusionary motif that was irregularly adapted to the dimensions of the space and created by square, "L-shaped" and hexagonal elements, reminds one of some Ostiense mosaics of 120-130 AD (see, for example BECATTI 1961, p. 102, n. 184, plate XXVI and pp. 123-124, n. 225, plate XXX).

[274] Four cinerary urns have been found underneath the mosaic preparation (which was removed for conservation reasons and subsequently replaced).

[275] The scene takes place on the bank of the River Styx. In the Greek world, this foul-smelling river was, however, intended as a female divinity, the daughter of Okeanos and Thesis (Hesiod) or Night and Erebus (Hyginus). Viceversa, the Acheron appears in masculine forms, as the son of Gaia, condemned to be an infernal river for having upset the Giants in the battle against the gods. The bearded personification, however, could also be a more general portrayal of Lake Averno, the volcanic lake of Campania which was believed to be the entrance to Hades.

[276] *De Acherontis Transitu* (VI, 384-425): "So they pursued their former journey, and drew near the river. Now when the Boatman saw them from the Stygian wave walking through the silent wood, and directing their footsteps towards its bank, he attacked them verbally, first, and unprompted, rebuking them: 'Whoever you are, who come armed to my river, tell me, from over there, why you're here, and halt your steps. This is a place of shadows, of Sleep and drowsy Night: I'm not allowed to carry living bodies in the Stygian boat. Truly it was no pleasure for me to take Hercules on his journey over the lake, nor Theseus and Pirithous, though they may have been children of gods, unrivalled in strength. The first came for Cerberus the watchdog of Tartarus, and dragged him away quivering from under the king's throne: the others were after snatching our Queen from Dis's chamber.' To this the prophetess of Amphrysian Apollo briefly answered: 'There's no such trickery here (don't be disturbed), our weapons offer no affront: your huge guard-dog can terrify the bloodless shades with his eternal howling: chaste Proserpine can keep to her uncle's threshold. Aeneas the Trojan, renowned in piety and warfare, goes down to the deepest shadows of Erebus, to his father. If the idea of such affection does not move you, still you must recognise this bough.' (She showed the branch, hidden in her robes.) Then the anger in his swollen breast subsided. No more was said. Marvelling at the revered offering, of fateful twigs, seen again after so long, he turned the stern of the dark skiff towards them and neared the bank. Then he turned off the other souls who sat on the long benches, cleared the gangways: and received mighty Aeneas on board. The seamed skiff groaned with the weight and let in quantities of marsh-water through the chinks. At last, the river crossed, he landed the prophetess and the hero safe, on the unstable mud, among the blue-grey sedge. Huge Cerberus sets these regions echoing with his triple-throated howling, crouching monstrously in a cave opposite. Seeing the snakes rearing round his neck, the prophetess threw him a pellet, a soporific of honey and drugged wheat. Opening his three throats, in rabid hunger, he seized what she threw and, flexing his massive spine, sank to earth spreading his giant bulk over the whole cave-floor. With the guard unconscious Aeneas won to the entrance, and quickly escaped the bank of the river of no return." The episode of help offered by the Sibyl to Aeneas, with the golden branch, was also narrated in Ovid's *Metamorphoses* (OV., *Met.*, XIV, 146-192, extracts taken from the English translated version by C. Martin, with introduction by B. Knox, Norton & Company Inc., New York, 2005): in this case, however, the mythical gift seems to only serve for leaving Hell which was alternatively easy to enter. "When he had sailed past these and left behind the walls of the Parthenope on his right, there, on his left side he beheld the tomb of Misenus, Aeolus' tuneful son, and the fertile lowlands' sedgey marsh on the coast of Cumae, where he stopped and entered the cave of the superannuated Sibyl to pray that he might journey through Avernus for consultation with his father's shade" (verses 146-154); "She spoke and showed him, deep within the wood of Prosperina, a shining golden branch and ordered him to break it from its tree" (verses 168-170); " 'Whether you are yourself a goddess, or are one who is most pleasing to the gods, you will seem always most divine to me. I will avow that my opportunity to tour the underworld and leave it alive has been your gift to me; and in exchange, when I return to where the air is fresh, I will erect a temple and establish a cult that will burn incense in your honour'" (verses 184-192).

[277] Instead, Aeneas' entrance in the Averno, appears in miniature form (about 400 AD) as illustrating the relative passage of Virgil found in the Vatican (Vatican Apostolic Library, *Vat. Lat.*, 3225, f. 52r).

[278] OV., *Met.*, VII, 416-488 in C. MARTIN, 2005). "Now, so that guile might not go out of fashion, Medea feigned a breakup with her husband and ran off as a suppliant to Pelias; since he himself was burdened with the weight of old age too, his daughters welcomed her; pretending friendship, the cunning Colchian took the girls in and shortly won them over. And while she entertained them all with stories of her remarkable accomplishments, she told at length of how she had restored Aeson to his prime. Her story raised the hope among her listeners that by such arts their father too could be rejuventated: they begged her aid, imploring her to name her own reward, however great it was. A moment's silence while she seemed in doubt, as by her fictive indecisiveness she kept the pleading girls in high suspense – but when she'd given them her word, she added, 'We'll have a demonstration, so that you may be more confident about this gift I offer you: your oldest sheep, the aged bellwether of your flock, will soon become, through my concoctions, a young lamb again.' Worn-out by his innumerable years, the woolly one, with great horns curving round his bulging temples, was brought forth at once; slitting his throat with her Thessalian blade (which his exhausted blood could barely stain) the sorcer woman quickly plunged his carcass into the cauldron, where the heat reduced it, and where his horns (and years) were burned away. A feeble *'Baa, baa'* comes from deep within: to their astonishment, a little lamb skips out and eagerly essays a bleat, then scampers off – to find a milky treat! The daughters of Pelias were dumbstruck then, for she had done exactly as she promised! Even more eagerly, they urged her on. Three times now Phoebus had unyoked his team after their plunge into the western stream; on the fourth night, the stars were glittering when the deceitful daughter of Aeetes brought up to boil a cauldron of clear water, and added to it herbs of no real power. A death-like sleep (produced by magic spells) had quite unstrung the king and his defenders. As ordered by the Colchian, his daughters, slipping across the threshold of his room, surround his bed: 'Slackers! Why hesitate? Unsheathe your swords and spill his ancient gore, and I'll refill his veins with youthful blood. Your aged father's life is in your hands; if you have any love for him at all, if you're not merely stirred by empty hopes, then give your father what you owe him, now: drive his old age off with your sharp weapons, let his blood out by plunging in your swords!' Urged on by her and by their piety, each child commits the worst crime that a child can possibly commit against a parent, and only to avoid a much worse crime! Unable nonetheless to watch themselves, they turn away and blindly strike at him. Bleeding profusely, leaning on one elbow, he struggles to get up, though slashed to ribbons, and as he raises arms in supplication amid a thicket of swords, cries out to them, 'What are you doing, daughters? Why arm yourselves to slay your father?' Their hands – and spirits – fall; he would have gone on speaking, but Medea slit his throat and plunged his mangled body into the cauldron full of boiling water."

[279] H. MEYER, *Medeia und die Peliaden*, 1980, pp. 15-16, plate 15,2-3; E. SIMON, in *LIMC*, VII, Zurich-Munich 1994, s.v. *Pelias*, p. 276, n. 22; V. SAMPAOLO, in *Pompei. Pitture e mosaici* IX (1999), p. 8, n. 10.

[280] M. SCHMIDT, *Der Basler Medeasarkophag*, 1968, p. 16, plate 29,3; H. MEYER, *Medeia und die Peliaden*, 1980, p. 14, plate 14,3; E. SIMON, in *LIMC*, VII, Zurich-Munich 1994, s.v. *Pelias*, p. 276, n. 23.

[281] On the iconography see, for example J. VALEVA, *The painted coffers of the Ostrusha Tomb*, Sofia 2005, pp. 79-85, fig. 1-5.

[282] See A. KOSSATZ-DEISSMANN, in *LIMC*, I, Zurich-Munich 1981, s.v. "*Achilleus*", pp. 147-161.

[283] Rich ceramics have been discovered inside including earthenware of the second century AD and several contemporary "Dressel 20" type *amphorae* (see above).

[284] LIVERANI, SPINOLA 2006, p. 74, fig. 79.

[285] LIVERANI, SPINOLA 2006, p. 76, fig. 80. Close to the tomb's façade outside, one sees a stele dedicated by *Theodorus Mnesteleris* to his son *Theodorion* who died at 10 years old, perhaps related to one of the deceased buried in the *columbarium*.

[286] Many cinerary urns conserve fine earthenware as part of their grave goods which mainly consisted of small, very fine vases.

[287] This type of decoration was rather common and finds numerous comparisons during this period such as three Ostian mosaics which are dated to between 110 and 130 AD (BECATTI 1961, p. 99, n. 175, p. 102, n. 185, plate XXXV and p. 125, n. 229, plate CCXXIV).

[288] The external brick wall of *columbarium* XVIII forms the back of the niches on the right wall of *columbarium* II. This support must have occurred in a period that was not too long after the construction of the *columbaria* previously described. However, it must be contained to the early years of the second century AD Parallel to the construction of *columbarium* II, the small window in the back wall of *columbarium* I was also closed off with a marble slab.

[289] LIVERANI, SPINOLA 2006, pp. 77-79, figs. 81-83. A stele is found outside of the tomb next to the entrance. It is dedicated by *Gellia* to his young brother *Nestor* and also indicates his tomb in that place. It is likely that the two figures were related to other deceased members inside the *columbarium*.

[290] At a later stage, the lower part of the niche was partially closed off by a small perforated brick wall.

[291] The area is free of masonry tombs but is densely occupied by cremations protected by "Spello" *amphorae* (50-150 AD) broken into two which were placed at a lower level to the landslide. Later on, the area was used once again for burials in graves, after the series of tombs presently discussed.

[292] Their foundations sunk into the gravelly layer of subsidence and, in some cases, were placed over previously buried tomb structures.

[293] LIVERANI, SPINOLA 2006, pp. 82-84, figs. 90-91.

[294] For example see M.E. BLAKE, in *MAAR*, XIII, 1936, pp. 126-127, plate 29, n. 3; ID., *ibidem*, XVII, 1940, p. 101, plate 12; C.C. VAN ESSEN, in *MededRome*, s. III, VIII, 1954, p. 76; BECATTI 1961, p. 14, nn. 6 and 7, plates XXII e XXVI, p. 165, n. 300, plate XXIV.

[295] See BECATTI 1961, p. 172, n. 319 and p. 194, n. 370, plate XL, pp. 201-202, nn. 380 and 383, plate XLI.

[296] LIVERANI, SPINOLA 2006, pp. 90-91, fig. 102; SPINOLA 2006, p. 45.

[297] See above. This tomb shares its back wall, which is partly against the ground, and the dividing lateral wall made of brick. One can also observe a marble slab of the bench belonging to the first phase of the *Natronii* below the right side of *columbarium* I. Furthermore, the tomb's front abuts against the anti-chamber's "little oven".

[298] Isodome work is a type of masonry, of distant Greek origin, which alternated, in staggered rows, of upright blocks and blocks placed sideways. A small pierced marble slab which links to an underground cinerary urn is found in the left corner at the back of the mosaic.

[299] See BECATTI 1961, p. 17, n. 16, plate XIV, pp. 42-44, n. 64, plate XV and p. 133, n. 267, plate XIII. All of the mosaics from Ostia are dated between AD 120 and 140 even if there are also similar examples that date to the first century AD. Slightly later (the second half of the second century AD) is the mosaic of Tomb 19 of Annona (see above) which bears a motif that repeats isodome work.

[300] The foundations cut through the previous stratigraphies. At the same time, two *columbaria* of the first century AD were completely levelled and covered under the western foundations, as were other older underlying tombs (with walls made of *opus reticulatum*) located in the southern area.

[301] TC 228. The dedication is arranged by the daughter *Sutoria Fortunata*, a freedman, *Lucius Sutorius Felix* and *Caius Iulius Augustalis* for them and their children and descendants. Originally, the inscription must have related to a tomb of a certain standing which was probably located not far away from the place of employment.
[302] TC 227. This is a dedication of the funerary statue of *Iulia Prima* (whose fingerprints can be seen on fixing pivots), placed there by his mother *Iulia Ampelis*, by her cohabiting partner *Blastus* and other figures who have yet to be identified (the base is in fact still buried).
[303] The ramp's slope can be reconstructed through the course of a layer of light-coloured plaster placed at the base of the external wall located north-east to Tomb XII.
[304] The ditches start from a street level at a level of about half a metre lower than that of the pathway and cut a wide plane of lime which could have been placed there in relation to the tomb's building site of 180-190 AD Only Tombs TF 6, 10 and 16 bear cover *a cappuccina*, whilst Altars TF 7, 8, 9, 10 11, 12, 13, 14, 15 and 17 are without a brick cover.
[305] LIVERANI, SPINOLA 2006, pp. 60-61. The tombs comprise of three single burial chambers, with three distinct entrances opening onto the east, all belong to the same building. In particular, Rooms XXIX and XII share the front and back of the same alignment and are only separated by a wall whilst Room IX with which Room XXIX shares a wall, ended up being decentralised. The tombs were accessed by means of a short flight of stairs (in Tomb XXIX connected to a central pilaster) but one cannot be certain that the tombs did not contain a higher level (which has not survived) with a second room setting.
[306] The colonnaded sarcophagus belongs to a type that originates in Asia Minor that is well documented in Rome above all by the end of the second century AD and all of the third century AD (on this type of sarcophagus, see for example R. BELLI, in A. GIULIANO (ed.), *Museo Nazionale romano. Le sculture*, I/8, Rome 1985, pp. 154-157, n. III,11; M. SAPELLI, *ibidem*, pp. 305-306, n. VI,15, pp. 316-317, n. VI,19, pp. 318-320, n. VI,20; N. AGNOLI, in G. KOCH (ed.), *Sarkophag-Studien*, 1, Akten des Symposiums "125 Jahre Sarkophag-Corpus", Marburg, 4-7 October 1995, Mainz am Rhein 1998, pp. 132 and 134, plates 66,7 and 70,1; A. AMBROGI, *Note su alcuni sarcofagi di tipo attico e microasiatico*, in G. KOCH (ed.), *Sarkophag-Studien*, 3, Akten des Symposiums des Sarkophag-Corpus, Marburg, 2-7 July 2001, Mainz am Rhein 2007, pp. 66-67, plate 26,7).
[307] LIVERANI, SPINOLA 2006, p. 94. Only the west side of the tomb, which originally must have had a square layout of almost 6 metres per side, has been conserved whilst the rest was cut down due to modern building works involved in the realisation of the Autoparco which occurred prior to the archaeological dig.
[308] LIVERANI, SPINOLA 2006, p. 90, fig. 101. Unfortunately, the tomb has been levelled down to the floor and a large part of it has been covered over by the Autoparco's modern structures.
[309] The term *sanctitas* can be found in many early Christian inscriptions but it is not exclusively used for these and also sporadically appears in pagan epigraphs. Furthermore, the deceased's title includes the definition of being a *h(onesta) f(emina)*, something that one comes across with a certain frequency in Christian inscriptions in Rome from the third century AD onwards. This was given as a title attributed to a matron of the Equestrian Order or of the municipal nobility, as was also given to the referent found in our inscription.
[310] Several burials were made inside abandoned tombs, such as Tomb I and Tomb III, by digging within the buried graves or chiselling niches in order to create crude *arcosolia* (see also Tomb 1b of the Galea area).
[311] TF 1 and TF 2.
[312] Only a part of the cement core has survived with a small tube inserted in the north-westerly part and inside the tomb. The red plaster-work covering is completely missing.
[313] Remarks have already been made about this ritual with concern to an infant burial in Tomb I located in the Autoparco area (see footnote 107 above with relative bibliography). Charon's *obol* is attested to in a *forma* of Tomb XXX in the Santa Rosa area as well as in a burial under the (TF 4) tomb *a semicappuccina* which leans against the external wall of the same tomb. The significance of various coins found in other settings during the excavation, sometimes in relation to cremation burials, is more difficult to explain.
[314] A layer of white plaster with red stripes was applied to visually unify the two different wall treatments.
[315] BURANELLI, LIVERANI, SPINOLA 2005-2005, pp. 459-464, figs. 7-11; LIVERANI, SPINOLA 2006, pp. 91-94, figs. 103-108; SPINOLA 2006, pp. 46-49. The building has survived to a noteworthy height with the exclusion of the area corresponding to the eastern corner which has mostly been damaged.
[316] J. TOYNBEE, J. WARD PERKINS, *The Shrine of St. Peter and the Vatican Excavations*, London-New York-Toronto 1956, pp. 51-57; H. MIELSCH, H. VON HESBERG, *Die heidnische Nekropolen unter St. Peter in Rom. Die Mausoleen E-I und Z-PSI*, *MemPontAcc*, XVI, 2, 1996, pp. 225-233; P. ZANDER, *La Necropoli sotto la Basilica di San Pietro in Vaticano*, Rome 2007, pp. 36-39, figs. 47-51.
[317] Two sarcophagi (one with winged Victories and the other belonging to *Publius Caesilius Victorinus*) were found *in situ* in front of the first *arcosolium* of the right wall (with regard to the entrance) whilst one can see signs of the bases of the other two on the mosaic along the back wall and left side.
[318] Only the red stripes on the white background which frame the walls and *arcosolia* have survived.
[319] Similar subjects are rather common and often appear throughout the ages (see, for example, *columbarium* 21 of the Annona area dated to the end of the first century AD – beginning of the second century AD). During the Severan Period, similar stylistic forms appear in both sepulchral and domestic architectural settings (see for example H. JOYCE, *The Decoration of Walls, Ceilings, and Floors in Italy in the Second and Third Centuries AD*, Rome 1981, p. 39, fig. 31, pp. 54-56, figs. 53 and 55, p. 79, fig. 80).
[320] For example, see J. BALTY, *ANRW*, II, 12.2, 1981, p. 363; C. AUGÉ, P. LINANT DE BELLEFONDS, *LIMC*, III, Zurich-Munich 1986, see entry *Dionysos (in peripheria orientali)*, p. 522, nn. 81-83.
[321] The composition (excluding the central scene of a drunken Dionysus) is very similar to the mosaic of Environment E (on the north side) of the *Insula dell'Aquila* at Ostia (see BECATTI 1961, pp. 195-196, n. 373, plate LXXXVII). This mosaic, however, contains more schematic forms with more rigid and less naturalistic figures than the Santa Rosa mosaic.
[322] The sarcophagus is iconographically and stylistically similar to other Roman productions executed around AD 220-240; see H. SICHTERMANN, *RM* 86, 1979, pp. 358-363, plates 95-100; G. KOCH, H. SICHTERMANN, *Römische Sarkophage*, Munich 1982, pp. 238-241, nn. 284 and 285; P. KRANZ, *Jahreszeiten-Sarkophage*, *Die antiken Sarkophagreliefs*, V, 4, Berlin 1984, pp. 211-213, nn. 96, 102, 107 and above all, 10 8 (which is iconographically pratically identical); G. SPINOLA, in P. LIVERANI (edited by), *Laterano 1. Scavi sotto la basilica di S. Giovanni in Laterano. I materiali*, Vatican City 1998, p. 32, n. 63, fig. 71. Severeal blocks from dismantled tombs have been reused underneath the trunk in order to make two bases, including a travertine pier in which the extent of the tomb plot was inscribed: perhaps it belonged to Tomb XI which was levelled in order to make way for the building of Tomb VIII.
[323] One seems to be able to see a group of hunters intent on driving out the prey on the left part of the raised area, beyond the angular grotesque mask. One is about to hurl the boulder that he holds on his shoulder and another is bent over, lighting a fire. A servant with a jug in hand who offers a cup to a seated guest appears on the right-hand side, next to the inscription. A reclining couple sat at the banquet, perhaps lying on a *stibadium* or *sigma* (a semicircular bed) appear just beyond. These subjects were frequently portrayed on the upper parts of sarcophagi towards the end of the third century and the first half of the following century (see I. RODÀ, *Sarcofagos cristianos de Tarragona*, in G. KOCH [ed.], *Sarkophag-Studien*, 1, Akten des Symposiums "125 Jahre Sarkophag-Corpus", Marburg, 4-7 October 1995, Mainz am Rhein 1998, pp. 155-157, plate 78,3). In particular, however, one finds stylistic assonances above all with works belonging to the late Severan Period and the middle of the third century AD (see, for example, R. AMEDICK, *Die Antike Sarkophagrelief*, IV,14, *Die Sarkophage mit Darstellungen aus dem Menschenleben. Vita privata*, Berlin 1991, pp. 157-158, 163-164, nn. 223, 260).
[324] It is interesting to note how the red overpainting has been conserved very well on the fragments that were reused upside down in order to fill in the gaps found in the mosaic floor. The parts that, on the other hand, were in direct contact with the sarcophagus' replenished layer have instead lost nearly all of their colour due to the acidity of the earth.
[325] P. LIVERANI, in J.M. NOGUERA CELDRÁN, E. CONDE GUERRI (edited by) *Escultura Romana en Hispania V* (Actas de la reunión internacional, Murcia, 9-11 November 2005), Murcia 2008, pp. 78-79.
[326] The iconography and style are very close to several sarcophagi dating to the first half-middle of the third century AD (see, for example, G. KOCH, *Meleager*, *Die Antike Sarkophagrelief*, XII,6, Berlin 1975, pp. 94 e 100, nn. 27, 52; F. VALBRUZZI, *Su alcune officine di sarcofagi in Campania*, in G. KOCH (ed.), *Sarkophag-Studien*, 1, Akten des Symposiums "125 Jahre Sarkophag-Corpus", Marburg, 4-7 October 1995, Mainz am Rhein 1998, pp. 123-124, plates 62-65). With regard to quality, the sarcophagus is comparable to better examples of the series such as the great Tiburtina sarcophagus of Palazzo dei Conservatori and that which contains an analogous subject to one at Woburn Abbey, both of which are dated to the second half of the third century AD (KOCH, *op. cit.*, pp. 102-103, n. 67 and p. 105, n. 71; J. BOARDMAN, *LIMC*, II, Zurich-Munich 1984, see entry *Atalante*, p. 942, n. 24).
[327] See D. BIELEFELD, *Die Antike Sarkophagrelief*, V,2,2, *Stadtrömische Eroten-Sarkophage. Weinlese- und Ernteszenen*, Berlin 1997, pp. 109, 116-117, 122, 136, nn. 50, 93, 129, 197. In reality, the comparisons refer to sarcophagi that are dated a few decades later compared to the chest with the Calydonian Boar hunting scene but are similar with regard to the compositional scheme.
[328] The decorative scheme is reversed compared to the tradional depiction were Eros caresses Psyche's face: here Psyche presses against Eros' cheek whilst Eros caresses the young girl's stomach. With regard to this rather unusual depiction, see F. GERKE, *Die christlichen Sarkophage der vorkostantinischer Zeit*, Berlin 1940, p. 69, plate 42,3; C. VERMEULE, in *Festschrift für F. Matz*, Mainz 1962, p. 104, plate 29,2; M. SAPELLI, in A. GIULIANO (edited by), *Museo Nazionale romano. Le sculture*, I/10,2, Rome 1988, pp. 122-123, n. 143.
[329] With regard to this type, see for example D. BIELEFELD, *Die Antike Sarkophagrelief*, V,2,2, *Stadtrömische Eroten-Sarkophage. Weinlese- und Ernteszenen*, Berlin 1997, pp. 103-104, 113, 116, nn. 25, 74, 92.
[330] See P. KRANZ, *Die antiken Sarkophagreliefs*, V,4, *Jahreszeiten-Sarkophage*, Berlin 1984, pp. 191, 200-201, 211, 213, 226, 243, nn. 27, 58, 96, 160, 108, 305. Comparisons are spread over the late Severan Period and the Gallienic Period although stylistically they appear closer to older examples.
[331] Sarcophagi of the first half of the third century AD are particularly close in style and the use of marble: their presence in the same family tomb could lead one to believe that they were bought from a single Roman workshop.
[332] Stylistically, the fragment bears similarities with sarcophagi of Severan production as seen with works executed shortly afterwards (see for example L. MUSSO, in A. GIULIANO (edited by), *Museo Nazionale romano. Le sculture*, I/10,2, Rome 1988, pp. 117-118, n. 138; M. SAPELLI, *ibidem*, I/10,1, Rome 1995, pp. 256-157, n. 104).
[333] One should note that a marble sarcophagus for an adult, with its relative cover, has an average weight of around one tonne.
[334] Following the excavation, a careful restoration of the floor was addressed due to the subtle and fragile layer upon which the *tesserae* were affixed. Therefore, one had to proceed with removing them in order to then consolidate the floor and, finally, to place it back. Nevertheless, since a series of depressions were present in the floor and imprints attest to the positioning of the supporting piers for the sarcophagi present in

the tomb, it was decided that the mosaic should not be levelled so that it did not loose these elements that constituted interesting evidence. To this end, prior to removing it, a cast of the entire floor surface was taken on top of which the mosaic was laid down in the laboratory thus ensuring the conservation of the original course of the mosaic surface. Following its removal, an excavation was carried out underneath the mosaic which resulted in bringing various parts of the original mosaic "rug" to light which corresponded to the relevant areas of the ancient restoration.

[335] Successive excavation attempts at removing the mosaic resulted in finding several frescoed fragments (which had perhaps crumbled off from the vault) underneath the restored parts of the mosaic floor. These were in direct contact with the treated mosaic surfaces that had originally collapsed. These traces of broken-off fresco leave open the possibility of the sepulchre being damaged during ancient times.

[336] J. STROSZECK, *Die antiken Sarkophagreliefs*, VI.1, *Löwen-Sarkophage,* Berlin 1998, p. 128, n. 175, p. 130, n. 192, p. 131, nn. 195 and 196.

[337] Fragments of the cover were found inside the *forma* behind the place where the chest was positioned. The cover's attribution is certain in as much that the cover is ovally shaped and the chest is a unique *lenòs* (tub) found in the tomb. Furthermore, the pierced holes and the imprints of the cramps that affixed the lid to the chest perfectly correspond to one another.

[338] See G. BARATTA, *La mandorla centrale dei sarcofagi strigilati. Un campo iconografico ed i suoi simboli*, in F. and T. HÖLSCHER (edited by), *Römische Bilderwelten. Von der Wirklichkeit zum Bild und zurück* (Kolloquium der Gerda Henkel Stiftung am Deutschen Archäologischen Institut Rom 15. – 17. März 2004), Heidelberg 2007, pp. 191-215. This type of amphora is rather common, as attested by the discovery of another dozen or so in other sarcophagi.

[339] See M. SAPELLI, in A. GIULIANO (edited by), *Museo Nazionale romano. Le sculture*, I/8, Rome 1985, pp. 242-245, n. V,11.

[340] With regard to this type of raised part, see for example A. RUMPF, *Die antiken Sarkophagreliefs*, V, 1, *Die Meerwesen*, Berlin 1939, pp. 90-92, nn. 303-323; M. SAPELLI, in A. GIULIANO (edited by), *Museo Nazionale romano. Le sculture*, I/7,2, Rome 1984, pp. 303-304, n. X,5; P. BALDASSARRI, *ibidem*, I/10,2, Rome 1988, pp. 11-12, n. 12, pp. 20-21, nn. 20 and 21, pp. 30-31, n. 32, pp. 33-34, n. 36, pp. 35-37, n. 38-40.

[341] M.L. CALDELLI, *Nota su* D(is) M(anibus) *e* D(is) M(anibus) S(acrum) *nelle iscrizioni cristiane di Roma*, in I. DI STEFANO MANZELLA (edited by), *Le iscrizioni dei cristiani in Vaticano*, Inscriptiones Sanctae Sedis, 2, Vatican City 1997, pp. 185-187 (with previous bibliography).

[342] Several fragments of heavy glazed-over medieval ceramic work was found inside this sepulchre's buried layers ("*Forum Ware*"). They almost touched the mosaic floor which indicates that this room was frequented during the eighth century and the ninth century.

CHAPTER FIVE

[*] A special word of gratitude to His Eminence Cardinal Angelo Comastri, president of the Fabric of St. Peter and His Excellency Mgr. Vittorio Lanzani, delegate of the same Fabric, for having encouraged the publication of this short contribution in the hope of offering a useful tool to those involved in the preservation and valorisation of our cultural heritage. My gratitude is naturally also directed to those who, with various skills and functions, were committed to the maintenance and fruition of the Vatican Necropolis. Finally, I would particularly like to thank the entire staff of the Fabric of St. Peter.

[1] See NICOLOSI 1949, pp. 310-317.

[2] By 1947, a robust floor made of iron and concrete to cover one of the necropolis' mausoleums had already been made. It had been set up and prepared in a way that then allowed for a ceiling of reinforced concrete to be "thrown" over the entire excavation site. This floor, which covers a surface area of 330 m^2, is made up of a series of 18 cm thick reinforced concrete slabs which have been further strengthened by stiffening them with large iron beams. The floor, which separates the grottoes from the underlying archeological excavations, was purposely made on two levels in order to respect every part of the pre-Constantinian necropolis. Following the completion of the reinforced concrete structure and relative floors in 1949, floors in the sacred grottoes were then laid down, using travertine in the naves of the central area and outbuildings in some parts whilst marble [was used] for the chapels and the majority of adjacent rooms. On this subject, see *L'Attività della Santa Sede nel 1947, 1948 e 1949*, and specifically pp. 233, 241 and 270.

[3] The recovery work was planned and launched by Cardinal Virgilio Noè, Chairman of the Fabric of St. Peter's between 1989 and 2002. It was initially carried out with funding from the company Enel which, split into two different restoration campaigns (1998-1999 and 2000), dealt with the area next to St. Peter's tomb and the tombs of the necropolis' western area. Thanks to the financial support provided by Fondazione Pro Musica Arte Sacra – Mercedes Benz, a serious restoration of Tomb H, the "Tomb of the *Valerii*" was subsequently carried out in 2007.

[4] Over the last ten years and with the Fabric of St. Peter's consent, Dr. Nazzareno Gabrielli and I have shared methodological choices taken over the conservation and restoration of the St. Peter necropolis' underground environments. I express my sincere gratitude to him as well as acknowledgement of his support and for his constant attention to conservation problems regarding the St. Peter excavations. Thanks to his gracious willingness and assistance, I owe the publication of this short essay to him, the contents of which have already been partly published in the magazine *Kermes*. On this subject, see GABRIELLI – ZANDER 2008, pp. 53-66.

[5] APOLLONJ GHETTI – FERRUA – JOSI – KIRSCHBAUM 1951; *L'Attività della Santa Sede nel 1951*, p. 393.

[6] The majority of these photographs have been reproduced in the following publications: PRANDI 1957; GUARDUCCI 1953; GUARDUCCI 1958; GUARDUCCI 1965.

[7] See MIELSCH – HESBERG – GAERTNER 1986 and 1995. The photographic campaign was carried out by the German Archeological Institute and includes the following tombs: A, B, C, D, E, F, G, H, Ψ, X, Φ, Z.

[8] See SPERANDIO – ZANDER 1999, pp. 18-25. Such an all-consuming and often difficult work was undertaken according to a carefully planned program of photographic film footage (black and white photographs and colour transparencies) by Mr. Marco Anelli who also personally oversaw the printing of the photographs. The preliminary photographic documentation of the restoration and subsequent documentation taken during conservative interventions was taken in black and white and colour whilst colour photographic reproductions were generally used for restoration interventions of a work in progress. The 1998-2000 photographic campaign dealt with the following tombs: Z, F, H, I, M, N, O, Q, R, R', S, T, U. In 2007, high resolution digital footage were taken inside of Tomb H or the "Tomb of *Valerii*".

[9] See *L'Attività della Santa Sede nel 1975*, p. 763.

[10] See ZANDER 2005, pp. 103-107; ZANDER 2008, pp. 102-113.

[11] See NICOLOSI 1941, p. 4.

[12] See APOLLONJ GHETTI – FERRUA – JOSI – KIRSCHBAUM 1951, p. XI.

[13] See MIELSCH – HESBERG – GAERTNER 1995, p. 150; ZANDER 2007 and 2009, pp. 80 and 82.

[14] See PRANDI 1957.

[15] See *L'Attività della Santa Sede nel 1979*, pp. 1259-1260. The study and architectonic survey of the necropolis' eastern area under St. Peter's Basilica was carried out by Professor Henner von Hesberg and architects Kai Gaertner, Rainer Roggensbuck, Jutta Weber and Woytek Bruszewski. In particular, the German Archaeological Institute conducted the campaign of architectonic survey on the following tombs: A, B, C, D, E, F, G, H, Ψ, X, Φ, Z. On the subject, see MIELSCH – HESBERG – GAERTNER 1986 and 1995.

[16] See SPERANDIO – ZANDER 1999, pp. 26-37; *L'Attività della Santa Sede, 1998*, p. 1199; 1999, p. 1274.

[17] The microclimatic monitoring, the acquisition of data and the study of environmental parametres of the St. Peter's necropolis was carried out by the company Lambda Scientifica of Vicenza. During the biennial of 1992-1994, the Fabric of St. Peter's gave them the task of continuously checking levels of relative humidity and temperature in some of the sepulchral structures (Tombs Z, B, H, I and Φ). This was done in order to increase knowledge concerning possible causes for the deterioration of pictorial decorations, stuccoes and perforated brick screens. On the subject, see *L'Attività della Santa Sede nel 1992*, pp. 1431-1432; SPERANDIO – ZANDER 1999, pp. 66-71.

[18] The amount of water vapour that can be contained in the air depends upon its temperature and pressure. A rise in temperature allows air to contain a greater amount of water vapour whilst a reduction in temperature causes a fall in the amount it can hold until it reaches the consistency of "dew". This represents the point at which vapour condenses and it separates in form from the water.

[19] During the initial phases of restoration, the laboratory analysis was conducted by Gabinetto di Ricerche Scientifiche dei Musei Vaticani (Institute of Scientific Research of the Vatican Museums). Diffractometric analysis of mortar and plaster was carried out by Professor Giacomo Chiari. See SPERANDIO – ZANDER 1999, p. 123.

[20] With regard to their quantities, the identified salifications are the following: chlorides, sulphates (*sodium decahydrate sulphates* and *sodium anhydrite sulphates* and *calcium sulphate dehydrates*), nitrates and fluorides. Furthermore, the investigation has revealed the presence of salifications of mixed carbonates and silicates. These salts formed particularly stubborn concretions and robustly adhered to the fresco surfaces. The carbonates are pertinent to rich calcium solutions which have permeated the decorative works over a long period of time; whilst the silicates should be considered soluble feldspars (orthoclase and albite) of clays and pozzolanas.

[21] In 1999 and during the subsequent interventions of restorations, instrumental and experimental checks were carried out in order to evaluate the air current trends within the St. Peter's necropolis. On the subject, see SPERANDIO – ZANDER 1999, p. 70; *L'Attività della Santa Sede nel 1999*, p. 1273.

[22] No viable solution was found for controlling the movement of air mass generated by a group of people who move around in a narrow, long and confined space. The same phenomenon is seen in metro stations when the train arrives.

[23] Automatic opening doors located at various points along the visitor path of the St. Peter's necropolis were placed at the following points: 1-2. East and west pathways in front of Tomb Z or tomb "of the Egyptians"; 2. *Iter*, between Tomb I or tomb "of the Quadriga" and Tomb L or "*Caetennii Minores*" tombs; 3. Pit in front of Tomb S.

[24] The trapdoors that were put in in 1979 inside of Tomb N and Tomb O were closed up with insulating panels whilst those located in Tomb Φ and in front of Tomb F and Tomb M were equipped with adjustable shutter fasteners to allow for eventual openings operated by automatic command. On the subject, see *L'Attività della Santa Sede nel 1979*, p. 1254, where the "Aeration of the Vatican Necropolis" is clearly discussed. See also: SPERANDIO – ZANDER 1999, p. 70; *L'Attività della Santa Sede nel 1999*, p. 1273.

[25] The space in-between the two panels of glass measures 20 mm. In order to avoid problems of condensation on the inside of the glass chamber (in the case of poor maintenance or old seals), silicone gel (perfectly anhydrous to the quantity of 20 kg per square metre and proportional to the "room"'s metric cubage) was inserted within the chamber. In addition to the silicone gel, the possibility of saturating the chamber with nitrogen was also planned, introducing it through a small reserve valve placed at the lower left-hand corner of the *visarm* glass and arranging a valve for the exit of air, diagonally positioned in the opposite upper corner.

[26] The aerobatic and phytosociological investigations were undertaken by the *RC-Scientifica* microbiology laboratory of Vicenza. On the subject, see SPERANDIO – ZANDER 1999, pp. 55-66; *L'Attività della Santa Sede nel 1999*, p. 1273.

[27] It was decided to repeat the use of selective biocides in order to overcome the growth of microorganisms. Naturally, ozone could not be used due to its harmful effects of oxidization which could have effected all of the material found in the necropolis and, above all, the metallic cramps belonging to the sarcophagi.

[28] The biocidal products tested were: *Preventol R80, Nipacide DDF, Nipacide DFX, Troysan 174, Troysan AF3, Traetex 225, Metatin 70/40, Metatin 58/10* and *4-cloro, 3-metilfenolo*.

[29] *Troysan 174* produced its best result when mixed with polar solvents: water and alcohol. As it was desirable to avoid the use of water, the best result was obtained using isopropanol, an alcohol which permits an optimum dilution and a good amount of direct contact with the works. Alternatively, *Metatin 70/40* can be diluted in mineral turpentine (white spirits) or, better still, in pure alkane fractions. Thanks to a study carried out by Dr. Nazzareno Gabrielli, it has been possible to verify that excellent results (a complete killing off of actinobacteria and microfungi) could be obtained by using a solution of *Metatin 70/40* at 3% in n-octane and applying it directly to the wall paintings. This product can be atomised even if a first treatment applied by brush is preferable. Finally, when applying *Troysan 174*, diluted with isopropanol, the application must always be preceded by *Metatin 70/40* diluted in octane. With regard to the disinfestation of non-frescoed surfaces (facings in brick, mosaics etc.), *Metatin 70/40* can be diluted with the simple use of white spirits.

[30] In order to evaluate the use of ultraviolet germicide lamps in the St. Peter necropolis, Dr. Nazzareno Gabrielli undertook specific tests and research. In particular, possible consequences of deterioration which could damage wall paintings with the use of germicide lamps that use ultraviolet radiation were carefully examined. Bearing in mind that the pictorial surfaces found in the St. Peter necropolis do not contain lacquer nor other organic-based pigments, it was decided to monitor the influence of pure ultraviolet light on mineral-based pigments by means of appropriate testing. To this end, fresco colours were applied to a small plastered tile. Following a complete and consolidated carbonisation, the fresco was placed under a 15 W germicide lamp at a distance of about a metre. In order to evaluate a possible change in pigments with the passing of time, the purity and brilliance of every colour was measured by means of colorimetric wavelength. Furthermore, half of every colour sample was covered with a strip of black polythene in order to demonstrate, after many hours of exposure (at least 1000 hours) eventual chromatic differences in pigment between the protected areas and those uncovered that had absorbed the ultraviolet radiation. Consequently, the measurements and checks carried out on both the colour samples exposed to ultraviolet and those that were protected from it produced a good experimental outcome. As such, it was possible to ponder over the eventual use of germicide lamps.

[31] In order to render the application of such panels on the sepulchral building roofs simpler and more practical, the decision was taken to apply a suitable silicate varnish rather than an anti-condensation plaster or rather a very porous plaster made from lime and perlite or of a lime and pozzolanic base. Despite having achieved satisfactory results, it is intuitive, therefore, that the application of an anti-condensation plaster can prevent problems of humidity condensation better, thus helping prevent the dangerous consequential effects of dripping onto the works. Insulating "cadorite" or "termanto" panels were placed on the inside of the following tombs: C, E, F, H, O, Z and T.

[32] In fact, it is well known that the process of ionization consists in the removal of external electrons by a molecule or an atom of atmospheric gas, thus forming a free electron and a positive ion and precisely N+, O+, N+2, O+2. The extracted electron can exist freely for a very short amount of time only. It easily attacks oxygen and nitrogen but since electro negativity of oxygen is greater than that of nitrogen, negative ions are essentially constructed of ionized oxygen as a consequence. Old apparatus indiscriminately produced positive ions, negative ions and often even ozone whilst latest generation ionizers ionized selectively negative air and did not produce ozone. Even though the mechanisms that lie at the root of the biological result are still to investigate thoroughly, many sustain that there are beneficial effects on the organism of negative ions. Various studies carried out in the field of respiratory problems have demonstrated that whilst positive ions made breathing difficult, negative ions helps one breathe better and improve the absorption of oxygen. The predisposition of devices for the negative ionization of air that circulates around the visitor path could therefore contribute to improving the quality of air in a confined atmosphere such as that of the St. Peter's necropolis.

[33] With regard to this, the experimentation of a small continuous air flow apparatus conceived by Dr. Nazzareno Gabrielli is currently underway. This apparatus inhales air in its lower part and pushes it upwards. During the ascension of the air, it comes across containers with permeable membranes first full of soda lime and then active carbon, exiting the upper part of the apparatus with the CO_2 having been removed. Furthermore, this aforementioned apparatus is equipped with ultraviolet germicide lamps which disinfect the exiting air. Once the functionality of this experimental machine is evaluated, the possibility of positioning similar "purifiers" in places where the highest concentrations of CO_2 have been registered will be considered. Such apparatus would naturally contain amounts of soda lime that were in proportion to the metric cubage of air present that requires cleansing.

[34] See *L'Attività della Santa Sede*, 1970-2008, which features tables charting monthly visitor frequency to the excavation site (subdivided into languages of affiliation: Italian, English, French, German and Spanish) in the Chapter dedicated to the Fabric of St. Peter's.

[35] Only a limited number of people above the age of 15 years old are allowed to access the excavation site due to the its particular location underneath the Basilica and its reduced dimensions. In order to join a guided tour, it is necessary to send a written request to the Fabric of St. Peter by fax (+39 06 69873017) or e-mail (scavi@fsp.va), indicating the number of people, language spoken, available dates and contact details in order the receive a reply. The visits to the excavation site take place from Monday to Saturday from 9.00 am to 6.00 pm with the exception of Sunday and festive holidays celebrated by the Vatican.

[36] *L'Attività della Santa Sede nel 1951*, p. 392.

[37] For the planning of the lighting system, the company Enel supported the "LED Studio Associato Cinzia Ferrara e Pietro Palladino". The aesthetic presentation of the system's components was curated by "Studio Associato di Architettura Adriana Annunziata e Corrado Terzi Architetti".

[38] Photosynthesis or carbon hydrate synthesis: transformation of luminous energy into chemical energy by means of chlorophyll.

[39] See SPERANDIO – ZANDER 1999, pp. 111-121.

[40] The restoration work in the St. Peter's necropolis was preceded by inspections of different disciplinary areas which were carried out by experts who were called in to give their professional opinionsof the situation so that a plan of intervention could be drawn up. With regard to this, the contribution provided by Professors Paolo and Laura Mora of the Istituto Centrale del Restauro (The Central Institute of Restoration) proved to be particularly significant. The role of 'Head of Building Works' for the Fabric of St. Peter's was assigned to the author of this essay and the architect Antonio Sperandio in 1998. Both were members of the Scientific Committee which was also composed of the following people: Cardinal Virgilio Noè, Monsignor Vittorio Lanzani, Sandro Benedetti, Margherita Cecchelli, Nazzareno Gabrielli, Paolo Liverani, Danilio Mazzoleni and Patrick Saint-Roch. The restoration work was carried out by Franco Adamo and Adele Cecchini (1999-2000; 2003; 2007-2009); Giorgio Capriotti, Lorenza D'Alessandro and Sabina Marchi (1999-2000), each of whom were assisted by their team of assistants. On the subject see SPERANDIO – ZANDER 1999, p. 1223.

[41] The restoration of Tomb M, the tomb "of the *Julii*" was carried out by Giorgio Capriotti in 1999.

[42] See PAPI 2008, pp. 423-436.

[43] The important restoration work was presented on the 27 May 2008 in the Fabric of St. Peter's library, located in the Vatican. The technical reports regarding the work carried out in this important tomb were introduced by Dr. Maria Cristina Carlo Stella, the Fabric of St. Peter's Office Manager. I would like to thank her for the attention she dedicated to the necropolis' conservative problems.

[44] The restoration of Tomb H or Tomb "of the *Valerii*" was carried out by Franco Adamo and Adele Cecchini, with the assistance of Paola Minoja, Corinna Ranzi, Sara Scioscia and Chiara Scioscia Santoro.

[45] Different types of frameworks and adhesion of stucco decorations have been identified. The small columns found at the sides of niches (which hold cinerary urns) were found to contain supports constructed of tubular elements of terracotta or wood axes. According to their projection and weight, stucco decorations were adhered to the wall with wooden nails and cramps of differing length. The study of holes left over from such supports has permitted the reconstruction of lost stucco sculptures of Tomb H, the Tomb "of the *Valerii*". Moreover graffiti found on the plaster, which was applied to help with the realisation of images in relief, are still visible.

[46] Interesting technical particularities concerning the execution of architectonic stucco decorations have emerged during the course of restoration work. Indeed, it has been possible to ascertain that templates were used for the simplest mouldings and, as such, succeeded in obtaining the desired profile with regard to length. What's more, stamps were used for [creating] repetitive decorative motifs which left their imprint in the fresh stucco.

[47] "PETRUS, ROGA XS HS/ PRO SANC[TI]S/ HOM[INI]BUS/ CHRESTIANIS AD/ CORPUS TUUM SEP[ULTIS]" ("Peter, pray for the Christian saints of Man buried next to your body". On the subject, see GUARDUCCI 1953.

[48] The multispectral works carried out in Tomb H or tomb "of the *Valerii*" were assigned by the Fabric of St. Peter's to Art-Test s.n.c. Such important optical measurements and the subsequent computerised elaborations were executed by Luciano Marras and Anna Pelagotti with the assistance of Marco Milano, Girolamo Carlucci, Anna Carloni and Fabio Remondino. To this end, a scientific photo-camera was used (chilled CCD), equipped with a set of interferential filters of medium band width (40 – 50 nm). The investigations were carried out in multi-band, using UV halogen lamps and exploiting the entire sensibility range of the silicon sensor (380-1125 nm) in order to verify the effects of reflection or fluorescence in relation to the narrow spectral intervals which can end up being visibly non-perceptible.

[49] In the presumed inscription of the word "HOM[INI]BUS" located in the central niche of the north wall, the first vertical stroke of the letter H and the second stroke coming off the letter M come up under fluorescent light. As such, they are clearly refer to part of the design. The second vertical stroke of the letter M seems pertinent to a sediment of colour.

[50] Following restoration work, the unstable microclimatic conditions not only brought about the phenomena of "normal settlement" but also the migration of soluble salts (in the form of natural impurities found in the clay used to make bricks or the mixture of mortar interstices) towards the outside surface, leaving salt traces there. This results in the lifting off of small flakes of brick. It is preferable to dust the salts off from the outset of their formations rather than intervene in removing them after a long amount of time. This is because, with the passing of time, salts become more stubborn to remove due to the phenomena of carbonisation. This results in making the process of cleaning a much longer and more difficult one.

BIBLIOGRAPHY

TOPOGRAPHIC SETTING

AE
L'Année Épigraphique
BullCom
Bullettino della Commissione archeologica comunale di Roma
Carta 2005
M.A. TOMEI – P. LIVERANI (eds), *Lexicon Topographicum Urbis Romae, Supplementum* I.1. *Carta Archeologica di Roma. Primo quadrante*, Rome 2005
CIL
Corpus Inscriptionum Latinarum
ICUR
Inscriptiones Christianae Urbis Romae
LIVERANI 1999
P. LIVERANI, *La topografia antica del Vaticano*, Vatican City 1999
LTUR
Lexicon Topographicum Urbis Romae I-VI, Rome 1993-2000
LTUR Sub
Lexicon Topographicum Urbis Romae. Suburbium I-V, Rome 2001-2008
MEFRA
Mélanges de l'Ecole française de Rome. Antiquité RendPontAcc
Rendiconti della Pontificia accademia romana di archeologia

THE RITUALS: ANTHROPOLOGICAL AND RELIGIOUS ASPECTS

ANGELUCCI *ET ALII* 1990
S. ANGELUCCI, I. BALDASSARRE, I. BRAGANTINI, M.G. LAURO, V. MANNUCCI, A. MAZZOLENI, C. MORSELLI, F. TAGLIETTI, *Sepolture e riti nella necropoli dell'Isola Sacra*, Bollettino di Archeologia 5-6, 1990, pp. 50-113.
DEICHMANN 1967
F.W. DEICHMANN (ed.), *Repertorium der christlich-antiken Sarkophage* I, Wiesbaden 1967.
HEINZELMANN, ORTALLI, WITTERER 2001
M. HEINZELMANN, J. ORTALLI, M. WITTERER (eds), *Römischer Bestattungsbrauch und Beigabensitten – Culto dei morti e costumi funerari romani*, Palilia 8, 2001.
KOCH, SICHTERMANN 1982
G. KOCH, H. SICHTERMANN, *Römische Sarkophage*, Munich 1982.
PELLEGRINO 1999
PELLEGRINO, *I riti funerari e il culto dei morti*, in *Dalle necropoli di Ostia. Riti ed usi funerari* (catalogue of the exhibition, Ostia, March 1998- July 1999), Ostia 1999, pp. 7-25.
SINN 1978
F. SINN, *Stadtrömische Marmorurnen*, Mainz 1978.
DUPONT 1985
DUPONT, F.: *Les morts et la mémoire. Le masque funèbre*, in *La mort, les morts et l'au-delà dans le monde romain* (Proceedings of the colloquium at Caen 20-22 November 1985), Caen 1987, pp. 167-172.
GUARNIERI 1993
GUARNIERI, C.: *La presenza dell'uovo nelle sepolture di Spina (Valle Trebba). Un problema aperto*, in *Studi sulla necropoli di Spina in Valle Trebba*, Conference [Ferrara] 15 October 1992 (Ferrara 1993) pp. 181-195.

THE NECROPOLIS UNDER ST PETER'S BASILICA

AE
L'Année Épigraphique
CALIÒ 2007
L.M. CALIÒ, *La morte del sapiente. La tomba di Valerius Herma nella necropoli vaticana*, in O.D. CORDOVANA – M. GALLI (eds), *Arte e memoria culturale nell'età della Seconda Sofistica*, Catania 2007, pp. 289-318
CASTAGNOLI 1992
F. Castagnoli, *Il Vaticano nell'età classica*, Vatican City 1992
CULLMANN 1965
O. CULLMANN, *San Pietro discepolo, apostolo, martire. Il problema storico e teologico di Pietro*, in O. CULLMANN *ET ALII, Il primato di Pietro*, Bologna 1965, pp. 1-349 (original edition: *Petrus. Jünger, Apostel, Märtyrer. Das historische und das theologische Petrusproblem*, Zürich-Stuttgart 1952; II ed. 1960)
D'AMELIO 2005
M.G. D'AMELIO, *Tra ossa polveri e ceneri: il «fuoriasse» del baldacchino di S. Pietro a Roma*, Annali di Architettura 17, 2005, pp. 127-136
ECK 1986
W. ECK, *Inschriften aus der Vatikanischen Nekropole unter St. Peter*, Zeitschrift für Papyrologie und Epigraphik 65, 1986, pp. 254-269
ECK 1996
W. ECK, *Tra epigrafia prosopografia e archeologia*, Rome 1996
Esplorazioni 1951
B.M. APOLLONJ GHETTI, A. FERRUA, E. JOSI, E. KIRSCHBAUM, *Esplorazioni sotto la Confessione di S. Pietro in Vaticano eseguite negli anni 1940-42*, Vatican City 1951
FERAUDI-GRUÉNAIS 2001a
F. FERAUDI-GRUÉNAIS, *Grabinschriften im archäologischen Kontext. Komplementarität von Schrift und Bild?*, in M. HEINZELMANN, J. ORTALLI, P. FASOLD,
M. WITTEYER (eds), *Römischer Bestattungsbrauch und Beigabensitten in Rom, Norditalien und den Nordwestprovin-*

zen von der späten Republik bis in die Kaiserzeit. Culto dei morti e costumi funerari romani. Roma, Italia settentrionale e province nord-occidentali dalla tarda Repubblica all'età imperiale (International Colloquium Rome 1-3 April 1998), *Palilia* 8, Wiesbaden 2001, pp. 203-213
FERAUDI-GRUÉNAIS 2001b
F. FERAUDI-GRUÉNAIS, *Ubi diutius nobis habitandum est. Die Innendekoration der kaiserzeitlichen Gräber Roms*, Wiesbaden 2001
GUARDUCCI 1953
M. GUARDUCCI, *Cristo e S. Pietro in un documento precostantiniano della Necropoli Vaticana*, Rome 1953
GUARDUCCI 1959
M. GUARDUCCI, *La tomba di Pietro*, Rome 1959
MIELSCH, VON HESBERG 1986
H. MIELSCH, H. VON HESBERG, *Die heidnische Nekropole unter St. Peter in Rom. Die Mausoleen A-D*, MemPontAcc XVI.1, 1986
MIELSCH, VON HESBERG 1996
H. MIELSCH, H. VON HESBERG, *Die heidnische Nekropoleunter St. Peter in Rom. Die Mausoleen E-I und Z-PSI*, MemPontAcc XVI.2, 1996
PAPI 2000-2001
C. PAPI, *Le iscrizioni della necropoli vaticana: una revisione*, Rendiconti della Pontificia Accademia Romana di Archeologia LXXIII, 2000-2001, pp. 239-265
PRANDI 1963
PRANDI, *La tomba di S. Pietro nei pellegrinaggi dell'età medievale* (II ed.), in *Pellegrinaggi e culto dei santi in Europa fino alla 1a Crociata* (Proceedings of the IV Conference, Todi 8-11 October 1961), Todi 1963, pp. 283-447
SINN 1987
F. SINN, *Stadtrömische Marmorurnen* (Beiträge zur Erschliessung hellenistischer und kaiserzeitlicher Skulptur und Architektur, 8), Mainz 1987
THÜMMEL 1999
H.G. THÜMMEL, *Die Memorien für Petrus und Paulus in Rom: Die archäologischen Denkmäler und die literarische Tradition*, Berlin-New York 1999
TOYNBEE – WARD PERKINS 1956
J. TOYNBEE – J.B. Ward Perkins, *The Shrine of St. Peter and the Vatican Excavations*, London 1956
ZANDER 2007
P. ZANDER, *La Necropoli sotto la Basilica di San Pietro in Vaticano*, s.l. 2007

THE VATICAN NECROPOLIS ON THE VIA TRIUMPHALIS

AA.VV. 1973
AA.VV., *Le iscrizioni della necropoli dell'Autoparco Vaticano*, ActaInstRomFin VI, 1973.
AE
Année Épigraphique.
ASMV
Archivio Storico dei Musei Vaticani.
BECATTI 1961
G. BECATTI, *Scavi di Ostia*, IV, *Mosaici e pavimenti marmorei*, Rome 1961.
BOSCHUNG 1987
D. BOSCHUNG, *Antike Grabaltäre aus den Nekropolen Roms*, Acta Bernensia X, Bern 1987.
BURANELLI, LIVERANI, SPINOLA 2005-2006
F. BURANELLI, P. LIVERANI, G. SPINOLA, *I nuovi scavi della necropoli della via Trionfale in Vaticano*, in *RendPontAcc*, LXXVIII, 2005-2006, pp. 451-472.
CAR
Carta archeologica di Roma I, Florence 1962.
Carta I
M.A. TOMEI, P. LIVERANI (eds), *LTUR, Supplementum* I.1. *Carta Archeologica di Roma. Primo quadrante*, Rome 2005.
CASTAGNOLI 1992
F. CASTAGNOLI, *Il Vaticano nell'antichità classica*, Studi e Documenti per la Storia del Palazzo Apostolico Vaticano pubblicati a cura della biblioteca Apostolica Vaticana, vol. VI, Vatican City 1992.
JOSI 1931
E. JOSI, *Scoperta di un sepolcreto romano nel territorio della Città del Vaticano*, in *IllVat*, 2, 3, 1931, pp. 26-35.
LIVERANI 1999
P. LIVERANI, *La topografia antica del Vaticano*, Vatican City 1999.
LIVERANI, SPINOLA 2006
P. LIVERANI, G. SPINOLA, *Mosaici in bianco e nero dal tratto vaticano della necropoli della via Trionfale*, in AISCOM. Proceedings of the V Colloquium of the Associazione Italiana per lo Studio e la Conservazione del Mosaico (Rome, 3-6 November 1997), Ravenna 1999, pp. 219-230.
LIVERANI, SPINOLA 2006
P. LIVERANI, G. SPINOLA, *La Necropoli Vaticana lungo la via Trionfale*, Rome 2006.
LIMC
Lexicon Iconographicum Mythologiae Classicae, I-VIII, Zürich-München 1981-1997.
LTUR
E.M. STEINBY (ed.), *Lexicon Topographicum Urbis Romae*, I-V, Rome 1993-1999.

MAGI 1958
F. MAGI, «Relazione preliminare sui ritrovamenti archeologici nell'area dell'autoparco vaticano», in *Triplice omaggio alla Sua Santità Pio XII*, Vatican City 1958, pp. 87-115.
Ostia I – II – III – IV
AA.VV., *Ostia I, Seminario di Archeologia e Storia dell'Arte Greca e Romana dell'Università di Roma*, «Studi Miscellanei», 13, Rome 1968; *Ostia II*, «Studi Miscellanei», 16, Rome 1970; *Ostia III*, «Studi Miscellanei», 21, Rome 1973; *Ostia IV*, «Studi Miscellanei», 23, Rome 1977.
SPINOLA 2006
G. SPINOLA, *Vivere (e morire) al tempo di Augusto*, in *Archeo*, 262, December 2006, pp. 36-49.
STEINBY 1987
E.M. STEINBY, *La necropoli della via Triumphalis. Pianificazione generale e tipologia dei monumenti funerari*, in *Römischen Gräberstraßen*, AbhMünchen, 96, 1987, pp. 85-110.
STEINBY 2003
E.M. STEINBY, *La necropoli della via Triumphalis. Il tratto sotto l'Autoparco vaticano*, Atti della Pontificia Accademia Romana di Archeologia, serie III, Memorie, vol. XVII, Rome 2003.

THE NECROPOLIS UNDERNEATH ST PETER'S BASILICA. CONSERVATION AND RESTORATION

APOLLONJ GHETTI, FERRUA, JOSI, KIRSCHBAUM 1951
M. APOLLONJ GHETTI, A. FERRUA, E. JOSI, E. KIRSCHBAUM, *Esplorazioni sotto la Confessione di San Pietro in Vaticano*, Vatican City 1951.
L'Attività della Santa Sede
L'Attività della Santa Sede, Vatican City 1941-2008.
GABRIELLI, ZANDER 2008
N. GABRIELLI, P. ZANDER, *La Necropoli sotto la Basilica di San Pietro in Vaticano. Interventi conservativi e opere di manutenzione*, in «Kermes», 20, 65, January-March 2007, pp. 53-66.
GUARDUCCI 1953
M. GUARDUCCI, *Cristo e San Pietro in un documento precostantiniano della Necropoli Vaticana*, Vatican City 1953.
GUARDUCCI 1958
M. GUARDUCCI, *I graffiti sotto la Confessione di San Pietro in Vaticano*, voll. 1-3, Vatican City 1958.
GUARDUCCI 1965
M. GUARDUCCI, *Le reliquie di Pietro sotto la Confessione della Basilica Vaticana*, Vatican City 1965.
MIELSCH, HESBERG, GAERTNER 1986
A. MIELSCH, H. VON HESBERG, K. GAERTNER, *Die Heidnische Nekropole unter St. Peter in Rom die Mausoleen A-D*, in «Atti della Pontificia Accademia Romana di Archeologia, serie 3, Memorie», 16, 1, Rome 1986.
MIELSCH, HESBERG, GAERTNER 1995
A. MIELSCH, H. VON HESBERG, K. GAERTNER, *Die Heidnische Nekropole unter St. Peter in Rom die Mausoleen E-I und Z-PSI*, in «Atti della Pontificia Accademia Romana di Archeologia, serie 3, Memorie», 16, 2, Rome 1995.
NICOLOSI 1941
G. NICOLOSI, *Lavori di ampliamento, risanamento e sistemazione delle Sacre Grotte Vaticane*, in «L'Osservatore Romano», 13 March 1941, p. 4.
NICOLOSI 1949
G. NICOLOSI, *Un decennio di lavori nelle Grotte Vaticane*, in «Ecclesia», IX, 6, 1949, pp. 310-317.
PAPI 2008
C. PAPI, *Il nome di Pietro nel presbiterio costantiniano della Basilica Vaticana. Una iscrizione inedita*, in *Epigrafia 2006. Atti della XIVe rencontre sur l'épigraphie in onore di Silvio Panciera con altri contributi di colleghi, allievi e collaboratori*, edited by M.L. Caldelli, G.L. Gregori, S. Orlandi, Rome 2008, pp. 423-436.
PRANDI 1957
A. PRANDI, *La Zona Archeologica della Confessio Vaticana*, Vatican City 1957.
SPERANDIO, ZANDER 1999
A. SPERANDIO, P. ZANDER (eds), *La tomba di San Pietro. Restauro e illuminazione della Necropoli Vaticana*, Milan 1999.
ZANDER 2005
P. ZANDER, tables 104-107, in *The Journey of Faith. Art and History from the Vatican Collections* (catalogue of the exhibition, Singapore, Asian Civilisations Museum, 17 June-9 October 2005), Singapore 2005, pp. 103-107.
ZANDER 2007
P. ZANDER, *La Necropoli sotto la Basilica di San Pietro in Vaticano*, Rome 2007.
ZANDER 2008
P. ZANDER, *La tomba di San Pietro e la Necropoli Vaticana, schede 52-54*, in *Magnificenze Vaticane. Tesori inediti della Fabbrica di San Pietro* (catalogue of the exhibition, Rome, Palazzo Incontro, 12 March-25 May 2008), edited by A.M. Pergolizzi, Rome 2008, pp. 102-113.
ZANDER 2009
P. ZANDER, *The Necropolis under St. Peter's Basilica in the Vatican*, Rome 2009 (English translation of the 2007 book with minor revisions)

Index of Names, Places and Subjects

Page numbers in italics refer to illustrations

Illustration Credits